JUDICIAL REVIEW AND THE HUMAN RIGHTS ACT

Cavendish
Publishing
Limited

London • Sydney

JUDICIAL REVIEW AND THE HUMAN RIGHTS ACT

Richard Gordon QC

Barrister at Brick Court Chambers, London, and Visiting
Professor in the Faculty of Laws at University College London

and

Tim Ward

Barrister at Monckton Chambers, London

Cavendish
Publishing
Limited

London • Sydney

First published in Great Britain 2000 by Cavendish Publishing Limited, The Glass House, Wharton Street, London WC1X 9PX, United Kingdom
Telephone: +44 (0)20 7278 8000   Facsimile: +44 (0)20 7278 8080
E-mail: info@cavendishpublishing.com
Visit our Home Page on http://www.cavendishpublishing.com

British Library Cataloguing in Publication Data

Gordon, RJF
Judicial review and the Human Rights Act
1 Civil rights – England 2 Civil rights – Wales
I Title II Ward, Tim
342.4'2'085

ISBN 1 85941 430 3

Printed and bound in Great Britain

'What are the Rights of Man and the Liberties of the World but Loose-Fish?'

Herman Melville, *Moby Dick*, Ch 89.

To Edmund and Adam

and

To Ethan

FOREWORD

The Rt Hon Lord Justice Brooke

Rights, they say, are coming home, even though English judges have been creating, shaping and defending our rights for nearly a thousand years. Experience has shown, however, that our freedom-based laws could not prevent some 'no-go' areas being created in which it has been hard for judges to perform their traditional role of doing right to all manner of man (and woman). The Human Rights Act aims to eliminate those 'no-go' areas.

From October 2000 onwards, every public authority, including every court, will be behaving unlawfully if it acts in a way which is incompatible with a Convention right. Courts and tribunals must take Convention jurisprudence into account whenever a question arises in connection with one of those rights. But Strasbourg jurisprudence is vast, and there are very few Human Rights Law Reports in circulation outside specialist corners of practice.

Hence the importance of this book. The new Act poses formidable challenges to practitioners in connection with both law and practice in the public law field. We are fortunate that Richard Gordon QC and Tim Ward have brought together into one place a mass of valuable material to help us find our way through the labyrinth we will all be entering. If we keep this book with us, we are far less likely to get lost in the maze.

Henry Brooke
Court of Appeal
September 2000

PREFACE

This book seeks to address the profound changes which the Human Rights Act 1998 will bring both to the practice of public law, and to the nature of judicial review itself.

Chapter 1 provides an analysis of the provisions of the Act and considers how it is likely to work in practice. Chapter 2, 'Claimants and Defendants', asks which bodies will be affected by the Act. There are important differences between the test for standing in 'ordinary' judicial review, and the requirement under the Human Rights Act that an applicant should have the status of 'victim'. If the domestic courts apply the Strasbourg case law, the test for standing under the Act will clearly be narrower than that which applies in 'ordinary' judicial review in certain important respects. In some circumstances, it is likely that the Convention may be brought to bear upon purely private disputes thereby further increasing its reach. It is also probable that there are bodies which are susceptible to challenge under the Act which have not been thought to be amenable to judicial review. Some 'obvious' public authorities (at least) face challenge under the Act in respect of functions such as, for example, those governed by employment law, which have previously been held to be outside the scope of judicial review. There is, therefore, little doubt that the broad approach to the question as to susceptibility to challenge under the Act will bring about a considerable widening of public law supervision.

Chapter 3 addresses 'Convention Concepts': the interpretative and analytical tools employed by the Strasbourg institutions. The Human Rights Act requires the domestic courts to 'take into account' the Strasbourg case law in determining any question which arises in connection with a Convention right. This cannot be done without also taking into account (at least some of) the concepts which are themselves integral to Strasbourg's reasoning. This conceptual framework brings the prospect of change to fundamental canons of domestic law, not least the doctrine of precedent. In some circumstances, the Wednesbury test may fail to satisfy the Court's doctrine of effectiveness and give rise to a breach of the closely related right to an effective remedy contained in Article 13.

Chapter 4 provides a brief exegesis of the substantive rights contained in the Convention. Article 6, the right to a fair trial, however, is of such significance for domestic public law that it is given separate treatment in Chapter 5. The substantive rights themselves have given rise to challenges to the sufficiency of judicial review. Aside from Article 6, questions have arisen as to the ability of judicial review to satisfy Article 5, the right to liberty and security, and, perhaps surprisingly, Article 1 of Protocol No 1, the right to property. The seed of such challenges can be found in the preamble to the Convention which emphasises the importance of the rule of law as part of the common heritage of the Contracting States. The Convention contains an explicit requirement that state action which serves to limit certain freedoms which are protected by the Convention must be 'lawful' and/or 'in accordance with the law'. The Strasbourg approach to the requirement of legality goes far beyond the Diceyan concept of the rule of law. In essence, the latter requires only adherence to the requirements of the law, such as they are. The European Court of Human Rights takes a substantive approach to the requirement of legality. It demands not merely adherence by the state to the rules of domestic law, but in addition, imposes requirements as to the 'quality' of domestic law. This requires adequate legal protection in domestic law against arbitrary interferences by public authorities with the rights safeguarded by the Convention. It is this prohibition on arbitrariness, inferred by the Court from the Convention requirement of legality, which gives rise to a control on the quality of judicial review.

In United Kingdom cases, applicants have typically alleged that the adherence by the judicial review courts to the *Wednesbury* test, and the absence of a substantive review of the exercise of public law powers entails that the quality of review does not provide sufficient protection against arbitrariness. As shall be seen, some – although by no means all – such challenges have succeeded in Strasbourg.

There are some circumstances in which judicial review in its current form cannot be said to give rise to a fair trial within the meaning of Article 6. This issue is considered in Chapter 5, as are two further questions of central importance. The first is the scope of the application of Article 6. Adherence by the domestic courts to the Strasbourg case law on this question may serve to exclude a number of important areas of domestic public law, such as immigration, from the ambit of Article 6 protection. The second question is the extent to which the requirements of Article 6 differ from those of the common law doctrine of natural justice. In many important respects, Article 6 is considerably more stringent in its demands.

The Human Rights Act introduces the possibility of a remedy in damages for a breach of Convention rights. There is no general right to damages in public law, and the new remedy may therefore be of great practical importance. The Act requires the domestic courts to take into account the principles applied by the Strasbourg Court in deciding whether to award damages for a breach of Convention rights, and the amount of such an award. In Chapter 7, the Strasbourg case law is analysed, and such principles as may be extracted from it are considered.

The final chapter of the book examines the relationship between the Convention and Community law. The European Court of Justice in Luxembourg applies the Convention in construing the fundamental rights which form part of the general principles in Community law. Important questions arise as to the role of the Convention in Community law, and indeed the best tactical approach to questions which engage fundamental rights but also fall within the scope of Community law.

We have endeavoured to state the law as at 1 August 2000. Later changes have been incorporated where possible. In particular, the new rules for judicial review contained in CPR Pt 54 have been considered.

Finally, we would like to thank our wives, Jane (for her endless patience) and Catherine (for inspiration during gestation).

Richard Gordon QC
Brick Court Chambers

Tim Ward
Monckton Chambers

CONTENTS

Foreword	*vii*
Preface	*ix*
Table of Cases	*xix*
Table of Statutes and Statutory Instruments	*xliii*
Table of European Legislation	*xlvii*

1 THE HUMAN RIGHTS ACT — 1

INTRODUCTION — 1

THE RIGHTS INCORPORATED — 1

THE INTERPRETATIVE OBLIGATIONS ON THE COURT — 3
The Strasbourg case law — 3
Interpretation of United Kingdom legislation — 4
The interpretative obligations and parliamentary sovereignty — 6

CLAIMANTS, DEFENDANTS AND FORUM — 7
Standing: who will be able to bring a Convention challenge? — 7
Defendants: who will be subject to a Convention challenge? — 8
Forum: where Convention points can be raised — 9

TIME LIMITS AND RETROSPECTIVE EFFECT OF
THE HUMAN RIGHTS ACT — 10
Time limits — 10
Retrospective effect — 11

EFFECT OF A BREACH OF THE CONVENTION IN
DOMESTIC LAW — 11
Primary legislation: declaration of incompatibility — 11
Subordinate legislation — 15
Administrative action — 15

THE STATUTORY DEFENCE — 16

DAMAGES — 17

SPECIAL PROTECTION FOR ARTICLES 9 AND 10 — 18

DEROGATIONS AND RESERVATIONS — 19

THE ROLE OF STRASBOURG — 21

2 CLAIMANTS AND DEFENDANTS — 23

STANDING TO CHALLENGE — 23
Standing in judicial review: sufficient interest — 23
Standing under the Human Rights Act: the 'victim' test — 26

DEFENDANTS: WHO WILL BE SUBJECT TO
   A CONVENTION CHALLENGE? 37
   Defendants under the Human Rights Act:
      public authorities 38
   The approach in domestic law: susceptibility
      to judicial review 38
   The Strasbourg case law 41
   Functions subject to challenge under the Human Rights Act 42
   Horizontal effect: the Convention in private disputes 47

3 CONVENTION CONCEPTS **49**

CONVENTION CONCEPTS IN DOMESTIC LAW 49

SCOPE OF APPLICATION OF
   CONVENTION CONCEPTS 51

INTERPRETING THE CONVENTION 51
   The Convention as an international treaty 51
   Principle of effectiveness 53
   Up to date interpretation 59
   Autonomous meaning of Convention terms 60
   Exceptions strictly construed 61

CONCEPTS AFFECTING APPLICATION OF
   THE CONVENTION 62
   General approach 62
   Principle of legality 63
   Legitimate aim 68
   Democratic values 69
   Proportionality 71
   Positive obligations 74

CONCEPTS INFORMING THE APPROACH
   OF THE COURT 78
   Margin of appreciation 78
   Subsidiarity 80
   Fourth instance principle 80
   Victim 81
   Burden of proof 82

4 CONVENTION RIGHTS **83**

ARTICLE 1: OBLIGATION TO RESPECT HUMAN RIGHTS 84

ARTICLE 2: RIGHT TO LIFE 85
   Health and medical issues 87
   Environment 89

Contents

ARTICLE 3: PROHIBITION OF TORTURE 89
The meaning of 'torture ... inhuman or degrading
    treatment or punishment' 90
Conditions of detention 91
Crime – extradition 92
Immigration and expulsion 93
Discrimination 94
Corporal punishment 95

ARTICLE 4: PROHIBITION OF SLAVERY AND
FORCED LABOUR 95

ARTICLE 5: RIGHT TO LIBERTY AND SECURITY 96
A right to liberty and security 97
A prohibition on the deprivation of liberty 98
Six cases in which deprivation of liberty is allowed 98
Judicial review, habeas corpus and Article 5(4) 110

ARTICLE 7: NO PUNISHMENT WITHOUT LAW 114

ARTICLE 8: RIGHT TO RESPECT FOR PRIVATE AND
FAMILY LIFE 115
Positive obligations and respect for Article 8 rights 117
A balancing exercise 118
Children 118
Divorce 120
Immigration 121
Sexuality 122
Personal data 124
Surveillance and investigation 125
Search and seizure of property 127
The environment 127
Article 8: rights of prisoners 128
Compulsory medical treatment 129

ARTICLE 9: FREEDOM OF THOUGHT, CONSCIENCE
AND RELIGION 129

ARTICLE 10: FREEDOM OF EXPRESSION 131
The scope of freedom of expression 131
Restrictions on freedom of expression 132
Subject matter 133
The press 134
Injunctions 135
Broadcasting 136

ARTICLE 11: FREEDOM OF ASSEMBLY
AND ASSOCIATION 137

Freedom of assembly	137
Freedom of association	138
ARTICLE 12: RIGHT TO MARRY	139
ARTICLE 13: RIGHT TO AN EFFECTIVE REMEDY	140
An arguable violation	141
The nature of a sufficient remedy	141
Article 13 and Article 6(1)	143
ARTICLE 14: PROHIBITION OF DISCRIMINATION	144
ARTICLE 15: DEROGATION IN TIME OF EMERGENCY	146
ARTICLE 16: RESTRICTIONS ON POLITICAL ACTIVITY OF ALIENS	148
ARTICLE 17: PROHIBITION OF ABUSE OF RIGHTS	149
ARTICLE 18: LIMITATION ON USE OF RESTRICTIONS ON RIGHTS	150
ARTICLE 1 OF PROTOCOL NO 1: PROTECTION OF PROPERTY	150
The first rule: peaceful enjoyment of possessions	151
The second rule: deprivation of possessions	152
The third rule: control of the use of property	154
Application	156
ARTICLE 2 OF PROTOCOL NO 1: RIGHT TO EDUCATION	158
Denial of the right to education	159
The rights of parents	159
Education and resources	161
Education and negligence	162
ARTICLE 3 OF PROTOCOL NO 1: RIGHT TO FREE ELECTIONS	162
ARTICLES 1 AND 2 OF PROTOCOL NO 6: THE DEATH PENALTY	164
5 ARTICLE 6, JUDICIAL REVIEW AND NATURAL JUSTICE	**165**
OVERVIEW	165
APPLICATION OF ARTICLE 6(1)	166
Civil cases	166
Criminal cases	171
ARTICLE 6(1), ADMINISTRATIVE DECISION MAKING AND JUDICIAL REVIEW	174

Contents

THE SUBSTANCE OF ARTICLE 6(1)   177
    Introduction   177
    Access to a court   177
    Procedural rights which extend beyond the scope of
        natural justice   183
    Rights which are co-extensive with natural justice   191
GUARANTEES IN CRIMINAL CASES   192
    Article 6(2): presumption of innocence   192
    Article 6(3): additional minimum safeguards
        in criminal cases   195

6 DAMAGES   **201**

INTRODUCTION   201
DAMAGES UNDER THE HUMAN RIGHTS ACT   202
    The power to award damages   203
    Civil proceedings only   204
    Discretionary nature of award of damages   204
    Damages for 'judicial acts'   205
    The role of the Strasbourg case law   206
THE STRASBOURG CASE LAW   206
    Who can receive just satisfaction   207
    Proof of loss   208
    Pecuniary and non-pecuniary loss   208
    The compensatory approach   209
    The equitable approach   211
    Quantum   211
    Mitigation   212
    Conduct of the applicant   213
    Causation – lost opportunities and
        procedural unfairness   213
    Judgment as sufficient reparation   215
    Non-compensatory awards   216
    Interest   216
    Costs and expenses   217

7 THE CONVENTION AND COMMUNITY LAW   **219**

OVERVIEW   219
THE ECHR IN COMMUNITY LAW   220
    The initial position   220
    Stages of change   220
    The modern view   222

Approach of the ECJ to the Strasbourg case law 223

THE SCOPE OF HUMAN RIGHTS PROTECTION
IN COMMUNITY LAW 226
The regulating principle 226
Extent of substantive ECHR protection in the ECJ cases 228

FUNDAMENTAL RIGHTS IN COMMUNITY LAW
AND THE HUMAN RIGHTS ACT 230

APPENDICES

1 THE HUMAN RIGHTS ACT 1998 233
2 THE EUROPEAN CONVENTION
ON HUMAN RIGHTS 263

Index 279

TABLE OF CASES

A

A and Others v Netherlands (1996) 22 EHRR 458 . . . . .212, 213

A Solicitor, Re [1993] QB 69 194

A v United Kingdom (1999) 27 EHRR 611 . . . . .90, 95

Abdulaziz, Cabales and Balkandali v United Kingdom
(1985) 7 EHRR 47 . . . . .94, 116, 117, 121, 145, 209

Acmanne v Belgium (1984) 40 DR 251 129

Adolf v Austria (1982) 4 EHRR 312 30

Adoui and Another v Belgian State [1982] ECR 1665 229

Advic v United Kingdom (1995) 19 EHRR CD 125 116

Aerts v Belgium (2000) 29 EHRR 50 . . . . .92, 104, 168

AGOSI v United Kingdom (1987) 9 EHRR 1 . . . . .58, 154, 155, 158, 173, 176

Agrotexim v Greece (1996) 21 EHRR 250 32

Ahmed v Austria (1997) 24 EHRR 278 94

Ahmed v United Kingdom (2000) 29 EHRR 1 163

Air Canada v United Kingdom (1995) 20 EHRR 150 . . . . .58, 154, 155, 158, 173, 176,

Airedale NHS Trust v Bland [1993] AC 789 88

Airey v Ireland (1979–80) 2 EHRR 305 . . . . .76, 120, 143, 178

Ait-Mouhoub v France (1998) unreported, 28 October 179

Akdivar v Turkey (1997) 23 EHRR 143 150

Aksoy v Turkey (1997) 23 EHRR 553 . . . . .89, 91, 143, 148

AKZO Chemie BV and AKZO Chemie UK Limited
v Commission (Case 53/85) [1986] ECR 2585 229

Albert and Le Compte v Belgium (1983) 5 EHRR 533 . . . . .175, 192

Alexandrou v Oxford [1993] 4 All ER 328 181

Allan Jacobsson v Sweden (1990) 12 EHRR 56 . . . . .154, 171

Allenet de Ribemont v France (1995) 20 EHRR 557 . . . . .195, 208, 216

American Cyanamid Co v Ethicon Ltd [1975] AC 396 18

Amuur v France (1996) 22 EHRR 533 . . . . .30, 66, 98, 104, 106, 216

Anderson v The Scottish Ministers (2000) The Times, 21 June 104

Andersson v Sweden (1998) 25 EHRR 722 124

Andronicou and Constantinou v Cyprus (1998) 25 EHRR 491 86

Anisminic v Foreign Compensation Commission
[1969] 2 AC 147 179

App No 10331/83 v United Kingdom (1984) 6 EHRR 583 42

App No 11189/84 v Sweden (1988) 10 EHRR 132 32

App No 7566/76 v United Kingdom (1976) 9 DR 124 163

App Nos 7572/76, 7586/76, 7587/76 (1979) 14 DR 67 33

Arrowsmith v United Kingdom (1981) 3 EHRR 218 .129, 130, 133

Artico v Italy (1981) 3 EHRR 1 ....27, 30, 53, 208, 209

Ashingdane v United Kingdom (1985) 7 EHRR 528 ....68, 82, 98, 103, 179

Associated Provincial Picture House Limited
    v Wednesbury Corporation [1948] 1 KB 223 ....13, 46, 56, 57, 58, 67, 155

Association X v United Kingdom (1978) 14 DR 31 85

Austria v Italy (1963) 6 YB 740 194

Autronic AG v Switzerland (1990) 12 EHRR 485 ....136, 137

Averill v United Kingdom (2000) The Times, 20 June 198

Aydin v Turkey (1998) 25 EHRR 251 ....77, 91, 143

B

B v Austria (1991) 13 EHRR 20 109

B v France (1994) 16 EHRR 1 ....118, 124

Balmer-Schafroth v Switzerland (1998) 25 EHRR 598 34

Baraona v Portugal (1991) 13 EHRR 329 169

Barberà Messegué and Jabaro v Spain (1989) 11 EHRR 360 ....177, 192

Barcelona Traction, Light and Power Company Ltd (1970) ICJ 39 32

Barfod v Denmark (1991) 13 EHRR 493 135

Barrett v Enfield Borough Council [1999] 3 WLR 79 201

Barrett v London Borough of Enfield [1999] 3 WLR 79 182

Barthold v Germany (1985) 7 EHRR 383 ....64, 131, 133

Beaumartin v France (1995) 19 EHRR 485 158

Beldjoudi v France (1992) 14 EHRR 801 ....121, 122

Belgian Linguistics Case (1979–80) 1 EHRR 252 ....144, 145, 159, 160, 161

Belilos v Switzerland (1988) 10 EHRR 466 161

Bendenoun v France (1994) 18 EHRR 54 ....158, 172, 189

Benham v United Kingdom (1996) 22 EHRR 293 ....100, 172, 178, 198, 218

Benthem v Netherlands (1986) 8 EHRR 1 ....167, 169, 170

Bergemann v Bundesanstalt für Arbeit [1988] ECR 5125 229

Berrehab v Netherlands (1989) 11 EHRR 322 ....94, 116

Bezicheri v Italy (1990) 12 EHRR 210 112

Bladet Tromsø and Stenaas v Norway (2000) 29 EHRR 125 135

Blastland v United Kingdom (1987) 52 DR 273 192

Bönisch v Austria (1987) 9 EHRR 191 191

Bouamar v Belgium (1989) 11 EHRR 1 ....102, 110

Bouchelkia v France (1998) 25 EHRR 686 ....121, 122

Boughanemi v France (1996) 22 EHRR 228 ....116, 122

Bourgoin SA v Minister of Agriculture,
    Fisheries and Food [1986] QB 716 201

Bowman v United Kingdom (1998) 26 EHRR 1 . . . . .31, 133, 162, 217

Boyle and Rice v United Kingdom (1988) 10 EHRR 425 . . . . .128, 141

Boyle v United Kingdom (1995) 19 EHRR 179 116

Bozano v France (1987) 9 EHRR 297 . . . . .98, 99

Brady v United Kingdom (1981) 3 EHRR 297 167

Brannigan and McBride v United Kingdom
    (1994) 17 EHRR 539 147

Brasserie du Pêcheur and Factortame
    (Cases C-46 and 48/93) [1996] ECR I-1029 202

Brincat v Italy (1993) 16 EHRR 591 209

Brind v United Kingdom (1994) 77 DR 42 137

Brogan v United Kingdom (1989) 11 EHRR 117 . . . . .100, 101, 107, 111, 113

Brozicek v Italy (1990) 12 EHRR 371 196

Bryan v United Kingdom (1996) 21 EHRR 342 . . . . .174, 176

Buchholz v Germany (1981) 3 EHRR 597 . . . . .186, 187

Buckley v United Kingdom (1997) 23 EHRR 101 . . . . .87, 116

Bullock v United Kingdom (1996) 21 EHRR CD 85 151

Bunkate v Netherlands (1995) 19 EHRR 477 215

Buscarini v San Marino (2000) 30 EHRR 208 130

C

C (Adult: Refusal of Medical Treatment), Re [1994] 1 WLR 290 .92

C Ltd v United Kingdom (1989) 61 DR 285 . . . . .135, 137

Camenzind v Switzerland (1999) 28 EHRR 458 . . . . .72, 127

Campbell and Cosans v United Kingdom (1982) 4 EHRR 293 . . . . .159, 160, 161

Campbell and Fell v United Kingdom (1985) 7 EHRR 165 . . . . .172, 173, 185

Campbell v United Kingdom (1993) 15 EHRR 137 . . . . .68, 95, 128

Canea Catholic Church v Greece (1999) 27 EHRR 521 212

Casado Coca v Spain (1994) 18 EHRR 1 . . . . .41, 42, 131, 133

Case concerning the factory at Chorzow, Series A No 17 209

Castells v Spain (1992) 14 EHRR 445 . . . . .133, 134

Chahal v United Kingdom (1997) 23 EHRR 413 .55, 93, 94, 104, 105,
                                                                            106, 111, 142, 143

Chappell v United Kingdom (1990) 12 EHRR 1 . . . . .116, 127

Chassagnou v France (2000) 29 EHRR 615 . . . . .60, 69, 155

Christians Against Racism and Fascism
    v United Kingdom (1980) 21 DR 138 138

Ciulla v Italy (1991) 13 EHRR 346 . . . . .100, 113

Clancy v Caird [2000] SLT 546 186

Clooth v Belgium (1992) 14 EHRR 717 108

Colman v United Kingdom (1994) 18 EHRR 119 . . . . .42, 133

Colozza v Italy (1985) 7 EHRR 516 214

Commission v Germany (Case C-62/90) [1992] ECR I-2575 225

Commission v Netherlands (Case C-62/90) [1992] ECR I-2575 229

Condron v United Kingdom (2000) The Times, 9 May 190

Consejo General de Colegios Oficiales de Economistas de
España v Spain (1995) 82-B 150 . . . . .36, 45

Cossey v United Kingdom (1991) 13 EHRR 622 . . . . .60, 123, 140

Costa v ENEL (Case 6/64) [1964] ECR 585 220

Costello-Roberts v United Kingdom (1995) 19 EHRR 112 . . . . .45, 84, 95, 118, 160

Council of Civil Service Unions v Minister for
the Civil Service [1985] AC 374 . . . . .39, 139

Council of Civil Service Unions v United Kingdom
(1988) 10 EHRR 269 . . . . .34, 139, 140

Credit and Industrial Bank and Moravec v Czech Republic
(1998) 26 EHRR CD 88 32

Croissant v Germany (1993) 16 EHRR 135 197

Cruz Varas v Sweden (1992) 14 EHRR 1 93

Cyprus v Turkey (1982) 4 EHRR 482 . . . . .98, 147

D

D v United Kingdom (1997) 24 EHRR 423 . . . . .56, 57, 87, 94

Dahanayake v United Kingdom (1983) 5 EHRR 144 30

Darby v Sweden (1991) 13 EHRR 774 . . . . .156, 210, 216, 217

Darnell v United Kingdom (1994) 18 EHRR 205 . . . . .186, 208, 212

De Becker v Belgium (1960) 2 YB 214 149

De Haes and Gijsels v Belgium (1998) 25 EHRR 1 . . . . .135, 191

De Jong, Baljet and Van den Brink v Netherlands
(1986) 8 EHRR 20 . . . . .30, 100, 113, 212

De Moor v Belgium (1994) 18 EHRR 372 215

De Wilde Ooms and Versyp v Belgium
(1979–80) 1 EHRR 379 . . . . .88, 99, 102, 109, 110

Defrenne v SABENA (Case 149/77) [1978] ECR 1365 229

Delcourt v Belgium (1979–80) 1 EHRR 355 70

Demeules v France (1990) 67 DR 166 163

Demicoli v Malta (1992) 14 EHRR 47 173

Demirel v Stadt Schwäbisch Gmünd (Case 12/86)
[1987] ECR 3719 227

Derbyshire CC v Times Newspapers [1992] QB 770 82
Detained Persons v Germany (1968) 11 YB 528 ....96, 171
Deumeland v Germany (1980) 8 EHRR 448 168
Deweer v Belgium (1979–80) 2 EHRR 439 ....33, 207
Dick v United Kingdom (1996) 21 EHRR CD 107 98
Dimes v The Proprietors of the Grand Junction Canal
  (1852) 3 HL Cas 759 183
Djeroud v France (1992) 14 EHRR 68 122
Dombo Beheer BV v Netherlands (1994) 18 EHRR 213 ....32, 45, 81, 191, 206, 214
Donnelly v United Kingdom (1975) 43 CD 122 28
Doorson v Netherlands (1996) 22 EHRR 330 198
Dudgeon v United Kingdom (1982) 4 EHRR 149 ....29, 71, 122, 123, 144
Dudgeon (Art 50) v United Kingdom (1983) 5 EHRR 573 ....215, 216, 217
Duke v GEC Reliance Ltd [1988] AC 618 5

E

E v Norway (1994) 17 EHRR 30 113
East African Asians v United Kingdom (1981) 3 EHRR 76 ....94, 97, 145
Eckle v Germany (1983) 5 EHRR 1 ....30, 171, 174, 187
Editions Periscope v France (1992) 14 EHRR 597 169
Edwards v United Kingdom (1992) 15 EHRR 417 ....175, 189
Elliniki Radiophonia Tileorassi AE v Dimotiki Etairia
  Pliroforissis (Case C-260/89) [1991] ECR I-2925 ....226, 227, 228
Emesa Sugar (Free Zone) NV v Aruba (Case C-17/98)
  (2000) The Times, 29 February 222
Engel v Netherlands (1979–80) 1 EHRR 647 ....61, 97, 98, 99, 100,
                                                              150, 171, 172, 173
Engel v Netherlands (No 2) (1979–80) 1 EHRR 706 ....212, 215
Erikkson v Sweden (1990) 12 EHRR 183 ....119, 120
Erkner and Hofauer v Austria (1987) 9 EHRR 464 152
Everest v United Kingdom (1997) EHRR 23 CD 180 42
Ewing v United Kingdom (1988) 10 EHRR 141 174
Ezelin v France (1992) 14 EHRR 362 ....135, 137, 138

F

F (In Utero), Re [1988] 2 All ER 193 88
F (Minors), Re (Care Proceedings: Contact)
  (2000) The Times, 22 June 119, 175
F v Switzerland (1988) 10 EHRR 411 ....72, 140

F v United Kingdom (1993) 15 EHRR CD 32 197

F v West Berkshire Health Authority [1990] 2 AC 1 92

Fayed v United Kingdom (1994) 18 EHRR 393 ....171, 180

Fédération Nationale des Infirmiers and Confédération
    Des Syndicats Médicaux Francais v France (1986) 47 DR 225 34

Feldbrugge v Netherlands (1986) 8 EHRR 425 ....167, 168

Findlay v United Kingdom (1997) 24 EHRR 221 ....186, 214, 217

Fischer v Austria (1995) 20 EHRR 349 ....175, 187

Fox, Campbell and Hartley v United Kingdom
    (1991) 13 EHRR 157 ....101, 106, 107, 215

Foxley v United Kingdom (2000) The Times, 4 July 117, 128

Francovich and Bonifaci v Italy (Cases C-6 and 9/90)
    [1991] ECR I-5357; (Cases C-46 and 48/93) [1996] ECR I-1029 202

Fratelli Costanzo SpA v Comune di Milano (Case 102/88)
    [1989] ECR 1839 17

Fredin v Sweden (1991) 13 EHRR 784 ....214, 215

Funke v France (1993) 16 EHRR 297 ....127, 174, 190

G

G v Netherlands (1993) 16 EHRR CD 38 117

Galloway v United Kingdom [1999] EHRLR 119 173

Gaskin v United Kingdom (1990) 12 EHRR 36 ....120, 124, 132

Gasus Dosier- und Födertechnik GmbH v Netherlands
    (1995) 20 EHRR 403 ....151, 155

Gay News Ltd and Lemmon v United Kingdom
    (1983) 5 EHRR 123 115

Gaygasuz v Austria (1997) 23 EHRR 364 ....151, 213

Geitling v High Authority (Joined Cases 36–38 and 40/59)
    [1960] ECR 423 220

General Mediterranean Holdings SA v Patel [2000] HRLR 54 124

Gillow v United Kingdom (1989) 11 EHRR 335 116

Gitonas v Greece (1998) 26 EHRR 691 163

Glasenapp v Germany (1987) 9 EHRR 25 133

Glimmerveen and Hagenback v Netherlands
    (1982) 4 EHRR 260 149

Goddi v Italy (1984) 6 EHRR 457 ....197, 214

Golder v United Kingdom (1979–80) 1 EHRR 524 ....52, 62, 68, 143, 177

Goodwin v United Kingdom (1996) 22 EHRR 123 ....72, 134

Govell v United Kingdom [1999] EHRLR 121 65

Gower v Bromley London Borough Council
(1999) unreported, 29 July 182
Graeme v United Kingdom (1990) 64 DR 158 161
Grare v France (1993) 15 EHRR CD 100 129
Greek Case (1969) 12 YB 1 147
Greenpeace Schweiz and Others v Switzerland
(1997) 23 EHRR CD 116 34
Gregory v United Kingdom (1998) 25 EHRR 577 185
Groppera Radio AG and Others v Switzerland
(1990) 12 EHRR 321 ....30, 64, 136, 137
GSM v Austria (1983) 34 DR 119 196
Guerra and Others v Italy (1998) 26 EHRR 357 ....76, 89, 125, 128
Guillemin v France (1998) 25 EHRR 435 ....153, 156, 158
Guleç v Turkey (1999) 28 EHRR 121 ....86, 87
Gustafsson v Sweden (1996) 22 EHRR 409 ....138, 139
Guzzardi v Italy (1981) 3 EHRR 333 ....98, 99, 100, 204, 210

H

H v Belgium (1988) 10 EHRR 339 ....169, 180, 208, 215
H v France (1990) 12 EHRR 74 209
H v United Kingdom (1988) 10 EHRR 95 ....119, 187
Hadjianastassiou v Greece (1993) 16 EHRR 219 188
Håkansson and Sturesson v Sweden (1991) 13 EHRR 1 214
Halford v United Kingdom (1997) 24 EHRR 523 ....45, 125, 126, 145, 216
Hamer v United Kingdom (1979) 24 DR 5 140
Handyside v United Kingdom (1979–80) 1 EHRR 737 ....18, 78, 80, 131, 134, 150
Hashman and Harrup v United Kingdom
(1999) The Times, 1 December 132
Hauer v Land Rheinland-Pfalz (Case 44/79)
[1979] ECR 3727 225
Hauschildt v Denmark (1990) 12 EHRR 266 185
Hentrich v France (1994) 18 EHRR 440 ....66, 153, 188
Herczegfalvy v Austria (1993) 15 EHRR 437 91
Hertel v Switzerland (1999) 28 EHRR 534 133
Hewitt and Harman v United Kingdom (1992) 14 EHRR 657 125
Hill v Chief Constable of West Yorkshire [1989] AC 53 181
Hilton v United Kingdom (1988) 57 DR 108 30
HLR v France (1998) 26 EHRR 29 90
Hodgson and Others v United Kingdom (1988) 10 EHRR 503 34

Hodgson v Commissioners of Customs and Excise
[1996] V & TR 200 172 172
Hodgson v United Kingdom (1987) 51 DR 136 . . . . .135, 137
Hoechst AG v Commission (Cases 46/87 and 227/88)
[1989] ECR 2859 224
Hoffman v Austria (1994) 17 EHRR 293 . . . . .116, 120
Hokannen v Finland (1995) 19 EHRR 139 119
Holy Monasteries v Greece (1995) 20 EHRR 1 . . . . .41, 152
Hood v United Kingdom (1999) The Times, 11 March 107
Howard v United Kingdom (1987) 52 DR 198 156
Hubert Wachauf v Federal Republic of Germany
(Case 5/88) [1989] ECR 2609 227
Hurtado v Switzerland (1994) A 280-A 91
Hussain v United Kingdom (1996) 22 EHRR 1 . . . . .109, 110
Huvig v France (1990) 12 EHRR 528 . . . . .65, 125, 126

I

Iatrides v Greece, Judgment 25 March 1999 63
Incal v Turkey (2000) 29 EHRR 449 . . . . .133, 176
Informatsionsverein Lentia v Austria (1994) 17 EHRR 93 . . . . .72, 136
Internationale Handelsgesellschaft mbH v Einfuhr- und
Vorratsstelle für Getreide und Futtermittel
(Case 11/70) [1970] ECR 1125 221
Inze v Austria (1988) 10 EHRR 394 . . . . .31, 60, 72, 144, 145,
208, 212, 213, 217
Ireland v United Kingdom (1979–80) 2 EHRR 25 . . . . .53, 84, 89, 90, 101,
107, 146, 147, 148
Iverson v Norway (1963) 6 YB 278 96

J

Jacobsson v Sweden (1990) 12 EHRR 56 170
James v United Kingdom (1986) 8 EHRR 123 . . . . .152, 153, 154, 155, 180, 181
Jamil v France (1996) 21 EHRR 65 115
Jarvis v Hampshire County Council [2000] Ed CR 1 182
Jersild v Denmark (1995) 19 EHRR 1 . . . . .131, 134, 136, 149
Jespers v Belgium (1981) 27 DR 61 197
Johansen v Norway (1997) 23 EHRR 33 . . . . .119, 120
Johnson v United Kingdom (1999) 27 EHRR 296 . . . . .103, 213
Johnston v Chief Constable of the Royal Ulster
Constabulary [1986] ECR 1651 179

Johnston v Ireland (1987) 9 EHRR 203 ....29, 52, 60, 120, 140
Jordan v United Kingdom (2000) The Times, 17 March 107

K

K v France (1993) 16 EHRR CD 23 150
Kalaç v Turkey (1999) 27 EHRR 552 ....45, 130
Kamasinski v Austria (1991) 13 EHRR 36 ....196, 197, 199
Kaplan v United Kingdom (1982) 4 EHRR 64 ....32, 166, 169
Kaya v Turkey (1999) 28 EHRR 1 87
Keegan v Ireland (1994) 18 EHRR 342 ....116, 118, 119, 208
Kemmache v France (1992) A 218 108
Khan v United Kingdom (2000) The Times, 19 May 65, 126, 142, 192
Khatun and Others v United Kingdom
    (1998) 26 EHRR CD 212 128
Kirkwood v United Kingdom (1984) 37 DR 158 93
Kjeldsen, Busk Madsen and Pederson v Denmark
    (1979–80) 1 EHRR 711 ....159, 160
Klass v Germany (1979–80) 2 EHRR 214............................8, 28, 29, 117,
    125, 126, 141, 142
Kleinwort Benson Ltd v Lincoln City Council
    and Others [1999] 2 AC 349 201
Kofler v Italy (1982) 30 DR 5 33
Kokkinakis v Greece (1994) 17 EHRR 397 ....18, 66, 70, 114,
    129, 130
Kolompar v Belgium (1993) 16 EHRR 197 105
König v Federal Republic of Germany
    (1979–80) 2 EHRR 170 ....166, 167, 186, 217
Konstantinidis v Stadt Altensteig-Standesamt and
    Landratsamt Calw, Ordnungsant (Case C-168/91)
    [1993] ECR I-1191 ....223, 228
Kopp v Switzerland (1999) 27 EHRR 91 126
Kosiek v Germany (1987) 9 EHRR 328 133
Koster v Netherlands (1992) 14 EHRR 396 215
KPD v Germany (1957) 1 YB 222 149
Kraska v Switzerland (1994) 18 EHRR 188 185
Kremzow v Austria (Case C-299/95) [1997] ECR I-2405 ....227, 228
Krone-Verlag GmbH and Mediaprint Anzeigen GmbH
    & Co KG v Austria (1997) 23 EHRR CD 152 173
Kruslin v France (1990) 12 EHRR 547 65
Kurt v Turkey (1999) 27 EHRR 373 ....31, 87, 150

L

Lasky, Jaggard and Brown v United Kingdom
(1997) 24 EHRR 39 . . . . .122, 123

Lawless v Ireland (1979–80) 1 EHRR 15 . . . . .101, 146, 147, 148, 149

LCB v United Kingdom (1999) 27 EHRR 212 . . . . .85, 88, 89

Le Compte, Van Leuven and De Meyere v Belgium
(1982) 4 EHRR 1 . . . . .138, 167, 169,
170, 174, 175, 184

Le Compte, Van Leuven and De Meyere v Belgium
(Art 50) (1983) 5 EHRR 183 . . . . .215, 216

Leander v Sweden (1987) 9 EHRR 433 . . . . .45, 72, 124, 125, 132, 142

Lechner and Hess v Austria (1987) 9 EHRR 490 208

Letellier v France (1992) 14 EHRR 83 108

Leudicke, Belkacem and Koç v Germany (No 2)
(1979–80) 2 EHRR 433 198

Liberal Party v United Kingdom (1980) 21 DR 211 164

Lightfoot v Lord Chancellor [2000] HRLR 33 170

Lindsay v United Kingdom (1986) 49 DR 181 . . . . .52, 157

Lingens v Austria (1986) 8 EHRR 407 . . . . .70, 133, 134, 193

Lithgow v United Kingdom (1986) 8 EHRR 329 . . . . .72, 152, 153, 154

Litwa v Poland, 4 April 2000 102

Lloyd v McMahon [1987] AC 625 187

Locabail Ltd v Bayfield Properties Ltd [2000] HRLR 292 . . . . .184, 185

Lopez-Ostra v Spain (1995) 20 EHRR 277 . . . . .75, 128

Lozidou v Turkey (1995) 20 EHRR 99 28

Lozidou v Turkey (1997) 23 EHRR 513 116

Luberti v Italy (1984) 6 EHRR 440 103

Lüdi v Switzerland (1993) 15 EHRR 173 . . . . .30, 126

Luedicke, Belkacem and Koç v Germany (1979–80) 2 EHRR 149 207

M

M v Spain (1991) 68 DR 209 36

Magee v United Kingdom (2000) The Times, 20 June 198

Malone v Metropolitan Police Commissioner [1979] Ch 244 63

Malone v United Kingdom (1985) 7 EHRR 14 . . . . .63, 65, 126

Mansur v Turkey (1995) 20 EHRR 535 108

Mantovanelli v France (1997) 24 EHRR 370 191

Marckx v Belgium (1979–80) 2 EHRR 330 . . . . .29, 76, 116, 117,
118, 144, 150

Markt Intern Verlag GmbH v Germany (1990) 12 EHRR 161 . . . . .131, 133, 136

Marleasing SA v La Comercial Internacional de
  Alimentación SA (Case C-106/89) [1990] ECR I-4135 5

Marshall v Southampton and South West Hampshire Health
  Authority (Teaching) (No 2) (Case C-271) [1993] ECR I-4367 202

Marthe Klensch v Secrétaire d'État à l'Agriculture
  et à la Viticulture (Cases 201 and 202/85) [1986] ECR 3477 227

Martins Moriera v Portugal (1991) 13 EHRR 517 214

Massa v Italy (1994) 18 EHRR 266 167

Masson and Van Zon v Netherlands (1996) 22 EHRR 491 .170, 180

Mathieu-Mohan and Clerfayt v Belgium (1988) 10 EHRR 1 . . . . .148, 162, 163, 164

Matos e Silva, Lda v Portugal (1997) 24 EHRR 573 . . . . .151, 156, 158, 209,
                                                                                                                      210, 211, 217

Matthews v United Kingdom (1999) 28 EHRR 361 . . . . .84, 163, 225

Matznetter v Austria (1979–80) 1 EHRR 198 108

Mauer v Austria (1998) 25 EHRR 91 213

MB, Re (Medical Treatment) [1997] 2 FLR 426 . . . . .88, 92

McCann v United Kingdom (1996) 21 EHRR 97 . . . . .54, 72, 85, 86,
                                                                                                                      87, 208, 213

McFeeley v United Kingdom (1980) 20 DR 44 128

McGonnell v United Kingdom (2000) The Times, 22 February .184

McGuinley and Egan v United Kingdom (1999) 27 EHRR 1 . . . . .77, 128

McLeod v United Kingdom (1999) 27 EHRR 493 127

McMichael v United Kingdom (1995) 20 EHRR 205 . . . . .72, 118

Mellacher v Austria (1990) 12 EHRR 391 . . . . .151, 154, 157

Mentes v Turkey (1997) 26 EHRR 595 . . . . .150, 217, 218

Mialhe v France (1993) 16 EHRR 332 127

Milasi v Italy (1988) 10 EHRR 333 113

Minelli v Switzerland (1983) 5 EHRR 554 194

Minister of Transport v Noort [1992] 3 NZLR 260 5

Modinos v Cyprus (1993) 16 EHRR 485 123

Monnell and Morris v United Kingdom (1988) 10 EHRR 205 . . . . .99, 188

Monsanto plc v Tilly and Others (1999) The Times, 30 November 170

Moody v United Kingdom 22613/93 (Rep) 16 January 1996 194

Moreira de Azevedov v Portugal (1991) 13 EHRR 721 170

Moustaquim v Belgium (1991) 13 EHRR 801 122

Müller v Switzerland (1991) 13 EHRR 212 . . . . .72, 131, 134

Murray v United Kingdom (1995) 19 EHRR 193 . . . . .79, 101, 105,
                                                                                                                      106, 107, 141

Murray v United Kingdom (1996) 22 EHRR 29 ....174, 190, 198

Murrell v British Leyland Trustees [1989] COD 389 45

N

Nasri v France (1996) 21 EHRR 458 122

National and Provincial Building Society and Others
    v United Kingdom (1998) 25 EHRR 127 ....151, 157, 167

National Panasonic v Commission (Case C-136/79)
    [1980] ECR 2033 225

National Union of Belgian Police v Belgium
    (1979–80) 1 EHRR 578 ....34, 139

Neilson v Denmark (1989) 11 EHRR 175 ....88, 102

Neimeitz v Germany (1993) 16 EHRR 97 ....116, 127

Neumeister v Austria (1979–80) 1 EHRR 91 ....99, 108, 109, 110, 167

Neumeister v Austria (No 2) (1979–80) 1 EHRR 136 212

Neves e Silva v Portugal (1991) 13 EHRR 535 169

New Horizons v Cyprus (1999) 27 EHRR CD 334 34

Nold v Commission of the European Communities
    (Case 4/73) [1974] ECR 491 221

Nölkenbockhoff v Germany (1991) 13 EHRR 360 33

Norris v Ireland (1991) 13 EHRR 186 123

O

O v United Kingdom (1988) 10 EHRR 82 169

Observer and Guardian v United Kingdom
    (1992) 14 EHRR 153 ....71, 132, 135, 136

Olsson v Sweden (1989) 11 EHRR 259 ....119, 207, 209

Open Door Counselling and Dublin Well Woman Centre
    v Ireland (1993) 15 EHRR 244 ....30, 132, 136, 208,
    210, 217, 218

Orkem v Commission [1989] ECR 3283 224

Osman v Ferguson [1993] 4 All ER 344 181

Osman v United Kingdom (2000) 29 EHRR 245 ....31, 75, 85, 86, 170,
    81, 182, 183, 201

Otto-Preminger-Institut v Austria (1995) 19 EHRR 34 134

Öztürk v Germany (1984) 6 EHRR 409 172

P

P v France (1993) 16 EHRR CD 29 33

P v S and Cornwall County Council (Case C-13/94)
    [1996] I ECR 2143 124

Pakelli v Germany (1984) 6 EHRR 1 ....208, 209
Papamichalopoulos v Greece (1993) 16 EHRR 440 152
Papamichalopoulos v Greece (just satisfaction)
(1996) 21 EHRR 439 ....209, 210, 211, 212
Parliament v Council (Radioactive Food) (Case C-70/88)
[1991] ECR I-4529 229
Paton v United Kingdom (1981) 3 EHRR 408 31
Paulsen-Medalen and Svensson v Sweden (1998) 26 EHRR 260 119
PD and LD v United Kingdom (1989) 62 DR 292 161
Pellisier and Sassi v France, Judgment of 25 March 1999 196
Pepper (Inspector of Taxes) v Hart [1993] AC 593 6
Pérez de Rada Cavanilles v Spain (2000) 29 EHRR 109 179
Perks v United Kingdom (2000) 30 EHRR 33 178
Pfeifer and Plankl v Austria (1992) 14 EHRR 692 178
Pham Hoang v France (1993) 16 EHRR 53 194
Phelps v Hillingdon London Borough Council
(2000) The Times, 28 July 162, 201
Philis v Greece (1991) 13 EHRR 741 208
Piermont v France (1995) 20 EHRR 301 148
Pierre-Bloch v France (1998) 26 EHRR 202 173
Piersack v Belgium (1983) 5 EHRR 169 ....184, 185
Pine Valley Developments Ltd v Ireland (1992) 14 EHRR 319 .....82, 145, 146, 156, 211
Platform 'Ärtze für das Leben' v Austria (1991) 13 EHRR 204 ....35, 137
Powell and Rayner v United Kingdom (1990) 12 EHRR 355 ....75, 128, 141, 180
Prager and Oberschlick v Austria (1996) 21 EHRR 1 135
Prais v Council (Case 130/75) [1976] ECR 1589 ....224, 229
Pressos Compania SA and Others v Belgium
(1996) 21 EHRR 301 ....151, 157
Pressos Compania SA and Others v Belgium
(just satisfaction) 26 June 1997 ....209, 212, 214
Pretto v Italy (1984) 6 EHRR 182 ....60, 188
Province of Bari, Sorrentino and Messini Nemaga v Italy
(1999) 27 EHRR CD 352 ....35, 36, 45
Purcell v Ireland (1991) 70 DR 262 137

Q

Quinn v France (1996) 21 EHRR 529 ....105, 212

R

R v Ministry of Agriculture, Fisheries and Food ex p Bostock
[1994] ECR I-955 . . . . .227, 228

R v Advertising Standards Authority ex p The Insurance
Service plc [1990] COD 42 40

R v Army Board of the Defence Council ex p Anderson
[1992] QB 169 187

R v Attorney General ex p Ferrante [1995] COD 18 39

R v Attorney General ex p ICI plc [1985] 1 CMLR 588 . . . . .24, 25

R v Bloomsbury and Marylebone County Court
ex p Blackburne (1985) 275 EG 1273 46

R v Bournewood Community and Mental Health Trust
ex p L [1998] 1 CCLR 390 98

R v Bow Street Metropolitan Stipendiary Magistrate
ex p Pinochet Ugarte (No 2) [2000] 1 AC 119 . . . . .37, 47, 183, 184

R v British Broadcasting Corporation ex p Lavelle
[1983] 1 WLR 23; [1983] 1 All ER 241 . . . . .36, 43, 44, 45

R v British Broadcasting Corporation ex p Pro-Life
Alliance Party [1997] COD 457 44

R v British Broadcasting Corporation ex p Referendum Party
[1997] COD 460 44

R v British Coal Corp and Roo Management
ex p GC Whittaker (Properties) [1989] COD 528 43

R v British Coal Corp ex p Price (No 2) [1993] COD 323;
(1993) The Times, 28 May 43

R v Broadcasting Complaints Commission ex p BBC
[1994] EMLR 497; [1994] COD 499 36

R v Broadcasting Standards Commission ex p BBC
[2000] 3 All ER 989 116

R v Brown [1994] 1 AC 212 123

R v Cambridgeshire Health Authority ex p B [1995] 25 BMLR 5 87

R v Central Criminal Court ex p Bright (2000) The Times, 26 July 60

R v Central London County Court ex p London
(1999) The Times, 23 March 46

R v Chief Rabbi of the United Hebrew Congregations of
Great Britain and the Commonwealth ex p Wachmann
[1992] 1 WLR 1036 . . . . .39, 41

R v Cleveland CC ex p Cleveland Care Homes [1994] COD 221 40

R v Code of Practice Committee of the British
Pharmaceutical Industry ex p Professional Counselling
(Aids) Ltd [1991] COD 228 40

R v Commissioner of Police of the Metropolis ex p Blackburn
[1968] 2 QB 118 39

R v Cornwall CC ex p Huntington [1994] 1 All ER 694 179

R v Criminal Injuries Compensation Board ex p Dickson
[1997] 1 WLR 158 187

R v Cripps ex p Muldoon and Others [1984] QB 68 46

R v Crown Prosecution Service ex p Hogg [1994] COD 237 43

R v Customs and Excise Commissioners ex p Lunn Poly Ltd
[1998] STC 649 DC 226

R v Department of Transport ex p Presvac Engineering Ltd
(1992) 4 Admin LR 121 25

R v Director of Public Prosecutions ex p Kebilene
[2000] HRLR 93 . . . . .19, 34, 73, 74, 78, 193

R v Director of Public Prosecutions ex p Manning
(2000) The Times, 19 May 188

R v Director of the Serious Fraud Office ex p Johnson
[1993] COD 58 24

R v Disciplinary Committee of the Jockey Club
ex p Aga Khan [1993] 1 WLR 909 . . . . .39, 40, 41, 44

R v East Sussex County Council ex p Tandy [1998] AC 714 161

R v Football Association Ltd ex p Football League Ltd
[1993] 2 All ER 833 . . . . .40, 44

R v Football Association of Wales ex p Flint Town United
Football Club [1991] COD 44 40

R v General Council of the Bar ex p Percival [1991] 1 QB 212 40

R v General Medical Council ex p Colman [1990] 1 All ER 489 . . . . .40, 42

R v Gough [1993] AC 646 183

R v Governor of Durham Prison ex p Hardial Singh [1984] 1 WLR 704 104

R v Hammersmith and Fulham LBC ex p Beddowes [1987] QB 1050 40

R v Hampshire County Council ex p Ellerton [1985] 1 All ER 599 194

R v Haringey Magistrates ex p Cragg [1997] COD 160 188

R v Harrow LBC ex p D [1989] 3 WLR 1239 39

R v Her Majesty's Treasury ex p Smedley [1985] 1 QB 657 25

R v Hertfordshire County Council ex p Green Industries Ltd
[2000] HRLR 368 190

R v Higher Education Funding Council ex p Institute of
Dental Surgery [1994] 1 WLR 242 188

R v Hull University Visitor ex p Page [1993] AC 682 42

R v IAT and Surinder Singh ex p Secretary of State for the
Home Department (Case C-370/90) [1992] ECR I-4265 229

R v Imam of Bury Park Jame Masjid Luton ex p Sulamain
[1994] COD 142 41

R v Inland Revenue Commissioners ex p Woolwich Equitable
Building Society [1990] 1 WLR 1400 ....157, 201

R v Inspectorate of Pollution ex p Greenpeace Ltd (No 2)
[1994] 4 All ER 329 ....25, 26

R v Institute of Chartered Accountants in England and Wales
ex p Andreou [1996] COD 489 40

R v Insurance Ombudsman Bureau ex p Aegon Life Assurance Ltd
[1994] COD 426 40

R v International Stock Exchange of the United Kingdom and
the Republic of Ireland Ltd ex p Else (1982) Ltd and Another
[1993] QB 534 40

R v IRC ex p National Federation of Self-Employed [1982] AC 617 ....24, 25

R v Kent Kirk [1984] ECR 2689 229

R v Khan [1997] AC 558 ....37, 192

R v Lambert (2000) The Times, 5 September 194

R v Law Society ex p Reigate Projects Ltd [1993] 1 WLR 1531 ....36, 40, 42

R v Legal Aid Board and Lord Chancellor's Department
ex p Mackintosh Duncan (A Firm)
(2000) unreported, 16 February 178

R v Legal Aid Board ex p Bateman [1992] 1 WLR 711 ....24, 25

R v Lewisham LBC ex p P [1991] 1 WLR 308 39

R v Lloyd's of London ex p Briggs [1993] 1 Lloyd's Rep 176;
[1993] COD 66 40

R v London Commodity Exchange (1986) Ltd
ex p Brearley [1994] COD 145 44

R v Lord Chancellor ex p Lightfoot [2000] 2 WLR 318 67

R v Lord Chancellor's Department ex p Witham [1998] QB 575;
[1997] 2 All ER 779 ....6, 67, 178

R v Manchester Crown Court ex p Director of
Public Prosecutions [1993] 1 WLR 1524 46

R v Mental Health Review Tribunal for South Thames Region
ex p Smith [1999] COD 148 103

R v Midlands Electricity Board ex p Busby
(1987) The Times, 28 October 40, 43

R v Ministry of Agriculture, Fisheries and Food
ex p British Pig Industry Support (2000) unreported, 27 July 226

R v Ministry of Agriculture, Fisheries and Food
ex p First City Trading Ltd [1997] 1 CMLR 250 ....73, 226

R v Ministry of Defence ex p Smith [1996] QB 541 ....56, 74

R v Ministry of Defence ex p Murray [1998] COD 134 74

R v Monopolies and Mergers Commission ex p Argyll Group plc
[1986] 1 WLR 763 ....25, 32

R v Norfolk CC ex p M [1989] QB 619 39

R v North and East Devon Health Authority ex p Coughlan
[2000] 2 WLR 622 ....37, 117, 156

R v Oxenden [1691] 1 Show 217 45

R v Panel of the Federation of Communication Services Ltd
ex p Kubis [1998] COD 5 40

R v Panel on Takeovers and Mergers ex p Datafin plc [1987] QB 815 39

R v Personal Investment Authority ex p Burns-Anderson
Network plc (1998) 10 Admin LR 57 40

R v Police Complaints Board ex p Madden [1983] 2 All ER 353 194

R v Poole BC ex p Beebee [1991] JPL 643 24

R v R [1992] 1 AC 599 114

R v Registrar of Companies ex p Central Bank of India
[1986] QB 1114 179

R v Registrar of Criminal Appeals ex p Pegg [1983] COD 192 45

R v Secretary of State for Defence ex p Sancto [1993] COD 144 ....24, 31

R v Secretary of State for Employment ex p Equal
Opportunities Commission [1995] 1 AC 1 35

R v Secretary of State for Foreign and Commonwealth Affairs
ex p Rees-Mogg [1994] 2 WLR 115 25

R v Secretary of State for Foreign and Commonwealth Affairs
ex p The World Development Movement Ltd [1995] 1 WLR 386 ....24, 25, 35

R v Secretary of State for Health ex p C (2000) The Times, 1 March 171

R v Secretary of State for Social Security ex p Sutton
(Case C-66/95) [1997] ECR I-2163 202

R v Secretary of State for Social Services ex p Child Poverty
Action Group [1990] 2 QB 540 25

R v Secretary of State for the Environment ex p Challenger
(2000) The Times, 11 July 178

R v Secretary of State for the Environment ex p Ostler
[1977] QB 122 179

R v Secretary of State for the Environment ex p Rose Theatre
Trust Co [1990] 1 QB 504 ....25, 26

R v Secretary of State for the Home Department ex p Bentley
[1994] QB 349 39

R v Secretary of State for the Home Department ex p Brind
[1991] 1 AC 696 ....5, 71, 137

R v Secretary of State for the Home Department ex p Bugdaycay
[1987] AC 514 56

R v Secretary of State for the Home Department ex p Chahal
(1999) The Times, 10 November 113

R v Secretary of State for the Home Department ex p McQuillan
[1995] 4 All ER 400 82

R v Secretary of State for the Home Department
ex p Mellor (2000) The Times, 5 September 128, 140

R v Secretary of State for the Home Department
ex p Pierson [1998] AC 67

R v Secretary of State for the Home Department
ex p Robb [1995] 1 All ER 677 92

R v Secretary of State for the Home Department
ex p Simms [1999] 3 WLR 328 . . . . .6, 67

R v Secretary of State for the Home Department
ex p Stafford [1999] 2 AC 38 67

R v Secretary of State for the Home Department
ex p Turgut [2000] HRLR 346 57

R v Secretary of State for Transport ex p Factortame Ltd
[1990] 2 AC 85 144

R v Secretary of State for Transport ex p Richmond LBC (No 1)
[1994] 1 WLR 74 35

R v Serious Fraud Office ex p Johnson [1993] COD 58 31

R v Servite Houses and the London Borough of Wandsworth Council
ex p Goldsmith and Chatting (2000) unreported, 12 May 44

R v Shemilt (A Taxing Officer) ex p Buckley [1988] COD 40 45

R v Solicitors Complaints Bureau ex p Curtin
(1994) 6 Admin LR 657 42

R v Somerset County Council and ARC Southern Ltd
ex p Dixon [1997] COD 323 . . . . .24, 25, 26, 35

R v Southend Stipendiary Magistrate ex p Rochford DC
[1995] Env LR 1 188

R v St Edmundsbury BC ex p Investors in Industry Commercial
Properties Ltd [1985] 1 WLR 1168 25

R v Stafford Justices ex p Imbert [1999] 2 Cr App R 276 78

R v Takeover Panel ex p Datafin plc [1987] 2 WLR 699 .8, 38, 42

R v The Independent Committee for the Supervision of
Telephone Information Services ex p Firstcode Ltd
[1993] COD 325 40

R v Tower Hamlets LBC ex p Thrasyvoulou [1991] COD 123 .24

R v United Kingdom (1988) 10 EHRR 74 119
R v Visitors to the Inns of Court ex p Calder and Persaud
  [1994] QB 1 42
R v Westminster CC and Others ex p M, P, A and X
  (1997) 1 CCLR 85 59
R v X, Y, Z (2000) The Times, 23 May 126
Racal Communications, Re [1981] AC 374 45
Radio ABC v Austria (1998) 25 EHRR 185 136
Rasmussen v Denmark (1985) 7 EHRR 371 . . . . .144, 145
Ravnsborg v Sweden (1994) 18 EHRR 38 173
Raymond v Honey [1983] 1 AC 1 67
Reckley v Minister of Public Safety and Immigration
  and Others (No 2) [1996] AC 527 39
Rees v United Kingdom (1987) 9 EHRR 56 . . . . .59, 60, 75, 118,
  123, 124, 140
Reid v Secretary of State for Scotland [1999] 2 WLR 28 104
Remli v France (1996) 22 EHRR 253 185
Reynolds v Times Newspapers [2000] HRLR 134 131
Ribitsch v Austria (1996) 21 EHRR 573 91
Ridge v Baldwin [1964] AC 40 206
Ringeisen v Austria (1979–80) 1 EHRR 455 . . . . .167, 170, 185
Ringeisen v Austria (No 2) (1979–80) 1 EHRR 504 212
Rioters' Case [1683] 1 Vern 175 45
Rowe and Davis v United Kingdom (2000) 30 EHRR 1 189
Ruis-Mateos v Spain (1993) 16 EHRR 505 192
Rutili v Ministre de l'Intérieur (Case 36/75) [1975] ECR 1219 . . . . .221, 222, 229

S

Salabiaku v France (1991) 13 EHRR 379 . . . . .193, 194, 231
Salesi v Italy (1998) 26 EHRR 187 . . . . .168, 212
Sanchez-Reisse v Switzerland (1987) 9 EHRR 71 . . . . .110, 112, 113
Santilli v Italy (1992) 14 EHRR 421 186
Saunders v United Kingdom (1997) 23 EHRR 313 190
Schenk v Switzerland (1991) 13 EHRR 242 192
Schiesser v Switzerland (1979–80) 2 EHRR 417 . . . . .101, 107
Schmidt and Dahlstrom v Sweden (1979–80) 1 EHRR 632 .139
Schmidt v Germany (1994) 18 EHRR 513 210
Schonenberger and Durmaz v Switzerland (1989) 11 EHRR 202 128
Schouten v Netherlands (1995) 19 EHRR 432 167

Schüler-Zgraggen v Switzerland
  (1993) 16 EHRR 405 ....168, 189
Schüler-Zgraggen v Switzerland (just satisfaction)
  (1995) A 305-A 217
Scottish Old People's Welfare Council, Petitioner 1987 SLT 179 25
Selçuk and Asker v Turkey (1998) 26 EHRR 477 ....89, 90
Selmouni v France (2000) 29 EHRR 403 ....90, 91
Sgarlata v Commission (Case 40/64) [1965] ECR 215 220
Sheffield and Horsham v United Kingdom
  (1999) 27 EHRR 163 ....59, 60, 123, 124, 140
Sibson v United Kingdom (1994) 17 EHRR 193 138
Sigurdur A Sigurjónsson v Iceland (1993) 16 EHRR 462 ....138, 139
Silver v United Kingdom (1983) 5 EHRR 347 ....54, 55, 63, 65, 69,
                                                                    86, 117, 128,
                                                                    141, 142, 143
Simmenthal v Commission (Case 92/78) [1979] ECR 777 220
Simpson v United Kingdom (1990) 64 DR 188 161
Skinner v Northallerton County Court Judge [1899] AC 439 46
Smalley, Re [1985] AC 622 46
Smith and Grady v United Kingdom (2000) 29 EHRR 493 ....54, 55, 56, 57,
                                                                    58, 72, 123, 142
Smith Kline and French Laboratories Ltd v Netherlands
  (1990) 66 DR 70 151
Smith v Secretary of State for Trade and Industry
  [2000] HRLR 83 186
Smith v United Kingdom (1996) 21 EHRR CD 74 172
Soering v United Kingdom (1989) 11 EHRR 439 ....28, 53, 55, 56, 57,
                                                                    60, 70, 71, 92,
                                                                    93, 94, 141, 171
SP, DP and T v United Kingdom (1996) 22 EHRR CD 148 31
Spadea and Scalbrino v Italy (1996) 21 EHRR 482 ....154, 157
Sporrong and Lönnroth v Sweden (1983) 5 EHRR 35 ....151, 152, 154,
                                                                    156, 158, 167, 211
Springer v United Kingdom (1983) 5 EHRR 141 29
SPUC v Grogan (Case C-159/90) [1991] ECR I-4685 ....224, 229
Stallinger and Kuso v Austria (1998) 26 EHRR 81 187
Starrs and Chalmers v Procurator Fiscal (Linlithgow)
  [2000] HRLR 191 186
Stauder v City of Ulm (Case 29/69) [1969] ECR 419 221
Steel and Others v United Kingdom (1999) 28 EHRR 603 ....131, 138

Table of Cases

Stefan v General Medical Council [2000] HRLR 1 188
Stögmüller v Austria (1979–80) 1 EHRR 155 108
Stork v High Authority (Case 1/58) [1959] ECR 17 220
Stran Greek Refineries v Greece (1995) 19 EHRR 293 ....151, 158, 216
Stubbings v United Kingdom (1997) 23 EHRR 213 179
Sunday Times v United Kingdom (1979–80) 2 EHRR 245 ....63, 64, 66, 114,
132, 134, 135
Sunday Times v United Kingdom (Art 50) (1981) 3 EHRR 317 ....204, 206, 208,
210, 217
Sunday Times v United Kingdom (No 2) (1992) 14 EHRR 229 ....132, 136
Sutherland v United Kingdom (1997) 24 EHRR CD 22 123
SW and CR v United Kingdom (1996) 21 EHRR 363 ....66, 114, 115
Swedish Engine Drivers' Union v Sweden (1979–80) 1 EHRR 617 ....139, 141

T

T (Adult: Refusal of Medical Treatment), Re [1992] 4 All ER 649 92
Taylor v United Kingdom (1994) 79-A DR 127 89
Tee v United Kingdom (1996) 21 EHRR CD 108 42
Tekin v Turkey, 9 June 1999, RJD 1998-IV 91
Ter Voort [1992] ECR I-5485 223
Tête v France (1987) 54 DR 52 ....163, 164
Thomas v Chief Adjudication Officer [1991] 2 QB 164 71
Thompson v Commissioner of Police for the Metropolis
[1998] QB 498 205
Thorgeirson v Iceland (1992) 14 EHRR 843 ....131, 134
Three Rivers District Council v Bank of England (No 3)
(2000) The Times, 19 May 201
Thynne Wilson and Gunnell v United Kingdom
(1991) 13 EHRR 666 ....111, 112
TI v United Kingdom (2000) 7 March 93
Timke v Germany (1995) 82-A DR 158 163
Tinnelly & Sons and Others and McElduff and Others
v United Kingdom (1999) 27 EHRR 249 179
Tolstoy Miloslavsky v United Kingdom (1995) 20 EHRR 442 ....132, 179, 217
Tomasi v France (1993) 15 EHRR 1 ....108, 109
Toth v Austria (1991) 14 EHRR 551 ....109, 110
Tre Traktorer Aktiebolag v Sweden (1991) 13 EHRR 309 169
Tyrer v United Kingdom (1979–80) 2 EHRR 1 ....59, 95

U

Umlauft v Austria (1996) 22 EHRR 76 175
UNECTEF v Heylens [1989] ECR 4097 229
Union Royale Belge des Sociétés de Football v Bosman
    [1995] ECR I-4291 229
United Communist Party of Turkey and Others v Turkey
    (1998) 26 EHRR 121 138
Uppal v United Kingdom (1981) 3 EHRR 391 167

V

V and T v United Kingdom (2000) 30 EHRR 120 . . . . .186, 190
Valenzuela Contreras v Spain (1999) 28 EHRR 483 . . . . .63, 65, 126
Valsamis v Greece (1997) 24 EHRR 294 . . . . .130, 160
Van de Hurk v Netherlands (1994) 18 EHRR 481 . . . . .188, 191
Van der Leer v Netherlands (1990) 12 EHRR 567 . . . . .106, 209
Van der Mussele v Belgium (1984) 6 EHRR 163 96
Van Droogenbroeck v Belgium (1982) 4 EHRR 443 . . . . .96, 99, 142
Van Gend en Loos v Nederlandse Administratie der Belastingen
    [1963] ECR 1 220
Van Marle v Netherlands (1986) 8 EHRR 483 169
Van Mechelen and Others v Netherlands (1998) 25 EHRR 647 61
Van Oosterwijck v Belgium (1981) 3 EHRR 557 123
Venditelli v Italy (1995) 19 EHRR 464 . . . . .154, 156, 158
Vereniging Weekblad Bluf! v Netherlands (1995) 20 EHRR 189 136
Vermiere v Belgium (1990) A 270-A 211
Vidal v Belgium (1992) A 235 198
Vijayanathan and Pusparajah v France (1993) 15 EHRR 62 29
Vilvarajah v United Kingdom (1992) 14 EHRR 248 . . . . .55, 56, 57, 93, 141
Vogt v Germany (1996) 21 EHRR 205 . . . . .72, 133
Volker Steam v Deutsche Bundespost (No 2) (Case C-132/93)
    [1994] I ECR 2715 226
von Colson v Land Nordrhein-Westfalen (Case 14/83)
    [1984] ECR 1891 5

W

W and DM v United Kingdom (1989) 37 DR 96 159
W and KL v Sweden (1985) 45 DR 143 160
W v Switzerland (1993) 17 EHRR 60 108

W v United Kingdom (1988) 10 EHRR 29 . . . . .116, 119, 167, 174, 175

W, X, Y and Z v Belgium (1975) 2 DR 110 163

Wachauf v The State [1988] ECR 2609 229

Wagner Miret v Fondo de Garantia Salaria (Case C-334/92)
    [1993] ECR I-6911 5

Waite and Kennedy v Germany (1999) 6 BHRC 499 179

Wasfi Suleman Mahmood, In re [1995] Imm AR 311 104

Watson v Bellmann (Case 118/75) [1976] ECR 1185 222

Webb v EMO Air Cargo (UK) Ltd [1993] 1 WLR 49 5

Weber v Switzerland (1990) 12 EHRR 508 . . . . .71, 172, 173

Weeks v United Kingdom (1988) 10 EHRR 293 . . . . .98, 99, 110, 111

Welch v United Kingdom (1995) 20 EHHR 247 115

Wemhoff v Germany (1979–80) 1 EHRR 55 . . . . .107, 108, 109

Widmer v Switzerland, App No 20527/92 88

Wingrove v United Kingdom (1997) 24 EHRR 1 134

Winterwerp v Netherlands (1979–80) 2 EHRR 387 . . . . .66, 98, 99, 102, 103,
    110, 111, 167, 170

Wood v United Kingdom (1997) 24 EHRR CD 69 42

Worm v Austria (1998) 25 EHRR 454 135

Wynne v United Kingdom (1995) 19 EHRR 333 112

X

X and Church of Scientology v Sweden (1979) 16 DR 68 .129, 130

X and Y v Netherlands (1986) 8 EHRR 235 . . . . .80, 116, 117

X and Y v United Kingdom (1983) 32 DR 220 123

X Ltd and Y v United Kingdom (1982) 28 DR 77 114

X v Austria (1967) 24 CD 8 187

X v Austria (1976) 7 DR 87 31

X v Austria (1989) 11 EHRR 112 101

X v Bedfordshire County Council [1995] 2 AC 633 . . . . .162, 183, 201

X v Belgium (1961) 4 YB 324 . . . . .115, 157

X v France (1983) 32 DR 266 . . . . .167, 208

X v France (1992) 14 EHRR 483 100

X v Germany (1975) 3 DR 92 33

X v Germany (1977) 9 DR 47 105

X v Germany (1983) 5 EHRR 512 92

X v Germany (1985) 7 EHRR 152 116

X v Iceland (1976) 5 DR 86 106

X v Switzerland (1979) 16 DR 85 159
X v Netherlands (1962) 5 YB 224 106
X v Netherlands (1966) 9 YB 474 129
X v United Kingdom (1975) 2 DR 50 130
X v United Kingdom (1976) 5 DR 100 160
X v United Kingdom (1978) 14 DR 179 88
X v United Kingdom (1980) 19 DR 244 159
X v United Kingdom (1980) 23 DR 228 159
X v United Kingdom (1982) 4 EHRR 188 ....67, 102, 109, 110,
111, 142, 207, 208
X v United Kingdom (1984) 6 EHRR 558 130
X v United Kingdom (1989) 64 DR 188 167
X, Y and Z v United Kingdom (1997) 24 EHRR 143 ....60, 123, 124

Y

Y v United Kingdom (1994) 17 EHRR 238 95
Yagci and Sargin v Turkey (1995) 20 EHRR 505 108
Yarrow plc and Three Shareholders v United Kingdom
(1983) 30 DR 155 32
Young v Ireland (1996) 21 EHRR CD 91 151
Young, James and Webster v United Kingdom
(1982) 4 EHRR 38 ....37, 69, 84, 138, 139
Young, James and Webster v United Kingdom (just satisfaction)
(1983) 5 EHRR 201 209

Z

Z v Finland (1998) 25 EHRR 371 ....124, 125
Z v United Kingdom (1999) 28 EHRR CD 65 ....162, 183
Zander v Sweden (1994) 18 EHRR 175 170
Zimmerman and Steiner v Switzerland (1984) 6 EHRR 17 ....113, 216
Zumbotel v Austria (1994) 17 EHRR 116 176

TABLE OF STATUTES AND STATUTORY INSTRUMENTS

Administration of Justice
Act 1973—
s 9(1)(c) 244
Air Force Act 1955 . . . . .247, 248
Ancient Monuments and
Archaeological Areas
Act 1979 26
Army Act 1955 . . . . .247, 248

Civil Aviation Act 1982—
s 76(1) 180
Civil Liability (Contributions)
Act 1978 244
Civil Procedure (Amendment
No 4) Rules 2000
(SI 2000/2092) 9, 127, 201,
204, 218
Companies Act 1985—
s 432(2) 190
Coroners Act 1988—
s 13 39
Court of Session Act 1988—
s 1(1) 244
Courts and Legal Services
Act 1990—
s 1 237
Courts Act 1971—
s 18 244
Criminal Justice Act 1987—
s 2(2) 31
Crown Proceedings Act 1947 246

Education Act—
s 9 161
European Communities
Act 1972
ss 2(1), (4) 144
s 3(1) 230

Financial Services Act 1986 42

Human Rights Act 1998 . . . . .1–21, 23,
26–27, 28, 36,
38, 42–45, 49,
54, 73, 98, 140,
186, 201, 219
s 1(1) 2, 19, 84,
140, 146, 233
s 1(2) 20, 146, 233
s 1(3) 2, 233
s 2 . . . . .3, 4, 49, 50,
60, 80, 230,
233, 245
s 2(1) 3, 4, 26,
38, 233
s 2(1)(b)–(d) .3, 233
s 3 . . . . .4, 5–6, 49, 60,
80, 81, 234
s 3(1) 3, 6–7, 11, 15,
17, 49, 234
s 3(2) 15, 49, 234
s 4 . . . . .11, 220, 234
s 4(2) 11, 234
s 4(4) 15, 235
s 4(5) 11, 235
s 4(6) 13, 235
s 5 . . . . .12, 235
s 5(2) 13, 235
s 6 . . . . .3, 4, 49, 60, 64,
73, 77, 80, 236
s 6(1) 7, 8, 13, 16,
38, 230, 236
s 6(2) .8, 13, 16, 236
s 6(3) 6, 7, 8, 38, 42,
45, 46, 49, 236
s 6(4) 43, 46, 236
s 6(5) 38, 236
s 6(6) 7, 46, 54,
77, 236
s 6(6)(b) 13, 236
s 6(7) 8
ss 6–8 . . . . .53, 236–38
s 7 . . . . .81, 236, 245

Human Rights Act
1998 CONTD—
s 7(1) 1, 7, 9, 26, 29,
204, 236,
238, 248
s 7(2) 9, 236
s 7(3) 1, 27, 81, 236
s 7(5) 10, 237
s 7(7) 1, 8, 26,
81, 237
s 7(11) 10, 203, 237, 245
s 8 . . . . .203, 238
s 8(1) 13, 16, 17, 238
s 8(2) 203, 204, 238
s 8(3) 17, 204–05, 238
s 8(4) 17, 206, 213, 238
s 9(1) 45, 47, 238
s 9(3) 205, 239
s 9(5) 206, 239
s 10(1)(a) 12, 239
s 10(1)(b) 12, 239
s 10(2) 12, 239
s 10(3)(b) 12, 239–40
s 10(4) 15, 240
s 11 . . . . .4, 240
s 12 . . . . .18–19, 240–41
s 13 . . . . .18, 241
s 14 . . . . .20, 241
s 14(3), (4) .20
s 15 . . . . .20, 241–42
s 15(3), (4) 20, 242
s 16(3) 20, 242
s 17(1) 20, 243
s 17(2) 20, 243
s 17(3) 20, 243
s 22(4) 11
Sched 1 . . . . .2, 49, 60, 170
Sched 1, Pt I 249–54
Sched 1, Pt II 254
Sched 1, Pt III 255
Sched 2, para 1(1) 13, 255
Sched 2, para 1(2) 14, 255

Sched 2, para 2(a) 14, 256
Sched 2, para 2(b) 14, 256
Sched 2, paras 3(1), 5 . . . . . .14, 256, 257
Sched 2, para 4(2) 14, 256
Sched 2, para 4(3) 14, 256
Sched 3, Pt I 19, 146, 257–59
Sched 3, Pt II 19, 161, 242, 259
Insolvency Act 1986—
s 371 117
Interpretation Act (Northern
Ireland) 1954—
s 41(6) 245

Law Reform (Miscellaneous
Provisions) (Scotland)
Act 1940 228
Leasehold Reform Act 1967 152

Marriage Act 1949 140
Marriage Act 1983—
s 1 140

Mental Health Act 1983 103
s 73 111
s 131 98

Ministers of the Crown
Act 1975 246

National Assistance Act 1948—
s 21 44
Naval Discipline Act 1957 . . . . . .247, 248
Northern Ireland Act 1998 246
Northern Ireland
Assembly Act 1973—
s 1 247
Northern Ireland
Constitution Act 1973—
s 38(1)(a) 246

Police Act 1997 . . . . .65, 126

Prevention of Terrorism
   (Temporary Provisions)
   Act 1984—
   s 16A 193

Sheriff Courts (Scotland)
   Act 1971 244

Supreme Court Act 1981—
   ss 2(1), 4(1) 243
   s 12(1)–(6) 243
   s 29(3) 46, 193,
                        195, 196
   s 31(3) 8, 23
   s 31(4) 201

War Crimes Act 1991 114

TABLE OF EUROPEAN LEGISLATION

Treaty Establishing the
European Economic
Community 1957
(EC Treaty)
(post-Amsterdam
numbers)

Arts 46, 55 228
Arts 48, 52, 59 228
Art 220 223
Art 234 231
Art 292 223
Art 307 224

European Convention on
Human Rights and
Fundamental Freedoms

Art 1 . . . . .2, 53, 77,
80, 84, 87,
90, 263
Art 2 . . . . .62, 75–77,
. . . . 83, 85–89,
. . . . .229, 263–64
Arts 2–12, 14 1
Arts 2, 3, 4(1), 7 . . . . .51, 146
Arts 2–18 . . . . .2, 84
Art 3 . . . . .55–58, 77, 83,
87, 88, 89–95,
145, 160,
229, 264
Art 4 . . . . .83, 95–96, 264
Art 5 . . . . .19, 30, 61,
62, 63, 66, 83,
96–113, 119, 149,
177, 205, 229,
239, 264–65
Art 6 . . . . .10, 33, 45, 51,
60–62, 68, 69,
70, 82, 83, 98,
108–10, 113, 119,
121, 149, 158,
165–99, 215, 227,
229, 265–66

Art 6(1) 143, 166–92,
214, 222, 265
Art 6(2) 192–95, 265
Art 6(3) 30, 189, 193,
194, 195–99,
265–66
Art 7 . . . . .60, 114–15,
229, 266
Art 8 . . . . .7, 51, 55, 63,
76–77, 83, 89,
95, 115, 120–29,
139, 143, 145, 160,
215, 216, 224, 225,
227, 229, 266
Arts 8–11 . . . . .51, 58, 59,
61, 62, 68, 69,
82–83, 86, 118,
221, 266–67
Art 9 . . . . .18, 70, 83,
129–30, 139,
159, 229, 266
Art 10 . . . . .18, 41, 72, 76,
131–37, 138, 139,
143, 149, 159,
224, 229, 266
Art 11 . . . . .61, 63, 137–39,
145, 229, 267
Art 12 . . . . .83, 139–40,
229, 267
Art 13 . . . . .2, 53–56, 58,
59, 80, 84,
140–43, 177,
229, 267
Art 14 . . . . .120, 144–46,
157, 229, 267
Art 15 . . . . .19, 96, 114,
146–48, 267–68
Art 16 . . . . .2, 148, 253, 268
Art 17 . . . . .149, 268
Art 18 . . . . .68, 150, 268
Art 19 268
Art 20 269

European Convention on
Human Rights and
Fundamental Freedoms
CONTD—
Art 21 269
Art 22 269
Art 23 .269–70
Art 24 270
Art 25 270
Art 26 .80, 270
Art 27 .233, 270
Art 28 271
Art 29 271
Art 30 271
Art 31 271
Art 32 .247, 271
Art 33 272
Art 34 . . . . .8, 21, 26, 28,
                                35, 41, 81,
                                237, 272
Art 35 . . . . .21, 272
Art 35(3) 141, 272
Art 36 272–73
Art 36(2) 37, 46, 273
Art 37 273
Art 38 273
Art 39 273
Art 40 273
Art 41 .113, 206,
                                207, 274
Art 42 274

Art 43 274
Art 44 274
Art 45 275
Art 46 .21, 275
Art 47 275
Art 48 275
Art 49 275
Art 50 275
Art 51 275
Art 52 276
Art 53 276
Art 54 .247, 276
Art 55 276
Art 56 .276–77
Art 57 277
Art 58 277
Art 59 .277–78
Protocol 1, Art 1 . . . . .31, 58, 60,
                                72, 83, 144,
                                150–58, 216, 229
Protocol 1, Arts 1–3 . . . . .1, 233
Protocol 1, Art 2 . . . . . . .19, 158–62, 241
Protocol 1, Art 3 . . . . . . .162–64, 225–26
Protocol 1, Arts 3, 10 149
Protocol 2, Art 1 95
Protocol 4, Art 2 . . . . .221, 230
Protocol 4, Art 2(3), (4) 63
Protocol 4, Art 3 230
Protocol 6, Arts 1, 2 . . . . .2, 164,
                                233, 255
Protocol 7, Art 1(1) 63

CHAPTER 1

THE HUMAN RIGHTS ACT

1.01 The central theme of this book is the relationship between the Human Rights Act 1998 and public law.

1.02 This chapter provides an overview of the Act and a general discussion of the problems that it raises. In some instances, where a more detailed exposition is provided elsewhere, cross-references are given.

1.03 The text of the Act itself is set out in Appendix 1, p 233.

INTRODUCTION

1.04 The preamble to the Human Rights Act states that its purpose is to 'give *further effect* to the rights and freedoms guaranteed under the European Convention on Human Rights' (emphasis added). On its face, the Act allows the raising of Convention issues to be raised only by the 'victim' of the unlawful acts (or proposed acts) of a public authority.[1] Ordinarily, such acts would be challenged by way of judicial review. The scheme of the Act suggests, however, that the Convention will impact upon almost all types of litigation, including that between private parties, and will extend well beyond the confines of judicial review. It will revolutionise the Courts' approach to both statutory construction[2] and development of the common law.[3]

THE RIGHTS INCORPORATED

1.05 Section 1 of the Human Rights Act defines the term 'Convention rights'. It provides:

In this Act 'the Convention rights' means the rights and fundamental freedoms set out in:

Articles 2 to 12 and 14 of the Convention;

Articles 1 to 3 of the First Protocol; and

---

1 HRA 1998, s 7(1), (3), (7). See paras 1.12–2.19.
2 See *ibid*, ss 3 and 6, at paras 1.23–1.38.
3 See *ibid*, ss 2 and 6, at paras 1.15–1.22.

> Articles 1 and 2 of the Sixth Protocol,
>
> as read with Articles 16 to 18 of the Convention.

1.06 The Articles referred to in s 1(1) of the Act are then set out in Schedule 1.[4] These rights are separately outlined in Chapter 4 of this book.

1.07   There are two important points to note about the manner in which the Convention has been given effect by the Human Rights Act. First, as shall be seen be seen later in this chapter, the way in which 'Convention rights' can be applied by the domestic courts is entirely dependent upon the structure of the Act itself. Many provisions in the Act restrict full implementation of the Convention. Secondly, not all the Convention provisions have been incorporated.

1.08   Articles 1 and 13 of the Convention are not among those Articles expressly given effect to by the Human Rights Act.[5] They provide:

> Art 1   The High Contracting Parties shall secure to everyone within their jurisdiction the rights and freedoms defined in Section I[6] of this Convention.
>
> Art 13 Everyone whose rights and freedoms as set forth in this Convention are violated shall have an effective remedy before a national authority notwithstanding that the violation has been committed by persons acting in an official capacity.

1.09 The exclusion of Article 1 from the Act is readily explained. Article 1 contains an international treaty obligation on Member States which (the government has stated) is now complied with by the Act itself. The omission of Article 13 appears to be because the Act was considered to afford an effective remedy against violations of the Convention and thereby rendered the specific incorporation of Article 13 itself unnecessary: see, for example, Lord Williams of Mostyn:

> Our view is, quite unambiguously, that Article 13 is met by the passage of the [Act].[7]

1.10 However, Article 13 is an important adjunct to challenging other Convention violations and is sometimes used by the European Court of Human Rights in Strasbourg to criticise existing domestic legal procedures for failing to provide an effective remedy against such violations. Judicial review has, in particular cases, been held by the Strasbourg Court not to afford an effective remedy under Article 13 (see paras 3.26 *et seq*).

---

4   HRA 1998, s 1(3).

5   ECHR, Arts 1 and 13 are analysed in Chapter 4 of this book. The Act also does not purport to incorporate those Protocols of the Convention which the United Kingdom has not ratified. For a table of Protocols and their ratification by signatory states, see the Strasbourg Court's website at www.echr.coe.int.

6   *Ibid*, Section I contains the substantive provisions of the Convention; ie, Arts 2–18.

7   *Hansard*, HL, 3 November 1997, col 1308.

THE INTERPRETATIVE OBLIGATIONS ON THE COURT

1.11 The Human Rights Act contains three sections that must be read together in order to understand the new interpretative obligations that now lie upon the courts.

1.12 Section 2(1) provides, materially, as follows:

> A court or tribunal determining a question which has arisen in connection with a Convention right must take into account any:
>
>> judgment, decision, declaration or advisory opinion of the European Court of Human Rights ...
>
> whenever made or given, so far as, in the opinion of the court or tribunal, it is relevant to the proceedings in which that question has arisen.[8]

1.12 Section 3(1) of the Act provides:

> So far as it is possible to do so, primary legislation and subordinate legislation must be read and given effect in a way which is compatible with the Convention rights.

1.13 Finally, s 6 provides, materially, that:

> It is unlawful for a public authority to act in a way which is incompatible with a Convention right.
>
> ...
>
> In this section, 'public authority' includes:
>
> a court or tribunal ...

1.14 The Act thus contains separate interpretative obligations which have the power to transform both statute and common law.

The Strasbourg case law

1.15 The effect of s 2 of the Human Rights Act is that a court or tribunal is required to take the Strasbourg case law into account, but is not bound by it. Further, the Act expressly states that the Strasbourg judgments (and other material)[9] must be taken into account 'whenever made or given'. It is clear that domestic courts will be able to depart from the Strasbourg case law and other material where, for example, Strasbourg has given no precise ruling on the matter.[10] The freedom to depart from this case law goes beyond this situation, however.

---

8   HRA 1998, s 2 recites other sources that must, on the same basis, be taken into account by domestic courts and tribunals being Commission reports and decisions and decisions of the Committee of Ministers: see s 2(1)(b)–(d).

9   See *ibid*, s 2(1)(b)–(d).

10 See, eg, *Hansard*, HL debates (committee stage), 18 November 1997, col 514.

1.16   The following points should be borne in mind when deploying s 2 of the Act.

1.17   Strasbourg's interpretative doctrines such as the principles of effectiveness and up to date interpretation (see paras 3.19–3.49) require the domestic courts to examine the current meaning of the words used in the Convention. The Strasbourg Court is not bound by a doctrine of precedent. Thus, reliance on an old Strasbourg case could be a breach of such principles and, hence, a breach of the court's obligations under s 6 of the Act. Section 2 of the Act would not require the old case to be followed.

1.18   The House of Lords has already ruled that one doctrine of the Strasbourg Court, namely, that of the margin of appreciation, is not strictly available to the national courts.[11]

1.19   There may also be circumstances where domestic law affords more protection than the Convention and where s 2 could never require adherence to the Strasbourg case law. Section 11 of the Act provides that reliance on a Convention right does not restrict any other right or freedom having effect in the United Kingdom.

1.20   There is a close relationship between ss 2 and 3 of the Act as the process of statutory construction may well entail consideration of the Strasbourg case law in order to give effect to the Court's obligations under s 3 to construe statutory provisions in so far as is possible compatibly with the Convention (see below).

1.21   Importantly, too, s 2 may have to be considered by the courts when developing the common law. The development of a tort of privacy may, for example, be a consequence of the Court's consideration of the Strasbourg case law when dealing with questions connected with Convention rights.

1.22   The obligations intrinsic to s 2 may require courts to depart from pre-Human Rights Act precedent when dealing with Convention issues. This would appear to follow from the combined effect of ss 2, 3 and 6 of the Act.

Interpretation of United Kingdom legislation

1.23   Domestic courts and tribunals are, by virtue of s 3 of the Human Rights Act, placed under a positive obligation of interpretation: they must actively seek out Convention-compatible meanings for legislation. On its face, s 3 extends to legislation whether passed before or after the coming into force of the Human Rights Act.

1.24   This provision is therefore of the utmost importance, but its meaning is unclear: what is meant by 'so far as possible'? It presumably cannot be inviting departure from the plain meaning of a statute. On the other hand, it cannot be

---

11   See *R v Director of Public Prosecutions ex p Kebilene* [2000] HRLR 93, pp 115–16, *per* Lord Hope of Craighead. See, also, paras 3.128–3.132.

intended to restrict such interpretation to situations where the statute bears two possible meanings. If the courts were only entitled to take into account the Convention where a statute is ambiguous, that would be little different from the pre-Human Rights Act position.[12] It has been suggested that this provision in effect enjoins the judiciary to find that legislation does comply with the Convention, thereby discouraging them from finding any breach.[13]

1.25   There is an important parallel to s 3 of the Act in European Community law. In *Marleasing SA v La Comercial Internacional de Alimentación SA*,[14] the European Court of Justice in Luxembourg held that national courts must as far as possible interpret domestic law in the light of the wording and purpose of a European Directive so as to achieve the result pursued by the Directive. In *Wagner Miret v Fondo de Garantia Salaria*,[15] the ECJ held that there was a presumption that the State intended to comply with Community law although this presumption was one that had to give way if domestic law could not be interpreted consistently with Community law.

1.26   The rigour of the *Marleasing* approach has been mitigated by the decision of the House of Lords in *Webb v EMO Air Cargo (UK) Ltd*.[16] There, the House of Lords held that it would only be possible to construe domestic law in accordance with Community law if it could be done without 'distorting' the meaning of domestic legislation, namely, where a domestic law was 'open to an interpretation consistent with the Directive whether or not it is also open to an interpretation inconsistent with it'.

1.27   The likely approach of the domestic courts to s 3 may, however, be more generous than in the Community law context. It has been foreshadowed both by decisions of the New Zealand courts in relation to that country's Bill of Rights and also by earlier decisions in this country.

1.28   In New Zealand, the courts have been both prepared to read words into legislative provisions in order not to construe domestic legislation in a manner that is incompatible with its Bill of Rights, and also to require a clear abrogation of the right in question before being prepared to construe such legislation inconsistently with the Bill of Rights.[17]

1.29   Domestic case law as to the construction of statutes involving human rights issues which pre-dates the Human Rights Act suggests that domestic courts

---

12   Ie, the position as set out in *R v Secretary of State for the Home Department ex p Brind* [1991] AC 696: the only difference would be that the HRA 1998 places a positive requirement upon the Court to seek out and resolve such ambiguity.

13   See Geoffrey Marshall, 'Interpreting interpretation in the Human Rights Bill' [1998] PL 167, pp 167 *et seq*.

14   Case C-106/89 [1990] ECR I-4135. See, also, Case 14/83 *von Colson v Land Nordrhein-Westfalen* [1984] ECR 1891.

15   Case C-334/92 [1993] ECR I-6911.

16   [1993] 1 WLR 49, *per* Lord Keith. See, also, *per* Lord Keith in *Duke v GEC Reliance Ltd* [1988] AC 618.

17   See, eg, *Minister of Transport v Noort* [1992] 3 NZLR 260.

will also require express provision to contrary effect before being prepared to construe a statute in a manner that is incompatible with the Convention.[18]

The interpretative obligations and parliamentary sovereignty

1.30 The Human Rights Act places at least two limitations on the conventional doctrine of parliamentary sovereignty.

1.31 The first lies in s 3 of the Act. As outlined above, it is apparent that this section requires the Court to employ the most flexible techniques of statutory interpretation when construing an Act of Parliament (whenever enacted) and including the Act itself after the Act becomes law. As Lord Cooke of Thorndon has observed, s 3(1):[19]

> ... definitely goes further than the existing common law rules of statutory interpretation, because it enjoins a search for possible meanings as distinct from the meaning which has been the traditional approach in the matter of statutory interpretation in the courts.

1.32 But, once the search for a range of possible meanings is sanctioned, indeed required, by the Act, it follows that the nature of the Court's function has changed. It is no longer searching for putative parliamentary intent in respect of the legislation being construed but is, rather, engaged in a wholly different enquiry, namely the enquiry as to whether the provision in question can be reconciled with a Convention meaning. The two functions are by no means the same. Section 3(1) may require the court to jettison the probable intention of Parliament where it appears to be incompatible with the Convention.

1.33 In *Pepper (Inspector of Taxes) v Hart*,[20] the House of Lords held that Hansard could be resorted to, for the purposes of statutory construction, where legislation is ambiguous, obscure or leads to an absurdity. Once there is ambiguity in a statute then, under s 3(1) of the Act, the possible Convention meaning must surely prevail. But, if this is so, it may no longer be material that *Hansard* may establish that Parliament actually intended the opposite.

1.34 The other significant aspect of s 3(1) is that the techniques of construction that it requires must be employed in relation to the Human Rights Act itself. For example, the definition of a 'public authority' is left open-ended in s 6(3) and refers, in somewhat circular fashion, to an authority certain of whose functions are of a 'public nature'. It has been assumed that this reference is

---

18 *R v Lord Chancellor's Department ex p Witham* [1997] 2 All ER 779, especially p 788e–g, *per* Laws J; *R v Secretary of State for the Home Department ex p Simms* [1999] 3 WLR 328.

19 *Hansard*, HL, 18 November 1997, col 533.

20 [1993] AC 593.

merely a reference back to those authorities susceptible to judicial review,[21] but s 3(1) is likely to require a much wider approach to jurisdiction for reasons which are addressed in Chapter 2.

1.35 The second significant limitation on Parliamentary sovereignty is created by s 6(1) of the Human Rights Act which has the effect that in the development of the common law the courts act unlawfully unless they act in a manner that is compatible with the Convention.

1.36 Although, as shall be seen (at paras 1.62–1.75), the Act does not permit the courts to strike down a statute which contravenes Convention rights, it has, as outlined above, given the courts the widest techniques of statutory interpretation in order to reach in a construction that is Convention-compliant. It seems probable that the Act may require the courts to give some protection against a failure to legislate. The Act does not permit a direct assault on Parliament's failure to do so.[22] But, if there is a legislative omission the courts may, in order to comply with s 6(1) of the Act, have to give effect to Convention rights (where appropriate) by developing the common law. The most obvious example, as suggested above, may be the creation of a new tort of privacy so as to effect compliance with Article 8 of the Convention.[23]

1.37 Further, it is clear that the courts can, and indeed must, apply Convention rights so as to cut down the scope of any statutory discretion capable of infringing those rights.

1.38 Thus, the Human Rights Act provides a new constitutional basis for the court's function in judicial review. No longer is the court searching for a solution to the fictional (and, essentially, passive) question of what Parliament actually intended and in reviewing the power found to have been conferred; from 2 October 2000, it is engaged in the (essentially active) exercise of seeking to protect designated Convention rights. This role is as much directed towards the substantive content (or omission) of the relevant law as it is of the application of that law by the relevant public authority.

CLAIMANTS, DEFENDANTS AND FORUM

Standing: who will be able to bring a Convention challenge?

1.39 Section 7(1) of the Human Rights Act states that only a person who is, or would be, a 'victim' of an action, or proposed action, by a public authority

---

21 Consider, eg, *Hansard*, HC, Vol 314, col 409, where the Home Secretary described the judicial review jurisdiction case law as the 'most valuable asset that we have to hand'.

22 HRA 1998, s 6(3), (6).

23 The Lord Chancellor has expressed a contrary view: *Hansard*, HL, 3 November 1997, col 755.

which is incompatible with the Convention can bring proceedings or rely on the Convention right or rights concerned.

1.40   The Act states that a person is a 'victim' only if he would be a victim for the purposes of Article 34 of the Convention.[24] That states that only a victim may bring an application before the Strasbourg Court. Thus, for these purposes, it appears to be mandatory for English courts and tribunals to follow the Strasbourg case law.[25]

1.41   The core concept is that there can be no challenge to the law in the abstract; the alleged victim must be directly, or indirectly at least, affected by the matter complained of.[26]

1.42   As has been widely commented on, this test may be narrower than the 'sufficient interest' test for judicial review, set out in s 31(3) of the Supreme Court Act 1981. These issues are considered at paras 2.03 *et seq*.

Defendants: who will be subject to a Convention challenge?

1.43 Section 6 (1) of the Human Rights Act states:

> It is unlawful for a public authority to act in a way which is incompatible with a Convention right.

1.44 A 'public authority' is defined to be 'any person whose functions are of a public nature'.[27]

1.45   The concept of a 'public authority' is a familiar one to judicial review lawyers. There is an extensive jurisprudence seeking to define its limits.[28] The 'public functions' test is – on the face of it at least – precisely the test for susceptibility to judicial review set out in *R v Takeover Panel ex p Datafin plc*.[29]

1.46   It might therefore be thought that the Act will apply in more or less the same situations as judicial review. Matters are, however, more complex than that, for two reasons at least.

1.47   First, the Act provides that a person is not to be regarded as a public authority in respect of acts which are by their nature private.[30] The implication would appear to be therefore that a public authority (in the sense familiar from the judicial review case law) is only susceptible to challenge under the Act in respect of the exercise of its public law powers. In fact, it is clear that that is not

---

24   HRA 1998, s 7(7).

25   For a discussion of the Strasbourg case law, see paras 2.20 *et seq*.

26   The leading case is *Klass v Germany* (1980) 2 EHRR 214. See para 2.23.

27   HRA 1998, s 6(3). The only body expressly excluded from this definition is Parliament itself: s 6(2). There can, therefore, be no challenge to Parliament for simply enacting legislation in contravention of Convention rights.

28   See the summary at paras 2.04 *et seq*.

29   [1987] 2 WLR 699, CA.

30   HRA 1998, s 6(7).

the government's intention. During the Act's passage through Parliament, statements were made by the Lord Chancellor and the Home Secretary to the effect that:

> Obvious public authorities, such as central government and the police, are caught in respect of everything they do.[31]

1.48 This approach is wholly different from that of the Administrative Court: one might challenge a local authority's planning decisions by way of judicial review, but not its decision to dismiss an employee. The latter have not been considered to be public functions. The parliamentary statements suggest that they would however fall to be considered under the Human Rights Act.

1.49 Secondly, in certain circumstances, a court determining a purely private dispute may be required to apply the Convention (see paras 3.142 *et seq*).

1.50 This has the potential to extend the reach of the court far beyond that of judicial review.

1.51 These issues are further explored at paras 2.71 *et seq*.

Forum: where Convention points can be raised

1.52 Use of the Convention is not restricted to proceedings for judicial review. Section 7(1) of the Human Rights Act states that parties will be able to rely upon the Convention in 'any legal proceedings'.

1.53 It does not, however, follow from this that a breach of the Convention can be relied upon as a *cause of action* in 'any legal proceedings'. The Act also provides that proceedings may only be brought in such 'appropriate court or tribunal' as may be determined by rules.[32]

1.54 The effect appears to be therefore that the Convention may be relied upon at least defensively in any legal proceedings, but that its use as a cause of action may be prescribed by the rules. The Lord Chancellor's Department Consultation Paper, *Human Rights Act 1998: Rules and Practice Directions*,[33] states:

> We propose that a free-standing case under s 7(1)(a) of the Act should be brought in the following ways:
>
> – using the existing judicial review procedures;
> – in the county court or in the High Court where a claim for damages is made (unless this is associated with a claim for judicial review).

In fact, no rule has as yet been enacted to this effect.[34]

---

31 The Home Secretary, *Hansard*, HC, 16 February 1998, col 775.
32 HRA 1998, s 7(2).
33 13 March 2000.
34 See the Civil Procedure (Amendment No 4) Rules 2000, SI 2000/2092, coming into force on 2 October 2000.

1.55   The implication appears to be therefore that normal jurisdictional rules apply, and that if a judicial review remedy is sought – such as a quashing order in respect of an impugned decision – a claim under the Human Rights Act will have to be brought by way of judicial review. Section 7(11) of the Act provides for the possibility that expanded remedies might be available outside the Administrative Court:

> The Minister who has power to make rules in relation to a particular tribunal may, to the extent he considers it necessary to ensure the tribunal can provide an appropriate remedy in relation to an act (or a proposed act) of a public authority which is (or would be) unlawful as a result of section 6(1), by order add to:
>
> (a) the relief or remedies which the tribunal may grant; or
>
> (b) the grounds on which it may grant them.

1.56 The Consultation Paper states, however, that there is no intention at this stage to draft any such rules. It is therefore inevitable that much litigation under the Human Rights Act will be conducted in the Administrative Court, notwithstanding that there may be cases in which that Court may fall foul of the requirements of Article 6 of the Convention unless the process of judicial review is expanded at least in certain areas (see Chapter 3, especially paras 3.19 et seq).

TIME LIMITS AND RETROSPECTIVE EFFECT OF THE HUMAN RIGHTS ACT

Time limits

1.57 Section 7(5) provides that proceedings under the Human Rights Act must be brought before the end of one year from the date the act complained of took place; there is however a discretion to extend time if the Court considers it just and equitable 'having regard to all the circumstances'. The operation of the court's discretion to extend time under s 7(5) of the Act must, itself, be exercised in a manner that is not incompatible with the Convention. Care may be needed in exercising such a discretion to ensure that the court complies with its obligations under Article 6 of the Convention (see Chapter 5, especially paras 5.61 et seq).

1.58   This period is subject to any rule imposing a stricter time limit in relation to the procedure used.[35] Thus, where, the proceedings are brought in the form of an application for permission to apply for judicial review, the three month time limit for such applications will be preserved.

---

35   HRA 1998, s 7(5).

Retrospective effect

1.59 A person may only rely upon Convention rights in legal proceedings, if the act which he contends contravened the Convention took place after section 7 of the Act comes into force, that is, 2 October 2000.[36]

1.60 This is however subject to an important exception. Section 22(4) of the Act provides that where proceedings are brought by or at the instigation of a public authority, a victim may rely on Convention rights 'whenever the act in question took place'. The effect is:

- the Convention cannot be relied upon as a cause of action by an aggrieved claimant except where the breach complained of takes place after 2 October 2000;
- a breach of Convention rights can be used defensively in proceedings after 2 October 2000, no matter when the breach complained of took place.

EFFECT OF A BREACH OF THE CONVENTION IN DOMESTIC LAW

1.61 The effect of a breach of Convention rights under the Act depends upon the type of breach which has occurred.

Primary legislation: declaration of incompatibility

1.62 The domestic courts cannot quash primary legislation which violates Convention rights.

1.63 As has already been seen, all legislation – whenever enacted – must be read so far as is possible to 'give effect to' it in a way which is compatible with Convention rights.[37]

1.64 Section 4 of the Act provides that where the legislation in question cannot be so read, a higher court[38] 'may make a declaration of that incompatibility'.[39] Thus, it is entirely a matter for the court's discretion whether to grant such a declaration.

---

36 HRA 1998, s 22(4). See paras 1.52 *et seq* for s 1.
37 *Ibid*, s 3(1).
38 Ie, the High Court or above: *ibid*, s 4(5). There is no suggestion that this remedy is confined to the Administrative Court.
39 *Ibid*, s 4(2).

1.65   Where a court is even considering whether to make a declaration of incompatibility, the Crown is entitled to notice, and the Minister is entitled to be joined as a party.[40]

1.66   If such a declaration is made, it is of little immediate value to the victim. Section 4(6) provides that such a declaration is not binding, and does not affect the continuing validity of the legislation. In itself, it makes no difference to the status of the impugned legislation. Its importance is that it triggers the possibility of a 'remedial order'.

Remedial orders

1.67   The effect of a remedial order is to provide a 'fast track' mechanism by which primary legislation can be amended, as shall be explained. There are three circumstances in which a Minister may make a remedial order pursuant to s 10 of the Act:

1   where a court has made a declaration of incompatibility, and there is to be no further appeal;[41]

2   where it appears to the Minister[42] that in the light of a finding of the Strasbourg Court after the Act comes into force, a provision of legislation is incompatible with the Convention;[43]

3   where, in the case of incompatible subordinate legislation, he considers it necessary to amend the primary legislation under which subordinate legislation was made, in order to enable the incompatibility to be removed.

1.68   A remedial order is not, however, an automatic consequence of any of these events. Section 10(2) of the Act provides:[44]

> If a Minister of the Crown considers that there are *compelling reasons* for proceeding under this section, he may by order make such amendments to the legislation as he considers necessary to remove the incompatibility. [Emphasis added.]

1.69   Thus, the Minister has a discretion whether or not to proceed. The words 'compelling reasons' were added during the Bill's progress through Parliament. The clear intention is therefore that there will be cases in which the

---

40   HRA 1998, s 5. In criminal proceedings, the Minister may appeal to the House of Lords against such an order (subject to leave).

41   *Ibid*, s 10(1)(a).

42   Or Her Majesty in Council: *ibid*, s 10(1)(b).

43   *Ibid*, s 10(1)(b).

44   *Ibid*, s 10(3)(b), which concerns amendment of primary legislation where necessary to remove an incompatibility in subordinate legislation is in substantially the same terms.

'fast track' procedure is not used. Failure to make a remedial order cannot itself be challenged under the Human Rights Act.[45]

.70   There appears to be little incentive to challenge primary legislation. A public authority found to have acted in breach of Convention rights has a complete defence if (broadly) the source of its breach was primary legislation which it applied.[46] If that is the case, the public authority will not have acted unlawfully, notwithstanding the proven breach of Convention rights[47] Section 8(1) of the Act provides that damages may only be awarded in respect of an act found by a court to be 'unlawful'. Plainly, therefore, there can be no award of damages if the fault lies with primary legislation.

.71   There is little prospect of any other useful relief. As has already been seen, the Act expressly provides that a declaration of incompatibility is not binding, and does not affect the continuing validity of the legislation.[48] It is therefore highly improbable that a court would conclude it had the power to disapply the legislation, pending consideration by the Minister of the declaration of incompatibility, and Parliament in due course. The Act plainly provides a comprehensive scheme in respect of the status of primary legislation. It is not even clear whether the applicant would benefit from any eventual change in the law which is made by Parliament. A remedial order may by made so as to take effect retrospectively,[49] but need not be.

.72   In practice, it may be that the issue of the compatibility of primary legislation is more likely to be raised by a defendant than a claimant. Where, for example, a claimant seeks to challenge the act of a local authority, that authority has a complete defence if as a result of one or more provisions of primary legislation it could not have acted differently.[50] It therefore has every incentive to contend that the breach of Convention rights, if made good, is founded on the provisions of primary legislation. Further, where the court is considering whether to make a declaration of incompatibility, the Crown is entitled to be joined to the proceedings on notice.[51] The defendant local authority would therefore obtain the benefit of fighting alongside another party.

---

45   HRA 1998, s 6(6)(b). It is at least conceivable however that in some circumstances such a refusal could be subject to challenge on *Wednesbury* grounds by way of judicial review.

46   *Ibid*, s 6(2). See, further, discussion at paras 1.86 *et seq*.

47   *Ibid*, s 6(1).

48   *Ibid*, s 4(6).

49   *Ibid*, Sched 2, para 1(1).

50   *Ibid*, s 6(2).

51   *Ibid*, s 5(2).

The fast track process for amending primary legislation

1.73 Schedule 2 to the Act governs the use of remedial orders. The power to make a remedial order is wide. It includes:

    (a) power to amend primary legislation (including primary legislation other than that which contains the incompatible provision); and

    (b) power to amend or revoke subordinate legislation (including subordinate legislation other than that which contains the incompatible provision.[52]

1.74 There are two procedures by which a remedial order may be made. Ordinarily, a draft of the order must be laid before Parliament together with an explanation of the incompatibility it seeks to remove and a statement of the reasons for utilising a remedial order.[53] There then follows a period of 60 days during which representations may be made.[54] If any such representations are made, the person making the remedial order must lay before Parliament a further statement summarising the representations and stating whether the order has been changed.[55] Once 60 days has passed since the order was laid (or, if the order was amended, since the further statement dealing with those representations was laid), it may be approved by a resolution of each House of Parliament.[56]

1.75 In urgent cases, such an order can be made without approval. The person making the order must however declare the urgency to be such that it is necessary to make the order without a draft being so approved.[57] Once made, it must, however, be laid before Parliament; just as in the 'ordinary' procedure, it must be accompanied by an explanation of the incompatibility it seeks to remove and a statement as to why a remedial order has been used.[58] There then follows a period of 60 days in which representations may be made; if they are, the order may be amended, and the order must again be laid before Parliament together with a summary of the representations and a statement as to any changes made as a result.[59] If the order has not been approved by each House of Parliament within 120 days of the date on which the original order was made, it ceases to have effect.

---

52 HRA 1998, Sched 2, para 1(2).
53 *Ibid*, Sched 2, paras 3(1), 5.
54 *Ibid*, Sched 2, paras 3, 5.
55 *Ibid*, Sched 2, para 4(2).
56 *Ibid*, Sched 2, para 2(a).
57 *Ibid*, Sched 2, para 2(b).
58 *Ibid*, Sched 2, paras 3(1), 5.
59 *Ibid*, Sched 2, para 4(2), (3).

Subordinate legislation

1.76 Nowhere in the Act is it expressly stated that subordinate legislation can be quashed (by an appropriate court, at least) if it contravenes Convention rights. That this is so, however, does seem clear by inference.

1.77   Section 3(1) provides that both primary and subordinate legislation must be read and given effect to in a way which is compatible with Convention rights (see the discussion above, at paras 1.23 *et seq*). Section 3(2) provides:

> This section:
>
> ...
>
> (b) does not affect the validity, continuing operation or enforcement of any incompatible primary legislation.

1.78 By inference, in the case of subordinate legislation, incompatibility with Convention rights does affect the 'validity, continuing operation or enforcement' of subordinate legislation.[60]

1.79   In other words, it can be quashed, or declared invalid if it inescapably contravenes Convention rights.

1.80   Not all subordinate legislation is subject to attack in this form. Incompatibility with Convention rights:

> ... does not affect the validity, continuing operation or enforcement of any incompatible subordinate legislation if (disregarding the possibility of revocation) primary legislation prevents the removal of the incompatibility.

1.81 On the face of it, this section raises the possibility that subordinate legislation could be 'ring-fenced'. Primary legislation could be used to expressly prohibit the possibility of challenge to subordinate legislation made pursuant to that primary legislation. It does not appear that this is what Parliament intended, however. The section is intended to prevent the court's quashing subordinate legislation where it is inevitably incompatible because of the terms of the parent statute.[61]

1.82   In such a case, the only remedy is a declaration of incompatibility.[62]

Administrative action

1.83 Courts may give relief against administrative action by a public authority which infringes Convention rights, except where:

---

60 Further support for this inference can be found in HRA 1998, s 10(4), which permits a remedial order where subordinate legislation has been quashed, or declared invalid, by reason of incompatibility with a Convention right.

61 Lord Chancellor, *Hansard*, HL, 3 November 1997, col 1230.

62 HRA 1998, s 4(4).

(1) the authority was bound to so act by primary legislation;

(2) the authority was acting to give effect to or to enforce provisions of, or made under primary legislation which cannot be read or given effect to in a way which is compatible with Convention rights.[63]

1.84 In those circumstances, the impugned administrative action is 'lawful'.[64] As stated above, no breach of the requirements of the Act is made out, and no damages will flow.[65]

1.85   The common law, however, must give way to Convention law when the actions of a public authority are considered. As has been seen, the Act states '[i]t is unlawful for a public authority to act in a way which is incompatible with a Convention right'.[66]

THE STATUTORY DEFENCE

1.86 Section 6(2) of the Act contains a statutory defence to a claim under s 6(1). A public authority may lawfully act in violation of Convention rights, where:

(a) as a result of one or more provisions of primary legislation, the authority could not have acted differently; or

(b) in the case of one or more provisions of, or made under, primary legislation which cannot be read or given effect in a way which is compatible with the Convention rights, the authority was acting so as to give effect to or enforce those provisions.

1.87 Thus, where a public authority has a duty to act under primary legislation which violates Convention rights, s 6(2)(a) provides that the authority has a complete defence to any claim under the Act. No damages[67] can be given against it.

1.88   Where a public authority acts to 'give effect to or enforce' infringing primary legislation (which cannot be read otherwise), s 6(2)(b) provides that it acts lawfully. The same defence applies where it acts upon subordinate legislation made under infringing primary legislation (where the primary legislation cannot be read otherwise). There is, however, an important lacuna in the statutory defence. It appears not to apply to an authority which gives effect to, or enforces subordinate legislation which offends Convention rights if that subordinate legislation was made under primary legislation which is itself compatible with the Convention. In those circumstances, it is at least arguable

---

63   HRA 1998, s 6(2).
64   *Ibid*, s 6(2).
65   *Ibid*, s 8(1).
66   *Ibid*, s 6(1).
67   *Ibid*, s 8(1).

that the authority should refrain from implementing the offending legislation.[68]

1.89   The resulting defence leaves a public authority with a difficult task. It must seek to construe subordinate legislation as far as possible in accordance with Convention rights.[69] Should it conclude this cannot be done, it must then carry out the same exercise in respect of the empowering provision of primary legislation. If it concludes that the primary legislation cannot be read compatibly, no violation of s 6(1) would occur if it acted upon the infringing subordinate legislation as it has a complete defence. If, however, it concludes that the primary legislation is compatible, it risks infringing s 6 of the Act if it gives effect to it.

DAMAGES

1.90   Damages may be awarded for the unlawful act of a public authority in breach of Convention rights.[70]

1.91   The Act states that no award of damages is to be made unless the court is satisfied that an award is necessary to afford just satisfaction, taking into account:

(a) any other relief or remedy granted, or order made, in relation to the act in question (by that or any other court); and

(b) the consequences of any decision of that or any other court in respect of that act.[71]

1.92   The court must also be satisfied that an award is necessary to afford just satisfaction.[72]

1.93   The Act provides that a court must 'have regard to' the principles applied by the Strasbourg Court under Article 41 when determining whether, and how much should be awarded in damages.[73] Article 41 of the Convention provides that:

> If the Court finds that there has been a violation of the Convention or the protocols thereto, and if the internal law of the High Contracting Party concerned allows only partial reparation to be made, the Court shall if necessary afford just satisfaction.

1.94   The principles to be derived from the Strasbourg case law are analysed at paras 6.27 *et seq*.

---

68   See, in the Community law context, Case 102/88 *Fratelli Costanzo SpA v Comune di Milano* [1989] ECR 1839.

69   HRA 1998, s 3(1).

70   *Ibid*, s 8(1).

71   *Ibid*, s 8(3).

72   *Ibid*, s 8(3).

73   *Ibid*, s 8(4).

SPECIAL PROTECTION FOR ARTICLES 9 AND 10

1.95 During the passage of the Act through Parliament, additional protection was added in respect of the right to freedom of religion (Article 9) and freedom of expression (Article 10).

1.96 Sections 12–13 of the Act provide that a court must have 'particular regard' to the importance of:

the right to freedom of expression;[74] and to

the right to freedom of thought, conscience and religion where its determination might affect the exercise by a religious organisation of that right.[75]

1.97 It is difficult to know precisely what is meant by 'particular regard'. If this section is intended merely to enjoin the courts to be vigilant in respect of these rights, it is arguably otiose. The Strasbourg Court itself consistently lays emphasis on the importance of these rights, stating that they are the essential foundations of a democratic society.[76] Thus, the Convention has have 'particular regard' to these rights anyway.

1.98 If, however, the section is intended to require the domestic courts to go further than the Strasbourg Court in the protection of these rights, it will lead the court to depart from the Strasbourg case law and substitute its own balancing exercise when it weighs these matters. Those who fall foul of these provisions may then go to Strasbourg where the Court will apply Articles 12 and 13 in its preferred way.[77]

1.99 Section 12 of the Act contains procedural safeguards apparently intended to reduce the risk that litigants will obtain oppressive late night injunctions. Where a court is considering whether to grant relief which might affect the exercise of Article 10 rights, it must not do so in the absence of the respondent unless satisfied that the applicant has taken all reasonable steps to notify the respondent, or there are compelling reasons why he should not be notified.[78]

1.100 Section 12(3) posits a higher threshold than that contained in the *American Cyanamid*[79] test: no such relief is to be granted so as to restrain publication unless the court is satisfied that the applicant is likely to establish that publication should not be allowed.

---

74 HRA 1998, s 12(4).

75 *Ibid*, s 13. See, also, Peter Cumper, 'The protection of religious rights under section 13 of the Human Rights Act 1998' [2000] PL 254.

76 *Handyside v United Kingdom* (1979–80) 1 EHRR 737; *Kokkinakis v Greece* (1994) 17 EHRR 397, para 31.

77 We envisage a case where for example an applicant's right to privacy has been 'trumped' by the English Court's 'particular regard' for freedom of expression.

78 HRA 1998, s 12(2).

79 *American Cyanamid Co v Ethicon Ltd* [1975] AC 396.

1.101   Section 12(4) provides that where proceedings relate to material which the respondent claims, or which appears to the court, to be journalistic, literary or artistic material,[80] the court must have 'particular regard' not only to the right to freedom of expression, but also to the extent to which the material has, or is about to become public; the public interest in publication; any relevant privacy code.

DEROGATIONS AND RESERVATIONS

1.102 As has been seen, the Act gives further effect to only some of the rights contained in the Convention.[81] Section 1(2) provides those Articles are to have effect for the purpose of the Act 'subject to any designated derogation or reservation'.

1.103   Article 15 of the Convention permits Contracting States to derogate from certain Articles of the Convention in time of war or other public emergency. Its provisions are considered elsewhere.[82]

1.104   Article 57 provides the means by which States may make a reservation in respect of a provision of the Convention:

1   Any State may, when signing this Convention or when depositing its instrument of ratification, make a reservation in respect of any particular provision of the Convention to the extent that any law then in force in its territory is not in conformity with the provision. Reservations of a general character shall not be permitted under this Article.

2   Any reservation made under this Article shall contain a brief statement of the law concerned.

1.105 Thus, a reservation may only be made at the time of signing or ratification of the Convention, or Protocols.

1.106   The United Kingdom has one derogation, made in 1988, from Article 5(3) in respect of the detention of suspected terrorists,[83] and has made one reservation, in respect of Article 2 of the First Protocol, the right to education.[84]

1.107   The Human Rights Act contains a mechanism designed to ensure that such derogations and reservations as may be made are kept under review, and subject to at least a degree of Parliamentary supervision.

1.108   The Act defines 'designated derogation' to mean the existing derogation referred to above, together with any other derogation which may be

---

80   Or conduct connected with such material: s 12(4).
81   Ie, Arts 2–12 and 14, Arts 1–3 of the First Protocol, and Arts 1 and 2 of the Sixth Protocol, as read with Arts 16–18 of the Convention: HRA 1998, s 1(1).
82   Its provisions are considered in detail at paras 4.219 *et seq*.
83   See HRA 1998, Sched 3, Pt I.
84   See *ibid*, Sched 3, Pt II. See paras 4.271 *et seq*.

designated by order by the Secretary of State in the future.[85] 'Designated reservation' is defined in a like manner.[86]

1.109 In the case of a derogation, a designation order will cease to have effect at the end of 40 days if not approved by resolution of both Houses of Parliament.[87]

1.110 The Act provides that where a designated derogation is amended or replaced, it ceases to be a designated derogation unless and until the Secretary of State makes a fresh designation order.[88] Similarly, if a reservation is withdrawn wholly or in part, it ceases to be a designated reservation, unless the Secretary of State makes a fresh designation order.[89]

1.111 If a designated derogation is not withdrawn, it ceases to have effect for the purposes of the Act five years after the coming into force of the relevant provision[90] of the Act in the case of the United Kingdom's current derogation, and, in the case of any future derogation, five years after the date on which the order designating it was made.[91] There is however provision for the Secretary of State to extend those periods by a further five years at any time before they come to an end.[92]

1.112 The Act requires the Minister to review the existing reservation within five years of the relevant section[93] of the Act coming into force, and in the case of any future reservation, within five years of the designation order coming into force.[94] When the Minister reviews a derogation, he must prepare a report and lay it before Parliament.[95] If the derogation is still in force, he must review it within five years of the last such report being laid before Parliament.[96]

---

85 HRA 1998, s 14.

86 *Ibid*, s 15. Whilst there could be no further reservation in respect of the Convention itself, the United Kingdom might in principle seek to make a reservation in respect of a protocol which it has not yet ratified.

87 *Ibid*, s 16(3).

88 *Ibid*, s 14(3), (4).

89 *Ibid*, s 15(3), (4).

90 Ie, *ibid*, s 1(2).

91 *Ibid*, s 16(1), (2).

92 *Ibid*, s 16(2).

93 Ie, *ibid*, s 1(2).

94 *Ibid*, s 17(1), (2).

95 *Ibid*, s 17(3).

96 *Ibid*, s 17(2).

THE ROLE OF STRASBOURG

1.113 The Act does not remove the right of individuals to petition the Strasbourg Court under Article 34. Indeed, it is submitted that the Act is likely to increase the frequency of such applications. Importantly, however, because only a 'victim' may petition the Strasbourg Court and the term 'victim' is defined as excluding governmental organisations,[97] only applicants and not respondents to human rights challenges may seek redress in Strasbourg.

1.114　　An applicant may only take a case to Strasbourg once domestic remedies are 'exhausted'.[98] The Act provides a new remedy (or remedies) which must be exhausted before Strasbourg may be petitioned. Notwithstanding its flaws, the Act will of course be relied on with success by many litigants. Even so, Strasbourg will remain a useful tool.

1.115　　A judgment of the Strasbourg court is final and binding pursuant to Article 46 of the Convention. In practice, it is a political impossibility for the government to ignore it. In many cases, amendment of legislation has followed. This is in marked contrast to the limited powers of the courts faced by a challenge to primary legislation.[99] The gaps in the protection that the Act leaves will inevitably encourage disappointed litigants to seek redress in Strasbourg. Further, as has already been seen in the period leading up to its coming into force, the Act is the catalyst for a vast expansion in human rights litigation, and indeed a dissemination of knowledge of its core principles.

97　See, further, paras 2.58 *et seq.*

98　ECHR, Art 35.

99　See above, paras 1.62 *et seq.*

CHAPTER 2

CLAIMANTS AND DEFENDANTS

2.01 Perhaps the most fundamental amongst the difficult procedural questions raised by the Human Rights Act 1998 are who can sue, and who can be sued? This chapter will explore the likely answers and the Convention case law which will serve to shape the approach of the domestic courts.

2.02 As shall be seen, there are important differences between the rules governing the domestic judicial review courts and the regime ushered in by the Human Rights Act.

STANDING TO CHALLENGE

2.03 The *actio popularis* in Roman law permitted any citizen to maintain an action for breach of a public wrong. Neither the domestic nor Convention case law permits this approach. Each jurisdiction imposes a 'standing' requirement. Whilst the rules on standing in judicial review have historically hampered the development of true public interest litigation, the courts generally now take a flexible and inclusive approach. The standing requirements at Strasbourg, apparently imported into domestic law by the Human Rights Act, are also flexible, and as shall be seen, in most cases they will not pose a problem to potential claimants for judicial review; in some ways, the approach in Strasbourg is more generous. Its case law is, however, demonstrably narrower[1] in at least two important respects: its application to public authorities, and, as has been much remarked, to interest groups and other forms of public interest litigation.

Standing in judicial review: sufficient interest

2.04 An applicant for judicial review must demonstrate a 'sufficient interest'. The rule is contained in s 31(3) of the Supreme Court Act 1981. It provides that the court shall not grant permission to move for judicial review:

> ... unless it considers that the applicant has a sufficient interest in the matter to which the application relates.

---

1 This feature was acknowledged this feature during the Bill's passage: *Hansard*, HL, 24 November 1997, col 830; *Hansard*, HC, 24 June 1998, col 1083.

2.05 The 'sufficient interest' requirement operates both at the permission stage and at any substantive hearing. In *R v IRC ex p National Federation of Self-Employed*,[2] the House of Lords held that the court must form a *prima facie*, or provisional, view as to the applicant's standing at the permission stage.[3]

2.06 If the matter proceeds to substantive hearing, the question of standing falls determined in the light of the substance of the application. In *IRC*, the majority view[4] was that the question of standing could not be considered in isolation from 'the matter to which the application relates', but must be taken together with merits, or 'legal and factual context'.[5]

2.07 Analytically, the test stated in *IRC* is problematic. It has been described judicially as 'something of a legal minefield'.[6] It introduced a factual and discretionary element[7] to the test of standing.[8] The benefit of this approach is that it has permitted the courts to apply the rules with great flexibility; in the years since *IRC*, the courts have taken an 'increasingly liberal approach to standing'.[9] Whilst the standing requirement may serve to 'prevent abuse by busybodies, cranks and other mischief-makers',[10] it is now most unusual for an otherwise well constituted and realistic challenge to fail on grounds of standing alone.[11]

2.08 Further, as the *IRC* case makes clear, the test of standing is inextricably linked to examination of the merits. Lord Fraser stated that standing may be easier to establish where an applicant relies upon 'some exceptionally grave or widespread illegality'.[12] The importance of the issue raised has also been held to be a factor mitigating in favour of sufficient interest.[13]

---

2 [1982] AC 617.

3 The threshold at the leave stage is set only at the height necessary to prevent abuse: *R v Somerset County Council ex p Dixon* [1997] COD 323, *per* Sedley J.

4 See the dissent of Lord Fraser: [1982] AC 617, p 645C.

5 *Per* Lord Wilberforce *ibid*, p 630E. See, also, Lord Fraser, *ibid*, p 645D and Lord Scarman, *ibid*, p 653F.

6 *R v Poole BC ex p Beebee* [1991] JPL 643, *per* Schiemann J, p 644.

7 It would be wrong, however, to see the standing test as one of pure discretion: *R v Attorney General ex p ICI plc* [1985] 1 CMLR 588, *per* Woolf J, p 618.

8 See Peter Cane, 'Standing, legality and the limits of public law' [1981] PL 322.

9 *R v Secretary of State for Foreign and Commonwealth Affairs ex p The World Development Movement Ltd* [1995] 1 WLR 386, *per* Rose LJ, p 395F.

10 *R v IRC ex p National Federation of Self-Employed* [1982] AC 617, *per* Lord Scarman, p 653G, as applied in *R v Legal Aid Board ex p Bateman* [1992] 1 WLR 711, *per* Nolan LJ, p 718C.

11 In *R v Attorney General ex p ICI plc* [1985] 1 CMLR 588, p 618, Woolf J stated 'it would be regrettable if a court had to come to the conclusion that in a situation where the need for the intervention of the court had been established this intervention was prevented by rules as to standing'. A finding of lack of standing generally accompanies an adverse conclusion on the merits of the application; see, eg, *R v Tower Hamlets LBC ex p Thrasyvoulou* [1991] COD 123; *R v Director of the Serious Fraud Office ex p Johnson* [1993] COD 58; *R v Secretary of State for Defence ex p Sancto* [1993] COD 144.

12 *R v IRC ex p National Federation of Self-Employed* [1982] AC 617, p 647B.

13 *R v Secretary of State for Foreign and Commonwealth Affairs ex p The World Development Movement Ltd* [1995] 1 WLR 386.

2.09   A direct legal or financial interest is, however, not required for standing,[14] although the presence of such an interest is plainly relevant.[15] Companies have been permitted to challenge decision addressed to competitors.[16] Pressure groups have been sometimes[17] found to have standing in reliance upon a wide range of factors. In *R v Secretary of State for Foreign and Commonwealth Affairs ex p World Development Movement Ltd*,[18] the applicant was held to have standing to challenge the grant of aid for the Pergau Dam project in Malaysia. Factors which were said to point to this conclusion were the importance of vindicating the rule of law, the importance of the issue raised, the likely absence of any other responsible challenger, the nature of the breach of duty against which relief was sought and the prominent role of the applicant in giving advice, guidance and assistance regarding aid.[19]

2.10   Individuals have been permitted to bring a challenge in an appropriate case, notwithstanding the absence of a direct relationship with the decision challenged, or any 'special private interest in the subject matter'.[20] In *R v Her Majesty's Treasury ex p Smedley* [1985] 1 QB 657, the applicant was held to have standing to challenge the Government's proposed contribution to the European Community 'if only in his capacity as taxpayer'.[21] In *R v Secretary of State for Foreign and Commonwealth Affairs ex p Rees-Mogg*,[22] the applicant who was said to have a 'sincere concern for the constitutional issues'[23] was held to have standing to challenge the ratification of the Maastricht Treaty.

2.11   This liberal approach is not uniform, however. In *R v Secretary of State for the Environment ex p Rose Theatre Trust Co*,[24] the applicant was a company, incorporated by campaigners seeking to save the remains of the *Rose Theatre*. Amongst them were a number of acknowledged experts. Schiemann J held

---

14 *R v IRC ex p National Federation of Self-Employed* [1982] AC 617, per Lord Fraser, p 646; *R v Secretary of State for the Environment ex p Rose Theatre Trust Co* [1990] 1 QB 504, per Schiemann J, p 520D.

15 *R v Legal Aid Board ex p Bateman* [1992] 1 WLR 711, per Jowitt J, p 721D.

16 Eg, *R v Attorney General ex p ICI* [1987] 1 CMLR 72; *R v Department of Transport ex p Presvac Engineering Ltd* (1992) 4 Admin LR 121; *R v St Edmundsbury BC ex p Investors in Industry Commercial Properties Ltd* [1985] 1 WLR 1168; *R v Monopolies and Mergers Commission ex p Argyll Group plc* [1986] 1 WLR 763.

17 In *R v Secretary of State for the Environment ex p Rose Theatre Trust Co* [1990] 1 QB 504, such a group was held to lack standing; see para 2.11.

18 [1995] 1 WLR 386.

19 *Ibid*, per Rose LJ, p 395E. See, further, *R v Inspectorate of Pollution ex p Greenpeace Ltd (No 2)* [1994] 4 All ER 329; *R v Secretary of State for Social Services ex p Child Poverty Action Group* [1990] 2 QB 540. Contrast, however, *Scottish Old People's Welfare Council, Petitioner* 1987 SLT 179.

20 *R v Somerset County Council and ARC Southern Ltd ex p Dixon* [1997] COD 323, p 330.

21 [1997] COD 323, per Slade LJ, p 760B.

22 [1994] 2 WLR 115.

23 *Ibid*, per Lloyd LJ, p 119D.

24 [1990] 1 QB 504.

that the company lacked standing to bring a challenge to the Secretary of State's refusal to protect the site.[25] The decision was by its nature one in respect of which no individual had standing to challenge; the incorporation of the company did not affect the position. The judgment appears to create a class of decisions which are beyond the scope of review,[26] but has been subject to criticism,[27] and not always followed.[28] In *R v Somerset County Council and ARC Southern Ltd ex p Dixon*,[29] Sedley J declined follow the *Rose Theatre* case, and stated that the court was not required to refuse leave to move for judicial review merely because the interest of the applicant is shared with the generality of the public. He held that, in certain cases of apparent abuse of power, any individual, simply as citizen, would have a sufficient interest to bring the matter before the court.

Standing under the Human Rights Act: the 'victim' test

2.12 The Human Rights Act imposes a narrower test for standing than that for judicial review. Only a person who is, or would be, a 'victim' of an action by a public authority which is, or would be, incompatible with a Convention right can bring proceedings or rely on the Convention right or rights concerned.[30]

2.13 As to the meaning of 'victim', the Human Rights Act provides that a person is a victim of an unlawful act *only* if he would be a victim for the purposes of Article 34 of the Convention if proceedings were brought in the European Court of Human Rights in respect of that Act.[31] Article 34 of the Convention itself embodies a 'victim' test. It states:

> The Court may receive applications from any person, non-governmental organisation or group of individuals claiming to be the victim of a violation by one of the High Contracting Parties of the rights set forth in the Convention or the protocols thereto ...

2.14 The effect of the Human Rights Act appears to be, therefore, that the English court must not only take the Strasbourg jurisprudence into account in this respect,[32] it must actually *follow* the Strasbourg jurisprudence under Article 34 as to the meaning of victim.

---

25 Pursuant to the Ancient Monuments and Archaeological Areas Act 1979.

26 Schiemann J was prepared to accept this consequence.

27 Eg, Peter Cane in [1990] PL 307; Clive Lewis in (1990) 49 CLJ 189.

28 *R v Somerset County Council and ARC Southern Ltd ex p Dixon* [1997] COD; *R v Inspectorate of Pollution ex p Greenpeace (No 2)* [1994] 4 All ER 329.

29 [1997] COD 323.

30 HRA 1998, s 7(1).

31 *Ibid*, s 7(7).

32 Ie, as required by *ibid*, s 2(1).

2.15   During the passage of the Human Rights Bill through Parliament, there were conflicting statements on this question. For example, the Lord Chancellor indicated that it was intended that persons should be able to rely upon Convention rights in 'precisely the same circumstances as they can rely upon them before the Strasbourg institutions'.[33] Much of what was said reflects this view. On the other hand, however, Mr Mike O'Brien[34] stated 'Our courts will develop their own jurisprudence on the issue'.[35]

2.16   As shall be seen, there are important differences between the Strasbourg and domestic case law.

The victim test and judicial review

2.17   The Lord Chancellor stated in Parliament that it was not intended to alter the rules of standing in judicial review by means of the Human Rights Act.[36] The Act provides that, where a claimant alleges an unlawful act under the Act by way of judicial review proceedings, he will be taken to have a sufficient interest in relation to the unlawful act complained of only if he is a victim.[37]

2.18   As the Lord Chancellor acknowledged, 'a consequence of that approach is that a narrower test will be applied for bringing applications by judicial review on convention grounds than will continue to apply in applications for judicial review on other grounds'.[38]

2.19   It if course likely, however, that many challenges will invoke both Convention and *Wednesbury* grounds for judicial review. Such a claimant may face two separate tests for standing: the 'sufficient interest' test in respect of conventional/*Wednesbury* grounds, and the narrower 'victim' test in respect of any human rights challenge. The court may therefore be placed in the position where it must consent to hear some, but not all, of the points advanced.

Victim: the Strasbourg case law

2.20   Strasbourg takes a flexible and pragmatic approach to the Convention. The Court has frequently stated that the Convention is intended to guarantee rights which are 'practical and effective', rather than 'theoretical or illusory':[39]

---

33 *Hansard*, HL, 24 November 1997, col 830. See, to similar effect, *Hansard*, HC, 20 May 1998, col 1084; 24 June 1998, col 1083.

34 Parliamentary Under Secretary of State for the Home Department.

35 *Hansard*, HC, 20 May 1998, col 1084.

36 *Hansard*, HL, 24 November 1997, col 834.

37 HRA 1998, s 7(3).

38 *Hansard*, HL, 24 November 1997, col 834.

39 *Artico v Italy* (1981) 3 EHRR 1, para 33.

> ... the object and purpose of the Convention as an instrument for the protection of individual human beings require that its provisions be interpreted and applied so as to make its safeguards practical and effective.[40]

2.21 That extends to both procedural and substantive protection.[41] As shall be seen, a flexible approach has generally been taken to the question of standing.

Basic principle: *no* actio popularis

2.22 As has been seen,[42] Article 34 permits applications from any person, non-governmental organisation or group of individuals claiming to be a victim of a violation of a Convention right by a contracting state.

2.23   The effect of this requirement is that there is no *actio popularis* in Convention law. In *Klass v Germany*,[43] the Court stated that an individual must be able to claim to have been 'actually affected by the violation he alleges'.[44] The right of individual petition:

> ... does not permit individuals to complain against a law *in abstracto* simply because they feel that it contravenes the Convention. In principle, it does not suffice for an individual applicant to claim that the mere existence of a law violates his rights under the Convention; it is necessary that the law should have been applied to his detriment.[45]

2.24 These *dicta* must, however, be treated with caution. Read in isolation, they suggest a much more restrictive approach than has been applied by the Court in practice.

Prima facie *case*

2.25 The applicant is not required to establish beyond doubt that he is a victim of an impugned practice in order to have standing to challenge. It is sufficient if he can show that there is at least *prima facie* evidence to that effect.[46]

Future events

2.26 The Human Rights Act provides that proceedings may be brought against a public authority which has acted, or proposes to act in breach of Convention

---

40 *Soering v United Kingdom* (1989) 11 EHRR 439, para 87. See, also, amongst others, *Lozidou v Turkey* (1995) 20 EHRR 99, para 72.

41 *SP, DP and T v United Kingdom* (1996) 22 EHRR CD 148.

42 See para 2.13.

43 (1979–80) 2 EHRR 214.

44 *Ibid*, para 33.

45 *Ibid*.

46 *Donnelly v United Kingdom* (1975) 43 CD 122, p 146.

rights.[47] The Convention case law similarly provides that a prospective harm may be sufficient to render an applicant a victim, provided it is sufficiently clear that it will take place. In *Vijayanathan and Pusparajah v France*,[48] the applicants were unsuccessful asylum seekers who had remained in France following rejection of their claims. They were subject to departure orders and liable to arrest and expulsion proceedings at any time. They could not, however, be removed until an 'expulsion order' had been made. No such orders had been made. Had an order been made, an appeal would have been open to the applicants. The Court concluded the applicants could not claim to be victims.

Potential effect of the impugned measure

2.27 There are circumstances in which an applicant can complain of legislation which may not yet have been applied to his detriment. In *Klass v Germany*[49] the applicants wished to challenge legislation which permitted state authorities to open mail and intercept telephone calls. All users of these services were potentially subject to this interference. The applicants complained that the legislation provided no absolute right to be notified after surveillance had occurred.

2.28 The Court accepted that a law might violate the rights of an individual if he was 'directly affected' by it in the absence of any specific measure of implementation. Under certain conditions,[50] an individual might claim to be the victim of a violation 'occasioned by the mere existence of secret measures' without having to establish that the measures were in fact applied to him.[51]

2.29 Thus, as the Court later put it, it is sufficient for an individual to contend that a measure violates the Convention if he 'run[s] the risk of being directly affected by it'.[52]

2.30 Applications have accordingly been entertained in a number of cases where the applicant could not claim to have been personally subject to the impugned measures. In *Johnston v Ireland*,[53] the challenge to the Irish prohibition on divorce, the government unsuccessfully argued that the applicants lacked standing on grounds of their 'tranquil domestic circumstances'.[54] In *Dudgeon v United Kingdom*,[55] the Court accepted that the

---

47 HRA 1998, s 7(1).
48 (1993) 15 EHRR 62. See, also, *Springer v United Kingdom* (1983) 5 EHRR 141.
49 (1979–80) 2 EHRR 214.
50 The conditions were not actually specified by the Court.
51 *Ibid*, para 34. On the facts, the claim succeeded.
52 *Marckx v Belgium* (1979–80) 2 EHRR 330, para 27.
53 *Johnston v Ireland* (1987) 9 EHRR 203.
54 *Ibid*, paras 41–42.
55 (1982) 4 EHRR 149.

existence of legislation that criminalised homosexual conduct itself constituted an interference with the applicant's private life. In the *Open Door Counselling*[56] case, the applicants brought a challenge to an injunction granted by an Irish court which prohibited the dissemination of information about abortion services available overseas. Two of the applicants were said to qualify as victims on the grounds that they belonged to a 'class of women of child-bearing age which may be adversely affected by the restrictions'.[57]

2.31　　There are limits to this flexible doctrine. The Commission has emphasised that there must be a reasonable likelihood that the applicant would be subject to the impugned measures.[58]

Prejudice

2.32　It follows that an applicant need not always show actual detriment arising from the impugned matter in order to be a victim. The Court has frequently stated that the existence of a violation of the Convention is 'conceivable' in the absence of prejudice.[59]

2.33　　In *Artico v Italy*,[60] the Court said (and has subsequently reiterated)[61] that prejudice is an issue which is 'only' relevant to the issue of just satisfaction. Thus, in that case, the applicant complained he had been deprived of access to a lawyer in breach of Article 6(3)(c). The Court rejected the government's contention that the lack of assistance must be shown to have caused prejudice. As the Court said, to hold otherwise would be to deprive the right 'in large measure of its substance'.[62]

2.34　　Where national authorities have acknowledged the breach of Convention rights, and afforded redress for the breach complained of, it may, however, be necessary to show prejudice.[63] Thus, in *De Jong v Netherlands*,[64] the applicant complained he had been detained in breach of Article 5. The Government contended he had not been prejudiced as the period of impugned detention was deducted from his sentence. The Court held that the apparent lack of

---

56　*Open Door Counselling and Dublin Well Woman Centre v Ireland* (1993) 15 EHRR 244.

57　*Ibid*, para 44.

58　*Hilton v United Kingdom* (1988) 57 DR 108, p 119.

59　*Artico v Italy* (1981) 3 EHRR 1, para 35. See, also, amongst others, *Adolf v Austria* (1982) 4 EHRR 312, para 37; *Groppera Radio AG and Others v Switzerland* (1990) 12 EHRR 321, para 47; *Lüdi v Switzerland* (1993) 15 EHRR 173, para 34; *Amuur v France* (1996) 23 EHRR 533, para 36.

60　(1981) 3 EHRR 1, para 35.

61　See, also, amongst others, *Adolf v Austria* (1982) 4 EHRR 312, para 37.

62　*Artico v Italy* (1981) 3 EHRR 1, para 35.

63　*Eckle v Germany* (1983) 5 EHRR 1, para 66; *Lüdi v Switzerland* (1993) 15 EHRR 173, para 34; *Amuur v France* (1996) 23 EHRR 533, para 36. The Commission has held an applicant can no longer claim to be a victim where the complaint has been remedied: eg, *Dahanayake v United Kingdom* (1983) 5 EHRR 144.

64　(1986) 8 EHRR 20, para 41.

prejudice did not in principle deprive him of his status as 'victim'. The matter might have been otherwise had the deduction been based upon an acknowledgment by the national court of a violation of the Convention.

2.35   Where the national authorities provide only partial redress, the applicant remains a victim.[65]

Indirect effect

2.36 There are situations in which the Court is prepared to entertain applications from those who are merely 'indirectly affected' by a breach of the Convention.

2.37   A close relative may be sufficiently indirectly affected to be considered a victim. Such relatives may include a spouse, or other family member. In *Kurt v Turkey*,[66] the applicant was able to bring a challenge in respect of the disappearance of her son. In *Paton v United Kingdom*,[67] a father of an unborn child was held to be so closely affected by the termination of his wife's pregnancy to claim to be a victim of the legislation governing abortion he complained of. By contrast, a man who was a husband and father lacked standing to challenge abortion legislation.[68]

2.38   Domestic law does not take such a generous approach. In *R v Secretary of State for Defence ex p Sancto*,[69] the applicants, who were the parents of a soldier who died in an accident during the Falklands conflict, were held to lack standing to challenge the Ministry of Defence's refusal to disclose an Army Board of Inquiry report into the incident.[70]

2.39   Litigation friends may also bring an individual petition to Strasbourg.[71]

Non-natural persons

2.40 It is clear beyond argument that companies and other non-natural persons can be victims under the Convention. Article 1 of the First Protocol expressly provides that legal persons have a right to property, but the Court has never shrunk from according the other rights and freedoms to companies in

---

65   *Inze v Austria* (1988) 10 EHRR 394; *Bowman v United Kingdom* (1998) 26 EHRR 1.

66   (1999) 27 EHRR 373. See, also, *Osman v United Kingdom* (2000) 29 EHRR 245.

67   (1981) 3 EHRR 408.

68   Case No 7045/75, *X v Austria* (1976) 7 DR 87.

69   [1993] COD 144.

70   See, similarly, *R v Serious Fraud Office ex p Johnson* [1993] COD 58: the applicant, who was charged with fraud, was held to lack standing to challenge a notice served upon his wife by the Director of the SFO under s 2(2) of the Criminal Justice Act 1987, requiring her to answer questions arising out of the SFO's investigations into the fraud charges against her husband.

71   See *SP, DP and T v United Kingdom* (1996) 22 EHRR CD 148; *Hansard*, HC, 20 May 1998, col 1084.

appropriate cases. In *Dombo Beeher BV v Netherlands*,[72] for example, a company successfully invoked the right to a fair trial in respect of the ruling made by a court in the course of civil litigation.

2.41   In very limited circumstances, the Strasbourg Court may be willing to 'pierce the corporate veil' to allow actions by shareholders. In *Agrotexim v Greece*,[73] the Court departed from earlier decisions of the Commission which permitted actions by shareholders on broad criteria. The Court expressly followed the approach of the International Court of Justice in the *Barcelona Traction, Light and Power Company Ltd*[74] case. The Court stated shareholders could not claim to be victims merely because a violation of the company's rights has caused a loss of value of their shares. It held that:

> ... the disregarding of a company's legal personality will be justified only in exceptional circumstances, in particular where it is clearly established that it is impossible for the company to apply to the Convention institutions through the organs set up under its articles of incorporation or – in the event of liquidation – through its liquidators.

2.42   Earlier decisions of the Commission on this point must therefore be considered doubtful.[75]

2.43   Domestic law is more flexible in this respect. In *R v Monopolies and Mergers Commission ex p Argyll Group plc*,[76] a minority shareholder in the company Distillers challenged a decision of the MMC which had freed the Guinness company to make a takeover bid for Distillers.

2.44   In *Credit and Industrial Bank and Moravec v Czech Republic*,[77] the Commission used an artificial but pragmatic approach in order to circumvent the rule in *Agrotexim*. The application concerned a bank which had been taken into compulsory administration. The application to Strasbourg had been filled in only by Mr Moravec, the President of its Board of Directors, and a shareholder. The Commission held that it appeared from the substance of the application that the bank wished to introduce an application through Mr Moravec. It therefore treated the application as if also brought by the bank. Thus, the application by the bank was declared admissible.

---

72   (1994) 18 EHRR 213.

73   (1996) 21 EHRR 250, paras 65, 66.

74   Judgment (1970) ICJ 39, pp 39 and 41, paras 56–58 and 66.

75   See, eg, *Kaplan v United Kingdom* (1982) 4 EHRR 64; *Yarrow plc and Three Shareholders v United Kingdom* (1983) 30 DR 155; *App No 11189/84 v Sweden* (1988) 10 EHRR 132.

76   [1986] 1 WLR 763.

77   (1998) 26 EHRR CD 88.

Death of the applicant

2.45 In some circumstances, the Strasbourg Court has gone on to consider an application following the death of the applicant.

2.46 Where an applicant dies in the course of proceedings, his heirs may in principle claim to be victims either as successors, or on their own behalf.[78] Whether they can do so depends on the nature of the breach alleged. There is, however, no general right for successors to do so. The Commission has said that what matters is whether the nature of the complaint is such that the interest can be considered to be transferable.[79] In practice, the presence of a financial element to the claim has proved to be important.

2.47 In *Deweer v Belgium*,[80] the applicant had complained of a number of breaches of Article 6 in respect of a fine he had paid. He died after his application had been declared admissible. His widow and daughters were held to have sufficient 'material and moral interest in seeing completed the proceedings instituted by their father'.[81] This case was followed in *Nölkenbockhoff v Germany*.[82] The applicant was the widow of a man who had died in the course of an appeal against a criminal conviction. As a result, the proceedings had been terminated. The applicant complained that the state's refusal to reimburse her late husband's costs was a contravention of the presumption of innocence in Article 6(2). The Court held that his widow had legitimate 'material interests' in her capacity has his heir, and a 'moral interest on behalf of herself and of the family in having her late husband exonerated from any finding of guilt'.

2.48 *P v France*,[83] however, was held to fall on the wrong side of the line. The applicant had been transferred from prison to a hospital whilst in the terminal stages of AIDS. He complained as to his treatment in hospital. Following his death, his parents sought to pursue his application to Strasbourg. The Commission held, however that his complaint was 'so closely bound up with the person of the deceased applicant that his parents could not allege a sufficient legitimate interest in continuing the action' and could not be considered victims.

2.49 In an exceptional case, a matter might in principle proceed notwithstanding that the surviving next of kin had no interest in it doing so if there were 'circumstances of a general character' which warranted it.[84]

---

78 *Deweer v Belgium* (1979–80) 2 EHRR 439, para 37; *App Nos 7572/76, 7586/76, 7587/76* (1979) 14 DR 67.
79 *Kofler v Italy* (1982) 30 DR 5, p 9.
80 (1979–80) 2 EHRR 439.
81 *Ibid*, para 37.
82 (1991) 13 EHRR 360.
83 (1993) 16 EHRR CD 29.
84 Eg, *X v Germany* (1977) 9 DR 47.

Convention law narrower than domestic law

2.50 There are two important areas in which the 'victim' test is demonstrably narrower than that for standing in judicial review.

2.51   As shall be seen, should the domestic courts adopt this approach, there would be at least a risk that worthwhile challenges would go unheard.

Groups, associations and public interest challenges

2.52 As a matter of Convention law, groups and associations, such trade unions[85] or political parties[86] may claim to be victims in principle, but only if they are themselves affected by the measure complained of. In *Hodgson and Others v United Kingdom*,[87] the applicants complained of an injunction granted to stop the broadcast of readings of transcripts from a trial during its progress. Whilst the Commission admitted an application by a journalist involved in the making of the programme, it declared the application by the National Union of Journalists to be inadmissible: the mere fact that one of its members was directly affected by the injunction was not sufficient to render the union itself a victim.

2.53   This rule does not wholly preclude such an organisation from bringing an action in a genuinely representative capacity. In order to do so, however, the applicant must identify the individuals it purports to represent and show that it had received specific instructions from each of them.[88]

2.54   The same approach applies to pressure groups. The group itself must be able to assert its status as a 'victim'. *Greenpeace Schweiz and Others v Switzerland*[89] illustrates where the line is drawn. The applicants included a number of associations and individuals. They complained of a breach of the right of access to a court in respect of a challenge brought to the renewal of a permit to run a nuclear power plant. Whilst the complaints of individuals who lived in the vicinity of the plant were declared admissible, the complaints of the remaining applicants were held inadmissible; they had 'failed to indicate whether they own, or lease, property, within the vicinity of the nuclear power plant'.[90]

---

85 *Council of Civil Service Unions v United Kingdom* (1988) 10 EHRR 269; *National Union of Belgian Police v Belgium* (1979–80) 1 EHRR 578.

86 *New Horizons v Cyprus* (1999) 27 EHRR CD 334.

87 (1988) 10 EHRR 503.

88 *Fédération Nationale des Infirmiers and Confédération Des Syndicats Médicaux Francais v France* (1986) 47 DR 225.

89 (1996) 23 EHRR CD 116.

90 See, to similar effect, *Balmer-Schafroth v Switzerland* (1998) 25 EHRR 598.

2.55   By contrast, in *Platform 'Ärtze für das Leben' v Austria*,[91] the applicant association had standing to complain about the sufficiency of police protection in respect of its anti-abortion demonstrations.

2.56   As has been seen (at paras 2.09 *et seq*), such groups have generally met with increasing sympathy from English judges in recent years when seeking to bring challenges for judicial review. The domestic courts have, however invoked factors which would be wholly immaterial at Strasbourg, such as the importance of the issue, or lack of any other likely challenger.[92] In *R v Somerset County Council and ARC Southern Ltd ex p Dixon*,[93] a local resident and activist had standing to challenge a decision to grant planning permission for the extension of a quarry, even assuming that the that he had no greater interest than that of the general public.

2.57   Such a pure public interest challenge would fail the 'victim' test, whether brought by a group or individual. In *Province of Bari, Sorrentino and Messini Nemaga v Italy*,[94] the President of the Province of Bari, in his capacity as a citizen of the city, could not claim to be a victim in respect of complaints arising out of the state's failure to restore the Bari Opera House after it was destroyed by fire.

Public authorities as victims

2.58   There is no obstacle in domestic law to public authorities bringing judicial review proceedings as claimants.[95] The wording of Article 34 of the Convention excludes challenge by at least some public authorities under Convention rights. It provides that an individual petition may be brought by:

> ... any person, non-governmental organisation or group of individuals claiming to be a victim ...

2.59   Thus, the Province of Bari itself lacked standing to bring a challenge in the case concerning its opera house: it was a pubic law authority which performed official duties assigned to it by the Constitution and legislation.[96]

2.60   The question this raises is which other bodies qualify as 'governmental organisations' so as to be excluded from reliance upon the Convention. As shall be seen, at paras 2.91 *et seq*, a wide range of bodies, including some private companies such as Railtrack, and those running nursing homes, are

---

91   (1991) 13 EHRR 204.

92   *R v Secretary of State for Foreign Affairs ex p The World Development Movement Ltd* [1995] 1 WLR 386.

93   [1997] COD 323.

94   (1999) 27 EHRR CD 352.

95   See, eg, *R v Secretary of State for Transport ex p Richmond LBC (No 1)* [1994] 1 WLR 74; *R v Secretary of State for Employment ex p Equal Opportunities Commission* [1995] 1 AC 1.

96   (1999) 27 EHRR CD 352.

likely to be treated as public authorities for the purposes of the Human Rights Act. Some bodies, such as the BBC, have appeared as both applicant and respondent in judicial review proceedings.[97] On the face of it, it would be invidious if, for example, the Law Society, which is subject to judicial review,[98] could not complain of a breach of Article 6 in the course of (for example) a trial over unpaid invoices.

2.61   Strasbourg takes a broad approach to the meaning of 'governmental body'. In one case,[99] the Commission held that the General Council of Official Economists' Associations in Spain, a public law corporation with statutory functions could not claim to be victim. The Commission stated that 'governmental organisation' included both government and the central organs of the state.[100] Further:

> Where powers are distributed along decentralised lines, no national authority exercising public functions can introduce an application.[101]

2.62   It might be argued that, although such bodies have 'public functions', they cannot be characterised as 'governmental' within the meaning of Article 34 of the Convention. As will be seen, however, domestic case law states that one of the tests for susceptibility to judicial review is whether a body has 'governmental functions' (see para 2.80).

2.63   Alternatively, it might be argued that a body such as the Law Society ought not to have the protection of the Convention *in respect of* its public, or governmental, functions, but should otherwise be free to have recourse to it. It is doubtful that such an approach would find favour in Strasbourg. In the *Province of Bari* case, the Commission, having held that the Province could not claim to be a victim, went on to say:

> This conclusion is also proved, arguing from the inverse, by the fact that acts, or failures to act, imputable to a province could engage the responsibility of the Italian State under the Convention if it were in breach of the latter.[102]

2.64   This *dictum* at least suggests that a 'governmental organisation' is excluded in all respects.

2.65   It is to be hoped that the domestic courts do not adopt so wide an approach; to do so would be to create a significant lacuna in the protection provided by the Human Rights Act.

---

97 Eg, *R v BBC ex p Lavelle* [1983] 1 WLR 23; [1983] 1 All ER 241; *R v Broadcasting Complaints Commission ex p BBC* [1994] EMLR 497; [1994] COD 499.

98 *R v Law Society ex p Reigate Projects Ltd* [1993] 1 WLR 1531.

99 *Consejo General de Colegios Oficiales de Economistas de España v Spain* (1995) 82-B 150.

100 See, also, *M v Spain* (1991) 68 DR 209.

101 *Ibid.*

102 *Province of Bari, Sorrentino and Messini Nemaga v Italy* (1999) 27 EHRR 352.

Third party intervention

2.66 Article 36(2) of the Convention expressly provides that the President of the Court may 'in the interests of the proper administration of justice' invite either a state or 'any person concerned who is not the applicant to submit written comments or to take part in hearings'. Rule 62(3) of the Court's Rules of Procedure provides that a request for leave to be heard may be made, provided that it is 'duly reasoned' and within a reasonable time after the fixing of the written procedure.[103] Thus, for example, in *Young, James and Webster v United Kingdom*,[104] the TUC was represented before the Court in a case concerning the legality of closed shop agreements.

2.67 Such intervention is unusual in domestic public law, but is becoming more common in the higher courts.[105]

2.68 During the passage of the Act through Parliament, the Lord Chancellor appeared to actively encourage the courts to develop this practice.[106] It was suggested that this would ameliorate the effects of the exclusion of pressure groups and the like from claiming the status of victim.

DEFENDANTS: WHO WILL BE SUBJECT TO A CONVENTION CHALLENGE?

2.69 It is clear that Parliament intended that the Human Rights Act should apply to a wide range of potential defendants,[107] including bodies which, hitherto, have fallen outside the scope of judicial review. Further, there are powers and functions of such bodies which have never previously been subject to control by the judicial review courts which are now subject to scrutiny on Convention grounds.

2.70 The effect is that the Human Rights Act brings with it a very considerable expansion of the scope of public law supervision.

---

103 For the procedural aspects of petitioning the Strasbourg Court, see Luke Clements, Nuala Mole and Alan Simmons, *European Human Rights: Taking a Case under the Convention*, 2nd edn, 1998, London: Sweet & Maxwell.

104 (1982) 4 EHRR 38, para 49.

105 For recent examples, see *R v Khan* [1997] AC 558; *R v North and East Devon Health Authority ex p Coughlan* [2000] 2 WLR 622; *R v Bow Street Metropolitan Stipendiary Magistrates ex p Pinochet Ugarte* [2000] 1 AC 1. See, now, CPR Pt 54.17.

106 *Hansard*, HL, 24 November 1997, cols 833–34.

107 See statements of the Lord Chancellor at *Hansard*, HL, 16 November 1997, col 1231.

Defendants under the Human Rights Act: public authorities

2.71 Section 6(1) of the Human Rights Act provides:

> It is unlawful for a public authority to act in a way which is incompatible with a Convention right.

2.72 Thus, only 'public authorities' are expressly stated to be potential defendants for the purposes of the Human Rights Act.

2.73 Although the Act does not define this notion exhaustively, some assistance with its meaning is given. It provides[108] that a 'public authority' is 'any person whose functions are of a public nature'. Such a person is not a public authority in respect of acts which are by their nature private.[109]

2.74 As has already been noted (at para 1.45), the 'public functions' test is – on the face of it at least – precisely the test for susceptibility to judicial review set out in *R v Takeover Panel ex p Datafin plc*.[110] The judicial review case law is, therefore, an important starting point in determining the meaning of this provision.[111]

2.75 As shall be seen, however, it is clear from parliamentary statements that the scope of the Human Rights Act goes beyond that of judicial review. Further, it must be recalled that the Human Rights Act requires that the Strasbourg case law should be taken into account in determining any question which arises in connection with a Convention right.[112] That requirement presumably extends to the determination of whether a body is capable of infringing a Convention right.

The approach in domestic law: susceptibility to judicial review

2.76 The courts rely (primarily at least) upon four factors in order to determine susceptibility to judicial review. No single factor is decisive in all cases.

---

108 HRA 1998, s 6(3).

109 *Ibid*, s 6(5).

110 [1987] 2 WLR 699, CA.

111 In Parliament, the Home Secretary described the domestic case law as 'the most valuable asset we have to hand' in this respect, but also, as something to be 'built upon': *Hansard*, HC, 17 June 1998, col 409.

112 HRA 1998, s 2(1).

Source of power

2.77 It is almost[113] axiomatic that a body exercising statutory or prerogative powers is subject to judicial review in respect of those powers.[114]

Public function

2.78 Whether or not a body is statutory, it is only susceptible to judicial review in respect of its 'public functions'. In *R v Panel on Takeovers and Mergers ex p Datafin plc*,[115] a non-statutory body which formed part of the self-regulatory framework of the City of London was held to be susceptible to judicial review. Whilst the Court recognised that the source of power would often, or even usually, be decisive, it was not the sole test of susceptibility to judicial review. If the body challenged exercised 'public law functions', or functions with 'public law consequences' that could be sufficient to bring that body within the reach of judicial review, notwithstanding the absence of a statutory source for its power.[116]

2.79   A body which is susceptible to judicial review can be challenged in respect of any of its public functions, not merely its express statutory powers.[117]

Governmental functions

2.80 A further test was introduced in the case of *R v Disciplinary Committee of the Jockey Club ex p Aga Khan*.[118] The Court of Appeal held that the Jockey Club was not susceptible to judicial review, notwithstanding that it controlled a significant national activity, on the grounds of the contractual source of its power, and the absence of a 'governmental' function[119] which was 'woven into

---

113 See, however, *R v Attorney General ex p Ferrante* [1995] COD 18: statutory functions of the Attorney General under the Coroners Act 1988, s 13, are immune from judicial review. The issue of jurisdiction did not arise in the subsequent appeal: (1995) *The Independent*, 3 April.

114 See *Council of Civil Service Unions v Minister for the Civil Service* [1985] AC 374, *per* Lord Diplock, p 490C. The subject matter of some prerogative powers excludes them from the remit of judicial review, *per* Lord Roskill, p 418B: treaty making, defence of the realm, prerogative of mercy, grant of honours, dissolution of Parliament and appointment of ministers are probably excluded. As to the prerogative of mercy, however, see *R v Secretary of State for the Home Department ex p Bentley* [1994] QB 349; *Reckley v Minister of Public Safety and Immigration and Others (No 2)* [1996] AC 527.

115 [1987] QB 815.

116 *Per* Lloyd LJ, p 847A–B.

117 See, eg, *R v Commissioner of Police of the Metropolis ex p Blackburn* [1968] 2 QB 118; *R v Norfolk CC ex p M* [1989] QB 619; *R v Harrow LBC ex p D* [1989] 3 WLR 1239; *R v Lewisham LBC ex p P* [1991] 1 WLR 308.

118 [1993] 1 WLR 909.

119 See, to similar effect, *R v Chief Rabbi of the United Hebrew Congregations of Great Britain and the Commonwealth ex p Wachmann* [1992] 1 WLR 1036, *per* Simon Brown J, p 1041D–E.

any system of governmental control'. Although the powers could be described as 'public', this was insufficient as they were in 'no sense governmental'.[120]

Consensual element

2.81 Where a body exercises statutory, and/or governmental powers, it is no obstacle to judicial review of those powers that it also has a contractual relationship with the claimant.[121] Where, however, a body's powers over the applicant solely derive from contract, without any 'governmental underpinning',[122] judicial review does not lie.[123]

2.82 The net effect of these overlapping tests is that a wide range of bodies have been held to be subject to judicial review, including The Law Society,[124] the Institute of Chartered Accountants,[125] the General Medical Council,[126] the Stock Exchange,[127] the Personal Investment Authority,[128] Lloyd's of London,[129] the Bar Council,[130] the Code of Practice Committee of the trade association of the British pharmaceutical industry,[131] the Advertising Standards Authority,[132] and a regulatory body set up by telephone operators to supervise the activities of certain service providers.[133]

---

120 [1993] 1 WLR 909, *per* Sir Thomas Bingham MR, p 923H.

121 Eg, *R v Cleveland CC ex p Cleveland Care Homes* [1994] COD 221; *R v Hammersmith and Fulham LBC ex p Beddowes* [1987] QB 1050; *R v Midlands Electricity Board ex p Busby* (1987) *The Times*, 28 October.

122 *R v Panel of the Federation of Communication Services Ltd ex p Kubis* [1998] COD 5.

123 *R v Insurance Ombudsman Bureau ex p Aegon Life Assurance Ltd* [1994] COD 426; *R v Lloyd's of London ex p Briggs* [1993] 1 Lloyd's Rep 176; [1993] COD 66; *R v Panel of the Federation of Communication Services Ltd ex p Kubis* [1998] COD 5; *R v Football Association of Wales ex p Flint Town United Football Club* [1991] COD 44; *R v Football Association Ltd ex p Football League Ltd* [1993] 2 All ER 833; *R v Disciplinary Committee of the Jockey Club ex p Aga Khan* [1993] 1 WLR 909. Cf, however, *R v The Independent Committee for the Supervision of Telephone Information Services ex p Firstcode Ltd* [1993] COD 325.

124 *R v Law Society ex p Reigate Projects* [1993] 1 WLR 1531.

125 *R v Institute of Chartered Accountants in England and Wales ex p Andreou* [1996] COD 489.

126 *R v General Medical Council ex p Colman* [1990] 1 All ER 489.

127 *R v International Stock Exchange of the United Kingdom and the Republic of Ireland Ltd ex p Else (1982) Ltd and Another* [1993] QB 534.

128 *R v Personal Investment Authority ex p Burns-Anderson Network plc* (1998) 10 Admin LR 57.

129 *R v Lloyd's of London ex p Briggs* [1993] Lloyd's Rep 176; [1993] COD 66.

130 *R v General Council of the Bar ex p Percival* [1991] 1 QB 212.

131 *R v Code of Practice Committee of the British Pharmaceutical Industry ex p Professional Counselling (Aids) Ltd* [1991] COD 228.

132 *R v Advertising Standards Authority ex p The Insurance Service plc* [1990] COD 42.

133 *R v The Independent Committee for the Supervision of Telephone Information Services ex p Firstcode Ltd* [1993] COD 325.

The Strasbourg case law

2.83 The Strasbourg organs do not approach the question of susceptibility to challenge in as analytical a manner as the domestic courts. A broad comparison of the Strasbourg and domestic case law shows that, in practice, there is a high degree of overlap as to the bodies considered to be susceptible to challenge, although Strasbourg has been prepared to entertain challenges in some circumstances in which judicial review would not lie.[134] Further, it is clear that, to some extent, the same factors are at issue. In *Casado Coca v Spain*,[135] for example, the applicant brought a challenge to the Barcelona Bar Council in respect of restrictions on his freedom to advertise. The complaint therefore engaged Article 10(1) which prohibits interference with free expression by 'public authority'. The Strasbourg Court concluded that the Spanish Bars were public authorities: not only were they 'public law corporations', but, as the Court put it:

> ... this status is further buttressed by their purpose of serving the public interest through the furtherance of free, adequate legal assistance combined with public supervision of the practice of the profession and of compliance with professional ethics.

2.84 Furthermore, appeal against the impugned decision lay to the competent courts.[136] In effect, both the source of the power and the nature of the function challenged were considered.

2.85 In *Holy Monasteries v Greece*,[137] the respondent State argued that the monasteries could not be regarded as 'non-governmental organisations' within the meaning of Article 34 (then Article 25) of the Convention. They therefore lacked the right of individual petition.[138] The Court rejected this argument on the grounds that the monasteries did not exercise 'governmental powers'; their objectives (spiritual and otherwise) were not such as to enable them to be classed with 'governmental organisations established for public administration purposes'.[139] This reasoning is clearly redolent of the 'governmental functions' test posited in the *Aga Khan* case.[140]

---

134 See para 2.99.

135 (1994) 18 EHRR 1.

136 *Ibid*, para 39.

137 (1995) 20 EHRR 1.

138 ECHR, Art 34 excludes 'governmental' bodies from the right of individual petition; see para 2.58.

139 (1995) 20 EHRR 1, para 49. See, to similar effect, *R v Chief Rabbi of the United Hebrew Congregations of Great Britain and the Commonwealth ex p Wachmann* [1992] 1 WLR 1036; *R v Imam of Bury Park Jame Masjid Luton ex p Sulamain* [1994] COD 142.

140 *R v Disciplinary Committee of the Jockey Club ex p Aga Khan* [1993] 1 WLR 909. See para 2.80.

2.86   As the *Casado Coca*[141] case makes clear, professional regulatory bodies are subject to control by Strasbourg, just as they are subject to judicial review. Both judicial review and challenge before Strasbourg lie against the General Medical Council,[142] the Law Society[143] and the Visitors to the Inns of Court General Council of the Bar.[144]

2.87   Strasbourg has found regulators to be difficult cases, as have the domestic courts. In *Tee v United Kingdom*,[145] the applicant complained about an investigation into his affairs by LAUTRO. The Financial Services Act 1986 provided LAUTRO with certain regulatory and investigatory powers. English courts would certainly view it as a public body for the purposes of judicial review,[146] and, following *Casado Coca,* it might reasonably expected that Strasbourg would too. In fact, the Commission expressly left the matter open, holding the application to be inadmissible on other grounds.

Functions subject to challenge under the Human Rights Act

2.88   Section 6(3) of the Human Rights Act states that a 'public authority' is 'any person whose functions are of a public nature'. Such a person is not a public authority in respect of acts which are by their nature private.[147] This is the language of the *Datafin*[148] test for susceptibility to judicial review (see para 2.74). It might therefore be thought that the Human Rights Act merely applied the familiar public law approach, namely, that a body exercising a public function was subject to judicial supervision in respect of that function, and nothing more.

2.89   It is quite clear, however, that this is not the intention of Parliament. *Hansard* reveals that the express intention is to create three categories of bodies.[149] The first is 'obvious' public authorities, 'all of whose functions are

---

141 (1994) 18 EHRR 1.

142 *Colman v United Kingdom* (1994) 18 EHRR 119; *R v General Medical Council ex p Colman* [1990] 1 All ER 489.

143 Eg, *R v Solicitors Complaints Bureau ex p Curtin* (1994) 6 Admin LR 657; *R v The Law Society ex p Reigate Projects* [1993] 1 WLR 1531; *Wood v United Kingdom* (1997) 24 EHRR CD 69.

144 *R v Visitors to the Inns of Court ex p Calder and Persaud* [1994] QB 1; *App No 10331/83 v United Kingdom* (1984) 6 EHRR 583; *Everest v United Kingdom* (1997) EHRR 23 CD 180. In *Calder and Persaud*, the Court of Appeal held that review of the visitorial jurisdiction was available, but only where the visitor acted in abuse of power, in breach of natural justice or in excess of jurisdiction, following the decision of the House of Lords in respect of a university visitor in *R v Hull University Visitor ex p Page* [1993] AC 682. There is no reason to suppose such jurisdictional limits apply in Strasbourg.

145 (1996) 21 EHRR CD 108.

146 The application to Strasbourg followed a judicial review which failed, although not on grounds of susceptibility to challenge.

147 HRA 1998, s 6(5).

148 *R v Takeover Panel ex p Datafin plc* [1987] 2 WLR 699, CA.

149 The Home Secretary, *Hansard*, HC, 17 June 1998, cols 409–10.

public'.[150] Such bodies are caught by the Human Rights Act 'in respect of everything they do'.[151] Examples given in Parliament include Government Departments, local authorities and the police.[152]

2.90   Viewed from the perspective of existing domestic law, there are no 'obvious' public authorities in the sense intended. Even central government has functions which have been traditionally regarded as outside the scope of public law control, such as matters arising out of a contract of employment.[153] The Parliamentary statements suggest that they would however fall to be considered under the Human Rights Act. This is a significant expansion of public law supervision. As shall be seen, at paras 2.99 *et seq*, however, this is in accordance with the approach of the Strasbourg Court.

2.91   Secondly, there are 'organisations with a mix of public and private functions'. Such bodies are susceptible to challenge only in respect of their public functions.[154]

2.92   This category appears to accord with the traditional approach of the judicial review courts, and indeed the overt language of s 6(4) of the Human Rights Act. It is clear, however, that the government intends that a wide range of bodies will fall within this category, some of which had been thought to be outside the scope of judicial review.

2.93   In Parliament, the Lord Chancellor cited Railtrack as a 'public utility',[155] as an example of a body only caught in respect of its public functions.[156] This echoes the statement in the Human Rights Act White Paper that the bodies subject to challenge under the human rights legislation included:

> ... to the extent that they are exercising public functions, companies responsible for areas of activity which were previously within the public sector, such as the privatised utilities.

2.94   Whilst it has long been thought analytically possible that a privatised utility could be subject to judicial review, we are unaware of any case where this has happened as yet. There are precedents for judicial review against utilities prior to privatisation,[157] and indeed for judicial review of private companies, at least

150 *Hansard*, HC, 17 June 1998, col 409.

151 The Home Secretary, *Hansard*, HC, 16 February 1998, col 775. See, also, the Lord Chancellor at *Hansard*, HL, 16 November 1997, col 1231; *Hansard*, HL, 24 November 1997, col 785.

152 The Home Secretary, *Hansard*, HC, 17 June 1998, cols 409–10.

153 *R v British Broadcasting Corporation ex p Lavelle* [1983] 1 WLR 23. Cf *R v Crown Prosecution Service ex p Hogg* [1994] COD 237.

154 The Lord Chancellor, *Hansard*, HL, 24 November 1997, col 785. See, also, The Home Secretary, *Hansard*, HC, 16 February 1998, col 775.

155 The Home Secretary, *Hansard*, HL, 24 November 1997, col 785.

156 *Ibid*, col 784.

157 Eg, *R v Midlands Electricity Board ex p Busby* (1987) *The Times*, 28 October; *R v British Coal Corp and Roo Management ex p GC Whittaker (Properties)* [1989] COD 528; *R v British Coal Corp ex p Price (No 2)* [1993] COD 323; (1993) *The Times*, 28 May.

where they perform a statutory and/or regulatory function.[158] Jack Straw MP stated that it was 'highly debatable' whether the Football Association, or Jockey Club had public functions;[159] both have been found to be outside the scope of judicial review.[160]

2.95   The BBC was also cited as an example of a body caught by the Human Rights Act in respect of its public functions.[161] Judicial review is probably available against the BBC (although the courts have avoided having decide the point),[162] at least in respect of those functions traditionally recognised as within compass of public law.[163]

2.96   The Home Secretary has suggested that nursing homes and housing associations may be subject to the Act in respect of some of their functions.[164] We are unaware of any case in which judicial review has been granted against such bodies.

2.97   If these statements of intention are given effect by the courts, a large number of bodies will be brought within the sphere of public law that have previously been thought beyond its reach, at least for the purposes of the Human Rights Act.

2.98   The third category of bodies contains those with no public functions. They fall entirely outside the scope of the Human Rights Act.[165]

The Strasbourg approach

2.99 The notion of 'obvious' public authorities susceptible to public law challenge in respect of all that they do is a novel one in domestic law. There are, however, Strasbourg cases that broadly mirror this approach. A number of

---

158 Eg, *R v London Commodity Exchange (1986) Ltd ex p Brearley* [1994] COD 145. The action was transferred to the Commercial Court, but not on grounds that the respondent was not susceptible to judicial review.

159 *Hansard*, HC, 17 June 1989, col 410.

160 *R v Football Association Ltd ex p Football League Ltd* [1993] 2 All ER 833; *R v Disciplinary Committee of the Jockey Club ex p Aga Khan* [1993] 1 WLR 909.

161 The Home Secretary, *Hansard*, HC, 16 December 1998, col 778.

162 *R v British Broadcasting Corporation ex p Referendum Party* [1997] COD 460 and *R v British Broadcasting Corporation ex p Pro-Life Alliance Party* [1997] COD 457.

163 In *R v British Broadcasting Corporation ex p Lavelle* [1983] 1 WLR 23, a challenge to its private law, contractual employment appeals procedure was held to be outside the scope of judicial review.

164 Speech to the Institute of Public Policy Research, 29 March 2000. In *R v Servite Houses and the London Borough of Wandsworth Council ex p Goldsmith and Chatting,* 12 May 2000, unreported, the High Court held that judicial review did not lie against a housing association undertaking functions under the National Assistance Act 1948, s 21.

165 The Home Secretary, *Hansard*, HC, 17 June 1998, cols 409–10. The Home Secretary noted that it was 'highly debatable' whether the Football Association and the Jockey Club had public functions; both have been held to be outside the scope of judicial review: *R v Football Association Ltd ex p Football League Ltd* [1993] 2 All ER 833; *R v Disciplinary Committee of the Jockey Club ex p Aga Khan* [1993] 1 WLR 909.

cases have dealt with employment disputes between an applicant and a public sector employer. Thus, for example, in *Halford v United Kingdom*,[166] the applicant was the former Assistant Chief Constable of Merseyside. She brought industrial tribunal proceedings alleging sex discrimination. The Strasbourg Court found that the interception by the police of calls made by her from her office telephone in order to gather information to use against her in the proceedings violated her Article 8 rights. It is very difficult to see how Ms Halford would have challenged this conduct by way of judicial review.[167]

2.100   Further, it is clear that Strasbourg recognises that bodies beyond the formal organs of government, such as professional regulatory organisations may exercise 'public functions' and thereby be liable to challenge under the Convention.[168]

2.101   It would accordingly be very surprising if the domestic courts did not give effect to the plain intention of Parliament in respect of the general approach at least to the issue of susceptibility to challenge.

Courts and tribunals

2.102 The Human Rights Act expressly defines 'public authority' to include courts and tribunals.[169] Thus, for example, decisions of courts may be challenged on the grounds of breach of Article 6.[170] Any such challenge must, however be brought by appeal, not by means of fresh proceedings.[171]

2.103   The right to challenge a court or tribunal under the Human Rights Act is far clearer and broader than the pre-existing right to bring (ordinary) judicial review of courts and tribunals. Superior courts are not susceptible to such judicial review at all.[172] This prohibition extends to the Supreme Court[173] and,

---

166 (1997) 24 EHRR 523. See, also, *Leander v Sweden* (1987) 9 EHRR 433; *Kalaç v Turkey* (1999) 27 EHRR 552; *Costello-Roberts v United Kingdom* (1995) 19 EHRR 112.

167 Eg, *R v British Broadcasting Corporation ex p Lavelle* [1983] 1 WLR 23.

168 *Province of Bari, Sorrentino and Messini Nemaga v Italy* (1999) 27 EHRR CD 352; *Consejo General de Colegios Oficiales de Economistas de España v Spain* (1995) 82-B 150; discussed at paras 2.39, 2.63.

169 HRA 1998, s 6(3).

170 Eg, *Dombo Beheer v Netherlands* (1993) 18 EHRR 213.

171 HRA 1998, s 9(1).

172 *The Rioters' Case* [1683] 1 Vern 175; *R v Oxenden* [1691] 1 Show 217; *Re Racal Communications* [1981] AC 374.

173 This includes the Registrar of Criminal Appeals (*R v Registrar of Criminal Appeals ex p Pegg* [1983] COD 192) and High Court Masters: *R v Shemilt (A Taxing Officer) ex p Buckley* [1988] COD 40; *Murrell v British Leyland Trustees* [1989] COD 389.

subject to important exceptions,[174] the Crown Court. Inferior courts, such as magistrates' courts, coroner's courts and county courts,[175] are subject to judicial review. In the case of statutory tribunals, it has been held that susceptibility to judicial review turns upon factors including whether the tribunal is presided over by a High Court judge, or whether it has 'a status so closely equivalent to the High Court that the exercise of the power of judicial review by the High Court is for that reason inappropriate'.[176] Any court or tribunal may be challenged at Strasbourg.[177]

Parliament

2.104 Section 6(3) of the Human Rights Act excludes Parliament from the definition of 'public authority'. The implication is therefore that there can be no challenge to Parliament for simply enacting legislation in contravention of Convention rights, or, indeed for failing to do so. The matter is in any event put beyond doubt by section 6(6). A failure to:

(a) introduce in, or lay before, Parliament a proposal for legislation; or

(b) make any primary legislation or remedial order ...

does not constitute an 'act' which may be held to be unlawful under s 6(1) of the Human Rights Act. The purpose of these provisions is to 'underpin parliamentary sovereignty'.[178]

2.105 There is no clear barrier in principle to a challenge by way of judicial review to the refusal of a minister to act on a declaration of incompatibility (see paras 1.67 *et seq*). Such a challenge could not proceed on Convention grounds, but could, conceivably, be brought on ordinary *Wednesbury* grounds. There can be little doubt that such a challenge would require exceptional facts in order to succeed.

2.106 Section 6(4) of the Human Rights Act expressly provides that 'Parliament' does not include the House of Lords acting in a judicial capacity. On the face of it, this provision is otiose. There is no scope in domestic law for a challenge to

---

174 Supreme Court Act 1981, s 29(3) provides: 'In relation to the jurisdiction of the Crown Court, other than its jurisdiction in matters relating to trial on indictment, the High Court shall have all such jurisdiction to make orders of mandamus, prohibition or certiorari as the High Court possesses in relation to the jurisdiction of an inferior court.' For the scope of this provision, see *Re Smalley* [1985] AC 622; *R v Manchester Crown Court ex p Director of Public Prosecutions* [1993] 1 WLR 1524. See, further, Richard Gordon, *Judicial Review and Crown Office Practice*, 1999, London: Sweet & Maxwell, paras 3-455 *et seq*.

175 Eg, *R v Bloomsbury and Marylebone County Court ex p Blackburne* (1985) 275 EG 1273; *R v Central London County Court ex p London* (1999) *The Times*, 23 March. Cf *Skinner v Northallerton County Court Judge* [1899] AC 439.

176 *R v Cripps ex p Muldoon and Others* [1984] QB 68, *per* Robert Goff LJ.

177 This is of course subject to the requirement that an applicant must exhaust domestic remedies: ECHR, Art 36.

178 The Lord Chancellor, *Hansard*, HL, 24 November 1997, col 814.

the judicial function of the House of Lords in any event.[179] Section 9(1) of the Human Rights Act provides that a claim that a judicial act contravenes Convention rights may only be brought by exercising a right of appeal. Thus, as now, a violation of Convention rights by the House of Lords Judicial Committee can only be remedied in Strasbourg.

Horizontal effect: the Convention in private disputes

2.107 In some circumstances, the Convention impacts upon disputes between two private bodies, or individuals. There are difficult questions as to the extent to which this 'horizontal effect' will occur under the Human Rights Act. These issues are discussed at paras 3.138 *et seq.*

---

179 Save perhaps in exceptional circumstances, as in *R v Bow Street Metropolitan Stipendiary Magistrates ex p Pinochet Ugarte (No 2)* [2000] 1 AC 119.

CHAPTER 3

CONVENTION CONCEPTS

CONVENTION CONCEPTS IN DOMESTIC LAW

3.01 As has been seen,[1] the Human Rights Act 1998 imposes important interpretative obligations on the courts. This is achieved, primarily, by a combination of ss 2, 3 and 6.

3.02 Section 2(1) of the Act requires the court in determining a question which has arisen in connection with a Convention right to take into account any judgment, decision, declaration, or advisory opinion of the European Court of Human Rights, opinion or decision of the Commission or decision of the Committee of Ministers whenever made or given so far as, in the opinion of the court or tribunal, it is relevant to the proceedings in which that question has arisen.

3.03 Section 3(1) and (2) of the Act provides that, so far as it is possible to do so, primary and subordinate legislation (whenever that legislation was enacted) must be read and given effect in a way which is compatible with the Convention rights.

3.04 Finally, s 6(1) makes it unlawful for a public authority to act in a way which is incompatible with a Convention right. Section 6(3) provides that the term 'public authority' includes a court or tribunal.

3.05 The combined effect of these sections is that the High Court is, in judicial review proceedings, as much a public authority as the defendant before it. In such proceedings where Convention rights are involved it has a duty, both when construing statutes and subordinate legislation and in developing the common law, to act in a manner which is compatible with the Convention rights enumerated in Sched 1.[2]

3.06 In carrying out their obligations under the Act, the domestic courts must have recourse to a number of Convention concepts as developed by the Strasbourg Court. Without careful consideration of the relevant Strasbourg case law in relation to these concepts, there will be a breach of s 2 and, in many instances, of ss 3 and 6 as well.

---

1   See Chapter 1.
2   See paras 1.11 *et seq.*

3.07   The Strasbourg case law is not determinative of the domestic courts' approach, however, for a number of reasons. First, s 2 of the Human Rights Act necessarily means that it is a guide rather than a tourniquet. It has to be taken into account but not always followed. Secondly, Strasbourg expects the national courts to apply the Convention standards in the first instance. Unlike the European Court of Justice in Luxembourg, applying European Community law,[3] the role of the Strasbourg Court is, essentially, supervisory. Finally, Convention rights operate as a floor rather than as a ceiling. Section 11 of the Human Rights Act provides that a person's reliance on a Convention right does not restrict any other right or freedom conferred on him by or under any law having effect in any part of the United Kingdom or his right to make any claim or bring any proceedings which he could make outside the Human Rights Act itself in domestic law.

3.08   Although not determinative in national law,[4] the Strasbourg case law provides an important framework for interpretation and application of the Convention. The concepts that it has developed over the years in relation to the Convention will, in large measure, be the concepts that the domestic courts will deploy in interpreting and applying the Convention in any individual case.

3.09   The Table below places the most important concepts utilised by the Strasbourg Court into three classes, namely, those material to: (a) interpretation of the Convention; (b) application of the Convention; and (c) informing the approach of the court.

Concepts affecting Convention interpretation	Concepts affecting application of the Convention	Concepts informing the approach of the court
1 An international treaty	6 Principle of legality ('prescribed by law')	11 Margin of appreciation
2 Principle of effectiveness	7 Legitimate aim	12 Subsidiarity
3 Up to date interpretation	8 Democratic values principle	13 Fourth instance
4 Autonomous meaning	9 Proportionality	14 Victim
5 Exceptions strictly construed	10 Positive obligations	15 Burden of proof

---

3   For which, in the context of human rights, see Chapter 7.
4   Save, of course, that, where Strasbourg has adjudicated in a particular case, the parties before it are bound in international law to give effect to the judgment.

SCOPE OF APPLICATION OF CONVENTION CONCEPTS

3.10 There are certain Convention rights which, on their face at least, are unqualified and do not fall to be balanced (see Articles 2, 3, 4(1) and 7). There are, however, rights which may be interfered with in accordance with certain prescribed exceptions (such as Articles 8–11). Further, certain Articles (for example, Article 6) contain implied limitations on the ambit of the right or the extent of permissible interference.

3.11   Different Convention concepts will be engaged depending on the right in question. In broad terms:

1   Of those concepts relevant to interpretation of the Convention: concepts 1–3 in the above Table apply to all Convention rights; concept 4 applies to specific terms (for example, 'civil rights and obligations' in Article 6); concept 5 applies only to those Articles which provide for some degree of limitation on the right.

2   Of those concepts relevant to application of the Convention: concept 7 (legitimate aim) applies where the Convention permits interference. Concept 6 (the principle of legality) also applies to all Convention rights even though the phrase 'prescribed by law' or 'in accordance with the law' is only used expressly in respect of certain provisions (see, for example, Article 5(1)). Concept 8, democratic values, applies throughout the Convention, at least to some degree. Concept 9, proportionality, applies wherever the Convention requires a balancing exercise. Concept 10 (positive obligations) applies, theoretically, to all Convention rights but (as will be seen) is most apposite to those rights which are regarded as the most fundamental and where special protection is thought to be required (as, for example, Articles 2 and 8).

3   Of those concepts relevant to informing the approach of the Court, they are (where material) equally applicable to all Convention rights, save for the doctrine of margin of appreciation which, in practice, is applied by the Court where either a balancing exercise is required, or an exception fails to be construed.

INTERPRETING THE CONVENTION

The Convention as an international treaty

3.12 Although the Human Rights Act contains its own principles of interpretation,[5] the domestic court may, on occasion, have to resort to the rules of public

---

5   See, especially, ss 2, 3 and 6 (above) and analysed at paras 1.11 *et seq*.

international law in interpreting the Convention. This is because the Convention is an international treaty and so falls to be interpreted, where appropriate, in accordance with the Vienna Convention on the Law of Treaties 1969.

3.13   The Strasbourg Court has confirmed that this is so. In *Golder v United Kingdom*,[6] it ruled that Articles 31–33 of the Vienna Convention (not then in force) should guide the Court in interpreting the European Convention on Human Rights because those Articles were declaratory of customary international law.

3.14   Article 31.1 of the Vienna Convention sets out the general rule of interpretation:

> ... a treaty shall be interpreted in good faith in accordance with the ordinary meaning[7] to be given to the terms of the treaty in their context and the light of its object and purpose.

3.15   Importantly, too, Article 31.3 requires the court to take into account amongst other things, together with the context, 'any subsequent practice in the application of the treaty which establishes the agreement of the parties regarding its interpretation'.

3.16   Further, Article 31.4 requires a special meaning to be given to a term if it is established that the parties so intended. In this way, both the Strasbourg case law and doctrines such as 'autonomous meaning' developed by that Court are consistent with Article 31 of the Vienna Convention as sources that the domestic court must take into account when interpreting the European Convention in proceedings before it.

3.17   The Vienna Convention also contains supplementary means of interpretation. Article 32 allows recourse to the preparatory work of a treaty either to confirm the conclusion reached by primary means of interpretation under Article 31 or to determine the meaning where Article 31 methods leave the meaning ambiguous or obscure or lead to a result which is manifestly absurd or unreasonable. Article 33 provides, in essence, that a treaty is equally authentic in each authenticated language and that any difference in meaning is to be resolved by adopting the meaning which best accords with the object and purpose of the treaty.[8]

3.18   Although the Strasbourg Court has not imposed a hierarchy in relation to the application of the Vienna Convention or the Convention concepts referred to in this Chapter for interpreting the European Convention, it is clear that it regards the Convention as possessing a special character, concerned as it is

---

6   (1979–80) 1 EHRR 524, para 29.

7   For examples of pure ordinary meaning construction adopted by the Strasbourg Court, see *Johnston v Ireland* (1987) 9 EHRR 203; *Lithgow v United Kingdom* (1986) 8 EHRR 329.

8   At the domestic level, of course, the only version of the Convention that has been given effect by the HRA 1998, Sched 1 is the English version.

with the protection of individual human rights as opposed to merely specifying the rights and obligations of Contracting States.[9] This suggests that the 'special object and purpose' part of Article 31.1 of the Vienna Convention represents an overarching principle that informs all the other principles of interpretation. This may, therefore, be the most significant of the Vienna Convention principles in interpreting the ECHR.

Principle of effectiveness

3.19 The principle of effectiveness requires that the provisions of the Convention be interpreted and applied so as to ensure effective safeguards for the protection of the rights recognised by the Convention.

3.20 In part, this principle is to be derived directly from the Convention itself. Article 1 stipulates that 'the High Contracting Parties shall secure to everyone within their jurisdiction the rights and freedoms defined in Section I of this Convention'. Article 13 provides that:

> ... everyone whose rights and freedoms as set forth in this Convention are violated shall have an effective remedy before a national authority notwithstanding that the violation has been committed by persons acting in an official capacity.[10]

3.21 However, neither Article 1 nor Article 13 have been included in Schedule 1 of the Human Rights Act as 'Convention rights'. The omission of Article 1 is readily explained: Article 1 operates on the level of state obligation and the Human Rights Act now represents the undertaking by the United Kingdom of that very obligation.[11]

3.22 The omission of Article 13 may be more significant. The government has contended that its inclusion is unnecessary given the extensive remedies contained in ss 6–8 of the Human Rights Act.[12]

3.23 Be that as it may, the fact that the Human Rights Act does not expressly incorporate Articles 1 and 13 does not mean that the principle of effectiveness is absent from domestic litigation. Parliamentary statements make clear that it is intended that the domestic courts may have regard to Article 13 and its case law.[13] The principle is also to be derived, as the Strasbourg Court has emphasised, from the object and purpose of the Convention.[14]

---

9   See, eg, *Ireland v United Kingdom* (1979-80) 2 EHRR 25; *Soering v United Kingdom* (1989) 11 EHRR 439.

10 ECHR, Arts 1 and 13 are analysed at paras 4.05–4.08; 4.198–4.210.

11 See *Hansard*, HL, 18 November 1997, col 475.

12 See, eg, *Hansard*, HC, 20 May 1998, col 20; *Hansard*, HL, 18 November 1997, col 475.

13 See *Hansard*, HL, 18 November 1997, col 475 and *Hansard*, HC, 20 May 1998, col 979.

14 See, especially, *Artico v Italy* (1981) 3 EHRR 1, para 33 (right to representation guaranteed by ECHR, Art 6(3) must be effective); *Soering v United Kingdom* (1989) 11 EHRR 439, para 87 (state cannot avoid responsibility under ECHR by expelling individual to a country where (s)he faces a real risk of treatment contrary to Art 3).

3.24   This principle has been used by the Strasbourg Court as a means not merely of defining the scope of particular express obligations in the Convention but also: (i) to develop the doctrine of positive obligations, considered below,[15] so as to require positive action to be taken to protect certain rights;[16] (ii) as a means of widening the ambit of state responsibility under the Convention;[17] (iii) to develop the right to independent scrutiny.[18]

3.25   There are two considerations that must be borne in mind in applying this principle in domestic litigation. First, the domestic courts are bound by any limitations intrinsic to the Human Rights Act. Thus, however much the principle of effectiveness may demand the imposition of a positive obligation in order to safeguard a 'Convention right', it cannot impose such obligation if it contravenes an express provision of the Act. The best instance of this is afforded by s 6(6) of the Human Rights Act which precludes liability on a public authority for failure to introduce a proposal before Parliament for legislation or to make any primary legislation. Since much of the effect of the doctrine of positive obligations (see below) is to require Member States to provide an effective legislative framework to prevent Convention violations, it seems likely that s 6(6) will place a significant limit upon the principle of effectiveness.

3.26   Secondly, the principle of effectiveness may in some cases require changes to judicial review. Article 13 provides a right to an effective domestic remedy in respect of an arguable claim to a violation of the Convention.[19] The Strasbourg case law suggests, generally, that a domestic remedy will not be an effective remedy unless each of the following tests are satisfied:[20]

1   The substantive arguments in respect of breach of the Convention can be advanced. In *Smith and Grady v United Kingdom*,[21] the Strasbourg Court observed that:

> The Court recalls that Article 13 guarantees the availability of a remedy at national level to enforce the substance of Convention rights and freedoms in whatever form they may happen to be secured in the domestic legal order. Thus, its effect is to require the provision of a domestic remedy allowing the competent national authority both to deal with the substance of the relevant Convention complaint and to grant appropriate relief ...

---

15 See paras 3.112–3.127.

16 See, eg, *McCann v United Kingdom* (1996) 21 EHRR 97 (effective official investigation of lethal force used by state in order to provide effective protection of the right to life under Art 2).

17 There would be a lack of effective protection if Member States could disclaim liability by accepting no responsibility for the actions of private bodies.

18 Apart from the discussion here, see paras 4.206 *et seq*.

19 *Silver v United Kingdom* (1983) 5 EHRR 347, para 113. See, further, paras 4.198 *et seq*. ECHR, Art 13 does not require that the Convention should be incorporated into domestic law. See para 4.303.

20 See, further, paras 4.198 *et seq*.

21 (2000) 29 EHRR 493, para 135.

2 There is effective relief that can be granted by the domestic court if the applicant's argument of Convention violation succeeds: this requirement appears in the above cited passage from *Smith and Grady v United Kingdom*;[22] the absence of interim relief by the court may not always be decisive if, in practice, such interim relief is not required.[23]

3 The decision maker has 'a sufficiently independent standpoint'.[24]

4 The applicant can, in practice avail himself of that which would otherwise constitute an effective remedy: in *Vilvarajah v United Kingdom*[25] (though the point did not, in the event, arise for decision by the Court because of its ruling that judicial review was an adequate remedy against the refusal of asylum), the Commission held that an appeal which could only be exercised after the affected individual had left the United Kingdom was not an effective remedy to test a claim that his deportation from the United Kingdom was in violation of Article 3 of the Convention.

3.27 In a number of cases, the Strasbourg Court has concluded that judicial review is not an effective remedy. In *Silver v United Kingdom*,[26] the applicant prisoners successfully contended that interference with their correspondence violated Article 8. The Court also found a violation of Article 13 in respect of these complaints. The applicants did not allege that the Home Office policy at issue was Wednesbury unreasonable, or otherwise contrary to domestic law. Judicial review could not, therefore, provide an effective remedy.

3.28 In *Chahal v United Kingdom*,[27] the applicant successfully challenged a deportation decision taken on grounds of national security on Article 3 grounds. The Strasbourg Court concluded that neither the advisory panel which considered the appeal against the deportation decision, nor the domestic court on judicial review, provided an effective remedy. Neither could (as Article 3 required) review the decision of the Secretary of State to deport the applicant solely by reference to the risk of ill treatment, leaving aside national security considerations. On the contrary, the domestic court's approach was to satisfy themselves that the Secretary of State had balanced the risk to the applicant against the danger to national security.

3.29 In *Smith and Grady v United Kingdom*,[28] the applicants challenged the Ministry of Defence policy of excluding homosexuals from serving in the armed forces. The Strasbourg Court found both a violation of Article 8, and of Article 13.

---

22 (2000) 29 EHRR 493.

23 See, eg, *Soering v United Kingdom* (1989) 11 EHRR 439, para 123 ('there is no suggestion that in practice a fugitive would ever be surrendered before his application to the Divisional Court and any eventual appeal therefrom had been determined').

24 *Silver v United Kingdom* (1983) 5 EHRR 347, para 116.

25 (1992) 14 EHRR 248.

26 (1983) 5 EHRR 347.

27 (1997) 23 EHRR 413.

28 (2000) 29 EHRR 493.

Judicial review proceedings had been brought, but were unsuccessful.[29] The Court of Appeal held it was bound to apply the *Wednesbury* test,[30] and the policy did not breach that test. The Strasbourg Court concluded that the test had been set 'so high that it effectively excluded any consideration by the domestic courts of the question whether the interference with the applicants' rights answered a pressing social need or was proportionate to the national security and public order aims pursued'.[31]

3.30   It should not, however, be inferred from these cases that judicial review, or, in particular, the *Wednesbury* test, invariably fails to satisfy Article 13. All such cases are decided on the facts of the particular complaint at issue, and in a number of cases, the Strasbourg Court has held judicial review to have satisfied the requirements of Article 13. It is, however, difficult to discern a consistent analytical basis upon which the Strasbourg Court decides, on the facts of a given case, whether judicial review is a sufficient remedy.

3.31   In *Soering v United Kingdom*,[32] the applicant challenged a decision to extradite him under Articles 3 and 13. The Strasbourg Court considered the extent of the judicial review court's powers and concluded that although the Convention was not itself part of domestic law the English courts could review the 'reasonableness' of an extradition decision in the light of the kind of factors relied on by the applicant before the Convention institutions in the context of Article 3. In *Vilvarajah v United Kingdom*,[33] the applicant challenged the refusal of asylum on the basis of Articles 3 and 13. The Strasbourg Court noted that, in the context of asylum law, the judicial review courts applied the 'anxious scrutiny' test,[34] and concluded that there were no material differences between that case and Soering. The Court stated that, whilst there were limitations on the powers of the courts in judicial review proceedings, those powers did provide an 'effective degree of control over the decisions of administrative authorities in asylum cases' and were sufficient to satisfy the requirements of Article 13.

3.32   Similarly, in the case of *D v United Kingdom*,[35] the Strasbourg Court held that the implementation of the decision to remove the applicant (who was an AIDS patient) to St Kitts would violate Article 3, as he would thereby lose access to vital medical treatment, was contrary to Article 3. As to the alleged violation of Article 13, the Court concluded there was no reason to depart from the cases of *Soering* and *Vilvarajah*.

---

29 *R v Ministry of Defence ex p Smith* [1996] QB 541.

30 The Court of Appeal held that, in applying the *Wednesbury* test, the human rights context was relevant: the more substantial the interference with human rights, the more the court would require by way of justification: *ibid*, p 564.

31 *Smith and Grady v United Kingdom* (2000) 29 EHRR 493, para 138.

32 (1989) 11 EHRR 439, para 121.

33 *Ibid*.

34 See *R v Secretary of State for the Home Department ex p Bugdaycay* [1987] AC 514.

35 (1997) 24 EHRR 423.

3.33   In *Smith and Grady v United Kingdom*,[36] the Strasbourg Court sought to distinguish *Soering* and *Vilvarajah* in the following way:

> ... The present applications can be contrasted with the cases of *SOERING* and *VILVARAJAH* cited above. In those cases, the Court found that the test applied by the domestic courts in applications for judicial review of decisions by the Secretary of State in extradition and expulsion matters coincided with the Court's own approach under Article 3 of the Convention.

3.34   The Strasbourg Court purported to explain the approach in *Vilvarajah* and *Soering*[37] on the underlying basis that:

> ... the courts have stressed their special responsibility to subject administrative decisions in this area to the most anxious scrutiny where an applicant's life or liberty may be at risk. Moreover, the practice is that an asylum seeker will not be removed from the UK until proceedings are complete once he has obtained leave to apply for judicial review.[38]

3.35   The doctrine of 'anxious scrutiny' was, clearly, available to the applicants in *Smith and Grady v United Kingdom*.[39] As has been seen, however, the criticism levied by the Strasbourg Court in that case was that the irrationality threshold applied by the domestic court effectively excluded any consideration by the domestic courts of the question of whether the interference with the applicants' rights answered a pressing social need or was proportionate to the aims pursued.

3.36   In *Smith and Grady*, the Court also pointed to a further purported distinction between that case and *Vilvarajah* and *Soering*:

> In those cases, the Court found that the test applied by the domestic courts in applications for judicial review of decisions by the Secretary of State in extradition and expulsion matters coincided with the Court's own approach under Article 3 of the Convention.

3.37   The distinguishing feature, therefore, is said to be that the approach of the domestic court in *Vilvarajah* and *Soering*, both Article 3 claims, 'coincides with' that of the Strasbourg Court, whereas, in *Smith and Grady* (a claim under Article 8), the *Wednesbury* doctrine could be equated with the proportionality doctrine. The difficulty with this analysis is that, in truth, in an asylum case (for example), the judicial review court does not perform the kind of primary fact finding function that the Strasbourg institutions undertake in determining an Article 3 challenge.

3.38   This issue has been considered by the Court of Appeal. In *R v Secretary of State for the Home Department ex p Turgut*,[40] the applicant was a Turkish Kurd

---

36   (2000) 29 EHRR 493, para 138.
37   See fn 32. See, also, *D v United Kingdom* (1997) 24 EHRR 423, referred to at para 3.32.
38   See *Vilvarajah v United Kingdom* (1992) 14 EHRR 248, para 125.
39   (2000) 29 EHRR 493, para 138.
40   (2000) HRLR 346.

who had been refused asylum. He sought to challenge by way of judicial review the refusal of the Secretary of State to grant him exceptional leave to remain, the Secretary of State having concluded that no substantial grounds existed for believing that the applicant would be at real risk of ill treatment under Article 3 if returned to Turkey. The Court of Appeal considered the correct approach to be taken in judicial review in the light of *Smith and Grady*.[41] Simon Brown LJ emphasised that the domestic court's role, even in a case involving fundamental human rights, remained essentially supervisory. He rejected the argument advanced on behalf of the applicant that the judicial review court should examine all the material before it and make its own assessment of risk, in the manner of the Strasbourg Court, in order to coincide with the Strasbourg Court's approach. He concluded that the Strasbourg Court well knew the nature of the judicial review process in Article 3 cases and *Smith and Grady* could not be taken to require a change of approach.

3.39   It is submitted that this was the correct result. *Smith and Grady* cannot be taken to have undermined the significant body of Strasbourg case law in which the Court has said that judicial review, in its *Wednesbury* form, satisfies Article 13 in relation to Article 3 challenges. Nevertheless, it is inescapable that the conclusion of the Strasbourg Court in the Article 3 cases that the approach taken on judicial review 'coincides with' that of Strasbourg is simply wrong. The approach of the two courts is quite different (as above).

3.40   The reasoning of the Strasbourg Court in these cases accordingly makes any extension of their application perilous. It seems likely that Articles 9–11 would fall to be considered in the same manner as Article 8, and, if so, the *Wednesbury* test may not always suffice. Further, it might reasonably be said that the Court would approach Article 2 in the same manner as Article 3: both these Articles contain rights which are not subject to any explicit balancing exercise. This result would be paradoxical: these rights lack qualification because of their importance. It would accordingly be surprising if Article 13 provided a lesser degree of supervision in these cases.

3.41   These cases are also difficult to reconcile with those of *AGOSI v United Kingdom*[42] and *Air Canada v United Kingdom*.[43] In each case, the applicants challenged the exercise of a discretion by Customs and Excise to seize certain goods. The applicants complained – unsuccessfully – that the limits on a *Wednesbury* review of the seizure were such that the measures offended the requirement of proportionality inherent to Article 1 of Protocol 1. In effect, therefore, the Court held that the use of a form of review which itself was not based on proportionality could form part of a proportionate regime.

---

41   (2000) 29 EHRR 493.

42   (1987) 9 EHRR 1.

43   (1995) 20 EHRR 150.

3.42   Thus, if, and to the extent, the domestic courts do give effect to Article 13, the effect on judicial review is difficult to predict with any degree of certainty.

3.43   There are significant parallels between the principle of effectiveness and the principle of legality. As shall be seen, that too has given rise to issues as to the adequacy of judicial review.

Up to date interpretation

3.44 Although there have been occasional suggestions that judicial review recognises a principle of construction that allows for the change in meaning of a statutory expression over time,[44] the reality is, in most instances, that domestic case law is grounded in the doctrine of precedent.

3.45   The position is very different so far as Strasbourg is concerned. To begin with, there is no doctrine of precedent under the Convention. Whilst relevant decisions are, in the interests of legal certainty, more likely to be followed,[45] this is by no means automatic.

3.46   Secondly, the Strasbourg Court recognises that the Convention is a 'living instrument'. By this is meant that it falls to be interpreted in the light of modern conditions.[46] In *Tyrer v United Kingdom*,[47] the Court was concerned with the issue of whether judicial birching was contrary to Article 3 of the Convention. It held that, in considering that question, it could not 'but be influenced by the developments and commonly accepted standards in the penal policy of the member states of the Council of Europe'. What was, in the Court's view, decisive were contemporary standards rather than those in force when the Convention was drafted. Thus, the Court has encouraged repeated applications in respect of the rights of transsexuals.[48]

3.47   Contemporary standards are generally to be derived from the domestic law and practice in the member states of the Council of Europe. In *Marckx v Belgium*,[49] for example, the Strasbourg Court accepted that the distinction between legitimate and illegitimate children was both permissible and normal at the time that the Convention was drafted. However, it looked at developments in the domestic law of the majority of the Contracting States and held that such a distinction was no longer compatible with the true interpretation to be given to Article 8 of the Convention at the time of the Court's judgment over 25 years later.

---

44 See the Court of Appeal in *R v Westminster City Council and Others ex p M, P, A and X* (1997) 1 CCLR 85.
45 See, eg, *Sheffield and Horsham v United Kingdom* (1999) 27 EHRR 163.
46 *Tyrer v United Kingdom* (1978) 2 EHRR 1, para 31.
47 *Ibid.*
48 See, eg, *Rees v United Kingdom* (1986) 9 EHRR 56, para 47.
49 (1979–80) 2 EHRR 330.

3.48   Strasbourg has been eclectic in its selection of appropriate sources from which to judge contemporary standards. Thus, it has been prepared to examine not merely the content of domestic law but also, for example, other international treaties and human rights instruments.[50] However, there is a relevant distinction to be drawn between the recognition of rights, by extension, that would have been in the contemplation of the drafters of the Convention on the one hand and, on the other, the creation of wholly new rights which were never intended to be so included.[51] Further, Strasbourg has been astute to wait for developments to occur in domestic law and practice rather than to seek to impose its own standards.[52]

3.49   The effect of ss 2, 3 and 6 of the Human Rights Act means that, in the human rights context, the doctrine of precedent will have only limited application.[53] In dealing with issues relating to 'Convention rights' as defined in Sched 1 to the Human Rights Act, the domestic courts must, in practice, follow the general Strasbourg approach to interpretation rather than always following the specific Strasbourg decision which may no longer reflect the correct position. So, too, the general Strasbourg approach to the reception of international human rights treaties means that the High Court will be required to take such instruments into account in undertaking its interpretative obligations.

Autonomous meaning of Convention terms

3.50   It is sometimes said that certain Convention terms have an 'autonomous' meaning.[54]

3.51   Certain key concepts have this character, such as 'civil right', 'criminal charge', 'tribunal' and 'witness' in Article 6, 'penalty' in Article 7, and 'possessions' in Article 1 of Protocol 1.[55]

3.52   It would contravene the principle of effectiveness, considered above, if the domestic law of a Contracting State could give a restrictive interpretation to

---

50 Of the many cases, see, eg, *Inze v Austria* (1988) 10 EHRR 394 (European Convention on the Status of Children Born out of Wedlock); *Pretto v Italy* (1984) 6 EHRR 182 (International Covenant on Civil and Political Rights). Equally, the techniques of comparative law in other relevant jurisdictions may be helpful in establishing commonly accepted principles for this purpose.

51 Consider, eg, *Johnston v Ireland* (1987) 9 EHRR 203, para 53 (right to divorce not intended by the drafters). Cf *Soering v United Kingdom* (1989) 11 EHRR 439 (abolition of death penalty could be invoked by Protocol 6 and this meant that no 'dynamic' interpretation could be given to Art 3 as now containing a general prohibition).

52 Note, especially, the changing approach of the Strasbourg Court in the transsexual cases: *Rees v United Kingdom* (1987) 9 EHRR 56; *Cossey v United Kingdom* (1991) 13 EHRR 622; *B v France* (1993) 16 EHRR 1; *X, Y and Z v United Kingdom* (1997) 24 EHRR 143; *Sheffield and Horsham v United Kingdom* (1999) 27 EHRR 163.

53 See, however, *R v Central Criminal Court ex p Bright* (2000) *The Times*, 26 May.

54 See, eg, *Chassagnou v France* (2000) 29 EHRR 615, para 100.

55 See, generally, Chapter 4.

Convention terms and, thereby, erode Convention rights. Thus, for example, the state's definition of what constitutes a 'criminal charge' is not decisive of whether particular proceedings will be subject to the guarantees contained in Article 6(2) and (3).[56]

3.53   Even where the meaning of a term is not expressly referred to as 'autonomous', the Strasbourg Court has invariably looked to the substance as opposed to the nomenclature of particular expressions in the Convention such as 'family' and 'private life' in Article 8.[57]

3.54   There are, however, certain terms, used in the Convention, that necessarily require consideration of the meaning accorded to them by domestic law. For example, the expression 'prescribed by law' that occurs in certain Articles,[58] and which is in any event a concept running through the Convention,[59] requires application of Convention principle to the domestic law in question. The domestic meaning of a term may also sometimes be a convenient starting point for determining the Convention meaning of that term.[60]

Exceptions strictly construed

3.55 In interpreting the Convention, Strasbourg has recognised the principle that the scope of legitimate interference with rights under the Convention will be strictly construed.

3.56   Thus, interference with the right to liberty under Article 5 is unlawful unless it falls within one or more of the specific sub-paragraphs of Article 5(1) which will be construed restrictively. As the Strasbourg Court held in *Ciulla v Italy*:[61]

> The government considered that when interpreting Article 5(1) in the instant case, it was necessary to have regard to the general background of the disputed detention.

> Certainly, the Court does not underestimate the importance of Italy's struggle against organised crime, but it observes that the exhaustive list of permissible exceptions in paragraph 1 of Article 5 of the Convention must be interpreted strictly ...

3.57 In *Van Mechelen and Others v Netherlands*,[62] the Court expressed itself thus:

> Having regard to the place that the right to a fair administration of justice holds in a democratic society, any measures restricting the rights of the defence

---

56 Ie, presumption of innocence (Art 6(2)) and specified minimum guarantees in Art 6(3) such as adequate time to prepare a defence.

57 See, generally, Chapter 4.

58 Most notably in Art 5(1). See, also, Art 11(2).

59 And considered separately at paras 3.62 *et seq*.

60 As, for example, in determining whether there is a 'criminal charge' under Art 6: *Engel v Netherlands* (1979–80) 1 EHRR 647, para 82.

61 (1991) 13 EHRR 346, para 41.

62 (1998) 25 EHRR 647, para 58.

should be strictly necessary. If a less restrictive measure can suffice, then that measure should be applied.

3.58 It must, however, be recalled that the doctrine of the margin of appreciation, and the approach taken by the Court to the words 'necessary in a democratic society' may permit a more generous reading of an exception than appears on the face of the Convention (see paras 3.89 *et seq*; paras 3.128 *et seq*).

CONCEPTS AFFECTING APPLICATION OF THE CONVENTION

General approach

3.59 Most of the concepts considered in this section principally become relevant where there is a restriction on a right otherwise conferred by the Convention. In order to determine whether the restriction is lawful, the judicial review court will have to examine a number of issues.

3.60 These are, essentially: (i) whether the right permits of any express or implied restriction;[63] (ii) the nature of any restriction permitted in Convention terms; (iii) whether the restriction is justified in domestic law by reference to the principle of legality or 'prescribed by law'; (iv) whether the restriction has been exercised in a manner that pursues a legitimate aim (by reference to any legitimate restriction on the right); (v) whether the restriction has been exercised in a manner that is necessary in a democratic society; (vi) whether the restriction has been exercised in a manner that is proportionate to such legitimate aim.[64]

3.61 The first two issues outlined in the previous paragraph require interpreting the Convention so as to determine the general ambit of the right in question and of the legitimate scope, under the Convention, for any interference with that right. Issues (iii)–(vi) are, however, concerned with the legality of the particular restriction by reference to its manner of exercise. The other Convention concept relevant to application of the Convention is that of 'positive obligations', namely, the principle that states may have to take positive steps in order to protect Convention rights. Unlike the other concepts

---

63 A few Convention rights (eg, Art 3: prohibition on torture or inhuman or degrading treatment) contain no express limitation provision. Others, such as Arts 2, 5 and 6, contain specified instances of where the right does not engage. The most important specified restrictions are those contained in Arts 8–11. Most rights (eg, the right to a fair trial under Art 6: *Golder v United Kingdom* (1979–80) 1 EHRR 524) also contain certain implied restrictions.

64 The Court has developed specific requirements of lawfulness in respect of certain provisions of the Convention; see Chapter 4.

considered in this section, positive obligations flow from the substance of a right, and are not a tool for construing restrictions on Convention rights. These concepts are now considered in more detail.

Principle of legality

3.62 The principle of legality is central to the Convention. Its preamble describes the rule of law as part of the 'common heritage' which the Member State signatories share. In *Iatrides v Greece*,[65] the Strasbourg Court described it as one of the 'fundamental principles of a democratic society'.

3.63 In essence, the principle requires that any state interference with Convention rights must, apart from the other requirements of the Convention,[66] be in conformity with the rule of law. It ousts the common law principle articulated in *Malone v Metropolitan Police Commissioner*[67] that anything that the law does not restrict is, necessarily, permitted.

3.64 Most of the relevant case law stems from consideration of express provisions in the Convention that reflect the principle of legality. Thus, the phrase 'prescribed by law' is used to qualify the scope of lawful interference in Articles 5(1), 9(2), 10(2) and 11(2). The phrase 'in accordance with the law' is similarly used in Article 8(2).[68] The word 'lawful' is used in other parts of the Convention.[69]

3.65 There are three fundamental rules that the cases have laid down for applying the principle of legality to state interferences.[70] These are:

1 the legal basis for such interference must be identified and established;

2 that legal basis must be accessible in the sense of being available and foreseeable to those affected, or potentially affected, by its application;

3 it must also be sufficiently clear and certain so that it is understood by those affected, or potentially affected, by its application.

3.66 Underlying these rules is protection against arbitrary action. For example, in *Valenzuela Contreras v Spain*,[71] the Strasbourg Court held that there had been a violation of Article 8 in monitoring the applicant's telephone line. The Court stated:

---

65 Judgment 25 March 1999, para 62.

66 Such as democratic values or legitimate aim (see below).

67 [1979] Ch 244.

68 See, also, Art 2(3) and (4) of Protocol 4 and Art 1(1) of Protocol 7 (not currently 'Convention rights' as defined in the HRA 1998, s 1(1)).

69 See, eg, Art 5(1)(a).

70 See, generally, *Sunday Times v United Kingdom* (1979–80) 2 EHRR 245, para 49; *Silver v United Kingdom* (1983) 5 EHRR 347, paras 85–90.

71 (1999) 28 EHRR 483, para 46(iii).

... Especially where a power of the executive is exercised in secret the risks of arbitrariness are evident. In the context of secret measures of surveillance or interception by public authorities, the requirement of foreseeability implies that the domestic law must be sufficiently clear in its terms to give citizens an adequate indication as to the circumstances in and conditions on which public authorities are empowered to take any such secret measures. It is essential to have clear, detailed rules on the subject, especially as the technology available for use is constantly becoming more sophisticated.

3.67 As to the existence of a legal basis for interference, the category of 'law' has been held to be sufficiently identified and established in many instances extending well beyond statute and secondary legislation and including the common law,[72] European Community law,[73] and even the rules of professional bodies.[74]

3.68   The latter presents potentially difficult problems. In *Barthold v Germany*,[75] the Strasbourg Court held that the Rules of Professional Conduct for Veterinary Surgeons in the Federal Republic of Germany were capable of constituting 'law' that must fulfill the requirements of the principle of legality. It stated:

The competence of the Veterinary Surgeons' Council in the sphere of professional conduct derives from the independent rule making power that the veterinary profession ... traditionally enjoys by parliamentary delegation ... Furthermore, it is a competence exercised by the Council under the control of the state ...

3.69 It is unclear whether the Court intended to hold that 'parliamentary delegation' or 'state control' were necessary features of 'law' so as potentially to legitimise interference with Convention rights. Unless, however, 'law' is more widely construed by the domestic courts there is the danger of inconsistency between the relatively wide notion of a 'public authority' as defined in s 6 of the Human Rights Act and the scope for any interference by such authority with Convention rights. This must be so since unless the published rules of such an authority constitute 'law' for the purpose of the principle of legality there can, under such rules, be no interference whatever with Convention rights.

3.70   In determining whether a measure is (for example) 'prescribed by law', it is important to distinguish between domestic recognition of the existence of a particular 'law' supporting the measure in question, and the separate Convention requirement that the 'law' must satisfy the principle of legality. The Convention is concerned with the 'quality' of domestic law. As the Court observed in *Malone v United Kingdom*:[76]

---

72 *Sunday Times v United Kingdom* (1979–80) 2 EHRR 245, paras 46–53.
73 *Groppera Radio AG v Switzerland* (1990) 12 EHRR 321.
74 *Barthold v Germany* (1985) 7 EHRR 383, para 46.
75 (1985) 7 EHRR 383.
76 (1985) 7 EHRR 14, para 67.

... the phrase 'in accordance with the law' does not merely refer back to domestic law but also relates to the quality of the law, requiring it to be compatible with the rule of law, which is expressly mentioned in the preamble to the Convention.

3.71 The linked rules of accessibility and certainty circumscribe the quality of the 'law' that is considered sufficient to justify interference with a Convention right.

3.72 In *Silver v United Kingdom*,[77] the Strasbourg Court gave expression to the need for both availability and foreseeability. It ruled thus:

... the law must be adequately accessible: the citizen must be able to have an indication that is adequate, in the circumstances, of the legal rules applicable to a given case ...

... a norm cannot be regarded as a 'law' unless it is formulated with sufficient precision to enable the citizen to regulate his conduct: he must be able – if need be with appropriate advice – to foresee, to a degree that is reasonable in the circumstances, the consequences which a given action may entail.

3.73 Thus, although the requirement of accessibility is not denied merely because an individual may need legal advice on the 'law' in question, there must be some means of obtaining access to the 'law' as well as a sufficient degree of precision according to the particular context.

3.74 Internal guidelines from government departments or other public bodies are likely to fail the accessibility rule if they are not published. So, too, even published guidelines will also be likely to fail the test if there are unavailable criteria by which such guidelines are to be interpreted.[78]

3.75 The Court's strict approach to accessibility and certainty in relation to 'secret' measures, such as surveillance, is exemplified by cases such as *Huvig v France*,[79] *Kruslin v France*,[80] and *Valenzuela Contreras v Spain*.[81] Most recently, in *Khan v United Kingdom*,[82] Strasbourg has reiterated this approach by holding that Home Office Guidelines on telephone tapping were unlawful. At para 27 of the Court's judgment, it observed thus:

At the time of the events in the present case, there existed no statutory system to regulate the use of covert listening devices, although the Police Act 1997 now provides such a statutory framework. The Home Office Guidelines at the

---

77 (1983) 5 EHRR 347, paras 87–88.

78 See, generally, *Silver v United Kingdom* (1983) 5 EHRR 347, paras 87–88 (prison orders and instructions); *Malone v United Kingdom* (1985) 7 EHRR 14, paras 66–68 (Home Office guidelines on telephone tapping); *Govell v United Kingdom* [1999] EHRLR 121 (internal police guidelines: a Commission decision).

79 (1990) 12 EHRR 527, para 32.

80 (1990) 12 EHRR 547, para 33.

81 (1999) 28 EHRR 483, para 46(iii).

82 (2000) *The Times*, 19 May.

relevant time were neither legally binding nor were they directly publicly accessible. The Court also notes that Lord Nolan in the House of Lords commented that under English law there is, in general, nothing unlawful about a breach of privacy. There was, therefore, no domestic law regulating the use of covert listening devices at the relevant time.

3.76 Context is, of course, important. As the Strasbourg Court observed in *Sunday Times v United Kingdom*:[83]

> ... whilst certainty is highly desirable, it may bring in its train excessive rigidity and the law must be able to keep pace with changing circumstances. Accordingly, many laws are inevitably couched in terms which, to a greater or lesser extent, are vague and whose interpretation and application are questions of practice.

3.77 Thus, for example, the incremental development of the common law over time does not breach the certainty rule provided that such development is reasonably foreseeable. In *SW and CR v United Kingdom*,[84] the Court held that the English Court decisions that removed the immunity of a husband from prosecution for rape did no more than continue a perceptible line of case law and that this evolution was consistent with the very essence of the offence and had reached a stage where it had become foreseeable.[85]

3.78   Inherent to the protection from arbitrary action which lies at the heart of the principle of effectiveness is the need for adequate legal safeguards against unlawful state action. In some contexts, the Court has imposed specific procedural requirements. For example, in *Hentrich v France*,[86] the state sought to exercise the right of 'pre-emption' to purchase land where it considered that the vendor proposed to sell for an undervalue. The Court held that such proceedings could not be legitimate in the absence of adversarial proceedings which complied with the equality of arms. In *Amuur v France*,[87] the Court considered whether the detention of asylum seekers under a legal regime contained in a 'brief circular' complied with Article 5(1)(f). It criticised not only the absence of any means to challenge the detention in the courts, but also the lack of any time limit on such detention, the absence of legal, humanitarian or social assistance, and the absence of procedures and time limits for access to such assistance. Where 'persons of unsound mind' are detained, Article 5(1)(e) embodies a right to a review of the medical basis of detention

3.79   In the case of detention of a person of unsound mind, protection from arbitrariness was held by the Court in *Winterwerp v Netherlands*[88] to require that, save in emergency cases, 'objective medical evidence should have reliably

---

83   (1979–80) 2 EHRR 245, para 49.
84   (1996) 21 EHRR 363, paras 43/41, 44/42.
85   See, also, eg, *Kokkinakis v Greece* (1994) 17 EHRR 397, para 52.
86   (1994) 18 EHRR 440.
87   (1996) 22 EHRR 533, para 53.
88   (1979) 2 EHRR 387.

shown' the person detained to have been of unsound mind.[89] Thus, the right to a speedy review of detention in such a case embodies a right to a review wide enough 'to bear on those conditions, which, according to the Convention, are essential' for lawful detention.[90] Thus, the adequacy of habeas corpus and judicial review proceedings has been successfully challenged by this means.[91] It has also been argued – without success – that *Wednesbury* judicial review provides an inadequate legal safeguard to challenge the seizure of property by Customs and Excise.[92]

3.80   It may, in any event, be thought that domestic judicial review has now come close to recognising a form of the principle of legality where fundamental human rights are in issue. For example, in *R v Lord Chancellor ex p Witham*,[93] the Divisional Court held that a wide enabling power in the statute ('may by order under this section prescribe the fees to be taken') could not authorise interference with the constitutional right of access to the Court save by express statutory authority.[94]

3.81   In *R v Secretary of State for the Home Department ex p Pierson*,[95] Lord Browne-Wilkinson held that:

> A power conferred by Parliament in general terms is not to be taken to authorise the doing of acts by the donee of the power which adversely affect the legal rights of the citizen or the basic principles on which the law of the United Kingdom is based unless the statute conferring the power makes it clear that such was the intention of Parliament.

3.82   In *R v Secretary of State for the Home Department ex p Simms*,[96] a case holding that the Home Secretary's and prison governors' ban on journalists from visiting prisoners to enable them to protect their innocence was unlawful, Lord Steyn gave full voice to the principle of legality. He held as follows:

> Literally construed, there is force in the extensive construction put forward. But one cannot lose sight that there is at stake a fundamental or basic right, namely, the right of a prisoner to seek through oral interviews to persuade a journalist

---

89 See paras 4.71 *et seq.*

90 *X v United Kingdom* (1982) 4 EHRR 188.

91 See paras 4.97 *et seq.*

92 See para 3.41.

93 [1998] QB 575.

94 Cf *R v Lord Chancellor ex p Lightfoot* [2000] 2 WLR 318, where Simon Brown LJ considered that a constitutional right might be abrogated by so construing a statute by necessary implication. Such an approach to construction is likely to fall away under the HRA 1998, s 3, and is, so far as access to the Court is concerned, inconsistent with earlier authority: see *Raymond v Honey* [1983] 1 AC 1.

95 [1998] AC 539, p 575D. See, also, *R v Secretary of State for the Home Department ex p Stafford* [1999] 2 AC 38, p 48C–D.

96 [1999] 3 WLR 328, p 340F–H.

to investigate the safety of the prisoner's conviction and to publicise his findings in an effort to gain access to justice for the prisoner. In these circumstances, even in the absence of an ambiguity, there comes into play a presumption of general application operating as a constitutional principle.

Legitimate aim

3.83　Even where a restriction on a Convention right satisfies the principle of legality, the Court may have to conduct a separate examination of the purpose of the restriction.

3.84　　As has been seen, Articles 8–11 of the Convention specify interests for the promotion or protection of which interference may be necessary in a democratic society. In order for such interference to be justified, the aim for which the interference is being imposed must be a specified ground of restriction. The interests so specified include public safety, national security, the protection of health and morals, and the economic well being of the country or the protection of the rights and freedoms of others. Potentially, they are very wide. Further, where the Contracting State seeks to rely on the principle of proportionality in order to justify a restriction on other Convention rights,[97] it must also demonstrate that the restriction pursues a legitimate aim.

3.85　　One of the means by which the protection afforded by the Convention is rendered practical and effective is by the requirement that any restriction invoking these interests must, genuinely, have those interests as its aim.[98] A different purpose is illegitimate.[99]

3.86　　If, in truth, a legitimate ground for interference is being used to camouflage the real purpose, then the measure would be unlawful. Under s 1(1) of the Human Rights Act, the specified 'Convention rights' are to be read with Articles 16–18 of the Convention. Article 18 provides that:

> The restrictions permitted under this Convention to the said rights and freedoms shall not be applied for any purpose other than those for which they have been prescribed.

3.87　However, Strasbourg has been careful not to exclude ancillary consequences if that is not the true purpose of the interference. For example, in *Campbell v United Kingdom*,[100] the applicant did not accept that the purpose of interference with his correspondence whilst a prisoner was, as asserted, the prevention of disorder or crime. He suggested that the true purpose was to assess the contents of letters before he did. Whilst upholding his claim that there had

---

97　Eg, *Ashingdane v United Kingdom* (1985) 7 EHRR 528, para 57 (Art 6(1)).

98　Another means of protection is to ensure that the restrictions are restrictively construed (see above).

99　*Golder v United Kingdom* (1979–80) 1 EHRR 524, para 44.

100　(1993) 15 EHRR 137, paras 39–41 and 60.

been a breach of Article 8 of the Convention, the Court saw no reason to doubt that there had been a legitimate aim for the interference.

3.88   Importantly, the concept of 'legitimate aim' is not solely directed towards interferences with rights on specified Convention grounds but applies to implied restrictions, such as those contained in Article 6(1).

Democratic values

3.89   Articles 8–11 expressly require that interference with the protected rights must be 'necessary in a democratic society' if it is to be legitimate. In *Silver v United Kingdom*,[101] the Court explained the meaning of this requirement:

(a) the adjective 'necessary' is not synonymous with 'indispensable', neither has it the flexibility of such expressions as 'admissible', 'ordinary', 'useful', 'reasonable' or 'desirable'.

(b) the contracting states enjoy a certain but not unlimited margin of appreciation in the matter of the imposition of restrictions, but it is for the Court to give the final ruling on whether they are compatible with the Convention.

(c) the phrase 'necessary in a democratic society' means that, to be compatible with the Convention, the interference must, inter alia, correspond to a 'pressing social need' and be 'proportionate to the legitimate aim pursued'.

3.90   Thus, as can be seen the concept of 'necessity' as applied by the Strasbourg Court is a great deal more flexible than the ordinary meaning of the term would suggest. There are, however, limits to this flexibility. As the Court observed in *Chassagnou and Others v France*:[102]

... in assessing the necessity of a given measure, a number of principles must be observed. The term 'necessary' does not have the flexibility of such expressions as 'useful' or 'desirable'. In addition, pluralism, tolerance and broadmindedness are hallmarks of a 'democratic society'. Although individual interests must on occasion be subordinated to those of a group, democracy does not simply mean that the views of a majority must always prevail: a balance must be achieved which ensures the fair and proper treatment of minorities and avoids any abuse of a dominant position. Lastly, any restriction imposed on a Convention right must be proportionate to the legitimate aim pursued.

3.91   As these formulations demonstrate, the concepts of legitimate aim, proportionality and democratic values are connected and are, in many ways, difficult to separate one from the other in practice.

---

101 (1983) 5 EHRR 347, para 97.

102 (2000) 29 EHRR 615, para 112. See, to similar effect, *Young, James and Webster v United Kingdom* (1982) 4 EHRR 38, para 63.

3.92   Even where the phrase 'necessary in a democratic society' is not expressly used, the concept of democratic values infuses the Convention and has often been referred to in the case law.

3.93   In *Soering v United Kingdom*,[103] for example, the Strasbourg Court said this:

> ... any interpretation of the rights and freedoms guaranteed has to be consistent with 'the general spirit of the Convention, an instrument designed to maintain and promote the ideals and values of a democratic society'.

3.94   So, too, in *Lingens v Austria*,[104] the Court observed that:

> Freedom of the press ... affords the public one of the best means of discovering and forming an opinion of the ideas and attitudes of political leaders. More generally, freedom of political debate is at the very core of the concept of a democratic society which prevails throughout the Convention.

3.95   That the notion of democratic values goes far wider than those specific Articles in which the phrase 'necessary in a democratic society' is used is exemplified by *Delcourt v Belgium*[105] where the Court used the idea of democracy to validate a liberal construction of Article 6. It held thus:

> In a democratic society within the meaning of the Convention, the right to a fair administration of justice holds such a prominent place that a restrictive interpretation of Article 6(1) would not correspond to the aim and purpose of that provision.

3.96   Whilst 'democratic values' have never been precisely defined, the notion clearly extends beyond the definition of a political system properly classifiable as a 'democracy'. It encompasses the true substance of the Convention rights which themselves connote a degree of pluralism and tolerance and respect for minorities as opposed to simple rule by the majority.

3.97   Thus, for example, in *Kokkinakis v Greece*,[106] the Court held that:

> As enshrined in Article 9, freedom of thought, conscience and religion is one of the foundations of a 'democratic society' within the meaning of the Convention ... The pluralism indissociable from a democratic society, which has been dearly won over the centuries, depends on it.

3.98   The importance accorded to the idea of grounded democratic values, within the meaning of the Convention, as the substantive basis of Convention rights is the link to the concept of that which must be necessary in the interests of democracy where interference with such rights is sought to be justified.

---

103 (1989) 11 EHRR 439, para 87.
104 (1986) 8 EHRR 407, para 42.
105 (1979–80) 1 EHRR 355, para 26.
106 (1994) 17 EHRR 397, para 31.

Proportionality

3.99 As indicated above, there is no precise demarcation in practice between the requirement that a measure must be no more than is necessary in a democratic society and that which requires it to be pursued in a manner that is proportionate to the legitimate aim pursued. The latter, the principle of proportionality, was not recognised in domestic judicial review prior to the coming into force of the Human Rights Act;[107] it is, however, applied by the domestic courts in considering Community law.[108]

3.100 Although the principle of proportionality is nowhere to be found in the text of the Convention, it is, nonetheless, fundamental to its case law. As the Court stated in *Soering v United Kingdom*:[109]

> ... inherent in the whole of the Convention is a search for a fair balance between the demands of the general interest of the community and the requirements of the protection of the individual's fundamental rights.

3.101 That 'fair balance' (which itself necessarily engages democratic values) can only result in a fundamental right being trumped by the general interest of the community if there is, in the language of the case law, a 'pressing social need' for the restriction in question.

3.102 Thus, for example, in *Dudgeon v United Kingdom*,[110] the Court held that the law, then in force in Northern Ireland, which made all homosexual conduct between males criminal regardless of age or consent breached the principle of proportionality. It ruled that:

> It cannot be maintained ... that there is a 'pressing social need' to make such acts criminal offences, there being no sufficient justification provided by the risk of harm to vulnerable sections of society requiring protection or by the effects on the public. On the issue of proportionality, the Court considers that such justifications as there are for retaining the law in force unamended are outweighed by the detrimental effects which the very existence of the legislative provisions in question can have on the life of a person of homosexual orientation like the applicant. Although members of the public who regard homosexuality as immoral may be shocked, offended or disturbed by the commission by others of private homosexual acts, this cannot on its own warrant the application of penal sanctions when it is consenting adults alone who are involved.[111]

---

107 *R v Secretary of State for the Home Department ex p Brind* [1991] 1 AC 696. See, especially, p 751E–F, *per* Lord Templeman; p 759D, *per* Lord Ackner; pp 762D–E, 766C–67G, *per* Lord Lowry. There have been many ingenious attempts to find the doctrine already embedded in judicial review but *Brind* remains the pre-HRA law.

108 *Thomas v Chief Adjudication Officer* [1991] 2 QB 164.

109 (1989) 11 EHRR 439, para 89.

110 (1982) 4 EHRR 149, para 60.

111 For other instances of there being no 'pressing social need' and hence a breach of proportionality, see, eg, *Observer and Guardian v United Kingdom* (1992) 14 EHRR 153, para 68 (injunctions were unjustified once the book had been published outside the United Kingdom); *Weber v Switzerland* (1990) 12 EHRR 508 (unjustified fine where 'confidential' information disclosed was already in the public domain).

3.103 Undoubtedly, a measure will be disproportionate where it affects 'the very essence' of the right being interfered with.[112] The Court has also emphasised that the state bears the burden of establishing that the measure in question is proportionate by reasons that are 'relevant and sufficient'.[113] The availability of a less restrictive alternative to achieve the objective is a further important factor and, in that context, the practice of other Contracting States may be relevant.[114] Finally, the manner in which the measure is implemented may breach proportionality. Thus, Strasbourg has classified measures as disproportionate in circumstances where there is either procedural unfairness,[115] or a lack of safeguards against abuse.[116]

3.104 Overall, proportionality is a fluid doctrine and the Strasbourg Court has often used it as the general basis for different levels of review of state interference in a way that makes it difficult to analyse the doctrine satisfactorily.

3.105 For example, the nature of the right infringed has affected the Court's level of review. Proportionality will be very strictly applied where the right to life is engaged.[117] So, too, the Court has, from time to time, stressed the importance of (for example) the right to private sexual relations,[118] or the role of the press in receiving and communicating information for the purpose of the rights enshrined in Article 10.[119] In contrast, the right to property under Article 1 of Protocol 1 has a far weaker proportionality threshold.[120]

3.106 Other factors which have also often affected the stringency of proportionality review include the extent of the interference: a more serious interference will require greater justification;[121] and the nature of the state interest sought to be protected: 'national security' is, for example, treated relatively deferentially.[122]

3.107 The Strasbourg Court sometimes seemingly uses the concepts of proportionality and margin of appreciation interchangeably. In fact, however,

---

112 *F v Switzerland* (1988) 10 EHRR 411, para 40.

113 See, eg, *Vogt v Germany* (1996) 21 EHRR 205, paras 32–37 (held: reasons relevant but not sufficient).

114 *Informationsverein v Austria* (1994) 17 EHRR 93 (held: grant of conditional licences was a less restrictive alternative to public monopoly); *Inze v Austria* (1988) 10 EHRR 394 (held: aim of legislation on inheritance could have been achieved by a less restrictive alternative than criteria of birth in and out of wedlock).

115 *McMichael v United Kingdom* (1995) 20 EHRR 205, para 87.

116 *Camenzind v Switzerland* (1999) 28 EHRR 458, para 45.

117 *McCann v United Kingdom* (1996) 21 EHRR 97, paras 149–50.

118 *Smith and Grady v United Kingdom* (2000) 29 EHRR 493, para 89.

119 *Goodwin v United Kingdom* (1996) 22 EHRR 123, para 39.

120 *Lithgow v United Kingdom* (1986) 8 EHRR 329, para 122.

121 *Smith and Grady v United Kingdom* (2000) 29 EHRR 493, para 90; *Muller v Switzerland* (1991) 13 EHRR 212, para 43.

122 Provided, always, that there are adequate procedural safeguards; see, eg, *Leander v Sweden* (1987) 9 EHRR 433, paras 58–67.

margin of appreciation (considered below)[123] is an international doctrine and is unlikely to be used (at least in the form it is applied by the Strasbourg Court) in domestic proceedings.[124] The domestic courts may, therefore, have to develop a distinctive approach to the doctrine of proportionality which disentangles it from the margin of appreciation.

3.108   The issue is whether or not proportionality requires a degree of deference by the domestic court to the decision maker, despite the absence of margin of appreciation from the domestic jurisprudence, as part of its review function or whether the Court (itself a 'public authority' under s 6 of the Human Rights Act) will have to engage in a form of primary decision making at least to the extent that reflects that the decision maker conforms to the proportionality principle.

3.109   There are, at present, differing views as to how, post the Human Rights Act, proportionality will work. In analysing its Community law counterpart in *R v MAFF ex p First City Trading*,[125] Laws J regarded the court's exercise in respect of Community law proportionality as one of secondary review. He said this:

> It is not the court's task to decide what it would have done had it been the decision maker, who (certainly in the case of elected government) enjoys a political authority, and carries a political responsibility, with which the court is not endowed. In the nature of things, it is highly unlikely that only one of the choices available to him will pass the test of objective justification: and the Court has no business to give effect to any preference for one possible measure over another when both lie within the proper legal limits. In this sense, it may be said that the decision maker indeed enjoys a margin of appreciation. The difference between *Wednesbury* and European review is that, in the former case, the legal limits lie further back. I think that there are two factors. First, the limits of domestic review are not, as the law presently stands, constrained by the doctrine of proportionality. Secondly, at least as regards a requirement such as that of objective justification in an equal treatment case, the European rule requires the decision maker to provide a fully reasoned case. It is not enough merely to set out the problem, and assert that within his discretion the Minister chose this or that solution, constrained only by the requirement that his decision must have been one which a reasonable Minister might make. Rather, the Court will test the solution arrived at, and pass it only if substantial factual considerations are put forward in its justification: considerations which are relevant, reasonable and proportionate to the aim in view. But as I understand the jurisprudence, the Court is not concerned to agree or disagree with the decision: that would be to travel beyond the boundaries of proper judicial authority, and usurp the primary decision maker's function. Thus, *Wednesbury* and European review are different models – one looser, one tighter – of the

---

123 See paras 3.128 *et seq.*

124 See *R v Director of Public Prosecutions ex p Kebilene* [2000] HRLR 93, pp 115–16; see, further, para 3.131.

125 [1997] 1 CMLR 250, p 278.

same juridical concept, which is the imposition of compulsory standards on decision makers so as to secure the repudiation of arbitrary power.

3.110 On the other hand, Simon Brown LJ in the Divisional Court in *R v Ministry of Defence ex p Smith* had observed thus:

> ... if the Convention for the Protection of Human Rights and Fundamental Freedoms were part of our law and we were accordingly entitled to ask whether the policy answers a pressing social need and whether the restriction on human rights involved can be shown proportionate to its benefits, then clearly the primary judgment (subject only to a limited 'margin of appreciation') would be for us and not others: the constitutional balance would shift. But that is not the position. In exercising merely a secondary judgment, this court is bound, even though adjudicating in a human rights context, to act with some reticence. Our approach must reflect, not overlook, where responsibility ultimately lies for the defence of the realm, and recognise too that Parliament is exercising a continuing supervision over this area of prerogative power.[126]

3.111 These differing formulations of the approach to proportionality both refer to the margin of appreciation. But if that doctrine is inappropriate to domestic review, the role of the court will have to be developed without reference to it. Whilst it is obvious that the court could never engage in primary decision making and that some form of deference will be likely to continue to be paid to the decision maker's expertise,[127] one may reasonably expect the parameters of review to be extended to the point where the Administrative Court will be far more interventionist and pro-active where the principle of proportionality brought in under the Human Rights Act is applicable than has previously been the case in domestic judicial review.

Positive obligations

3.112 As has been seen, the majority of Convention obligations are negative in nature. They prevent unjustified interferences save on strictly established grounds.

3.113 There is, however, an increasing tendency on the part of the Strasbourg Court to interpret certain rights as conferring positive obligations on the Contracting State to take steps to prevent Convention breaches by third parties. On the international level, this enables state liability to engage in circumstances where individual liability could not. The doctrine of 'positive obligations' has extended the reach of the Strasbourg case law into disputes between private individuals. A wide range of private activity which would be wholly unregulated by ordinary judicial review is, accordingly, vulnerable to intervention on human rights grounds.

---

126 [1996] QB 517, p 541.
127 *R v Director of Public Prosecutions ex p Kebilene* [2000] HRLR 93, pp 115–16. See para 3.131.

3.114   There is an important relationship between the proportionality principle (discussed above) and the doctrine of positive obligations. Both principles derive from the need to create a 'fair balance' between the individual on the one hand and the community on the other. As the Court observed in *Rees v United Kingdom*:[128]

> In determining whether or not a positive obligation exists, regard must be had to the fair balance that has to be struck between the general interest of the community and the interests of the individuals.

3.115 The scope of the positive obligations imposed will differ according to the case. There are two broad categories; first, those that are designed to prevent a Convention breach and, secondly, those that are designed to afford a timeous response to a breach.

3.116   Most of the case law concerns the first category which can itself be subdivided into obligations to: (i) provide an adequate legal framework or other measures; (ii) take particular steps.

3.117   In *Osman v United Kingdom*,[129] whilst rejecting the argument that the state had failed to take adequate measures to protect the lives of the second applicant and his father, the Court laid down a general statement of principle as to the scope of the positive obligations doctrine in the context of Article 2. It said this:

> In the opinion of the Court, where there is an allegation that the authorities have violated their positive obligation to protect the right to life in the context of their above mentioned duty to prevent and suppress offences against the person, it must be established to its satisfaction that the authorities knew or ought to have known at the time of the existence of a real and immediate risk to the life of an identified individual or individuals from the criminal acts of a third party and that they failed to take measures within the scope of their powers which, judged reasonably, might have been expected to avoid that risk. The Court does not accept the government's view that the failure to perceive the risk to life in the circumstances known at the time or to take preventive measures to avoid that risk must be tantamount to gross negligence or wilful disregard of the duty to protect life ...

3.118 In *Lopez Ostra v Spain*,[130] the applicant complained that a waste treatment plant had been built 12 metres away from her home. The town already had a heavy concentration of leather industries. The plant began to operate without a licence, releasing fumes and smells which caused nuisance and health problems to local residents. Although the Spanish authorities were not directly responsible for the emissions in question, the town had allowed the plant to be

---

128 (1987) 9 EHRR 56, para 37. See, to similar effect, *Powell and Rayner v United Kingdom* (1990) 12 EHRR 355, para 41.

129 (2000) 29 EHRR 245, especially para 116.

130 (1995) 20 EHRR 277, especially para 51.

built on its land and the state had subsidised the plant's construction. The Court accordingly found the state to be in violation of Article 8.

3.119 The Strasbourg Court analysed the state's liability both in terms of the doctrine of positive obligations and interference under Article 8(2). It stated as follows:

> Severe environmental pollution may affect individuals' well being and prevent them from enjoying their homes in such a way as to affect their private and family life adversely without ... seriously endangering their health.

> Whether the question is analysed in terms of a positive duty on the state – to take reasonable and appropriate measures to secure the applicant's rights under paragraph 1 of Article 8 – as the applicant wishes in her case, or in terms of an 'interference by a public authority' to be justified in accordance with paragraph 2, the applicable principles are broadly similar. In both contexts, regard must be had to the fair balance that has to be struck between the competing interests of the individual and of the community as a whole ...

3.120 There are also cases in which the Court has held a state's existing legislative regime to be inadequate. In *Marckx v Belgium*,[131] for example, it was held that Belgian law contravened Article 8 in that there was a lack of any objective and reasonable justification for the differences of treatment between the legitimate and illegitimate family. In *Airey v Ireland*,[132] the Court held that effective respect for family life obliged Ireland to make legal aid available so that she could be legally represented to petition for a decree of judicial separation.[133] In both cases, therefore, the state was held to be under a positive, albeit unspecified, obligation to ensure that their legislative regimes addressed the rights in question.

3.121 Particular positive steps that have been required by Strasbourg to prevent breaches of the Convention include the provision of information. In *Guerra and Others v Italy*,[134] the applicants lived approximately 1 km from a chemical factory. In 1976, a serious arsenic poisoning accident had occurred. In 1988, the factory was classified as high risk. A 1988 technical report criticised standards at the factory. The applicants complained that the lack of practical measures to lower the risks posed by the factory violated their rights to Article 8 and Article 2 (the right to life). They also complained that the authority's failure to inform the public about the hazards and the procedures to be followed in the event of a major accident infringed their right to 'freedom of information' under Article 10 (the right to freedom of expression).

3.122 The Court rejected the complaint under Article 10. It found that Article 10 could not be construed as imposing on a state positive obligations to collect and disseminate information. The claim under Article 8, however, was made

---

131 (1979–80) 2 EHRR 330, paras 55, 59 and 62.

132 (1979–80) 2 EHRR 305, para 33.

133 The Court emphasised that the right to legal aid was not a general right but depended upon the facts of each case (see *ibid*, para 26).

134 (1998) 26 EHRR 357.

out. The failure to provide essential information itself breached the obligation to secure the applicants' Article 8 rights. For a case engaging similar reasoning and underlining the principle that Article 8 may raise an issue as to the state being required to take positive steps to provide requisite environmental information, see *McGinley and Egan v United Kingdom*.[135]

3.123 There is sometimes a positive obligation on states to respond to breaches of the Convention. This is certainly so for breaches of particularly significant rights such as those in Articles 2 (right to life) and 3 (prohibition against torture or inhuman or degrading treatment or punishment). For example, in *Aydin v Turkey*,[136] the Court observed that the provision of an effective remedy under Article 13 required a comprehensive response to violations of Article 3. It said this:

> ... where an individual has an arguable claim that he or she has been tortured by agents of the state, the notion of an 'effective remedy' entails, in addition to the payment of compensation where appropriate, a thorough and effective investigation capable of leading to the identification and punishment of those responsible and including effective access for the complainant to the investigatory procedure.

3.124 The doctrine of positive obligations translates somewhat uneasily to domestic litigation. First, Articles 1 (obligation to respect human rights) and 13 (provision of an effective remedy) underpin some of the case law on positive obligations: as has been seen, there are difficult issues as to how these may be invoked in the domestic court since they are not a 'Convention right' as defined in s 1 of the Human Rights Act.[137] Secondly, it is difficult to see how the Human Rights Act will be of assistance to an applicant who alleges a breach of a positive obligation where the allegation is that there is inadequate legislative protection. To the extent that there is an inadequate legislative regime in place, there is no effective remedy that the domestic court can provide by way of the imposition of a positive obligation. Section 6(6) of the Human Rights Act stipulates that failure to introduce before Parliament a proposal for legislation or make any primary legislation is not actionable under the Human Rights Act. However, in cases where the positive obligation could be met by the exercise of an administrative discretion, the doctrine may prove a powerful one.

3.125 The more difficult issue is whether, at least in the context of positive obligations, the court would be able, and indeed bound as a public authority under s 6 of the Human Rights Act, to require individual third parties to act positively under the Convention to protect Convention rights. This would

---

135 (1999) 27 EHRR 1.
136 (1998) 25 EHRR 251, para 103.
137 See paras 1.08–1.10. Most Strasbourg cases in which positive obligations are invoked do not explicitly rely on either Art 1 or 13.

achieve a form of 'horizontal effect' in that individuals as well as public authorities would be brought within the ambit of the Convention.

3.126 This issue does not directly affect judicial review since the defendant will always be a public body.

3.127 There are competing views on this issue but the overall consensus is that the Human Rights Act will result in some 'horizontal effect' on this footing.[138] Horizontal effect is further discussed below.[139]

CONCEPTS INFORMING THE APPROACH OF THE COURT

Margin of appreciation

3.128 The margin of appreciation is the phrase used in the Strasbourg case law to signify the deference given by Strasbourg, as an international court, to the Contracting State in deciding Convention issues.

3.129 The scope of the margin of appreciation principle was outlined by the Strasbourg Court in *Handyside v United Kingdom*.[140] The Court said this:

> By reason of their direct and continuous contact with the vital forces of their countries, state authorities are in principle in a better position than the international judge to give an opinion on the exact content of these requirements as well as on the 'necessity' of a 'restriction' or 'penalty' intended to meet them ... Nevertheless [Article 10(2)] does not give the Contracting States an unlimited power of appreciation. The Court, which, with the Commission, is responsible for ensuring the observance of those States' engagements, is empowered to give the final ruling ... The domestic margin of appreciation thus goes hand in hand with a European supervision ...

3.130 The doctrine cannot therefore be applied directly in domestic judicial review.[141] This does not mean, however, that there is no scope for deferential review by the Administrative Court of decision making that involves the Convention.

3.131 The role of margin of appreciation in domestic litigation has already been given detailed consideration by the House of Lords in *R v Director of Public Prosecutions ex p Kebilene*.[142] Lord Hope of Craighead there observed as follows:

---

138 Consider Murray Hunt [1998] PL 423 and HWR Wade (1998) EHRLR 522 (both advocates of horizontal effect) with Ian Leigh [1999] ICLQ 57 (who takes a more limited view).

139 See paras 3.138 *et seq*.

140 (1979–80) 1 EHRR 737, paras 48–49.

141 *R v Stafford Justices ex p Imbert* [1999] 2 Cr App R 276, *per* Buxton LJ.

142 [2000] HRLR 93, pp 115–16.

... The doctrine of the 'margin of appreciation' is a familiar part of the jurisprudence of the European Court of Human Rights. The European Court has acknowledged that, by reason of their direct and continuous contact with the vital forces of their countries, the national authorities are in principle better placed to evaluate local needs and conditions than an international court ... The extent of this supervision will vary according to such factors as the nature of the Convention right in issue, the importance of that right for the individual and the nature of the activities involved in the case.

This doctrine is an integral part of the supervisory jurisdiction which is exercised over state conduct by the international court. By conceding a margin of appreciation to each national system, the court has recognised that the Convention, as a living system, does not need to be applied uniformly by all states but may vary in its application according to local needs and conditions. This technique is not available to the national courts when they are considering Convention issues arising within their own countries. But in the hands of the national courts also the Convention should be seen as an expression of fundamental principles rather than as a set of mere rules. The questions which the courts will have to decide in the application of these principles will involve questions of balance between competing interests and issues of proportionality.

In this area, difficult choices may have to be made by the executive or the legislature between the rights of the individual and the needs of society. In some circumstances, it will be appropriate for the courts to recognise that there is an area of judgment within which the judiciary will defer, on democratic grounds, to the considered opinion of the elected body or person whose act or decision is said to be incompatible with the Convention ... It will be easier for such an area of judgment to be recognised where the Convention itself requires a balance to be struck, much less so where the right is stated in terms which are unqualified. It will be easier for it to be recognised where the issues involve questions of social or economic policy, much less so where the rights are of high constitutional importance or are of a kind where the courts are especially well placed to assess the need for protection. But, even where the right is stated in terms which are unqualified, the courts will need to bear in mind the jurisprudence of the European Court which recognises that due account should be taken of the special nature of terrorist crime and the threat which it poses to a democratic society: *Murray v United Kingdom* (1994) 19 EHRR 193 at 222, para 47.

3.132 Thus, it is clear that the doctrine of margin of appreciation should not, strictly, be applied by the domestic court. Nevertheless, the scope of the 'area of judgment within which the judiciary will defer', as identified by Lord Hope, may prove to be indistinguishable in practice from the margin afforded by the Strasbourg Court.

Subsidiarity

3.133 The subsidiarity principle is to the effect that it is the Member States who have the primary role in safeguarding human rights within their jurisdiction. As the Strasbourg Court observed in *Handyside v United Kingdom*:[143]

> ... the machinery of protection established by the Convention is subsidiary to the national systems of safeguarding human rights.

3.134 This principle is reflected in Articles 1 (duty on Member States to secure fundamental rights and freedoms), 13 (duty on Member States to provide an effective remedy for Convention violations) and 26 (requirement of prior exhaustion of domestic remedies) of the Convention.

3.135   Although these Articles are not, themselves, incorporated into domestic law by the Human Rights Act, ss 2, 3 and 6 of the Human Rights Act (the interpretative obligation sections)[144] also reflect the subsidiarity principle in that they impose a direct obligation on public authorities (including the Court) to safeguard Convention rights, whilst placing the Strasbourg Court in a subsidiary position to that of the domestic court by ranking the Strasbourg case law as secondary to domestic interpretation of the Convention and as material which must be taken into account rather than generally inflexibly adhered to.

Fourth instance principle

3.136 The Strasbourg Court does not operate as a court of appeal. It has repeatedly stated that it is not its task to take the place of the competent national courts in the interpretation of domestic law.[145] This is known as the fourth instance principle. It is related to the principle of subsidiarity: it follows from the fact that it is the Member States who bear primary responsibility for safeguarding human rights that the Strasbourg organs perform a 'review' function rather than a merits examination of domestic court decisions.

3.137   Nevertheless, it must be recalled that, where the Convention requires that action by the state be 'lawful', the Strasbourg Court undertakes a measure of supervision in respect of compliance with domestic law.[146]

---

143 (1979–80) 1 EHRR 737, para 48.
144 See paras 1.15 *et seq*.
145 Eg, *X and Y v Netherlands* (1986) 8 EHRR 235, para 29.
146 See paras 3.70 *et seq*.

Victim

3.138 Only a person who is, or would be, a 'victim' of an action by a public authority which is incompatible with the Convention can bring proceedings or rely on the Convention right or rights concerned (s 7(1) of the Human Rights Act).

3.139 The Human Rights Act states that a person is a 'victim' only if he would be a victim for the purpose of Article 34 of the Convention (s 7(7)). Where an applicant alleges an unlawful act under the Human Rights Act by way of judicial review proceedings, he will be taken to have a sufficient interest in relation to the unlawful act complained of only if he is a victim (s 7(3)).

3.140 It follows that it is the Convention concept of 'victim' that must inform the approach of the domestic court as to an applicant's true standing on human rights issues. This issue and its effect on judicial review is examined in Chapter 2.

3.141 An important question is whether, despite absence of 'victim' status, a domestic court may, having regard to its obligations under s 6(1), 6(3) of the Human Rights Act as a 'public authority', have to examine Convention issues raised in proceedings before it even as between private parties. This has been referred to as the possible 'horizontal effect' of the Human Rights Act.[147] To allow non-victims to raise such issues might, however, erode the 'victim' requirement of standing in s 7 of the Human Rights Act itself.

3.142 There are, however, at least three circumstances in which Convention issues may be relevant even if the claimant is not a 'victim' under s 7 of the Human Rights Act and Article 34 of the Convention.

3.143 First, it is difficult to see how the domestic court could fail but implement, as a 'public authority', its own Convention obligations towards any party before it. Thus, for example, where determining 'civil rights and obligations' on judicial review,[148] the procedures adopted would have to be consistent with Article 6 of the Convention.[149]

3.144 Secondly, given its interpretative obligations under s 3 of the Human Rights Act to construe statutes and subordinate legislation in a manner that is, so far as is possible, compatible with Convention rights (not merely the Convention rights legitimately before the Court raised by a 'victim'), it is difficult to see how the court could do other than hear argument on the Convention issues raised by the Act or statutory instrument in question by whomsoever raised if relevant to the outcome of the challenge.

---

147 For horizontal effect, see, further, para 3.125. Sedley LJ has, extra-judicially, described the term 'horizontal effect' as an 'inappropriate geometric metaphor' preferring the phrase 'cascade effect'.

148 See Chapter 5, especially paras 5.08 *et seq*.

149 See, eg, *Dombo Beheer BV v Netherlands* (1993) 18 EHRR 213.

3.145   Thirdly, Convention issues have, in the past, come to be litigated in judicial review proceedings either (for example) because there was an overlap between the common law and the Convention or, more recently, because the Court had come to accept that the Convention is relevant to of the exercise of an administrative discretion as well as being an influence on the development of the common law.[150] The numerous ways in which the Convention had been given partial effect prior to the entry into force of the Human Rights Act was well summarised by Lord Bingham in his maiden speech in the House of Lords.[151] These grounds will, on any view, continue to be available to non-victims in judicial review proceedings whatever their status under the Human Rights Act.[152]

Burden of proof

3.146 In judicial review, the applicant ordinarily bears the burden of establishing that the respondent has acted unlawfully, irrationally or unfairly. This principle is subject to important qualification in the context of Convention rights. As has been seen, the Convention permits a degree of interference with most of the interests which it protects. Such interference is either expressly permitted, as in the case of Articles 8–11, or, as in the case of Article 6(1), for example, has been held to be implicit by the Strasbourg Court.[153] Such interferences must, *inter alia*, be proportionate to a legitimate aim.[154] Where such competing interests are relied on by the state, it bears the burden of proof in this respect.[155]

---

150 Of the many cases, see, eg, *R v Secretary of State for the Home Department ex p McQuillan* [1995] 4 All ER 400 (administrative discretion); *Derbyshire CC v Times Newspapers* [1992] QB 770, pp 812, 830 (affirmed on other grounds at [1993] AC 534).

151 *Hansard*, HL, 3 July 1996, Vol 574, col 1466.

152 As to the question whether the doctrine of positive obligations could give rise to horizontal effect, see paras 3.125 *et seq.*

153 *Ashingdane v United Kingdom* (1985) 7 EHRR 528, para 57.

154 See paras 3.83 *et seq.*

155 See, eg, *Pine Valley Developments Ltd v Ireland* (1992) 14 EHRR 319, para 64. See, also, the burden on the state under Art 3 (para 4.33) and Art 14 (para 4.218).

CHAPTER 4

CONVENTION RIGHTS

4.01 This chapter provides a brief overview[1] of the core Strasbourg case law on the substantive rights provided by the Convention and those Protocols to it which have been ratified by the United Kingdom. Articles 1 and 13 are also considered.

4.02 The principles by which Convention rights are to be interpreted and applied are set out in Chapter 3. Article 6 and, in particular, its relationship with judicial review and the doctrine of natural justice, is dealt with in Chapter 5. The Convention's relationship with European Community law is dealt with in Chapter 7.

4.03 In what follows, illustrations of the Convention's application are drawn, where possible, from the central areas of domestic public law practice. The Strasbourg case law has principally engaged the following areas of domestic public law:

Children and family	Arts 6, 8;
Commercial	Art 6, Art 1 Protocol No 1;
Crime	Arts 3, 4, 5, 6, 7;
Education	Art 2 Protocol No 1, Art 9;
Environment	Arts 2, 8, Art 1 Protocol No 1;
Housing	Art 8, Art 1 Protocol No 1;
Immigration	Arts 3, 5, 8;
Health	Arts 3, 5, 8;
Mental health	Arts 2, 3, 5, 8;
Planning	Arts 6, 8, Art 1 Protocol No 1;
Prisoners' rights	Arts 3, 4, 5, 6, 8, 9, 12;
State benefits	Art 6;
Tax	Art 1 Protocol No 1.

---

1 The best detailed exegesis of the Convention case law is to be found Harris, DJ, O'Boyle, M and Warbrick, C, *Law of the European Convention on Human Rights*, 1995, London: Butterworths. For the Strasbourg cases themselves, see Gordon, R, Ward, T and Eicke, T, *The Strasbourg Case Law – Leading Cases from the European Human Rights Reports*, 2000, London: Sweet & Maxwell.

4.04 It must be emphasised, however, that one of the likely effects of the Human Rights Act 1998 is that public law litigation will spill into new areas, previously beyond the reach of judicial review (see paras 2.88 *et seq*).

ARTICLE 1: OBLIGATION TO RESPECT HUMAN RIGHTS

4.05 Article 1 provides:

> The High Contracting Parties shall secure to everyone within their jurisdiction the rights and freedoms defined in Section I of this Convention.

4.06 This right is not amongst those 'Convention rights' given further effect to by the Human Rights Act. It places an obligation upon Contracting States to 'secure' the rights set out in Section I of the Convention, namely, Articles 2–18, all of which, save for Article 13 are 'Convention rights' pursuant to the Human Rights Act (s 1(1)). A breach of Article 1 follows automatically from, but adds nothing to, a breach of any of the Articles contained in Section I of the Convention.[2]

4.07 In order to secure the enjoyment of those rights and freedoms, as Article 1 requires, the Contracting State must prevent or remedy any breach at 'subordinate levels'.[3] Further, as the Court held in *Young, James and Webster v United Kingdom*,[4] 'if a violation of one of those rights and freedoms is the result of non-observance of that obligation in the enactment of domestic legislation, the responsibility of the state for that violation is engaged'. This doctrine of 'positive obligations' may require the state to intervene in relations between private bodies to ensure that Convention rights are secured.[5] This issue is explored elsewhere.[6]

4.08 The exclusion of Article 1 from the provisions of the Convention incorporated by means of the Human Rights Act might – in theory at least – be said to give rise to potential interpretative difficulties when the domestic courts come to consider the Strasbourg case law concerning the scope of the Convention's application and the doctrine of positive obligations in particular. In practice, however, the Strasbourg organs rarely draw explicitly upon this provision:[7] non-incorporation of Article 1 should rarely present the domestic courts with practical problems.

---

2   *Ireland v United Kingdom* (1979–80) 2 EHRR 25, para 239.
3   *Ibid.*
4   (1982) 4 EHRR 38, para 49.
5   Eg, *Costello-Roberts v United Kingdom* (1995) 19 EHRR 112: state responsibility for corporal punishment administered at a private school. See, further, para 4.267.
6   See paras 3.112 *et seq*.
7   See, however, *Matthews v United Kingdom* (1999) 28 EHRR 361, para 33.

ARTICLE 2: RIGHT TO LIFE

4.09 Article 2 provides:

> (1) Everyone's right to life shall be protected by law. No one shall be deprived of his life intentionally save in the execution of a sentence of a court following his conviction of a crime for which this penalty is provided by law.
>
> (2) Deprivation of life shall not be regarded as inflicted in contravention of this article when it results from the use of force which is no more than absolutely necessary:
>
> > (a) in defence of any person from unlawful violence;
> >
> > (b) in order to effect a lawful arrest or to prevent the escape of a person lawfully detained;
> >
> > (c) in action lawfully taken for the purpose of quelling a riot or insurrection.

4.10 The right to life enshrined by Article 2 has been described by the Court as 'one of the most fundamental provisions in the Convention'.[8] The state is required not only to refrain from the intentional and unlawful taking of life, but also to take appropriate steps to preserve life.[9] It is not necessary to show that the state has sought intentionally to deprive a person of his life in order to establish a breach of Article 2.[10]

4.11 The obligations upon the state are not, however, absolute; the Court has stated that Article 2(1) must be interpreted in a way that does not impose an impossible or disproportionate burden on the authorities.[11] Not every claimed risk to life requires the authorities to take measures to prevent that risk from occurring; where such steps are required, they need not guarantee the safety of those they are intended to protect. In *Osman v United Kingdom*,[12] the applicants complained that the police had failed to take adequate and appropriate steps to protect them following warnings in respect of the conduct of a man who later shot one of the applicants, and killed his father. The Court rejected the Government's submission that it was necessary to show gross negligence or wilful disregard of duty to protect life. To make out such a complaint it must be shown to the Court's satisfaction that:

> ... the authorities knew or ought to have known at the time of the existence of a real and immediate risk to the life of an identified individual or individuals from the criminal acts of a third party and that they failed to take measures

---

8   *McCann v United Kingdom* (1996) 21 EHRR 97, para 146. ECHR, Art 15 provides that no derogation is permitted from Art 2, except in respect of deaths resulting from lawful acts of war.

9   *Osman v United Kingdom* (2000) 29 EHRR 245, para 115; *LCB v United Kingdom* (1999) 27 EHRR 212, para 36; *Association X v United Kingdom* (1978) 14 DR 31, p 32.

10 *LCB v United Kingdom* (1999) 27 EHRR 212, para 36.

11 *Osman v United Kingdom* (2000) 29 EHRR 245, para 116.

12 *Ibid.*

within the scope of their powers which, judged reasonably, might have been expected to avoid that risk.[13]

4.12 On the facts, the Court held the police could not be criticised for failing to act.

4.13 Article 2(2) permits the taking of life in certain situations, including the death penalty.[14] These exceptions to the general prohibition contained in Article 2(1) must be strictly construed.[15] In *McCann v United Kingdom*,[16] the Court stated that this provision applies both to intentional killing and to situations where the state is permitted to use force which may result in the unintended deprivation of life, such as, as on the facts of that case, the apprehension of suspected terrorists who were killed by the SAS.

4.14 The force used must be no more than 'absolutely necessary' for the achievement of one of the purposes set out in Article 2(2). The Court made clear that this is a more rigorous standard than applies elsewhere under the Convention:[17]

> ... a stricter and more compelling test of necessity must be employed from that normally applicable when determining whether state action is 'necessary in a democratic society' under paragraph 2 of Articles 8 to 11 of the Convention. The force used must be strictly proportionate to the achievement of the aims set out in sub-paragraphs 2(a), (b) and (c).[18]

4.15 In seeking to determine whether the use of force was genuinely necessary, the Court is prepared to consider the wider factual matrix, including the planning and control of the actions under examination.[19] These factors gave rise to a breach of Article 2 in the case of *McCann*. The conduct of the soldiers who actually carried out the shooting was exonerated. The Court accepted that the soldiers honestly believed, in the light of the information they had been given, that it was necessary to shoot the suspects in order to prevent them from detonating a bomb. It was sufficient that the use of force was based on an honest belief which was perceived to be valid at the time which subsequently turned out to be mistaken. To hold otherwise would impose an unrealistic burden on the state.[20]

---

13 *Osman v United Kingdom* (2000) 29 EHRR 245, para 116. The Court further emphasised that it was necessary to bear in mind the difficulties involved in policing modern societies and the need to ensure the police respected due process and other legitimate restraints on their scope of activity.

14 The Convention's Sixth Protocol, which has now been ratified by the United Kingdom, requires its abolition during peacetime. See, further, paras 4.482 *et seq*.

15 *McCann v United Kingdom* (1996) 21 EHRR 97, para 147.

16 *Ibid*, para 148.

17 See, eg, *Silver v United Kingdom* (1983) 5 EHRR 347, para 97.

18 (1996) 21 EHRR 97, para 149. See, also, *Guleç v Turkey* (1999) 28 EHRR 121.

19 *McCann v United Kingdom* (1996) 21 EHRR 97, para 150.

20 See, also, *Andronicou and Constantinou v Cyprus* (1998) 25 EHRR 491.

4.16   Where individuals have been killed by the use of force by the agents of the state, the obligation to protect the right to life, read in conjunction with the state's general duty under Article 1 of the Convention to 'secure to everyone within their jurisdiction the rights and freedoms defined in the Convention', requires some form of effective official investigation.[21] Without a review procedure, the general legal prohibition on arbitrary killing by the state would, in the Court's view, be ineffective.[22]

Health and medical issues

4.17 Applicants have argued for the right to life-sustaining medical treatment under Article 2. Such claims are difficult to make out, save perhaps on extreme facts. Where, for example, a state-administered vaccination programme in fact resulted in the deaths of a number of children, the Commission rejected the claim on the grounds that 'adequate and appropriate steps' had nonetheless been taken.[23]

418   It may be, however, that Article 2 will sometimes be apt to impose a positive obligation on the state to provide treatment. In *R v Cambridgeshire Health Authority ex p B*,[24] Laws J, at first instance, accepted that the right to life in domestic law potentially recognised such an obligation. However, his judgment was overruled by the Court of Appeal who held that issues of clinical decision making of this kind were not justiciable.[25] It is to be expected, post Human Rights Act, that the Courts will be invited to revisit such issues.

4.19   Certainly, if a disabled person were to be refused treatment solely because of disability this would be likely to infringe Article 2 together with Article 14 of the Convention.

4.20   A breach of Article 2 might in principle also arise from administration of treatment. In *Buckley v United Kingdom*,[26] the applicant's son had died at Broadmoor hospital after receiving drugs administered without consent. The applicant had been unable to establish negligence on the part of the hospital; in

---

21   This obligation is only triggered where there is 'concrete evidence' that would establish beyond reasonable doubt a killing has in fact taken place: *Kurt v Turkey* (1999) 27 EHRR 373, para 108.

22   *McCann v United Kingdom* (1996) 21 EHRR 97, para 161. The Court accordingly considered the adequacy of the inquests held in respect of the killings. See, also, *Kaya v Turkey* (1999) 28 EHRR 1; *Guleç v Turkey* (1999) 28 EHRR 121.

23   *McCann v United Kingdom* (1996) 21 EHRR 97, para 161. In *D v United Kingdom* (1997) 24 EHRR 423, para 59, the Court found a breach of Art 3 where the State sought to deport an AIDS patient who would lose access to essential treatment, and did not, therefore, go on to consider his complaint under Art 2.

24   [1995] 25 BMLR 5.

25   [1995] 1 WLR 898.

26   (1997) 23 EHRR CD 129.

the particular case, however, the Commission concluded that the facts did not disclose any substantive or procedural failure to protect the applicant's right to life.

4.21   Article 2 may give rise to an obligation upon the state to warn of potential health risks. In *LCB v United Kingdom*,[27] the applicant's father had been present at nuclear tests at Christmas Island in 1957 and 1958. The applicant suffered from leukaemia and complained that the authorities' failure to warn her of her father's alleged exposure to radiation had prevented earlier diagnosis and treatment of her illness. The Court stated that the question was whether the state 'did all that could have been required of it to prevent the applicant's life being avoidably put at risk'.[28] The claim failed on its facts, but the Court accepted that it was 'perhaps arguable that, had their been reason to belief that she was in danger of contracting a life-threatening disease owing to her father's presence on Christmas Island, the state authorities would have been under a duty to have made this known'.[29]

4.22   The issue of euthanasia also engages Article 2. The question is whether the positive obligations upon the state oblige it to provide life-saving treatment against the wishes of a patient, or whether consent can curtail that obligation.[30] In *Widmer v Switzerland*,[31] the Commission held that Article 2 does not require that passive euthanasia – allowing a person to die by withholding treatment – should be a crime. This appears to be broadly in line with the English case law.[32]

4.23   The question whether a patient is entitled to refuse treatment engages issues under Article 3 is discussed below at paras 4.34 *et seq*.

4.24   Abortion has raised issues under the Convention. It is not clear whether, and to what extent an unborn child has rights under the Convention. Even if a foetus does have a right to life, however, it is subject to implied limitation by the need to protect the health of its mother.[33] This too broadly reflects the position in English law.[34]

---

27 (1999) 27 EHRR 212.

28 *Ibid*, para 36.

29 *Ibid*, para 40.

30 In other contexts, consent can dramatically curtail convention rights, see, eg, *Neilson v Denmark* (1989) 11 EHRR 175, although cf *De Wilde, Ooms and Versyp v Belgium* (1979–80) 1 EHRR 373.

31 *App No 20527/92*, cited in *op cit*, Harris, O'Boyle and Warbrick, fn 1, p 38.

32 See *Airedale NHS Trust v Bland* [1993] AC 789.

33 *X v United Kingdom* (1980) 19 DR 244.

34 *Re F (In Utero)* [1988] 2 All ER 193; *Re MB (Medical Treatment)* [1997] 2 FLR 426.

4.25   The Commission has rejected an attempt to rely upon Article 2 to challenge 'wider issues' as to the organisation and funding of the NHS; it concluded that such issues lay outside the scope of the Convention.[35]

Environment

4.26   The positive obligations upon the state to preserve life could in principle extend to providing protection from environmental hazards. In *Guerra and Others v Italy*,[36] the applicants complained that the failure of the authorities to reduce the risk to health posed by a chemical plant infringed their Article 2 rights. The Court found for the applicants on the basis of Article 8, and did not go on to determine the challenge under Article 2. As the case of *LCB v United Kingdom*[37] (discussed above) shows, Article 2 may also require the provision of a warning where such an environmental hazard may have been created.

ARTICLE 3: PROHIBITION OF TORTURE

4.27   Article 3 states:

> No one shall be subjected to torture or to inhuman or degrading treatment or punishment.

4.28   On its face, this right is unqualified. No derogation from it is permitted.[38] The Court has held that even in the most difficult circumstances such as the fight against organised terrorism and crime, the prohibitions contained in Article 3 are absolute.[39] This lack of qualification has to some extent determined the approach taken to Article 3 in Strasbourg. Ill treatment must reach a minimum level of severity to amount to a breach; the assessment of that minimum depends on all the circumstances of the case, such as the duration of the treatment, its physical or mental effects and, in some cases, the sex, age and state of health of the victim.[40] Thus, although it is frequently invoked, a breach of Article 3 is rarely made out.

---

35 *Taylor v United Kingdom* (1994) 79-A DR 127.

36 (1989) 26 EHRR 357.

37 (1999) 27 EHRR 212. See para 4.21.

38 ECHR, Art 15.

39 *Aksoy v Turkey* (1997) 23 EHRR 553 para 62. Thus, in *Selçuk and Asker v Turkey* (1998) 26 EHRR 477, a case concerning the alleged burning of the applicants' village by security forces, the Court held that, even if the acts in question were carried out to prevent the applicants' homes being used by terrorists or as a discouragement to others, this would not provide a justification for the ill treatment.

40 *Ireland v United Kingdom* (1979–80) 2 EHRR 25, para 162.

4.29   A breach of Article 3 generally requires proof beyond a reasonable doubt,[41] although 'such proof may follow from the co-existence of sufficiently strong, clear and concordant inferences'.[42] In some circumstances, however, a breach may be made out on grounds that the applicant faces 'real risk' of such ill treatment in the future.[43]

4.30   A breach of Article 3 may be made out where the direct perpetrators of the impugned treatment do not act on behalf the state. The Court has held that the obligation on the High Contracting Parties under Article 1 of the Convention to secure Convention rights and freedoms to everyone within their jurisdiction, taken together with Article 3 required states to take measures designed to ensure that individuals within their jurisdiction are not subject to forms of treatment prohibited by Article 3 administered by private individuals. 'Children, and other vulnerable individuals, in particular are entitled to state protection, in the form of effective deterrence against such serious breaches of personal integrity.[44]

The meaning of 'torture ... inhuman or degrading treatment or punishment'

4.31 'Torture', 'inhuman' and 'degrading' have distinct meanings, although the difference between them is to some extent a matter of degree. In *Ireland v United Kingdom*,[45] the applicant complained of techniques used to interrogate terrorist suspects: they were forced to stand against a wall in an uncomfortable position, hooded, subjected to continuous loud noise and deprived of food and sleep. The Court stated that 'torture' was 'deliberate inhuman treatment causing very serious and real suffering'. The matters complained of did not satisfy the definition, but caused 'intense physical and mental suffering' and led to 'acute psychiatric disturbances during interrogation', and thereby qualified as 'inhuman treatment'.[46] They were also 'degrading' as they aroused in their victims 'feelings of fear anguish and inferiority capable of humiliating and debasing them and possibly breaking their physical or moral resistance'. The Court has recently warned, however, that acts it has classified

---

41 *Ireland v United Kingdom* (1979–80) 2 EHRR 25, para 161.

42 *Selmouni v France* (2000) 29 EHRR 403, para 88.

43 See paras 4.42 *et seq*. See, further, para 4.33 in respect of injuries suffered in police custody.

44 *A v United Kingdom* (1999) 27 EHRR 611, para 22 (beating of a child by a parent); *HLR v France* (1998) 26 EHRR 29 (threat posed to deportee by non-State agents in destination country). ECHR, Art 1 is not amongst the Convention rights given effect by the HRA 1998. See, further, paras 4.05 *et seq*.

45 (1979–80) 2 EHRR 25.

46 See *Selçuk and Asker v Turkey* (1998) 26 EHRR 477: burning of applicants' village by security forces amounted to inhuman treatment.

in the past as 'inhuman and degrading treatment' as opposed to torture could be classified differently in the future.[47]

Conditions of detention

4.32   Article 3 is frequently invoked in challenges to the conditions of detention, both by prisoners and in mental health cases. The Court has said that in the case of a person deprived of his liberty, recourse to physical force which has not been made strictly necessary by his own conduct diminishes human dignity and is in principle an infringement of Article 3.[48] In *Aksoy v Turkey*,[49] a finding of torture was made where the applicant had been stripped naked, his arms tied together behind his back and then suspended by the arms. Rape of a detainee by an official of the state has been held to constitute torture.[50]

4.33   Where a prisoner sustains injuries whilst in custody, the state is placed under an obligation to provide a plausible explanation as to the cause of the injuries, and assaults by police in the course of detention have been held to violate Article 3.[51]

4.34   Failure to provide medical treatment to a prisoner may breach Article 3. In *Hurtado v Switzerland*,[52] the applicant suffered broken ribs in the course of arrest, but did not see a doctor until he had been detained for eight days. The Commission found the delay violated Article 3.[53]

4.35   The Court is receptive to medical justifications for impugned treatment. In *Herczegfalvy v Austria*,[54] the applicant, who was detained as a 'mentally deranged offender', went on hunger strike in protest against his detention, and refused all contact and treatment. He was forcibly given food and drugs, isolated and handcuffed to his bed for around four weeks. The Court rejected his claim under Article 3, holding that 'a measure which is a therapeutic necessity cannot be regarded as inhuman or degrading'.[55]

4.36   On the face of it, this test appears to be higher than that prevailing in English law. Medical intervention is permitted in cases where a patient lacks

---

47   *Selmoumi v France* (2000) 29 EHRR 403, para 101.

48   *Ribitsch v Austria* (1996) 21 EHRR 573, para 38. See, also, *Tekin v Turkey*, 9 June 1999, RJD 1998-IV p 1504, para 53.

49   (1997) 23 EHRR 553.

50   *Aydin v Turkey* (1998) 25 EHRR 251.

51   *Ribitsch v Austria* (1996) 21 EHRR 573; *Aksoy v Turkey* (1997) 23 EHRR 553.

52   (1994) A 280-A.

53   The case settled before it was considered by the Court.

54   (1993) 15 EHRR 437.

55   *Ibid*, para 82.

capacity if in the 'best interest' of a patient.[56] For example, eating breakfast might be said to be in a patient's best interest, even if not 'a therapeutic necessity'. If asked to decide, however, the Strasbourg Court would, it is submitted, uphold the 'best interest' test.[57]

4.37   In one respect, English law clearly provides a more rigorous safeguard of the interests of a detainee. In *X v Germany*,[58] a prisoner (apparently of full capacity) who went on hunger strike was tied to a chair and force-fed. The Commission accepted that in 'certain circumstances' force-feeding a patient may amount to degrading treatment. On the facts, the authorities acted 'solely for the best interests' of the applicant, the actions in question being taken 'with a view to securing his health and even saving his life'. They subjected the applicant to no more constraint than was necessary to achieve that goal. The complaint under Article 3 was accordingly manifestly ill founded. Such intervention in the case of a detainee with capacity would be plainly unlawful as a matter of domestic law.[59]

4.38   A failure to provide a suitable therapeutic environment may itself breach Article 3, although the threshold is high. In *Aerts v Belgium*,[60] the applicant, who was detained in a psychiatric wing of a prison complained he had not received any regular medical or psychiatric attention. The complaint was rejected on the facts as, whilst the conditions in the wing were 'unsatisfactory and not conducive to the effective treatment of inmates',[61] the Court held he had not shown that the matters he complained of had 'such serious effects on his mental health as would bring him within the scope of Article 3'.[62]

Crime – extradition

4.39   Applicants subject to extradition proceedings have contended that they would be subject to treatment in breach of Article 3 should they be returned to the requesting state. In *Soering v United Kingdom*,[63] the Court it made clear that in

---

56   See, especially, *F v West Berkshire Health Authority* [1990] 2 AC 1. There is a rebuttable presumption that every adult (whether or not suffering from mental disorder) has capacity and may decide for himself/herself however irrational the decision reached: *Re T (Adult: Refusal of Medical Treatment)* [1992] 4 All ER 649. For other important cases on the essential elements of capacity, see, eg, *Re C (Adult: Refusal of Medical Treatment)* [1994] 1 WLR 290; *Re MB (Medical Treatment)* [1997] 2 FLR 426.

57   There is sufficient flexibility in the concept of 'necessity' as applied by the Strasbourg Court to permit this. See paras 3.89 *et seq*.

58   *X v Germany* (1985) 7 EHRR 152.

59   See Stephen Livingstone, Tim Owen and Lord Steyn, *Prison Law*, 2nd edn, 1998, Oxford: OUP, para 6.16; and *R v Secretary of State for the Home Department ex p Robb* [1995] 1 All ER 677.

60   (2000) 29 EHRR 50.

61   *Ibid*, para 65.

62   *Ibid*, para 65.

63   (1989) 11 EHRR 439.

some cases, the mere risk of ill treatment may be sufficient to establish a breach of Article 3, even where that ill treatment would be at the hands of third parties. In *Soering*, the applicant was a German national. The United States sought his extradition from the United Kingdom to face a murder charge. The Court held that a Contracting State could not surrender a fugitive where there were 'substantial grounds'[64] for believing he would be subjected to treatment in breach of the Convention. On the facts, there was a 'real risk' of a death sentence and, accordingly, exposure to the 'death row phenomenon'. Whilst the Convention permitted capital punishment, the six to eight years the applicant could expect to spend on death row meant that the decision to extradite gave rise to a breach of Article 3.

4.40   The *Soering* doctrine is a narrow one.[65] The 'serious and irreparable harm'[66] threatened was central to the Court's reasoning. It rejected an argument that the absence of legal aid available in Virginia denied the applicant a fair trial within the meaning of Article 6.[67]

Immigration and expulsion

4.41 Whilst the prohibition provided by Article 3 is absolute in expulsion cases,[68] as elsewhere, the Court's approach to the issues raised by such cases is conditioned to some extent by its recognition that Contracting States have the right to control the entry, residence and expulsion of aliens.[69]

4.42   Article 3 has been relied upon by applicants who claim (pursuant to the *Soering*[70] principle) to be at risk of harm at the hands of another state if removed or deported. In such cases, the risk must be assessed at the date of the Court's consideration.[71]

4.43   In *Vilvarajah v United Kingdom*,[72] the Court held that the risk of ill treatment in Sri Lanka faced by returned Tamil asylum seekers was not sufficient to give

---

64 (1989) 11 EHRR 439, para 88.

65 See *Cruz Varas v Sweden* (1992) 14 EHRR 1.

66 *Soering v United Kingdom* (1989) 11 EHRR 439, para 90. Cf *Kirkwood v United Kingdom* (1984) 37 DR 158.

67 The Court stated, however, that it could not exclude the possibility that the risk of a 'flagrant denial of a fair trial' in the requesting country could exceptionally raise the risk of a breach of Art 6. The breach of Convention rights threatened on the facts was not sufficient.

68 See *Chahal v United Kingdom* (1997) 23 EHRR 413, paras 80, 81.

69 Eg, *Vilvarajah v United Kingdom* (1992) 14 EHRR 248, para 102.

70 *Soering v United Kingdom* (1989) 11 EHRR 439.

71 *Chahal v United Kingdom* (1997) 23 EHRR 413

72 (1992) 14 EHRR 248. Such claims also failed in *Cruz Varaz v Sweden* (1992) 14 EHRR 1 and *HLR v France* (1998) 26 EHRR 29 (non-state agents). See, also, *TI v United Kingdom*, 7 March 2000: complaint as to removal to Germany under the Dublin Convention inadmissible.

rise to a breach. In *D v United Kingdom*,[73] however, the *Soering* principle was invoked successfully, on the basis of the non-availability of medical treatment. The application arrived in the United Kingdom from St Kitts in possession of prohibited drugs. He was refused leave to enter, imprisoned, and removal directions were made. He was in the advanced stages of AIDS. It was accepted that his removal would hasten his death, and there was a serious danger it would subject him to 'acute mental and physical suffering'. The Court held that, in those 'exceptional circumstances', removal of the applicant would amount to inhuman treatment.

4.44   Once a real risk of ill treatment risk is established, it is not permissible for the state to seek to balance against other factors which may militate in favour of removal, such as the conduct of the individual 'however undesirable or dangerous'.[74]

4.45   Where the suffering relied upon consists solely of the emotional consequences of immigration decisions which have the effect of dividing applicants from their families, such treatment has been held on the facts to fall short of the level of severity which breaches Article 3.[75]

4.46   In *Abdulaziz, Cabales and Balkandali v United Kingdom*,[76] a complaint that an immigration decision was degrading was rejected on the basis that the immigration controls at issue was not designed to, and did not humiliate or debase (despite the applicants' assertion to the contrary) but was intended solely to achieve legitimate immigration aims.

Discrimination

4.47   The Convention contains no general prohibition on discrimination.[77] In *East African Asians v United Kingdom*,[78] however, the Commission held that discrimination based on race could, in certain circumstances, of itself amount to degrading treatment within the meaning of Article 3.

---

73   (1997) 24 EHRR 423. The *Soering* argument also succeeded in *Chahal v United Kingdom* (1997) 23 EHRR 413 and *Ahmed v Austria* (1997) 24 EHRR 278.

74   *Chahal v United Kingdom* (1997) 23 EHRR 413.

75   See, eg, *Berrehab v Netherlands* (1989) 11 EHRR 322.

76   (1985) 7 EHRR 471.

77   For ECHR, Art 14, see paras 4.211 *et seq*.

78   (1981) 3 EHRR 76, para 207.

Corporal punishment

4.48 Corporal punishment may constitute a violation of Article 3, provided that it attains a level of severity higher than that inherent in any punishment.[79] In *Tyrer v United Kingdom*,[80] the Court held that the judicial birching of a juvenile violated Article 3; whilst the punishment was held not to be either torture or inhuman treatment, in the circumstances of the case, 'the element of humiliation attained the level inherent in the notion of degrading punishment'. Punishment administered in schools has not always been considered to amount to a sufficient level of severity to breach Article 3.[81] Corporal punishment in private schools falls within the supervisory jurisdiction of the Court in principle: the state has an obligation to secure to pupils in private schools the rights guaranteed in Articles 3 and 8, as well as the right to education under Article 2 of Protocol No 1 to pupils in private schools.[82] In *A v United Kingdom*,[83] the state's failure to protect a boy from beatings by his stepfather gave rise to a violation.

ARTICLE 4: PROHIBITION OF SLAVERY AND FORCED LABOUR

4.49 Article 4 provides:

(1) No one shall be held in slavery or servitude.

(2) No one shall be required to perform forced or compulsory labour.

(3) For the purpose of this article the term 'forced or compulsory labour' shall not include:

    1 any work required to be done in the ordinary course of detention imposed according to the provisions of Article 5 of this Convention or during conditional release from such detention;

    2 any service of a military character or, in the case of conscientious objectors in countries where they are recognised, service exacted instead of compulsory military service;

    3 any service exacted in case of an emergency or calamity threatening the life or well being of the community;

    4 any work or service which forms part of normal civic obligations.

---

79 *Tyrer v United Kingdom* (1979–80) 2 EHRR 1.

80 *Ibid*, para 35.

81 *Costello-Roberts v United Kingdom* (1995) 19 EHRR 112; *Campbell v United Kingdom* (1982) 4 EHRR 293. In that case, the Court found a violation of Art 2 of Protocol No 1. Contrast *Y v United Kingdom* (1994) 17 EHRR 238, where the Commission found a breach of Art 3 on the facts.

82 *Costello-Roberts v United Kingdom* (1995) 19 EHRR 112, paras 26–28.

83 (1999) 27 EHRR 611.

4.50 Perhaps unsurprisingly, and indeed thankfully, this Article has not proven to be of great significance in practice. The Court has never found a breach of Article 4.

4.51 The prohibition on 'slavery and servitude' is absolute.[84] 'Servitude' requires, however, a 'particularly serious' form of 'denial of freedom';[85] it was not established in a case concerning an applicant who had a long history of criminal offences and was detained as a criminal recidivist and forced to work.[86] 'Forced labour' is that carried out under 'physical or mental constraint'; 'compulsory labour' is work carried out not merely under legal compulsion or obligation, but must be 'exacted under the menace of a penalty' and against the will of the person concerned.[87] The Commission has said that in the case of forced or compulsory labour, such work should be unjust, oppressive, or involve avoidable hardship.[88] Thus, complaints by a dentist at having to perform public service[89] and by a lawyer against a requirement to perform *pro bono* work[90] were rejected.

4.52 Article 4(3) provides that 'forced and compulsory labour' excludes work in the ordinary course of detention, military, emergency or civic service. Challenges by prisoners to (for example) lack of payment for prison work[91] have accordingly not succeeded.

ARTICLE 5: RIGHT TO LIBERTY AND SECURITY

4.53 Article 5 states:

(1) Everyone has the right to liberty and security of the person. No one shall be deprived of his liberty save in the following cases and in accordance with a procedure prescribed by law:

(a) the lawful detention of a person after conviction by a competent court;

(b) the lawful arrest or detention of a person for non-compliance with the lawful order of a court or in order to secure the fulfilment of any obligation prescribed by law;

(c) the lawful arrest or detention of a person effected for the purpose of bringing him before the competent legal authority on reasonable suspicion of having committed an offence or when it is reasonably

---

84 No derogation is permitted from Art 4(1) under Art 15.
85 *Van Droogenbroeck v Belgium* (1982) 4 EHRR 443, para 58.
86 *Ibid.*
87 *Van der Mussele v Belgium* (1984) 6 EHRR 163, para 34.
88 *Iverson v Norway* (1963) 6 YB 278.
89 *Ibid.*
90 *Van der Mussele v Belgium* (1984) 6 EHRR 163.
91 *Detained Persons v Germany* (1968) 11 YB 528.

considered necessary to prevent his committing an offence or fleeing after having done so;

(d) the detention of a minor by lawful order for the purpose of educational supervision or his lawful detention for the purpose of bringing him before the competent legal authority;

(e) the lawful detention of persons for the prevention of the spreading of infectious diseases, of persons of unsound mind, alcoholics or drug addicts or vagrants;

(f) the lawful arrest or detention of a person to prevent his effecting an unauthorized entry into the country or of a person against whom action is being taken with a view to deportation or extradition.

(2) Everyone who is arrested shall be informed promptly in a language which he understands, of the reasons for his arrest and of any charge against him.

(3) Everyone arrested or detained in accordance with the provisions of paragraph (1)(c) of this article shall be brought promptly before a judge or other officer authorised by law to exercise judicial power and shall be entitled to trial within a reasonable time or to release pending trial. Release may be conditioned by guarantees to appear for trial.

(4) Everyone who is deprived of his liberty by arrest or detention shall be entitled to take proceedings by which the lawfulness of his detention shall be decided speedily by a court and his release ordered if the detention is not lawful.

(5) Everyone who has been the victim of arrest or detention in contravention of the provisions of this article shall have an enforceable right to compensation.

4.54 Thus, Article 5 defines the conditions in which the state may deprive a person of their liberty. It contains in essence:

- the right to liberty and security of the person;
- a general prohibition against deprivation of liberty;
- six provisos: cases in which deprivation of liberty is allowed;
- four rights which arise out of arrest and/or detention.

These components will be considered in turn.

A right to liberty and security

4.55 Article 5(1) provides that everyone has the right to liberty and security of the person. In practice, a clear distinction has not been established between 'liberty' and 'security'.[92] 'Liberty' means 'liberty of the person'.[93] Similarly, 'security'

---

92 In *East African Asians v United Kingdom* (1981) 3 EHRR 76, para 220, the Commission suggested that 'liberty and security of the person' should be read as a whole.

93 *Engel v Netherlands* (1979–80) 1 EHRR 647, para 58.

does not refer to any form economic rights: the 'security' in question is the right to 'security of the person'.[94]

A prohibition on the deprivation of liberty

4.56 Article 5(1) states that 'no one shall be deprived of his liberty'. The question as to what amounts to a 'deprivation of liberty' is one of fact and degree. In *Guzzardi v Italy*,[95] the Court stated that the difference between deprivation of liberty and a mere restriction upon liberty is one of degree or intensity, and not one of nature or substance.[96] The line between the two is not easy to draw; some borderline cases 'are a matter of opinion'.[97]

4.57 In *R v Bournewood Community and Mental Health Trust ex p L*,[98] the House of Lords divided 3:2 on the question of whether L, an autistic patient, had been 'detained' when taken to the Accident and Emergency Unit of the local hospital, sedated and then admitted informally under s 131 of the Mental Health Act 1983. The majority held that he had not been detained, but it may be doubted whether the same conclusion would have been reached had the Human Rights Act then been in force.

Six cases in which deprivation of liberty is allowed

4.58 As has already been seen, Article 5(1)(a) sets out six provisos to the general prohibition on the deprivation of liberty. They are exhaustive of the situations in which the Convention permits deprivation of liberty[99] and must be construed narrowly.[100] All are, however, expressly subject to the limit set out in Article 5(1), namely, that deprivation must be 'in accordance with a procedure carried out by law'. This requires not only that domestic law must itself be complied with, but in addition:

---

94 *Bozano v France* (1987) 9 EHRR 297, para 54.

95 (1981) 3 EHRR 333, para 92.

96 See by way of illustration *Guzzardi* itself (confinement within 2.5 km^2 of an island not deprivation; cf *Dick v United Kingdom* (1996) 21 EHRR CD 107); *Engel v Netherlands* (1979–80) 1 EHRR 647 (military disciplinary penalties a matter of degree); *Weeks v United Kingdom* (1988) 10 EHRR 293 (prisoner released on licence; revocation of licence a deprivation of liberty); *Cyprus v Turkey* (1982) 4 EHRR 482 (curfew not a deprivation of liberty); *Ashingdane v United Kingdom* (1985) 7 EHRR 528 (compulsory detention on an open ward of a psychiatric hospital constituted detention); *Amuur v France* (1996) 22 EHRR 533 (asylum seekers held at airport with option of leaving the country was a restriction on liberty).

97 (1981) 3 EHRR 333, para 93.

98 [1998] 1 CCLR 390.

99 *Engel v Netherlands* (1979–80) 1 EHRR 647, para 57.

100 *Winterwerp v Netherlands* (1979–80) 2 EHRR 387, para 37. ECHR, Art 5 is, however, subject to derogation under Art 15. See paras 4.219 *et seq*.

... the domestic law must itself be in conformity with the Convention, including the general principles expressed or implied therein. The notion underlying the term in question is one of fair and proper procedure, namely, that any measure depriving a person of his liberty should issue from and be executed by an appropriate authority and should not be arbitrary.[101]

4.59 The deprivation of liberty must also be 'lawful'. This requires both conformity with domestic law, and the purpose of the provision of Article 5 relied upon,[102] namely to protect the individual from arbitrary arrest and detention.[103]

4.60 The six provisos will be considered briefly in turn.

Article 5(1)(a): lawful detention of a person
after conviction by a competent court

4.61 A 'court' is a body which possesses a judicial character and is independent of the executive and of the parties to the case.[104] It must provide adequate guarantees of judicial procedure, although the forms of procedure required by the Convention need not be identical in every case.[105] There can only be a 'conviction' by a competent court where there has been a finding of guilt for a specific offence[106] and the imposition of a penalty or other measure involving deprivation of liberty.[107]

4.62 There must be a close causal and temporal connection between the conviction and the deprivation of liberty complained of.[108] A substantial lapse of time may not, however, always break the connection. In *Weeks v United Kingdom*,[109] the applicant had been released on licence after spending 10 years of a life sentence in prison, but that licence had been revoked a year after his release. The Court found the connection between his original conviction and subsequent recall sufficient to satisfy Article 5(1)(a). In *Monnell and Morris v United Kingdom*,[110] the Court of Appeal had refused leave to appeal against the applicants' criminal convictions and had directed that time spent by the applicants in prison pending consideration of the appeals should not count towards their sentences. Before the Strasbourg Court, it was argued that the

---

101 *Winterwerp v Netherlands* (1979–80) 2 EHRR 387, para 45.

102 *Ibid*, para 39. For the principle of legality generally, see paras 3.62 *et seq*.

103 *Bozano v France* (1987) 9 EHRR 297, para 54.

104 *Neumeister v Austria* (1979–80) 1 EHRR 91, para 24.

105 *De Wilde, Ooms and Versyp v Belgium* (1979–80) 1 EHRR 373, para 78. The guarantees required by Art 5(1) are not always co-extensive with the requirements of Art 6: *Engel v Netherlands* (1979–80) 1 EHRR 647, para 68.

106 *Guzzardi v Italy* (1981) 3 EHRR 333, para 100.

107 *Van Droogenbroeck v Belgium* (1982) 4 EHRR 443, para 35.

108 *Ibid*.

109 (1988) 10 EHRR 293.

110 (1988) 10 EHRR 205.

loss of time constituted a further period of imprisonment imposed not for a criminal offence, but for unmeritoriously seeking leave to appeal. The argument was rejected. The sanction of loss of time was used to reduce the time spent in custody by those with meritorious appeals. The Court held, however, that this was an inherent part of the criminal appeal process following conviction of an offender; there was accordingly a 'sufficient and legitimate connection' with the original conviction.[111]

Article 5(1)(b): lawful arrest or detention of a person for non-compliance with the lawful order of a court or in order to secure the fulfilment of any obligation prescribed by law

4.63 Article 5(1)(b) permits lawful arrest or detention for either non-compliance with the order of a court, or in order to secure the fulfilment of any obligation prescribed by law. The first limb, 'non-compliance' applies to arrest and detention for contempt of court, and has been applied, for example, to refusal to comply with a court-ordered medical examination.[112]

4.64 The second limb, 'obligation prescribed by law' has been interpreted narrowly. To fall within it, arrest or detention must be in order to compel the person arrested 'to fulfil a specific and concrete obligation which he has until then failed to satisfy'.[113] By contrast, the obligation to live in a particular place[114] or to pay 'community charge'[115] have been held to amount to relevant 'obligations'. This provision does not serve to justify detention imposed as a punishment. If it did, 'this would deprive such punishments of the fundamental guarantees of sub-paragraph (a)' of Article 5(1).[116]

Article 5(1)(c): the lawful arrest or detention of a person effected for the purpose of bringing him before the competent legal authority on reasonable suspicion of having committed an offence or when it is reasonably considered necessary to prevent his committing an offence or fleeing after having done so

4.65 This proviso consists of three situations where lawful arrest and detention of a suspect may be permitted in connection with criminal proceedings:[117]

---

111 (1988) 10 EHRR 205, para 48.

112 *X v Germany* (1975) 3 DR 92.

113 *Engel v Netherlands* (1970–80) 1 EHRR 647, para 69; *Guzzardi v Italy* (1981) 3 EHRR 333, para 101; *Ciulla v Italy* (1991) 13 EHRR 346, para 101.

114 *Ciulla v Italy* (1991) 13 EHRR 346.

115 *Benham v United Kingdom* (1996) 22 EHRR 293.

116 *Engel v Netherlands* (1979–80) 1 EHRR 647, para 69.

117 *Ciulla v Italy* (1991) 13 EHRR 346, para 38. In *Brogan v United Kingdom* (1989) 11 EHRR 117, para 51. The Court concluded that a statutory power of arrest for involvement in terrorism, defined to mean 'use of violence for political ends' fell within this definition. Military proceedings are also included: *De Jong, Baljet and Van den Brink v Netherlands* (1986) 8 EHRR 20.

(a) on reasonable suspicion of having committed an offence;

(b) when reasonably considered necessary to prevent an offence;

(c) when reasonably considered necessary to prevent a person fleeing after committing an offence.

4.66 In each case, the arrest and/or detention must be for the purpose of bringing the suspect before the 'competent legal authority'.[118] This means 'a judge or other officer authorised by law to exercise legal power' as required by Article 5(3).[119]

4.67 It does not follow, however, that an applicant must in fact be brought before a court for detention to fall within the scope of this provision: all that is required is that this should be the purpose of the arrest or detention. In *Brogan v United Kingdom*,[120] the Court accepted that Article 5(1)(c) does not even presuppose the existence of sufficient evidence to bring charges, either at the point of arrest, or whilst the person is in custody.

4.68 Arrest or detention pursuant to Article 5(1)(c) requires objective justification. Whilst there is no requirement that an offence should actually have been committed[121] 'reasonable suspicion' presupposes the existence of facts or information which would satisfy an objective observer that the person concerned may have committed the offence.[122] The honesty and *bona fides* of the suspicion constitute an indispensable element of its reasonableness.[123] Honesty is not, however, enough on its own.[124] In *Fox, Campbell and Hartley v United Kingdom*,[125] the Court rejected the Government's attempt to justify detention of terrorist suspects under this provision as it had failed to provide any information which would allow it to conclude that the suspicions were reasonable. Thus, whilst Article 5(1)(c) permits detention for the purpose of prevention of an offence, this does not justify preventative detention generally.[126]

---

118 *Lawless v Ireland* (1979–80) 1 EHRR 15, para 14.

119 *Ireland v United Kingdom* (1979–80) 2 EHRR 25, para 199; *Schiesser v Switzerland* (1979–80) 2 EHRR 417, para 29. See paras 4.86 *et seq* for Art 5(3).

120 *Brogan v United Kingdom* (1989) 11 EHRR 117, para 53.

121 *X v Austria* (1989) 11 EHRR 112.

122 *Fox, Campbell and Hartley v United Kingdom* (1991) 13 EHRR 157, para 32. What may be regarded as 'reasonable' will however depend upon all the circumstances, and terrorist crime may not fall to be judged by the same standards as are applied to conventional crime. The length of deprivation of liberty which the applicant may face is also material to the level of suspicion required: *Murray v United Kingdom* (1995) 19 EHRR 193, para 56.

123 *Murray v United Kingdom* (1995) 19 EHRR 193, para 61.

124 *Fox, Campbell and Hartley v United Kingdom* (1991) 13 EHRR 157, para 35.

125 (1991) 13 EHRR 157, paras 33, 34.

126 *Lawless v Ireland* (1979–80) 1 EHRR 15, para 14.

Article 5(1)(d): the detention of a minor by lawful order for
the purpose of educational supervision or his lawful detention for
the purpose of bringing him before the competent legal authority

4.69 This proviso permits the detention of a minor for two reasons: for educational supervision, or in order to be brought before a competent legal authority.[127]

4.70 Detention may be 'for the purpose' of educational supervision even if education is not given during detention itself. In *Bouamar v Belgium*,[128] the Court held that detention of a minor in an adult remand prison did not necessarily contravene Article 5 provided the detention was a means of ensuring he speedily received educational supervision.

Article 5(1)(e): mental health: the lawful detention of persons
for the prevention of the spreading of infectious diseases, of persons
of unsound mind, alcoholics or drug addicts or vagrants

4.71 Most of the cases under Article 5(1)(e) have concerned detention of 'persons of unsound mind'.[129] In *Winterwerp v Netherlands*,[130] the leading case, the Court stated that the term could not be given a definitive interpretation: both the treatment of and societies attitudes to mental illness are changing. That does not mean, however that a person falls within the definition 'simply because his views or behaviour deviate from the norms prevailing in a particular society'.[131]

4.72 A patient who submits to detention on the grounds permitted by Article 5(1)(e) does not thereby forfeit the protections afforded by Article 5. In *De Wilde, Ooms and Versyp v Netherlands*,[132] the applicants were 'vagrants' who had been detained at 'vagrancy centres'. The Court held that the fact they had given themselves up to be taken into detention did not deprive them of the protection of Article 5.

4.73 Detention on mental health grounds may only be justified under Article 5(1)(e) if effected in a hospital, clinic or 'other appropriate institution

---

127 Although minors are only expressly referred to in Art 5(1)(d), the remaining provisions of Art 5 also apply: *Neilson v Denmark* (1989) 11 EHRR 175, para 58. As that case shows, where a parent gives consent to the detention of a minor, the protection offered by Art 5 is dramatically curtailed.

128 (1989) 11 EHRR 1.

129 Although see *De Wilde, Ooms and Versyp v Netherlands* (1979–80) 1 EHRR 373. See also *Litwa v Poland*, 4 April 2000, detention in a sobering up centre. Other provisions of Art 5 may also be relevant to persons detained under mental health legislation, especially, Art 5(2) and (4), below. In the case of a patient detained under s 37 of the Mental Health Act 1983 following criminal conviction, both Arts 5(1)(a) and 5(1)(e) must be satisfied: *X v United Kingdom* (1982) 4 EHRR 188, para 39.

130 (1979–80) 2 EHRR 387.

131 (1979–80) 2 EHRR 387, para 37.

132 (1979–80) 1 EHRR 373, para 65.

authorised for the purpose'.[133] Detention at either a secure hospital, or a local psychiatric hospital have been held to fall within the scope of Article 5.[134]

4.74 In order to be 'lawful', detention must meet the test set out in *Winterwerp*:[135]

(a) save in emergency cases, 'objective medical expertise' must have 'reliably shown' a person to be of an unsound mind;[136]

(b) the mental disorder must be of a 'kind or degree warranting compulsory confinement';[137]

(c) the validity of continuing detention depends upon the persistence of such a disorder;

(d) detention must be in accordance with domestic law, and must not be arbitrary.[138]

4.75 It is not necessary that a patient be released immediately once he or she is no longer suffering from the form of illness which led to confinement. Authorities retain a discretion as to what action is most appropriate, provided that discharge is not unreasonably delayed. In *Johnson v United Kingdom*,[139] a Mental Health Review Tribunal was satisfied that the applicant no longer suffered from mental illness wished to discharge him from Rampton conditionally, but efforts to find a suitable hostel had failed. The Court held that the Tribunal were entitled to defer immediate discharge, but his eventual discharge (almost three years later) was unreasonably delayed.[140]

4.76 Article 5(1)(e) is not in principle concerned with suitable treatment or conditions.[141] Thus, in *Ashingdane v United Kingdom*,[142] the Court rejected the applicant's complaint that his authorised move from Broadmoor, a secure special hospital to a 'more appropriate' local psychiatric hospital was delayed for two years. A breach of Article 5(1) may, however, be made out if the

---

133 *Ashingdane v United Kingdom* (1985) 7 EHRR 528, para 44.

134 *Ibid*.

135 *Winterwerp v Netherlands* (1979–80) 2 EHRR 387, paras 38–40.

136 Where medical evidence is produced in order to justify detention, an applicant will need compelling arguments in order to persuade the Court to go behind it. See the unsuccessful challenges in *Ashingdane v United Kingdom* (1985) 7 EHRR 528; *Luberti v Italy* (1984) 6 EHRR 440. In emergency cases, a person may be detained without the benefit of medical opinion. In *Winterwerp* itself, the Court held permissible a six week period of 'emergency' detention.

137 This is reflected in the detention provisions of the Mental Health Act 1983: see *R v Mental Health Review Tribunal for South Thames Region ex p Smith* [1999] COD 148.

138 For further discussion of this requirement, see paras 3.62 *et seq*.

139 (1999) 27 EHRR 296.

140 The right to a review of detention under Art 5(4) applies in the context of mental health, and is discussed below.

141 *Ashingdane v United Kingdom* (1985) 7 EHRR 528, para 46.

142 *Ibid*.

patient's regime is actually injurious. In *Aerts v Belgium*,[143] the applicant was detained in a prison psychiatric wing. The Mental Health Board considered he was not receiving the treatment he required and that his situation was harmful to him. The Strasbourg Court held that 'there must be some relationship between the ground of permitted deprivation of liberty relied on and the place and conditions of detention'.[144] It concluded that, on the facts, the 'proper relationship between the aim of the detention and the conditions in which it took place was therefore deficient'.[145] In some respects, the domestic regime for detention of mentally disordered patients may be more liberal than the Convention requires, since, for example, save in Scotland, psychopathic patients who are not treatable must be discharged.[146]

Article 5(1)(f): immigration: the lawful arrest or detention of a person to prevent his effecting an unauthorized entry into the country or of a person against whom action is being taken with a view to deportation or extradition

4.77   This provision governs the use of detention in immigration control. It is not necessary in order to justify detention it should be considered 'reasonably necessary' in order to prevent the commission of an offence, or the subject's flight.[147] The only substantive requirements of Article 5(1)(f) are that action is taken with a view to deportation or extradition, and that the arrest or detention should be 'lawful'.[148] The requirement of lawfulness does not extend to consideration of whether the underlying decision to expel can be justified under national or Convention law.[149]

4.78   Just as in domestic law,[150] there, however, are implied limits on the duration of such detention.[151] Expulsion proceedings must actually be in progress,[152] and detention may in any event cease to be lawful if proceedings

---

143 (2000) 29 EHRR 50.

144 *Ibid*, para 46.

145 *Ibid*, para 50.

146 *Reid v Secretary of State for Scotland* [1999] 2 WLR 28; see *Anderson v The Scottish Ministers* (2000) *The Times*, 21 June.

147 *Chahal v United Kingdom* (1997) 23 EHRR 413, para 112. The Court accepted that this provided a different level of protection to Art 5(1)(c). Cf *Immigration Service Instruction on Detention*, 3 December 1991, 20 September 1994: Butterworths Immigration Law Service, D [971].

148 See paras 3.62 *et seq* for a discussion of the meaning of the principle of legality. In the case of asylum seekers, the requirements that the domestic law be sufficiently accessible and precise are of fundamental importance: *Amuur v France* (1996) 22 EHRR 533, para 50.

149 *Chahal v United Kingdom* (1997) 23 EHRR 413, para 112.

150 *R v Governor of Durham Prison ex p Hardial Singh* [1984] 1 WLR 704; *In re Wasfi Suleman Mahmood* [1995] Imm AR 311.

151 The Court has been prepared, however, to sanction lengthy delay: *Chahal v United Kingdom* (1997) 23 EHRR 413.

152 *Ibid*, para 113.

are not conducted with the necessary diligence.[153] In *Chahal v United Kingdom*,[154] the Court took account of the 'extremely serious and weighty nature' of the considerations raised by the proposed deportation of the applicant in determining that a lengthy period of detention was not unlawful. Where delay is not due to any fault of the detaining state, no complaint under Article 5(1) will lie. This is so whether the delay is due to the fault of another state[155] or the conduct of the applicant himself.[156]

Judicial review, habeas corpus and Article 5(1)(f)

4.79 As has been seen, the Article 5(1) requirement of 'lawfulness' implies protection against arbitrariness on the part of the state.[157] In *Chahal v United Kingdom*,[158] judicial review and habeas corpus proceedings were held not to be sufficient for the purposes of Article 5(1)(f). The applicant had been detained, pending a proposed deportation on national security grounds. He had challenged his detention by means of habeas corpus and judicial review proceedings. The Secretary of State's evidence was that he 'remained satisfied that a threat to national security existed and ... his temporary release from detention would not be justified'. Macpherson J had concluded that the detention was lawful. He noted that he had not seen all the material on which the decision to detain had been made, but accepted that, 'in certain circumstances, the Executive must be able to keep secret matters which they deem necessary to keep secret'. The Strasbourg Court accepted that as a result, the domestic courts were not in a position to effectively review the justification for the decision. For substantially the same reasons, the Court found that the judicial review and habeas corpus proceedings did not provide an adequate safeguard for the purpose of Article 5(1)(f).[159] It found however, that the

---

153 *Kolompar v Belgium* (1993) 16 EHRR 197; *Quinn v France* (1996) 21 EHRR 529.

154 (1997) 23 EHRR 413, para 117.

155 *X v Germany* (1983) 5 EHRR 512.

156 *Kolompar v Belgium* (1993) 16 EHRR 197.

157 See para 4.59 and, generally, paras 3.62 *et seq.*

158 (1997) 23 EHRR 413, para 120.

159 The Court is not always so unsympathetic to the state's wish to maintain confidentiality in respect of some of the grounds for detention. In *Murray v United Kingdom* (1995) 19 EHRR 193, paras 58, 59, the Court noted that the use of confidential information was 'essential' in combatting terrorism, and, on the facts of that case, accepted that 'some credence' could be attached to the governments' 'declaration concerning the existence of reliable but confidential information' which it had sought to rely upon (pursuant to Art 5(1)(c) as grounds for its 'reasonable suspicion' that the applicant had committed an offence). (See further, para 4.68.) In *Chahal*, the Court was in part influenced by consideration of the Canadian procedure whereby such evidence is considered by the judge in camera, in the absence of the applicant and his representative, but in the presence of security-cleared counsel instructed by the court: see para 144.

immigration advisory panel procedure (which was able to fully review the evidence relating to the alleged national security threat) was sufficient.[160]

4.80   Whilst *Chahal* itself turned on the absence of any review of confidential material, there are suggestions that Strasbourg is taking an increasing rigorous approach to the requirements of Article 5(1)(f). In *Amuur v France*,[161] the Court held that Article 5(1)(f) imposed a requirement that domestic law concerning asylum seekers should be of 'sufficient quality' to provide adequate legal safeguards against arbitrariness, including not just a right to challenge their detention through the courts, but also 'legal, humanitarian and social assistance'.

Article 5(2): rights on arrest

4.81   Article 5(2) provides:

> Everyone who is arrested shall be informed promptly in a language which he understands of the reasons for his arrest and of any charge against him.

4.82   This provision does not only apply to criminal cases: 'arrest' bears an autonomous Convention meaning, and this safeguard applies to those detained on mental health grounds.[162]

4.83   The information required by this measure goes beyond a bare indication of the legal basis for the arrest; Article 5(2) requires that the person detained must be told 'in simple non-technical language that he can understand, the essential legal and factual grounds for his arrest, so as to be able, if he sees fit, to apply to a court to challenge its lawfulness in accordance with paragraph (4)'.[163]

4.84   The Convention does not require that the information be given in writing, or in any particular form;[164] it may be sufficient if this information emerges in the course of interrogation.[165]

4.85   'Promptly' does not mean 'immediately': the requisite information need not be conveyed at the moment of arrest.[166] Whilst a delay of 10 days has been

---

160 The panel did not, however, suffice to meet the requirements of Art 5(4): see para 4.101.

161 (1996) 22 EHRR 533, paras 50–54.

162 *Van der Leer v Netherlands* (1990) 12 EHRR 567, para 28. A person charged with a criminal offence has the right pursuant to Art 6(3) to be informed in sufficient detail as to the nature and cause of the accusation against him.

163 *Fox, Campbell and Hartley* (1991) 13 EHRR 157, para 40. ECHR, Art 5(4) provides a right to bring proceedings to challenge the lawfulness of detention, and is discussed at paras 4.95 *et seq*.

164 *X v Netherlands* (1962) 5 YB 224, at 228; *X v Netherlands* (1966) 9 YB 474, at 480.

165 *Fox, Campbell and Hartley* (1991) 13 EHRR 157, para 41. See, also, *Murray v United Kingdom* (1995) 19 EHRR 193, para 78.

166 *Fox, Campbell and Hartley* (1991) 13 EHRR 157, para 40.

held to be too long,[167] a delay of a few hours may be lawful.[168] The extent of permissible delay depends, however, upon the circumstances of the case.[169]

Article 5(3): release pending trial

4.86 Article 5(3) provides that a person arrested or detained:

> ... shall be brought promptly before a judge or other officer authorised by law to exercise judicial power; shall be entitled to trial within a reasonable time or to release pending trial; and release may be conditioned by guarantees to appear for trial.

4.87 In essence, this provision contains three rules which will be considered in turn.

(a) Right to be brought promptly before a judge or other officer

4.88 The requirement of promptness is strict, but is to be interpreted according to the 'special features' of each case.[170] In *Brogan v United Kingdom*,[171] a breach of Article 5(3) was made out where terrorist suspects were detained[172] for a period of just over four days, and not brought before a magistrate. In *Schiesser v Switzerland*,[173] the Court held that a 'judge or other officer' must be independent of the executive and the parties. Article 5(3) further imposes some additional procedural and substantive requirements upon him: he must hear the party detained, review the circumstances militating against detention, and decide 'by reference to legal criteria' whether there are reasons justifying detention; if not, he must order release.[174]

4.89 No violation of this provision can arise if the arrested person is released 'promptly before any judicial control of his detention would have been feasible'.[175]

---

167 *Van der Leer v Netherlands* (1990) 12 EHRR 567, para 31.

168 *Fox, Campbell and Hartley v United Kingdom* (1991) 13 EHRR 157, para 42; *Murray v United Kingdom* (1995) 19 EHRR 193, para 78.

169 *Fox, Campbell and Hartley v United Kingdom* (1991) 13 EHRR 157, para 40.

170 *Wemhoff v Germany* (1979–80) 1 EHRR 55, para 10. It is more strict that the requirement in the second half of Art 5(3), 'reasonable time', and that in Art 5(4), 'speedily': *Brogan v United Kingdom* (1989) 11 EHRR 117, para 58.

171 (1989) 11 EHRR 117. The Court expressly declined to state whether the same period would have been acceptable in an 'ordinary criminal case': para 60.

172 Pursuant to the Prevention of Terrorism (Temporary Provisions) Act 1984.

173 (1979–80) 2 EHRR 417, paras 29–31. A soldier's commanding officer does not fulfil this requirement: *Hood v United Kingdom* (1999) *The Times*, 11 March; *Jordan v United Kingdom* (2000) *The Times*, 17 March.

174 (1979–80) 2 EHRR 417, paras 29–31. The judge must have the power to order release if appropriate: *Ireland v United Kingdom* (1970–80) 2 EHRR 25, para 199.

175 *Brogan v United Kingdom* (1989) 11 EHRR 117, para 58.

(b) Trial within a reasonable time or release pending trial

4.90 The wording of Article 5(3) suggests the state has a choice between trial within a reasonable time release pending trial and a prompt trial. This is not so: Article 5(3) does not provide the state the option to postpone trial indefinitely if release is granted.[176]

4.91 Detention prior to trial must not extend beyond a reasonable time: Article 5(3) requires the accused's provisional release once detention ceases to be reasonable.[177] The reasonableness of the time spent in detention must be assessed in the light of the very fact of detention, and according to the special features of each case.[178] There is no maximum permissible length of detention.[179] The persistence of a reasonable suspicion is a 'condition *sine qua non* for the validity of the continued detention', but, after a certain lapse of time, it no longer suffices.[180] The burden is then upon the state to show 'relevant and sufficient' reasons.[181] The following grounds have been held to be sufficient justification: the risk the accused will abscond,[182] the danger of interference with the course of justice,[183] that the accused will re-offend,[184] and that his release would be likely to cause a public disturbance.[185] The mere fact that any sentence imposed would be severe does not of itself provide such grounds.[186] The 'state of the evidence', that is, the existence of serious indications of guilt is a relevant factor, but may not justify continuing detention on its own.[187]

4.92 Where the reasons given by the state are relevant and sufficient, it is also necessary to consider whether the authorities displayed 'special diligence in the conduct of proceedings'.[188] During the period prior to trial, the person

---

176 *Wemhoff v Germany* (1979–80) 1 EHRR 55, para 5. The right to trial within a reasonable time is guaranteed for all suspects, whether detained or otherwise by Art 6(1). See paras 5.90 *et seq*.

177 *Neumeister v Austria* (1979–80) 1 EHRR 91, para 4.

178 *Wemhoff v Germany* (1979–80) 1 EHRR 55, paras 5, 10.

179 *W v Switzerland* (1993) 17 EHRR 60, para 30.

180 *Stögmüller v Austria* (1979–80) 1 EHRR 155, para 4.

181 See the much repeated formulation in *Letellier v France* (1992) 14 EHRR 83, para 35.

182 *Wemhoff v Germany* (1979–80) 1 EHRR 55, para 14. Detention would not, however, be justified for this reason if the concern could be met by bail or other guarantees: para 15. See, also, *Tomasi v France* (1993) 15 EHRR 1, para 96.

183 *Wemhoff v Germany* (1979–80) 1 EHRR 55, para 14; *Tomasi v France* (1993) 15 EHRR 1, para 95.

184 *Matznetter v Austria* (1979–80) 1 EHRR 198, para 9. The danger must be 'a plausible one and the measure appropriate in the light of circumstances of the case and, in particular, the past history and the personality of the person concerned': *Clooth v Belgium* (1992) 14 EHRR 717, para 40.

185 *Letellier v France* (1992) 14 EHRR 83, para 51; *Tomasi v France* (1993) 15 EHRR 1, para 92.

186 *Letellier v France* (1992) 14 EHRR 83, para 43.

187 *Yagci and Sargin v Turkey* (1995) 20 EHRR 505, para 53; *Mansur v Turkey* (1995) 20 EHRR 535, para 56; *Kemmache v France* (1992) A 218.

188 *Matznetter v Austria* (1979–80) 1 EHRR 198, para 12.

detained must be presumed to be innocent; a detained person is entitled to have his case given priority and treated with expedition.[189] Thus, where lengthy periods of delay are due to inactivity on the part of the state, a breach of Article 5(3) may be made out.[190]

4.93 For the purposes of Article 5(3), the relevant period runs from arrest or detention, up until judgment at the end of the accused's trial at first instance; it does not include the period of any appeals.[191] The legality of detention after conviction is governed by Article 5(1)(a).[192]

(c) Bail: 'guarantees to appear for trial'

4.94 Article 5(3) provides that release may be conditional upon 'guarantees to appear for trial'; in other words, bail. The conditions imposed must, however, be designed to ensure the presence of the accused at trial, and not some other purpose. Thus, in *Neumeister v Austria*,[193] the Court held it was impermissible to set the amount of a surety by reference the financial losses imputed to the accused, rather than by reference to what would be sufficient to ensure his attendance. If the only reason for detaining the accused is concern he will abscond, he must be released if there are guarantees which would ensure his appearance at trial.[194]

Article 5(4): the right to a review of detention

4.95 Article 5(4) provides a right to review detention:

> Everyone who is deprived of his liberty by arrest or detention shall be entitled to take proceedings by which the lawfulness of his detention shall be decided speedily by a court and his release ordered if the detention is not lawful.

4.96 'Court' has a much wider meaning under the Convention than in English law. It is satisfied by an independent body[195] with a judicial character.[196] Whilst review by the Secretary of State does not satisfy this criteria, review by the Mental Health Review Tribunal may.[197] The requirement of judicial character

---

189 *Wemhoff v Germany* (1979–80) 1 EHRR 55, para 17. Greater expedition may therefore be required than under Art 6(1).

190 See, eg, *Toth v Austria* (1991) 14 EHRR 551 (almost one year); *Tomasi v France* (1993) 15 EHRR 1.

191 *Wemhoff v Germany* (1979–80) 1 EHRR 55, para 9; *B v Austria* (1991) 13 EHRR 20.

192 See paras 4.61 *et seq.*

193 (1979–80) 1 EHRR 91, para 14.

194 *Wemhoff v Germany* (1979–80) 1 EHRR 55, para 15.

195 It must be independent of both the parties and the executive: *De Wilde, Ooms and Versyp v Belgium* (1979–80) 1 EHRR 373, para 78.

196 *Neumeister v Austria* (1979–80) 1 EHRR 91, para 24. A criminal trial satisfies Art 5(4) in principle at least.

197 *X v United Kingdom* (1982) 4 EHRR 188, para 61. The Parole Board has been held not to satisfy Art 5(4); see, eg, *Hussain v United Kingdom* (1996) 22 EHRR 1.

embodies further procedural requirements, both for the initial hearing and any appeal that may be provided.[198] The Court has stated that the proceedings need not always be attended by the same guarantees as those required under Article 6(1).[199] The scope of Article 5(4) protection is not identical for every kind of deprivation of liberty:[200] '... in order to determine whether a domestic procedure provides adequate guarantees, regard must be had to the particular circumstances of the case.'[201] In practice, however, almost all the requirements of Article 6(1) have been held, on the facts of a particular case, to apply to Article 5(4): reasons,[202] full disclosure,[203] legal representation,[204] an adversarial procedure,[205] equality of arms,[206] an oral,[207] and a public hearing.[208]

Judicial review, habeas corpus and Article 5(4)

4.97   There have been a number of successful challenges to the adequacy of judicial review and habeas corpus for the purposes of Article 5(4). In order to satisfy its requirements, proceedings must provide the applicant with the means to challenge the 'lawfulness' of his detention, that is, to challenge both its compliance with domestic law, but also its 'arbitrariness'.[209]

4.98   In the case of detention of a person of unsound mind, protection from arbitrariness was held by the Court in *Winterwerp v Netherlands*[210] to require that save in emergency cases, objective medical evidence should have reliably shown' the person detained to have been of unsound mind.[211] Thus, in *X v*

---

198 *Toth v Austria* (1992) 14 EHRR 551, para 84.

199 *Winterwerp v Netherlands* (1979–80) 2 EHRR 387, para 60.

200 *Bouamar v Belgium* (1989) 11 EHRR 1, para 60.

201 *Winterwerp v Netherlands* (1979–80) 2 EHRR 387, para 57.

202 *X v United Kingdom* (1982) 4 EHRR 188, para 66.

203 *Weeks v United Kingdom* (1987) 10 EHRR 293, para 68.

204 *Bouamar v Belgium* (1989) 11 EHRR 1, para 60; *Hussain v United Kingdom* (1996) 22 EHRR 1, para 60.

205 *Hussain v United Kingdom* (1996) 22 EHRR 1, para 60; *Sanchez-Reisse v Switzerland* (1987) 9 EHRR 71, para 51.

206 *Sanchez-Reisse v Switzerland* (1987) 9 EHRR 71, para 51.

207 *Winterwerp v Netherlands* (1979–80) 2 EHRR 387, para 60. In *Hussain v United Kingdom* (1996) 22 EHRR 1, para 60, the Court held that a hearing before the Parole Board failed to comply with Art 5(4) for want of 'an oral hearing in the context of an adversarial procedure with legal representation and the possibility of calling and questioning witnesses'.

208 Cf *De Wilde Ooms and Versyp v Belgium* (1979–80) 1 EHRR 379, p 409, para 79 and *Neumeister v Austria* (1979–80) 1 EHRR 91, para 23.

209 See paras 3.62 *et seq*.

210 (1979–80) 2 EHRR 387.

211 See para 4.74.

United Kingdom,[212] a case concerning the detention of a person of unsound mind, habeas corpus proceedings were held to be insufficient for the purposes of Article 5(4). The applicant had been conditionally discharged from Broadmoor secure hospital, but had been recalled by the Secretary of State. He wished to challenge whether his mental disorder still persisted. The Strasbourg Court held that such proceedings must, in order to satisfy Article 5(4), be wide enough 'to bear on those conditions, which, according to the Convention, are essential' for lawful detention.[213] The Court noted that:[214]

> ... when the terms of a statute afford the executive a discretion, whether wide or narrow, the review exercisable by the courts in habeas corpus proceedings will bear solely upon the conformity of the exercise of that discretion with the empowering statute.

4.99 The Court concluded that whilst this narrow form of review might suffice in the case of emergency detention – which may be lawful even in the absence of any medical opinion[215] – it would not suffice in the case of continuing confinement. Whilst the Court accepted that domestic review proceedings need not permit the court to substitute its own discretion on all aspects of the case, it was necessary for the review to 'bear upon those conditions which, according to the Convention, are essential for the "lawful" detention of a person on the ground of unsoundness of mind'. It was necessary that a court be able to examine whether the patient's mental disorder still persisted. Whilst the Mental Health Review Tribunal was able to provide an appropriate form of review, its function was, at that time, only advisory in the case of a restricted patient, and it accordingly lacked the power to order release.[216]

4.100 The Court applied similar reasoning in the case of *Weeks v United Kingdom*.[217] That case concerned a challenge to a decision of the Secretary of State to recall a prisoner who had been released on licence during the term of a discretionary life sentence. The Court concluded that the scope of judicial review was insufficient to bear upon the 'conditions essential for the "lawfulness" of Mr Weeks' detention'.[218] By contrast, in *Brogan v United Kingdom*,[219] the applicants had been detained for periods of four to six days without being charged, or brought before a court. They complained of breaches of Articles 5(3) and 5(4). As to the latter, the Court found that the practice of the Northern Ireland courts permitted examination of 'the

212 (1982) 4 EHRR 188.

213 *Ibid*, para 58.

214 *Ibid*, para 56. Contrast *E v Norway* (1994) 17 EHRR 30.

215 *Winterwerp v Netherlands* (1979–80) 2 EHRR 387, para 39.

216 This position subsequently changed; see Mental Health Act 1983, s 73.

217 (1988) 10 EHRR 293, para 69.

218 *Ibid*, para 69. See, also, *Thyme, Wilson and Gunnell v United Kingdom* (1991) 13 EHRR 666.

219 (1989) 11 EHRR 117, paras 63–65.

procedural and substantive requirements which are essential for the "lawfulness" in the sense of the Convention, of their deprivation of liberty'.[220]

4.101   In *Chahal v United Kingdom*,[221] the applicant was detained following a decision to deport him on national security grounds.[222] The Court found that in those circumstances the national courts were not in a position to review whether his detention was justified on national security grounds, and accordingly, neither habeas corpus, nor judicial review proceedings satisfied the requirements of Article 5(4).[223]

Review at reasonable intervals

4.102 Article 5(4) provides for a review of detention at reasonable intervals where the reasons for detention may cease to exist;[224] at least where there is no automatic review of a judicial character,[225] detention on remand calls for short intervals between reviews.[226] Where, however, a prisoner is subject to a mandatory life sentence, imposed automatically and irrespective of considerations of the dangerousness of the offender, the Court has held that the guarantee contained in Article 5(4) is satisfied by the original trial procedure.[227] By contrast, discretionary life prisoners are entitled to take review proceedings under Article 5(4): such a sentence takes into account factors which are susceptible to change with passage of time, such as mental instability and dangerousness.[228] In *V and T v United Kingdom*,[229] the Court held a breach of Article 5(4) had occurred where the applicants, who were detained at Her Majesty's Pleasure, had had their sentence tariffs set by the Home Secretary quashed by the House of Lords, without any fresh tarrif being substituted. The Court held that the failure to set a new tarrif meant that the applicant's entitlement to access to a tribunal for periodic review of their detention remained 'inchoate'.

4.103   The acceptable duration of such proceedings depends upon the circumstances of the case.[230] The Strasbourg Court has been prepared to hold

---

220 The Court stated that review by the Northern Ireland courts included consideration of the reasonableness of suspicion.

221 (1997) 23 EHRR 413, para 130.

222 See, further, para 3.28.

223 The immigration advisory panel lacked the power to give a binding decision and could not be considered a court within the meaning of Art 5(4): para 130.

224 *Winterwerp v Netherlands* (1979–80) 2 EHRR 387, para 50.

225 *X v United Kingdom* (1982) 4 EHRR 188, para 207.

226 *Bezicheri v Italy* (1990) 12 EHRR 210, para 21.

227 *Wynne v United Kingdom* (1995) 19 EHRR 333, para 35.

228 *Thynne Wilson and Gunnell v United Kingdom* (1990) 13 EHRR 666, para 73; *Wynne v United Kingdom* (1995) 19 EHRR 333, para 33.

229 (2000) 30 EHRR 120.

230 *Sanchez-Reisse v Switzerland* (1987) 9 EHRR 71, para 56.

unlawful delays of 31 and 46 days,[231] and, in another case, eight weeks.[232] The workload of the courts does not necessarily excuse delay. Whilst a temporary backlog of work will not render the state liable provided prompt remedial action is taken,[233] Contracting States are under a duty to organise their legal systems so as to enable the courts to comply with the requirements of the Convention.[234]

Article 5(5): a right to compensation

4.104 Article 5(5) provides:

> Everyone who has been the victim of arrest or detention in contravention of the provisions of this Article shall have an enforceable right to compensation.

4.105 Article 41 of the Convention gives the Strasbourg Court a power to make an award of compensation in respect of any violation of the Convention (see paras 6.27 *et seq*). Article 5(5) is the only provision which requires that a domestic court should have the power to do so.[235] If breached, the Strasbourg Court may award just satisfaction.[236]

4.106 The Court will consider a complaint under Article 5(5) alongside a complaint of a breach of the substantive provisions of Article 5 without requiring the applicant to exhaust domestic remedies in respect of Article 5(5).[237]

4.107 In *R v Secretary of State for the Home Department ex p Chahal*,[238] the English Court of Appeal accepted that it might be perverse for the Secretary of State to refuse to offer compensation in advance of an ECHR examination of a claim under Article 5(5) if the inevitable result of such a claim was that it would succeed.

ARTICLE 6: RIGHT TO A FAIR TRIAL

4.108 Article 6 is considered in detail in Chapter 5.

---

231 *Sanchez-Reisse v Switzerland* (1987) 9 EHRR 71.

232 *E v Norway* (1994) 17 EHRR 30. See, also, *De Jong, Baljet and Van den Brink v Netherlands* (1986) 8 EHRR 20: breach of Art 5(4) where servicemen prevented from petitioning a military court for 14 days a breach of Art 5(4).

233 *Zimmerman and Steiner v Switzerland* (1984) 6 EHRR 17, para 29.

234 *Milasi v Italy* (1988) 10 EHRR 333, para 18; *Bezicheri v Italy* (1990) 12 EHRR 210, para 25.

235 *Brogan v United Kingdom* (1989) 11 EHRR 117, para 67; *Fox, Campbell and Hartley* (1991) 13 EHRR 157.

236 *Brogan v United Kingdom* (1989) 11 EHRR 117, para 67.

237 *Ciulla v Italy* (1991) 13 EHRR 346, para 45.

238 (1999) *The Times*, 10 November.

ARTICLE 7: NO PUNISHMENT WITHOUT LAW

4.109 Article 7 provides:

(1) No one shall be held guilty of any criminal offence on account of any act or omission which did not constitute a criminal offence under national or international law at the time when it was committed. Nor shall a heavier penalty be imposed than the one that was applicable at the time the criminal offence was committed.

(2) This article shall not prejudice the trial and punishment of any person for any act or omission which, at the time when it was committed, was criminal according to the general principles of law recognised by civilised nations.

4.110 This provision prohibits both conviction for a retroactive offence,[239] and the imposition of a retroactively increased penalty. No derogation from this provision is permissible under Article 15 (see para 4.219).

4.111   Whilst the principle of non-retroactivity is hardly alien to domestic law, there is an analytic tension between this rule of Convention law and a common law system whereby principles evolve through case law. The word 'law' as it appears in Article 7 embodies the same guarantees of accessibility and foreseeability as are implicit in the words 'according to law' elsewhere in the Convention.[240] The Court has stated:

... the criminal law must not be extensively construed to an accused's detriment, for instance by analogy; it follows from this that an offence must be clearly defined in law. This condition is satisfied where the individual can know from the wording of the relevant provision and, if need be, with the assistance of the courts' interpretation of it, what acts and omissions will make him liable.[241]

4.112 In practice, Article 7 litigation generally concerns the issue of legal certainty, rather than overtly retrospective legislation.[242] In *SW and CR v United Kingdom*,[243] the Court considered the reversal by the House of Lords of the long standing common law rule[244] which provided that a husband could not be found guilty of raping his own wife.[245] The Strasbourg Court stated that however clearly drafted a legal provision may be, there is an inevitable need for interpretation and adaptation to changing circumstances. Article 7 could not be read as outlawing the gradual clarification of the rules of criminal

---

239 Except where the conduct complained of was in any event a crime under international law: Art 7(2). See War Crimes Act 1991.

240 *SW and CR v United Kingdom* (1996) 21 EHRR 363, para 35/33. See *Sunday Times v United Kingdom* (1979–80) 2 EHRR 245, para 49 and paras 3.62 *et seq*.

241 *Kokkinakis v Greece* (1994) 17 EHRR 423, para 52.

242 See, eg, *X Ltd and Y v United Kingdom* (1982) 28 DR 77.

243 (1996) 21 EHRR 363.

244 The rule is stated in *Hale's History of the Pleas of the Crown*, 1736.

245 *R v R* [1992] 1 AC 599.

liability 'provided that the resultant development is consistent with the essence of the offence and could be reasonably foreseen'.[246] The Court concluded that the judgment of the House of Lords 'did no more than continue a perceptible line of case law'.[247] The substance of the change in the law brought about by the House of Lords overtly influenced the Court: it was held to be in conformity with the 'fundamental objectives of the Convention, the very essence of which is respect for human dignity and human freedom'.[248] It may be that on different facts so stark a change in the law would not have been acceptable.

4.113   Article 7(1) also prohibits retroactively increased penalties. This provision only applies to a penalty following conviction for a criminal offence. The terms 'penalty' and 'criminal offence' have autonomous Convention meanings.[249] Confiscation orders imposed on drug traffickers have been held to fall within the scope of Article 7.[250]

4.114   Article 7(2) exempts from the scope of Article 7(1) the 'trial and punishment of any person for any act or omission which, at the time when it was committed, was criminal according to the general principles of law recognised by civilised nations'. The *travaux préparatoires* show that this provision was included to make clear that Article 7 did not affect measures enacted to punish war crimes at the end of the Second World War.[251]

ARTICLE 8: RIGHT TO RESPECT FOR PRIVATE AND FAMILY LIFE

4.115 Article 8 provides:

(1) Everyone has the right to respect for private and family life, his home and his correspondence.

(2) There shall be no interference by a public authority with the exercise of this right except such as in accordance with the law and is necessary in a democratic society in the interests of national security, public safety or the economic well-being of the country, for the prevention of disorder or crime, for the protection of health or morals, or for the protection of the rights and freedoms of others.

---

246 *SW and CR v United Kingdom* (1996) 21 EHRR 363, para 36/34.

247 (1996) 21 EHRR 363, para 43/41. See, also, *Gay News Ltd and Lemmon v United Kingdom* (1983) 5 EHRR 123, para 9.

248 (1996) 21 EHRR 363, para 44/42.

249 *Jamil v France* (1996) 21 EHRR 65, paras 30, 31.

250 *Ibid*; see, also, *Welch v United Kingdom* (1995) 20 EHHR 247.

251 See *X v Belgium* (1961) 4 YB 324.

4.116 The Court has not provided tight definitions of the interests protected by Article 8. As is obvious, they are to some extent overlapping. 'Home' is not limited to residences which are lawfully established.[252] Nor is actual occupation necessary.[253] In *Neimeitz v Germany*,[254] the applicant was a lawyer whose offices had been searched for information about the whereabouts of a third party who was subject to criminal proceedings. The Court stated that it was neither possible or necessary to attempt an exhaustive definition of the notion of 'private life'. It was, however, consonant with the essential object and purpose of Article 8 to interpret 'private life' and 'home' as including certain professional or business activities or premises.[255] Private life extends to a person's physical and moral integrity, including their sexual life.[256] It also implies the right 'to establish and develop relationships with other human beings, especially in the emotional field for the development of one's own personality'.[257]

4.117 The concept of 'family' is also broad and flexible. What matters is the closeness of the relationship, rather than its legal status. It encompasses what the Court calls '*de facto*' family ties where parties live together outside marriage[258] and (at least as between parents and children) can survive divorce.[259] Where there is a lawful and genuine marriage, the concept 'family' must include such a relationship.[260] Family life may between child and parents, even if they are separated[261] or if there is no cohabitation.[262] Taking a child into the custody of the state does not bring to an end the rights of the child and his or her parents to respect for their family life.[263] Exceptional circumstances are required to break the tie between parent and child.[264] Family life may also exist between children and other relatives such as grandparents, or an uncle;[265]

---

252 *Buckley v United Kingdom* (1997) 23 EHRR 101.

253 *Gillow v United Kingdom* (1989) 11 EHRR 335. In *Lozidou v Turkey* (1997) 23 EHRR 513, para 66, the Court held 'home' did not extend to land where it was intended to build a home; nor did it extend to include an area where a person grew up, and where his family had roots, but no longer lived.

254 (1993) 16 EHRR 97. In *Chappell v United Kingdom* (1989) 12 EHRR 1, para 36, the Court accepted that an Anton Piller order executed at premises where the applicant both lived and operated his business constituted interference with both 'private life' and 'home'.

255 (1993) 16 EHRR 97, para 31. For privacy of a company, see *R v Broadcasting Standards Commission ex p BBC* [2000] 3 All ER 989, CA.

256 *X and Y v Netherlands* (1985) 8 EHRR 235, para 22.

257 *X v Iceland* (1976) 5 DR 86.

258 *Keegan v Ireland* (1994) 18 EHRR 342, para 44.

259 Eg, *Hoffman v Austria* (1994) 17 EHRR 293. No distinction is drawn between 'legitimate' and 'illegitimate' family: *Marckx v Belgium* (1980) 2 EHRR 330, para 31.

260 *Abdulaziz, Cabales and Balkandali v United Kingdom* (1985) 7 EHRR 471, para 62.

261 *Berrehab v Netherlands* (1988) 11 EHRR 322.

262 *Boughanemi v France* (1996) 22 EHRR 227.

263 *W v United Kingdom* (1987) 10 EHRR 29, para 59.

264 *Boughanemi v France* (1996) 22 EHRR 227.

265 *Boyle v United Kingdom* (1995) 19 EHRR 179.

whether it does so is a question of fact and degree.[266] There may be family life between a parent and an adult child provided there are 'elements of dependency, involving more than the normal emotional ties'.[267]

4.118 The protection of correspondence under Article 8 has been most frequently invoked by those in detention.[268] In *Foxley v United Kingdom*,[269] the applicant successfully invoked Article 8 where his correspondence had been redirected to his trustee in bankruptcy pursuant to s 371 of the Insolvency Act 1986 and letters to from his legal advisors had been read and copied before being forwarded to him. This right extends to telephone conversations,[270] and, as shall be seen, it has also been invoked in cases concerning surveillance.

4.119 An example of the application of Article 8 by a domestic court is afforded by the facts of *R v North and East Devon Health Authority ex p Coughlan*.[271] There, the Applicant had left a hospital where she was a long stay patient in reliance upon a promise that the hospital to where she moved would be her 'home' for the rest of her life. The Court of Appeal held that the judge at first instance had been entitled to find that the Respondent Health Authority had violated the Applicant's right to respect for her home contrary to Article 8.

Positive obligations and respect for Article 8 rights

4.120 There are positive obligations inherent in an effective respect for family life.[272] The effect is that the state is required to take steps to secure respect for private life in the sphere of relations between private individuals.[273] As shall be seen, this doctrine is of central importance to the Court's regulation of child welfare matters.

4.121 The Court has stated that the notion of 'respect' is not clear cut. Its requirements will vary from case to case, and accordingly, the Contracting States enjoy a wide margin of appreciation.[274] There is no clear test as to when such a positive obligation exists, or its extent: the Court has stated only that in determining whether it does, regard must be had to 'the fair balance that has to

---

266 In *G v Netherlands* (1993) 16 EHRR CD 38, the Commission concluded there was no family life between an applicant sperm donor, despite the fact he had contact with the child following the birth.

267 *Advic v United Kingdom* (1995) 19 EHRR CD 125 at 126.

268 Eg, *Silver v United Kingdom* (1983) 5 EHRR 347.

269 20 June 2000.

270 *Klass v Germany* (1979–80) 2 EHRR 214, para 41.

271 [2000] 2 WLR 622.

272 *Marckx v Belgium* (1979–80) 2 EHRR 330, para 31. The doctrine of positive obligations is discussed at paras 3.112 *et seq.*

273 *X and Y v Netherlands* (1986) 8 EHRR 235, para 23.

274 *Abdulaziz v United Kingdom* (1985) 7 EHRR 471, para 67. For margin of appreciation, see paras 3.128 *et seq.*

be struck between the general interest of the Community and the interest of the individual'.[275] The Court has said that the boundaries between the state's positive and negative obligations under Article 8 do not lend themselves to precise definition.[276] Even where the Court does identify a situation where the state falls under positive obligations, it is generally not prepared to say what the state should do to rectify the breach.[277]

A balancing exercise

4.122 Not all interference with interests protected by Article 8 amounts to a breach of Article 8(1).[278] Even where such interference is made out, it is capable in principle of justification, provided it can be shown to be in accordance with the law, necessary in a democratic society and proportionate to one of the aims set out in Article 8(2). Substantially the same balancing exercise must be carried out in respect of Articles 9–11, and its nature is considered in detail in Chapter 3.

Children

4.123 As has been seen at para 4.117, the concept of family life is sufficiently flexible to apply to a wide range of relationships involving children. The Court has stated that where the existence of a family tie with a child has been established, the state must act in a manner calculated to enable that tie to be developed and legal safeguards must be created that render possible from the moment of birth the child's integration in his family.[279] Most cases in this area arise from measures by the state to take children into care, or otherwise regulate a parent's access to their child. Cases of this kind are by their nature driven by value-laden assessments of complex factual situations. The state is afforded a wide margin of appreciation in these matters and it is relatively uncommon for the Court to interfere with the substance of such a decision. As shall be seen, however, the Court has bolstered the protection offered by Article 8 by reading into it procedural safeguards which apply in respect of child welfare measures. It has less frequently engaged the substance of such disputes.

4.124 The decision making process leading to interference in child welfare cases must be fair and such as to afford due respect to the interests safeguarded by Article 8.[280] Whilst national authorities are permitted some discretion as to the

---

275 *Rees v United Kingdom* (1987) 9 EHRR 56, para 37.

276 *Keegan v Ireland* (1994) 18 EHRR 342, para 49.

277 Eg, *B v France* (1993) 16 EHRR 1.

278 See, eg, *Costello Roberts v United Kingdom* (1995) 19 EHRR 112: corporal punishment at school insufficiently severe to fall within scope of Art 8.

279 *Marckx v Belgium* (1979–80) 2 EHRR 330, para 31.

280 *McMichael v United Kingdom* (1995) 20 EHRR 205, para 87.

nature of the process, parents must be involved to a degree which is sufficient to protect their interests.[281] Thus, in *W v United Kingdom*,[282] the Court found a breach of Article 8 where parents had not been informed or consulted in advance before their child was placed with long term foster parents with a view to adoption, nor of a decision to terminate the parents' access. Similarly, in *Keegan v Ireland*,[283] the Court held that provisions of Irish law which allowed adoption to take place without either the knowledge or the consent of the child's father interfered with the father's right to respect for his family life.

4.125 Just as with Articles 5 and 6, procedural delay can itself result in a breach of Article 8: '... effective respect for family life requires that future relations between parent and child be determined solely in the light of all relevant considerations and not by the mere effluxion of time.'[284] 'Exceptional diligence' is required in ensuring the progress of proceedings concerning restrictions on access between a parent and a child taken into public care.[285] The reasonableness of the length of proceedings is to be assessed in the light of the complexity of the case and the conduct of the applicant and the authorities.[286] In *H v United Kingdom*,[287] the Court found a breach of Article 8 on the grounds that court proceedings concerning access to a child taken into care had taken two years to resolve.

4.126 Importantly, the right of access to, or custody of a child are 'civil rights' for the purposes of Article 6, the right to a fair trial. That Article is accordingly frequently invoked alongside Article 8 in cases where challenges to procedural fairness are brought by parents.[288] Article 6 is discussed in Chapter 5.

4.127 The Court has repeatedly emphasised that in regulating custody and access issues, its role is not to substitute itself for the competent national authorities, but rather to review the decisions taken by those authorities in exercise of their 'power of appreciation'.[289] Nevertheless, it has engaged in the substance of such disputes on occasion. The Court requires that such decisions 'must be supported by sufficiently sound and weighty considerations of the welfare of the child'.[290] A violation of Article 8 may accordingly be made out in the

---

281 *W v United Kingdom* (1988) 10 EHRR 29, para 64.

282 (1988) 10 EHRR 29. In *Re F (Minors) (Care Proceedings: Contact)* (2000) *The Times*, 22 June, Wall J cautioned against reliance on Strasbourg cases which pre-dated the Children Act 1989.

283 See, also, *H v United Kingdom* (1988) 10 EHRR 95.

284 *W v United Kingdom* (1988) 10 EHRR 29, para 65.

285 *Johansen v Norway* (1997) 23 EHRR 33, para 88; *Paulsen-Medalen and Svensson v Sweden* (1998) 26 EHRR 260, para 39. In those cases, the issue of delay was considered pursuant to Art 6(1).

286 (1988) 10 EHRR 95.

287 (1988) 10 EHRR 95. See, also, *R v United Kingdom* (1988) 10 EHRR 74.

288 Eg, *Erikkson v Sweden* (1990) 12 EHRR 183; *Keegan v Ireland* (1994) 18 EHRR 342.

289 *Hokannen v Finland* (1995) 19 EHRR 139, para 55.

290 *Olsson v Sweden* (1989) 11 EHRR 259, para 72.

absence of 'relevant and sufficient reasons' which would justify the interferences at issue.[291]

4.128   In *Johanssen v Norway*,[292] the Court held that the taking of a child into care should normally regarded as a temporary measure to be discontinued as soon as circumstances permit. A measure such as a permanent placement of a child in a foster home with a view to adoption should only be taken in 'exceptional circumstances' and 'if motivated by an overriding requirement pertaining to a child's best interests'. The interests of the child are of 'particular importance' and may override those of the parent.[293]

4.129   In cases concerning the compulsory taking of a child into public care, Article 8 includes a right for a parent to have measures taken with a view to being reunited with the child. In *Eriksson v Sweden*,[294] the Court found a breach of Article 8 where a local authority had prohibited the applicant from removing her daughter from a foster home for an indefinite period.[295]

4.130   In *Hoffman v Austria*,[296] The applicant complained of a court ruling which awarded custody of her children to her husband, on grounds, amongst other things, that the Applicant was a Jehovah's Witness. The Court found a violation of Article 8 in conjunction with the Article 14 prohibition of discrimination.

4.131   A refusal to provide access to records kept in respect of a period spent by a child in care may also breach Article 8. In *Gaskin v United Kingdom*,[297] the applicant contended he had been abused whilst in care; he sought access to local authority records. The authority disclosed only those parts of the records in respect of which consent had been obtained from the person who compiled them. The Court held a violation had been made out: the requirement of consent could in principle be compatible with Article 8, but only if there was an independent authority which could decide whether to allow access where consent was improperly withheld, or a contributor was not available.

Divorce

4.132 There is no express right to divorce under the Convention and, in *Johnston v Ireland*,[298] the Court refused to read such a right into Article 8. In *Airey v*

---

291 (1989) 11 EHRR 259, para 68.

292 (1997) 23 EHRR 33, para 78.

293 *Ibid*.

294 (1990) 12 EHRR 183.

295 See, also, *Olsson v Sweden* (1989) 11 EHRR 259.

296 (1994) 17 EHRR 293.

297 *Gaskin v United Kingdom* (1989) 12 EHRR 35.

298 (1987) 9 EHRR 203.

Ireland,[299] the Court held, however, that the protection of private life may sometimes necessitate a husband and wife being relieved from the duty to live together. In that case the applicant complained that legal aid was not available for judicial separation proceedings. The Court held that not only was her right of access to a court (Article 6) infringed, but that there was also a breach of Article 8.

4.133   As has already been noted (at para 4.117), divorce does not necessarily bring family life to an end between parent and child.

Immigration

4.134 Whilst the Convention does not guarantee the right of a foreign national to enter or remain in a country, issues may arise under Article 8 where the effect of an immigration control measure is to exclude a person from the state where members of his family are living.[300]

4.135   When considering whether such an applicant can claim to have enjoyed private and family life within the meaning of the Convention, the Strasbourg Court will assess the applicant's position at the date that the contested immigration measure was applied.[301] Thus, it will not avail an applicant to argue that a subsequent marriage has strengthened, or created, family ties which would be interfered with by his expulsion.[302] In *Abdulaziz, Cabales and Balkandali v United Kingdom*,[303] the applicants were women who were lawfully and permanently settled in the United Kingdom. Their husbands (who were non-UK nationals) were refused permission to join (or remain with) them. In each case, the applicants had married after becoming settled in the United Kingdom. The Court held there was no general obligation on the part of the Contracting State to respect the choice by married couples of the country of their matrimonial residence and to accept the non-national spouses for settlement in that country. On the facts, the applicants had not shown that there were obstacles to establishing family life in their own or their husbands' home countries.[304]

4.136   Applicants have invoked Article 8 in challenges to removal decisions taken as a result of the applicant's criminal conduct. Typically, it is argued by the state that the interference with family life can be justified under Article 8(2) on the grounds of the prevention of disorder or crime. Where the applicant has

---

299 (1979–80) 2 EHRR 305, para 32.

300 *Abdulaziz, Cabales and Balkandali v United Kingdom* (1985) 7 EHRR 471, para 60

301 *Bouchelkia v France* (1998) 25 EHRR 686, para 41.

302 The current policy of the UK Government adopts a broadly similar approach; see DP 3/96, Butterworths Immigration Law Service, D [551].

303 (1985) 7 EHRR 471.

304 Cf *Beljoudi v France* (1992) 14 EHRR 801.

strong family ties which would be imperilled by the deportation decision, the Court has found deportation to be in breach of Article 8(2). This can be so even where the criminal conduct in question is violent,[305] serious or prolific. *Beldjoudi v France*[306] concerned an Algerian national who had been born in France, but lost his French nationality in 1963 (when Algeria became independent). His mother and four siblings all lived in France and he had been married to a French citizen for over 20 years. He had been convicted of criminal offences on six different occasions and had served a total of 10 years in prison. The Court found that his deportation would be disproportionate: he had spent his whole life in France, and had no links with Algeria except for his nationality; if his wife were to follow her husband to Algeria, she might face real practical or legal obstacles. The interference in question might therefore have imperilled the unity or even the very existence of the marriage.[307]

4.137   By contrast, in *Bouchelkia v France*,[308] the Court found no breach of Article 8. The applicant was an Algerian, deported from France after serving a prison sentence for aggravated rape. He had re-entered France illegally, married and fathered a child. At the time of the deportation order, however, he was single, and lived with his family.[309] He had lived in France since the age of two; he had only returned to Algeria when he had been deported. Nevertheless, the majority of the Court found that deportation order was not disproportionate to the aim of the prevention of disorder or crime.

Sexuality

4.138 Whilst it is clear that sexual orientation and activity engage the right to private life,[310] the Court has expressed doubts as to whether all sexual activities would fall within its sphere.[311] It has not always been robust in the protection of such interests: it is at times restrained by a perceived lack of common ground between Contracting States, and has accordingly granted a wide margin of appreciation in this area.[312]

---

305 *Nasri v France* (1996) 21 EHRR 458.

306 (1992) 14 EHRR 801.

307 *Beldjoudi v France* (1992) 14 EHRR 801. See, further, *Moustaquim v Belgium*, (1991) 13 EHRR 801 and *Djeroud v France* (1992) 14 EHRR 68 (friendly settlement).

308 (1998) 25 EHRR 686. See, also, *Boughanemi v France* (1996) 22 EHRR 228; *Nasri v France* (1996) 21 EHRR 458.

309 The Court held that the applicant's position had to be assessed at the time of the deportation order: para 41. The subsequent strengthening of his family ties was accordingly irrelevant.

310 *Dudgeon v United Kingdom* (1982) 4 EHRR 149, para 52.

311 *Lasky, Jaggard and Brown v United Kingdom* (1997) 24 EHRR 39, para 36.

312 Eg, *Rees v United Kingdom* (1987) 9 EHRR 56, para 37.

4.139   In the past, the Commission has taken the view that a same sex couple cannot be said to have a family life within the meaning of the Convention.[313] A more flexible approach may however, be beginning to emerge. In *X, Y and Z v United Kingdom*,[314] the Court considered an application by a transsexual, his partner he had lived with for 13 years, and their baby. On the facts, the applicants had demonstrated the existence of *de facto* family ties.[315]

4.140   The Court has consistently held that prohibitions on consensual homosexual activity falls foul of the Convention.[316] It has rejected a challenge based on differences in the age of consent between homosexual and heterosexuals,[317] but found that 'exceptionally intrusive' investigations by military police into the sexuality of members of the armed forces, and subsequent dismissal from the forces on grounds of their sexuality violated Article 8.[318] The state is, however, entitled to use the criminal law to seek to regulate sexual activities which cause physical harm.[319] In *Lasky, Jaggard and Brown v United Kingdom*,[320] the Court considered convictions for assault occasioning actual bodily harm and unlawful wounding as a result of sado-masochistic activities carried out by consent, in private, and without inflicting any injury which required medical treatment. The House of Lords held (by a majority) that consent was no defence.[321] On the facts, the Strasbourg Court accepted the measures were necessary for the protection of health, and held that the conditions contained in Article 8(2) were satisfied.[322]

4.141   The Court has considered a series of applications from transsexuals seeking legal recognition for their gender reassignment. Such applications have been generally refused.[323] The Court has repeatedly asserted that states must be afforded a wide margin of appreciation when dealing with the issues raised, in view of the lack of common ground between Contracting States, and the

---

313 *X and Y v United Kingdom* (1983) 32 DR 220.

314 (1997) 24 EHRR 143.

315 *Ibid*, para 37.

316 *Dudgeon v United Kingdom* (1982) 4 EHRR 149. See, also, *Norris v Ireland* (1991) 13 EHRR 186, *Modinos v Cyprus* (1993) 16 EHRR 485.

317 *Dudgeon v United Kingdom* (1982) 4 EHRR 149, para 62. The Commission has recently reached a different view: *Sutherland v United Kingdom* (1997) 24 EHRR CD 22.

318 *Smith and Grady v United Kingdom* (2000) 29 EHRR 493.

319 *Lasky, Jaggard and Brown v United Kingdom* (1997) 24 EHRR 39, para 42.

320 (1997) 24 EHRR 39.

321 *R v Brown* [1994] 1 AC 212, HL.

322 It was common ground before the Strasbourg Court that the prosecution and conviction amounted to interference with the applicants' rights to respect for private life. The Court did however express doubt as to whether this concession was rightly made: para 36

323 *Van Oosterwijck v Belgium* (1981) 3 EHRR 557 (inadmissible for failure to exhaust domestic remedies); *Rees v United Kingdom* (1987) 9 EHRR 56; *Cossey v United Kingdom* (1991) 13 EHRR 622; *X, Y and Z v United Kingdom* (1997) 24 EHRR 143; *Sheffield and Horsham v United Kingdom* (1999) 27 EHRR 163.

transitional stage of the law.[324] As a consequence, it has shied away from any clear assertion of transsexual rights.[325] It has, however, encouraged repeated applications by asserting the need to keep legal measures in this area under review[326] and, in one case, *B v France*,[327] found a violation of Article 8. The French authorities refused to allow the applicant to change the civil status register and official identity papers to reflect her changed gender. The Court distinguished its earlier case law on the grounds that the applicant faced daily difficulties as a result (with, for example, dealing with banks) to a level which was not compatible with respect for her private life.

Personal data

4.142 The Court has asserted that the protection of personal data is of fundamental importance of to a person's enjoyment of his her right to respect for private and family life under Article 8.[328] Where information is held in a secret register in circumstances where the subject cannot obtain access, a breach of Article 8 may be made out. In *Leander v Sweden*,[329] the applicant had been refused employment at the Naval Museum on the grounds that he was a security risk. as a result of information about him provided from a secret police register. The Court held that both the storing and release of such information, coupled with a refusal to allow the applicant an opportunity to refute it, breached of his right to respect for his private life. The Court has stopped short, however, of declaring any general right of access to such records.[330]

4.143 Article 8 may also be engaged by the disclosure of such confidential information to third parties. The rights of the subject to the confidentiality of such data are not absolute: in a suitable case they may be outweighed by other interests. In *Andersson v Sweden*,[331] the applicant complained that a psychiatrist she had consulted disclosed his findings to social welfare authorities without

---

324 *Rees v United Kingdom* (1987) 9 EHRR 56, para 37; *X, Y and Z v United Kingdom* (1997) 24 EHRR 143, para 44; *Sheffield and Horsham v United Kingdom* (1999) 27 EHRR 163, para 58.

325 Cf the approach of the ECJ in Case C-13/94 *P v S and Cornwall County Council* [1996] I-ECR 2143, which was cited to the Strasbourg Court in *X, Y and Z v United Kingdom* (1997) 24 EHRR 143.

326 Most recently, *Sheffield and Horsham v United Kingdom* (1999) 27 EHRR 163, para 60.

327 (1994) 16 EHRR 1.

328 *Z v Finland* (1998) 25 EHRR 371, para 95.

329 (1987) 9 EHRR 433.

330 *Gaskin v United Kingdom* (1989) 12 EHRR 35, para 36. No such right arises under Art 10 either: see para 4.167. For disclosure of privileged material under the CPR, see *General Mediterranean Holdings SA v Patel* [2000] HRLR 54.

331 (1998) 25 EHRR 722. The Court also rejected a complaint under Art 6(1) that the Applicant had been given no opportunity to challenge the communication before a court before it occurred. The Court concluded that the applicant had no 'right' to prevent the communication of data under domestic law, and therefore, Art 6(1) was not applicable.

her knowledge or consent. The psychiatrist was obliged under domestic law to make the disclosure as he considered it was necessary for the protection of her son, a minor. The Court concluded no arguable claim arose under Article 8.[332] The measure had been notified to the applicant, and the information remained confidential. Further, there was independent evidence which supported the psychiatrist's concern.[333]

4.144   Article 8 may also give rise to an obligation upon the authorities to disclose other kinds of information. In *Guerra and Others v Italy*,[334] the Court held that the authorities had a positive obligation to disclose information to the applicants as to the environmental risks posed by a chemical factory near to their homes.

Surveillance and investigation

4.145 Article 8 is engaged by investigative techniques such as the interception of post[335] or the monitoring of telephone calls,[336] whether made from home or the office.[337]

4.146   Where covert surveillance cases takes place,[338] there is generally little difficulty in establishing a breach of Article 8(1). The question whether such interference can be justified pursuant to Article 8(2). Governments enjoy a wide margin of appreciation in choosing the means to protect national security,[339] and the Court accepts that states must be able to engage in secret surveillance in order to meet 'highly sophisticated forms of espionage and terrorism'.[340]

4.147   Such measures are generally only permissible 'under exceptional conditions'.[341] The central issue is generally whether there are adequate safeguards to prevent abuse.[342] In *Malone v United Kingdom*,[343] the Court

---

332 (1998) 25 EHRR 722, para 42.

333 See, also, *Z v Finland* (1998) 25 EHRR 371: disclosure of medical records of HIV positive applicant in the course of proceedings to which she was not a party.

334 (1998) 26 EHRR 357.

335 *Hewitt and Harman v United Kingdom* (1992) 14 EHRR 657.

336 In *Klass v Germany* (1979–80) 2 EHRR 214, para 41, the Court decided that telephone conversations fall within the ambit of private life and correspondence.

337 Eg, *Huvig v France* (1990) 12 EHRR 528; *Halford v United Kingdom* (1997) 24 EHRR 523.

338 In some circumstances, an applicant can claim to be a victim of measures which permit such surveillance without having to prove that it has taken place. See, further, paras 2.77 *et seq*.

339 *Leander v Sweden* (1987) 9 EHRR 433, para 59.

340 *Klass v Germany* (1979–80) 2 EHRR 214, para 48.

341 *Ibid*.

342 In *Valenzuela Contreras v Spain* (1999) 28 EHRR 483, para 46, the Court set out the minimum safeguards required for such measures. See, also, *Kopp v Switzerland* (1999) 27 EHRR 91, para 50.

343 (1984) 7 EHRR 14.

found a violation where the metering[344] and interception of communications were authorised as a matter of administrative discretion. The Court held it could not be said with reasonable certainty what elements of the power to intercept were incorporated within legal rules, and what elements remained within the discretion of the executive.[345] A range of procedural safeguards were subsequently introduced by means of the Interception of Communications Act 1985.

4.148   A lacuna in that framework was considered by the Court in *Halford v United Kingdom*.[346] The applicant (who was conducting sexual discrimination proceedings against her employer, the Merseyside Police) complained that calls made from her office telephones were intercepted for the purpose of obtaining information to use against her in the discrimination proceedings. The Court found that the interference could not be justified under Article 8(2). The 1985 Act did not apply to an internal communication system.[347] As such, there was no system of regulation at all; the interference was therefore not in accordance with the law. In *Khan v United Kingdom*,[348] the applicant had been convicted of drug dealing on the basis of evidence obtained by a secret listening device installed by the police. At the time, there had been no statutory regime applicable to the use of the device, merely Home Office guidelines.[349] The Court held that the interference with the applicant's Article 8 rights could not be said to be in accordance with the law.

4.149   Such safeguards should normally include a form of judicial supervision.[350] *Klass v Germany*[351] concerned legislation which permitted the German authorities to open the mail and listen to the telephone conversations of any person in the Federal Republic without their ever knowing. Further, the applicants complained that German law provided no remedy against the use of the legislation. The Court considered that the surveillance had a legitimate aim (namely, to safeguard national security and/or to prevent disorder or

---

344 Ie, the practice of recording the number, time and duration of a call, but not the call itself.

345 *Malone v United Kingdom* (1984) 7 EHRR 14, para 79. See, also, *Kopp v Switzerland* (1999) 27 EHRR 91.

346 *Halford v United Kingdom* (1997) 24 EHRR 523. See, also, *R v X, Y, Z* (2000) *The Times*, 23 May: foreign telephone intercepts admissible.

347 The Interception of Communications Act 1985 only applied to communications transmitted by post or by means of a public telecommunications system: s 1(1).

348 (2000) *The Times*, 19 May.

349 See, now, the Police Act 1997.

350 *Klass v Germany* (1979–80) 2 EHRR 214, para 55. It need not always: see *Huvig v France* (1990) 12 EHRR 528, where judicial supervision was held on the facts to be insufficient to meet the requirements of the Convention.

351 (1979–80) 2 EHRR 214. See, further, *Lüdi v Switzerland* (1993) 15 EHRR 173.

crime) and was necessary in a democratic society: initial control by an official qualified for judicial office, and subsequent review provided by Parliament were sufficient safeguards against abuse.

Search and seizure of property

4.150 Search and seizure measures are permissible in principle, but must be justified by relevant and sufficient reasons, must be proportionate, and there must be adequate and effective procedural safeguards against abuse.[352] In *Funke v France*,[353] the applicant's house had been searched by Customs officers, and documents seized. No prior judicial authorisation was required for the use of such powers, and the Court found the safeguards in place to be insufficient. Judicial authorisation may not always be enough to render such a measure lawful, however: in *Neimeitz v Germany*,[354] a judicial warrant which authorised a search was found by the Court to be too broadly drawn to satisfy the requirements of Article 8.

4.151   In *Chappell v United Kingdom*,[355] the Court considered the legality of an Anton Piller order,[356] which allows one party to enter the premises of another without notice to inspect and remove documents. The applicant did not challenge the lawfulness of the order in principle. His complaints centred on the manner of execution of the order: 16 people had searched his premises, and a number of usual safeguards were missing. The Court stated that although the manner of the execution of the search was 'disturbing', 'unfortunate and regrettable',[357] the shortcomings were not so serious that the complaint was made out.

The environment

4.152 Article 8 has been invoked in environmental nuisance claims. Where a nuisance, such as aircraft noise, is generated in pursuit of a legitimate aim, it is relatively easy to justify. Where the state has taken measures to control, abate or compensate for such a nuisance, the Court has held that a fair balance has

---

352 *Camenzind v Switzerland* (1999) 28 EHRR 458, para 45.

353 *Funke v France* (1993) 16 EHRR 297. See, also, *Mialhe v France* (1993) 16 EHRR 332. Cf, however, *Camenzind v Switzerland* (1999) 28 EHRR 458, para 45.

354 *Neimeitz v Germany* (1993) 16 EHRR 97.

355 *Chappell v United Kingdom* (1990) 12 EHRR 1. See, also, *McLeod v United Kingdom* (1999) 27 EHRR 493: entry by police officers in order to prevent a breach of the peace contrary disproportionate.

356 Now known as a 'search order': CPR Pt 25.1.

357 (1990) 12 EHRR 1, para 63.

been struck between the competing interests of the individual and the community.[358]

4.153   In an appropriate case, the state may be obliged to disclose environmental risks faced by those who live near to an environmental hazard.[359]

Article 8: rights of prisoners

4.154 Prisoners can lay claim to family life in principle[360] although such claims have generally not met with success. The Commission has rejected a number of applications from prisoners seeking transfer from English prisons to Northern Ireland in reliance upon Article 8. In *Boyle and Rice v United Kingdom*,[361] the Court accepted that a challenge under Article 8 might arise in principle in respect of limits to the number of visits a prisoner was entitled to receive in a year.

4.155   The right to association with others implicit in Article 8 extends to prisoners, although removal of prisoners from association as a form of punishment may be justified.[362]

4.156   The right to correspondence has been successfully invoked by prisoners. In *Silver v United Kingdom*,[363] the Court found a breach of Article 8 where the interference with mail was insufficiently foreseeable to be 'in accordance with the law'. In *Campbell v United Kingdom*,[364] the Court upheld a complaint that the authorities had opened correspondence between the applicant and his solicitor. Whilst some limited measure of control of prisoners' mail was compatible with the Convention, correspondence with legal advisors was privileged and as a matter of principle should not be read.[365]

---

358 *Powell and Rayner v United Kingdom* (1990) 12 EHRR 355 (aircraft noise); *Khatun and Others v United Kingdom* (1998) 26 EHRR CD 212 (nuisance caused by road construction). Cf, however, *Lopez-Ostra v Spain* (1995) 20 EHRR 277 (a failure to adequately regulate a waste treatment plant failed to strike a fair balance).

359 *Guerra and Others v Italy* (1998) 26 EHRR 357; *McGuinley and Egan v United Kingdom* (1999) 27 EHRR 1.

360 *Boyle and Rice v United Kingdom* (1988) 10 EHRR 425. There is no right to artificial insemination: *R v Secretary of State for the Home Department ex p Mellor* (2000) *The Times*, 5 September.

361   (1988) 10 EHRR 425.

362   *McFeeley v United Kingdom* (1980) 20 DR 44.

363   (1983) 5 EHRR 347. See, also, *Foxley v United Kingdom* (2000) *The Times*, 4 July.

364   (1993) 15 EHRR 137. See, also, *Schonenberger and Durmaz v Switzerland* (1989) 11 EHRR 202: the stopping of an unsolicited letter from a legal advisor requesting authority to act for detainee was contrary to Art 8.

365 The protection also extends to correspondence with the Strasbourg institutions themselves: *Campbell v United Kingdom* (1993) 15 EHRR 137, para 64.

Compulsory medical treatment

4.157 Challenges to compulsory medical treatment have been brought unsuccessfully under Article 8. In *Acmanne v Belgium*,[366] the applicants challenge to compulsory tuberculosis screening failed: although there was interference with private life, it was justified as proportionate and necessary to protect health. In *Grare v France*,[367] the applicant was a voluntary patient in a psychiatric hospital and complained he had been subjected to a treatment regime with unpleasant side effects. The Commission held that even if the treatment could have been considered an invasion of the applicant's private life, it was justified by the need to preserve public order and the protection of the applicant's health.

ARTICLE 9: FREEDOM OF THOUGHT, CONSCIENCE AND RELIGION

4.158 Article 9 provides:

(1) Everyone has the right to freedom of thought, conscience and religion; this right includes freedom to change his religion or belief and freedom, either alone or in community with others and in public or private, to manifest his religion or belief, in worship, teaching, practice and observance.

(2) Freedom to manifest one's religion and beliefs shall be subject only to such limitations as are prescribed by law and are necessary in a democratic society in the interests of public safety, for the protection of public order, health or morals, or for the protection of the rights and freedoms of others.

4.159 Article 9 guarantees freedom of thought, conscience and religion.[368] Article 9 rights primarily protect individuals. Whilst a church or other association with religious objectives may rely on Article 9,[369] the Commission has held that a company may not.[370]

4.160   A wide range of beliefs are protected.[371] The Court has stated that in its religious dimension, Article 9 is:[372]

---

366 *App No 10435/83*, 40 DR 251.

367 (1993) 15 EHRR CD 100.

368 For the provisions of the HRA 1998 dealing expressly with Art 9, see paras 1.95 *et seq*.

369 *X and Church of Scientology v Sweden* (1979) 16 DR 68.

370 *X v Switzerland* (1979) 16 DR 85.

371 Including, eg, pacifism: *Arrowsmith v United Kingdom* (1981) 3 EHRR 218.

372 *Kokkinakis v Greece* (1994) 17 EHRR 397, para 31.

... one of the most vital elements that go to make up the identity of believers and their conception of life, but it is also a precious asset for atheists, agnostics, sceptics and the unconcerned.

4.161 Whilst the freedom to hold protected beliefs is absolute, Article 9(2) permits the curtailment of freedom to manifest those beliefs. 'Manifestation' includes 'the right to try and convince one's neighbour, for example, through teaching'.[373] The nature of manifestation of belief is critical in determining whether a restriction placed upon it is lawful. In *Kokkinakis v Greece*,[374] the Court upheld[375] the applicants' complaints that their convictions for proselytising violated Article 9. The Court distinguished 'bearing Christian witness' and 'improper prostelytism' which might involve the use of 'improper pressure ... violence or brainwashing' which might not be compatible with the religious freedoms of others.[376]

4.162 Restrictions on the manifestation of belief arising from situations entered into voluntarily may be permissible. In *Kalaç v Turkey*,[377] the Court rejected a complaint brought by a military 'judge advocate' who had undergone 'compulsory retirement' on the grounds that he held 'unlawful fundamentalist opinions'. In choosing to pursue a military career, the applicant accepted of his own accord a system of military discipline that by its nature implied the possibility of limitations on his rights and freedoms which could not be imposed on civilians. In *Buscarini v San Marino*,[378] however, the Court held a breach of Article 9 was made out where the applicants were required to swear an oath on the Gospels on pain of forfeiting their parliamentary seats.

4.163 A certain degree of robustness in these matters is expected by the Court. In *Valsamis v Greece*,[379] it rejected a complaint in respect a child suspended from school for refusing to participate in a Greek National Day parade on grounds of pacifist beliefs. The Court found there was nothing in the parade which constituted an interference with her freedom of religion.

4.164 A number of complaints under Article 9 have been brought by prisoners complaining of partial restrictions upon religious practice. The Commission has generally been willing to find such measures to be justified under Article 9(2).[380] The balancing exercise required by Article 9(2) is explained in Chapter 2.

---

373 *Kokkinakis v Greece* (1994) 17 EHRR 397, para 31.

374 (1994) 17 EHRR 397.

375 Albeit by a majority.

376 (1994) 17 EHRR 397, para 48. Freedom of manifestation has been held not to extend to a refusal to pay taxes: *X v United Kingdom* (1984) 6 EHRR 558, nor to 'advertisements of a purely commercial nature': *X and Church of Scientology v Sweden* (1979) 19 DR 68, p 72, or to the distribution of pacifist leaflets to soldiers: *Arrowsmith v United Kingdom* (1981) 3 EHRR 218.

377 (1999) 27 EHRR 552, para 28.

378 (2000) 30 EHRR 208.

379 (1997) 24 EHRR 294.

380 See, eg, *X v United Kingdom* (1976) 5 DR 100.

ARTICLE 10: FREEDOM OF EXPRESSION

4.165 Article 10 provides:[381]

(1) Everyone has the right to freedom of expression. This right shall include freedom to hold opinions and to receive and impart information and ideas without interference by state authority and regardless of frontiers. This article shall not prevent States from requiring the licensing of broadcasting, television or cinema enterprises.

(2) The exercise of these freedoms, since it carries with it duties and responsibilities, may be subject to such formalities, conditions, restrictions or penalties as are prescribed by law and are necessary in a democratic society, in the interests of national security, territorial integrity or public safety, for the prevention of disorder or crime, for the protection of health or morals, for the protection of the rights of others, for preventing the disclosure of information received in confidence, or for maintaining the authority of the judiciary.

The scope of freedom of expression

4.166 Freedom of expression is said by the Court to be one of the essential foundations of a democratic society, 'one of the basic conditions for its progress and for the development of every man'.[382] The right is wide enough to encompass political,[383] artistic,[384] and commercial expression, such as advertising.[385] It applies not only to the inoffensive, but (in theory at least) also to ideas which 'offend, shock or disturb the state or any sector of the population'.[386] The Court has never suggested that any particular media of expression is excluded from Article 10's reach. In *Steel v United Kingdom*,[387] the Court held that a protest which took the form of 'physically impeding activities of which the applicants disapproved' amounted to an expression of opinion within the meaning of Article 10.

---

381 For provisions of the HRA 1998 dealing expressly with Art 10, see paras 1.95 *et seq*.

382 *Handyside v United Kingdom* (1979–80) 1 EHRR 737, para 49.

383 Eg, *Barthold v Germany* (1985) 7 EHRR 383. 'Political' expression is not to be distinguished from that dealing with other matters of public concern: *Thorgeirson v Iceland* (1992) 14 EHRR 843, para 64. Cf *Reynolds v Times Newspapers* [2000] HRLR 134.

384 *Müller v Switzerland* (1991) 13 EHRR 212.

385 *Markt Verlag GmbH v Germany* (1990) 12 EHRR 161, para 26; *Casado Coca v Spain* (1994) 18 EHRR 1, paras 35–36.

386 *Handyside v United Kingdom* (1979–80) 1 EHRR 737, para 49. For a lack of robustness on the part of the Court in defence of the controversial, see *Markt Intern Verlag v Germany* (1990) 12 EHRR 161. Racist expression may not be protected by Art 10: *Jersild v Denmark* (1995) 19 EHRR 1, para 35.

387 (1999) 28 EHRR 603, para 92.

4.167 Article 10 also embodies a right to receive information that others may be willing to impart.[388] It does not, however, place any obligation upon the state to provide information, or provide access to information to individuals.[389] Thus, in *Guerra v Italy*,[390] the Court held that Article 10 placed no obligation upon the authorities to collect or disseminate information about the hazards to health posed by a chemical factory to neighbouring residents.

Restrictions on freedom of expression

4.168 Freedom of expression may potentially collide with other important interests, and indeed, other Convention rights; in particular, the right to a private life. Article 10(2) expressly states that the exercise of this freedom carries with it duties and responsibilities, and freedom of expression may accordingly be subject to the restrictions permitted by Article 10(2).[391] Such interference must however be in accordance with the law,[392] proportionate to the aim pursued, and no greater than is necessary in a democratic society. These concepts are analysed in Chapter 2.

4.169 The justification for a restriction on freedom of expression may be undermined over time. In *Observer and Guardian Newspapers v United Kingdom*,[393] the applicants challenged injunctions upheld by the House of Lords to prevent the publication of extracts of the book '*Spycatcher*'. The Strasbourg Court accepted that the injunctions were justified until the book was published abroad.[394] Once the book had been published, however, the injunctions could no longer be considered necessary in a democratic society.[395]

---

388 *Sunday Times v United Kingdom* (1979–80) 2 EHRR 245, paras 65, 66.

389 *Leander v Sweden* (1987) 9 EHRR 433, para 74. ECHR, Art 8 may, however, be more helpful in this respect: *Gaskin v United Kingdom* (1990) 12 EHRR 36, paras 37, 52: paras 4.142 *et seq.*

390 (1998) 26 EHRR 357. See, also, paras 4.142 *et seq.*

391 These exceptions are to be interpreted narrowly: *Sunday Times v United Kingdom* (1979–80) 2 EHRR 245, para 65.

392 In *Sunday Times v United Kingdom* (1979–80) 2 EHRR 245, para 52, the Court accepted that the English common law of contempt was sufficiently certain to satisfy this requirement. See, also, *Tolstoy Miloslavsky v United Kingdom* (1995) 20 EHRR 442: unsuccessful challenge to award of damages in a libel trial. In *Hashman and Harrup v United Kingdom* (1999) *The Times*, 1 December, the Court held an order binding over two hunt saboteurs to be of good behaviour was insufficiently precise to be prescribed by law.

393 (1992) 14 EHRR 153. See, also, *Sunday Times v United Kingdom (No 2)* (1992) 14 EHRR 229.

394 *Ibid.*

395 Once information is in the public domain, such restrictions will rarely be justified; see, eg, *Open Door Counselling and Dublin Well Woman Centre v Ireland* (1993) 15 EHRR 244, para 76.

Subject matter

4.170 The subject matter of the expression at issue in part determines the degree of protection afforded at Strasbourg. The Court is relatively vigilant in respect of political expression.[396] It has emphasised the importance of a free press and political debate[397] and, as shall be seen (at paras 4.174 et seq), is generally protective of journalists. It has defended political activists,[398] and found a violation where a teacher dismissed on grounds of active membership of the Communist party.[399] In Bowman v United Kingdom,[400] a violation of Article 10 was found where the applicant was convicted under election law[401] when she arranged for the distribution of leaflets outlining candidates' views on abortion.

4.171 Commercial expression is accorded less weight. A wide margin of appreciation is provided.[402] Even the publication of items which are true and describe real events may under certain circumstances be prohibited, where, for example the obligation to respect privacy or commercial confidentiality are in play.[403] In challenges to restrictions upon advertising by professionals, Strasbourg has upheld absolute prohibitions in a number of cases.[404]

4.172 Where, however, commercial speech engages in a debate of general interest the margin of appreciation is reduced.[405] Thus, in Barthold v Germany,[406] the Court found a breach of Article 10 where a veterinary surgeon who made critical statements to the press about the local emergency services was prosecuted for breaching a prohibition on publicity: there was a risk that members of the profession would be discouraged from contributing to public debate.

---

396 See Castells v Spain (1992) 14 EHRR 445, paras 42 et seq (freedom of expression especially important for an elected representative); Incal v Turkey (2000) 29 EHRR 449 (freedom of expression is particularly important for political parties and their members).

397 Lingens v Austria (1986) 8 EHRR 407, para 42.

398 Incal v Turkey (2000) 29 EHRR 449. Cf Arrowsmith v United Kingdom (1981) 3 EHRR 218.

399 Vogt v Germany (1996) 21 EHRR 205; although cf Glasenapp v Germany (1987) 9 EHRR 25; Kosiek v Germany (1987) 9 EHRR 328.

400 (1998) 26 EHRR 1.

401 Representation of the People Act 1983, s 75, which prohibited expenditure of more than £5 by an unauthorised person during the period before an election on conveying information to electors with a view to promoting or procuring the election of a candidate.

402 Markt Intern Verlag v Germany (1990) 12 EHRR 161.

403 Ibid.

404 Eg, Colman v United Kingdom (1993) A 258-D, para 39 (prohibition on advertising by a doctor upheld); Casado Coca v Spain (1994) 18 EHRR 1 (written warning given to a lawyer for advertising upheld).

405 Hertel v Switzerland (1999) 28 EHRR 534, para 47.

406 (1985) 7 EHRR 383.

4.173   The Court has asserted the importance of 'pluralism, tolerance and broadmindedness' in a democratic society.[407] It has not always, however, been vigilant in protecting artistic expression, particularly where it comes into conflict with obscenity law. A wide margin of appreciation applies.[408] The 'duties and responsibilities' of artists under Article 10 include 'an obligation to avoid as far as possible expressions that are gratuitously offensive to others'.[409] In *Müller v Switzerland*,[410] the Court concluded that the confiscation of paintings held to be obscene for a period of eight years by a national court was justifiable. A wide margin of appreciation also applies in respect of blasphemous works. In *Wingrove v United Kingdom*,[411] the Court upheld the refusal to grant a classification to a video work on the grounds that it was blasphemous.

The press

4.174 The Strasbourg Court has emphasised the particular importance of the safeguards afforded to the press. Whilst the press must not overstep the bounds set, *inter alia*, in the interest of the protection of the rights of others, it is incumbent upon it to impart information and ideas of public interest, which, in turn the public has a right to receive.[412] In *Jersild v Denmark*,[413] the applicant was a journalist prosecuted for broadcasting an interview which contained racist remarks made by the subject. The Court held there had been a breach of Article 10; it was not for the Court or the national courts to substitute their own views for those of the press as to what technique of reporting should be adopted.

4.175   The Court has been protective of a journalist who wished to conceal his source,[414] and has criticised the use of criminal libel laws to protect politicians.[415]

4.176   Article 10 does not, however, guarantee a wholly unrestricted freedom of expression even with respect to press coverage of matters of serious public

---

407 *Handyside v United Kingdom* (1979–80) 1 EHRR 737, para 49.

408 (1979–80) 1 EHRR 737, para 48.

409 *Otto-Preminger-Institut v Austria* (1995) 19 EHRR 34.

410 (1991) 13 EHRR 212. See, also, *Otto-Preminger-Institut v Austria* (1995) 19 EHRR 34 (seizure of film on grounds of 'disparaging religious doctrines' upheld); *Wingrove v United Kingdom* (1996) RJD 1996-IV, p 1937 (refusal to certify a video considered to be blasphemous upheld).

411 (1997) 24 EHRR 1.

412 *Sunday Times v United Kingdom* (1979–80) 2 EHRR 245, para 65; *Jersild v Denmark* (1995) 19 EHRR 1, para 31.

413 (1995) 19 EHRR 1, para 31.

414 Eg, *Goodwin v United Kingdom* (1996) 22 EHRR 123.

415 Eg, *Lingens v Austria* (1986) 8 EHRR 407; *Castells v Spain* (1992) 14 EHRR 445, para 46; *Thorgeirson v Iceland* (1992) 14 EHRR 843 (allegations against the police).

concern. In *Bladet Tromsø and Stenaas v Norway*,[416] the Court stated that by reason of the 'duties and responsibilities' inherent in the exercise of freedom of expression, the safeguard afforded to journalists by Article 10 is subject to the proviso that they are acting in good faith in order to provide accurate and reliable information in accordance with the ethics of journalism. In that case, a newspaper was found to have published defamatory statements. The statements in question were factual, and were based on the contents of an official report which the newspaper had not checked. The Strasbourg Court held that the press should normally be entitled to rely on the contents of such a report when contributing to matters of public debate. Otherwise, 'the vital public watchdog role of the press would be undermined'.[417]

4.177   There are, further, limits to freedom of the press in respect of the judiciary. Whilst the press has a duty to impart information and ideas concerning matters that come before the courts,[418] the Strasbourg Court has emphasised that the courts must enjoy public confidence, and that therefore they must be protected from unfounded 'destructive attacks ... especially in view of the fact that judges are subject to a duty of discretion that precludes them from replying to criticism'.[419] It has accordingly upheld findings of defamation where judges have been criticised,[420] as well as measures taken in respect of contempt of court.[421]

Injunctions

4.178 Whilst Article 10 does not prohibit the use of injunctions to prevent publication, the Strasbourg Court applies 'the most careful scrutiny' to such restraints.[422] On occasion, it has been prepared to protect expression in circumstances where the English courts have not. The *Sunday Times*[423] case concerned articles published in the course of proceedings concerning the drug thalidomide. The purported aim of the articles was to assist the parents of victims to obtain a more generous settlement. The Attorney General had obtained an injunction against publication (on grounds of contempt of court)

---

416 (2000) 29 EHRR 125, para 65.

417 *Ibid*, para 68.

418 *Sunday Times v United Kingdom* (1979–80) 2 EHRR 245, para 65.

419 *De Haes and Gijsels v Belgium* (1998) 25 EHRR 1, para 37.

420 *Barfod v Denmark* (1991) 13 EHRR 493; *Prager and Oberschlick v Austria* (1996) 21 EHRR 1; *De Haes and Gijsels v Belgium* (1998) 25 EHRR 1, para 37. Contrast *Ezelin v France* (1992) 14 EHRR 362.

421 *Worm v Austria* (1998) 25 EHRR 454; *Hodgson v United Kingdom* (1987) 51 DR 136; *C Ltd v United Kingdom* (1989) 61 DR 285; although see *Sunday Times v United Kingdom* (1979–80) 2 EHRR 245.

422 *Observer and Guardian v United Kingdom* (1992) 14 EHRR 153, para 60.

423 *Sunday Times v United Kingdom* (1979–80) 2 EHRR 245.

which had been quashed by the Court of Appeal and restored by the House of Lords. The Strasbourg Court held that the restriction was neither proportionate to a legitimate aim nor necessary in a democratic society.[424]

4.179   The terms of such an injunction are critical to whether it can be justified. In the *Open Door Counselling*[425] case, the Court found that an injunction which prevented clinics which counselled pregnant women from imparting information about abortion facilities outside Ireland breached Article 10. The Court held that the absolute and 'perpetual' nature of the injunction was enough to render the restriction over-broad and disproportionate.[426]

4.180   Further, once the information for which protection is sought is in the public domain, or has ceased to be confidential, the justification for such a measure may no longer suffice.[427]

4.181 Where commercial speech is in issue the Court has been less vigilant. In *Markt Intern Verlag GmbH v Germany*,[428] it upheld an injunction granted to prevent a retail newsletter from criticising the practices of a mail order firm.

Broadcasting

4.182 Article 10(1) expressly permits the licensing of broadcasting,[429] television or cinema enterprises. The purpose of this provision is to make clear that states are permitted to regulate the way in which broadcasting is organised, particularly in its technical aspects.[430] This does not, however, mean that licensing measures are free of the requirements of Article 10(2).[431] The Court has accordingly intervened where it considers licensing regimes to be over-restrictive[432] or monopolistic,[433] even where such a regime is 'capable of contributing to the quality and balance of programmes'.[434]

---

424 See, similarly, *Observer and Guardian v United Kingdom* (1992) 14 EHRR 153; *Sunday Times v United Kingdom (No 2)* (1992) 14 EHRR 229 which concerned the prohibition on the publication of the book '*Spycatcher*' and *Open Door Counselling and Dublin Well Woman Centre v Ireland* (1993) 15 EHRR 244 at para 73.

425 *Open Door Counselling and the Dublin Well Woman Centre v Ireland* (1993) 15 EHRR 244.

426 (1993) 15 EHRR 244, para 73.

427 *Ibid*, para 76; *Vereniging Weekblad Bluf! v Netherlands* (1995) 20 EHRR 189, para 44.

428 (1990) 12 EHRR 161.

429 This includes programmes broadcast over the air and cable transmission: *Groppera Radio AG v Switzerland* (1990) 12 EHRR 321, para 55. Reception of programmes by a satellite dish is also protected: *Autronic AG v Switzerland* (1990) 12 EHRR 485, para 47.

430 *Groppera Radio AG v Switzerland* (1990) 12 EHRR 321, para 61.

431 *Ibid*.

432 Eg, *Autronic AG v Switzerland* (1990) 12 EHRR 485.

433 *Radio ABC v Austria* (1998) 25 EHRR 185.

434 *Informatsverein Lentia v Austria* (1994) 17 EHRR 93, para 37.

4.183   Article 10 also applies to the means of reception of broadcast material. In *Autronic AG v Switzerland*,[435] the Court held that a refusal to allow a company to receive television materials from a satellite breached Article 10.

4.184   The substance of broadcast material may also engage Article 10 rights. In *Jersild v Denmark*,[436] the Court found a violation were journalists were prosecuted for reporting racist remarks. In the *Brind*[437] litigation, the Commission found a ban on broadcasting the voices of members of Sinn Fein struck a fair balance.

ARTICLE 11: FREEDOM OF ASSEMBLY AND ASSOCIATION

4.185 Article 11 provides:

(1) Everyone has the right to freedom of peaceful assembly and to freedom of association with others, including the right to form and join trade unions for the protection of his interests.

(2) No restrictions shall be placed on the exercise of these rights other than such are prescribed by law and are necessary in a democratic society in the interests of national security or public safety, for the protection of disorder or crime, for the protection of health or morals or for the protection of the rights and freedoms of others. This article shall not prevent the imposition of lawful restrictions on the exercise of those rights by members of the armed forces, or of the police or of the administration of the state.

4.186 Article 11 contains two distinct rights: of freedom of assembly, and of freedom of association.

Freedom of assembly

4.187 Freedom of assembly is protected by Article 11(1) provided it is 'peaceful'. The freedom to take part in a peaceful assembly 'is of such importance that it cannot be restricted in any way'.[438] There are positive duties upon the state to protect this freedom. In *Platform 'Artze für das Leben' v Austria*,[439] the applicants complained that anti-abortion demonstrations had been disrupted by counter-demonstrators. The Court held whilst there was a positive obligation upon the state to take reasonable and appropriate measures, it could not be required to

---

435 (1990) 12 EHRR 485. Cf, however, *Groppera Radio AG v Switzerland* (1990) 12 EHRR 321.

436 (1995) 19 EHRR 1. For cases concerning the prevention, or postponement of broadcasts, see *Hodgson v United Kingdom* (1987) 51 DR 136 (postponement under s 4(2) of the Contempt of Court Act 1981); *C Ltd v United Kingdom* (1989) 61 DR 285.

437 *R v Secretary of State for the Home Department ex p Brind* [1991] AC; *Brind v United Kingdom* (1994) 77 DR 42. See, also, *Purcell v Ireland* (1991) 70 DR 262.

438 *Ezelin v France* (1992) 14 EHRR 362, para 53.

439 (1991) 13 EHRR 204, para 30.

guarantee that those measures would succeed.[440] Even a general ban on all public processions may be justified, however, 'if there is a real danger of their resulting in disorder which cannot be prevented by other less stringent measures'.[441]

4.188   Article 11 protection can extend beyond the act of assembly itself, to consequences of it. In *Ezelin v France*,[442] the applicant lawyer had demonstrated against two court judgments. The Court held that the subsequent imposition of a fine breached Article 11.

Freedom of association

4.189 Although trade unions are expressly mentioned in Article 11, this is only 'one example among others of the form in which the right to freedom of association may be exercised'.[443] A religious group may also fall within the scope of this provision.[444] In *Le Compte, Van Leuven and De Meyere v Belgium*,[445] the Court held, however, that a professional association founded by the legislature which exercised 'public control over the practice of medicine' did not fall within Article 11.

4.190   Just as with freedom of assembly, there are positive obligations inherent in freedom of association. Thus, Article 11 extends to the regulation of the activities of private employers. In *Young, James and Webster v United Kingdom*,[446] the applicant railway workers complained they had lost their jobs when they refused to join a trade union after a 'closed shop' agreement had been reached with British Rail. At that time, British Rail was publicly owned. The Strasbourg Court stated, however, that it need not determine whether the state was responsible on the grounds that it was the employer, or that British Rail was under its control: it was the domestic law in force at the time that made lawful the treatment of which they complained. The Court has since confirmed that in certain circumstances, Article 11 may oblige the state to intervene in relationships between private individuals,[447] and has considered complaints in respect of the activities of unions in a private workplace.[448]

---

440 Participation in a demonstration may also amount to the expression of opinion, and fall to be protected by Art 10: *Steel and Others v United Kingdom* (1999) 28 EHRR 603.

441 *Christians Against Racism and Fascism v United Kingdom* (1980) 21 DR 138, p 150.

442 (1992) 14 EHRR 362.

443 *United Communist Party of Turkey and Others v Turkey* (1998) 26 EHRR 121, para 24.

444 *Ibid*.

445 (1982) 4 EHRR 1, paras 64–65. Cf, however, *Sigurdur A Sigurjónsson v Iceland* (1993) 16 EHRR 462: taxi drivers' association held to be an association within the meaning of Art 11 notwithstanding public law functions.

446 (1982) 4 EHRR 38.

447 *Gustafsson v Sweden* (1996) 22 EHRR 409.

448 *Sibson v United Kingdom* (1994) 17 EHRR 193; *Gustafsson v Sweden* (1996) 22 EHRR 409.

4.191   In *Young, James and Webster*, the Court was prepared to assume that Article 11 did not guarantee a right not to be compelled to join a trade union, but held that the threat of dismissal for failure to join struck at the 'very substance of the freedom guaranteed by Article 11'.[449] The Court has subsequently held that Article 11 does encompass a right of non-association.[450]

4.192   Article 11 requires the state to put into place conditions which 'permit and make possible' the 'conduct and development' of trade union activities.[451] This obligation does not, however, extend to a right to an unqualified right to strike;[452] nor does it require states to consult with trade unions,[453] or to enter into collective agreements.[454] The members of a trade union have a right that the union be heard, but Contracting States have a free choice as to how they bring about this end.[455]

4.193   There is one respect in which employees in the private sector enjoy stronger protection than some in the public sector. Article 11(2) permits interference with Article 11(1) rights not only on grounds of the kind of competing policy considerations to be found in Articles 8, 9 and 10, but also permits 'the imposition of lawful restrictions on the exercise of those rights by members of the armed forces, or of the police or of the administration of the state'. In the *GCHQ* case, the House of Lords upheld a ban on trade union membership of employees at the Government's Communications Headquarters.[456] The Commission also rejected the complaint, concluding that the restrictions imposed were 'lawful restrictions on the exercise of those rights by members ... of the administration of the state'.[457]

ARTICLE 12: RIGHT TO MARRY

4.194 Article 12 provides:

Men and women of marriageable age have the right to marry and to found a family, according to the national laws governing the exercise of this right.

---

449 (1982) 4 EHRR 38, para 55.

450 *Sigurdur A Sigurjónsson v Iceland* (1993) 16 EHRR 462, para 35. The right is, of course, not absolute.

451 *National Union of Belgian Police v Belgium* (1979–80) 1 EHRR 578, para 39.

452 *Schmidt and Dahlstrom v Sweden* (1979–80) 1 EHRR 632.

453 *Ibid*.

454 *Swedish Engine Drivers' Union v Sweden* (1979–80) 1 EHRR 617. ECHR, Art 11 does not guarantee the right not to enter into a collective agreement: *Gustafsson v Sweden* (1996) 22 EHRR 409.

455 *National Union of Belgian Police v Belgium* (1979–80) 1 EHRR 578, para 39.

456 *Council of Civil Service Unions v Minister for the Civil Service* [1985] AC 374.

457 *Council of Civil Service Unions v United Kingdom* (1988) 10 EHRR 269.

4.195 The Court has stated that the right to marriage refers to the 'traditional marriage between persons of the opposite biological sex'.[458] In *Rees v United Kingdom*,[459] it concluded that the right to marry did not extend to transsexuals. The stated justification was (at least in part) that Article 12 is mainly concerned to protect marriage as the basis of the family.[460]

4.196 Article 12 permits the regulation of the right to marry and to found a family 'according to the national laws governing the exercise of this right'. Strasbourg retains a supervisory jurisdiction over the content of those laws, however. Such limitations must not restrict or reduce the right to marry in such a way or to such an extent that its very essence is impaired.[461] In *F v Switzerland*,[462] the applicant was a three times divorced man who wished to remarry. A court had ordered that he could not do so until three years had passed since his divorce. The Strasbourg Court stated that, where divorce is allowed, the right to remarry must be without unreasonable restrictions, and a breach of Article 12 was made out. The Court has however refused to read a right to divorce into Article 12.[463]

4.197 The right to marry was relied upon successfully in a number of challenges by prisoners to UK legislation[464] which effectively prevented them from marrying by restricting marriage to certain specified places, excluding prisons.[465]

ARTICLE 13: RIGHT TO AN EFFECTIVE REMEDY

4.198 Article 13 provides:

> Everyone whose rights and freedoms are set forth in this Convention are violated shall have an effective remedy before a national authority notwithstanding that the violation has been committed by persons acting in an official capacity.

4.199 Article 13 is not amongst those rights given further effect by the Human Rights Act.[466] Parliamentary statements, however, make clear that the Government's

---

458 *Council of Civil Service Unions v United Kingdom* (1988) 10 EHRR 269, para 49.

459 (1987) 9 EHRR 56.

460 *Ibid*, para 49. See, also, to similar effect, *Cossey v United Kingdom* (1991) 13 EHRR 622, para 46. This position was recently reaffirmed by the Court in the case *Sheffield and Horsham v United Kingdom* (1999) 27 EHRR 163, paras 66–70.

461 *Rees v United Kingdom* (1987) 9 EHRR 56, para 50.

462 (1988) 10 EHRR 411.

463 *Johnston v Ireland* (1987) 9 EHRR 203.

464 Marriage Act 1949.

465 Eg, *Hamer v United Kingdom* (1979) 24 DR 5. Marriage inside prison is accordingly now permitted: Marriage Act 1983, s 1. See, also, *R v Secretary of State for the Home Department ex p Mellor* (2000) *The Times*, 5 September: artificial insemination by prisoners.

466 See HRA 1998, s 1(1).

intention was that the Human Rights Act itself would satisfy its requirements,[467] and that the domestic courts would be free to have regard to Article 13.[468]

An arguable violation

.200 Read literally, it might be thought that Article 13 only applies where a breach of another Convention right has been established, that is, where Convention rights 'are violated'. If so, it would, in a sense, be otiose. In fact, the Court has made clear that an applicant need not establish a breach of another right in order to invoke Article 13. In *Klass v Germany*,[469] the Court held that Article 13 requires that where an individual 'considers himself to have been prejudiced by a measure allegedly in breach of the Convention' he should have a remedy before a national authority to determine his claim, and if appropriate, to obtain redress. Article 13 requires an effective remedy for 'everyone who *claims* that his rights and freedoms under the Convention have been violated' (original emphasis). The Court subsequently stated that test is whether the claim is arguable;[470] this is said to be the same test as that as to whether a claim is 'manifestly ill founded' applied by the Court at the admissibility stage pursuant to Article 35(3).[471]

.201   Effectiveness does not, therefore, require that the applicant should obtain a favourable outcome.[472] Article 13 requires only that 'appropriate relief' should be available in 'meritorious cases'.[473]

The nature of a sufficient remedy

.202 Effectiveness also requires that remedy should allow 'the competent "national authority" ... to deal with the substance of the relevant Convention complaint'.[474] There have been a number of challenges to the sufficiency of judicial review invoking Article 13. This issue is considered at paras 3.26 *et seq.*

.203   Article 13 does not require that Contracting States should adopt any particular means of implementation of the Convention.[475] Contracting States

---

467 *Hansard*, HL, 3 November 1997, col 1318.

468 *Hansard*, HL, 18 November 1997, col 475; *Hansard*, HL, 20 May 1998, col 979.

469 (1979–80) 2 EHRR 214, para 64.

470 *Silver v United Kingdom* (1983) 5 EHRR 347, para 113; *Boyle and Rice v United Kingdom* (1988) 10 EHRR 425, para 52.

471 *Powell and Rayner v United Kingdom* (1990) 12 EHRR 355.

472 *Vilvarajah v United Kingdom* (1992) 14 EHRR 248, para 122

473 *Murray v United Kingdom* (1995) 19 EHRR 193, para 100.

474 *Soering v United Kingdom* (1989) 11 EHRR 439, para 120.

475 *Swedish Engine Drivers' Union v Sweden* (1979–80) 1 EHRR 617, para 50.

are afforded a margin of appreciation in conforming with their obligations under this provision.[476] It accordingly does not require that the Convention be implemented in domestic law;[477] nor does it guarantee a remedy which would allow the state's laws as such to be challenged before a national authority on grounds that they are contrary to the Convention.[478]

4.204   It is not necessary that any single remedy should satisfy Article 13.[479] The Court will 'take a comprehensive view of the whole system, as apparent shortcomings in one procedure may be remedied by safeguards available in other procedures'.[480]

4.205   The remedy provided by the state for violation of Convention rights and freedoms need not be necessarily in the form of a judicial authority.[481] If it is not, however, the powers and the guarantees which the authority which provides the remedy affords are relevant in determining whether the remedy before it is effective.[482] Some degree of enforceability is required. In *Silver v United Kingdom*,[483] for example, the applicant prisoners complained of interference with their correspondence. The Court concluded that an application to the Prison Board of Visitors did not amount to an effective remedy, as it lacked the power to enforce its conclusions. It may not, however, be necessary that the determination of the remedial authority be legally binding.[484]

4.206   Article 13 also requires independent scrutiny of the applicant's contentions.[485] In the *Silver* case, the Court concluded that the Home Secretary lacked sufficient independence to provide an effective remedy where a prisoner wished to challenge the Home Secretary's directives on prison correspondence, but the position would have been otherwise had a prisoner alleged that one of those directives was being misapplied.[486]

4.207   The scope of the obligation under Article 13 varies depending on the nature of the applicant's complaint under the Convention. Thus, in *Klass v Germany*,[487]

---

476 *Smith and Grady v United Kingdom* (2000) 29 EHRR 493, para 135.

477 *Ibid.*

478 *Leander v Sweden* (1987) 9 EHRR 433, para 77. It is therefore difficult to see how the provisions of the HRA 1998 itself could be subject to challenge under Art 13.

479 The Court takes a similar approach to Art 6(1). See para 5.42.

480 *X v United Kingdom* (1982) 4 EHRR 188, para 60; *Van Droogenbroeck v Belgium* (1982) 4 EHRR 443, para. 56.

481 *Leander v Sweden* (1987) 9 EHRR 433, para 77. In some circumstances, a judicial authority may not satisfy the requirements of Art 13: *Greek Case* (1969) 12 YB 1.

482 *Klass v Germany* (1979–80) 2 EHRR 214, para 67.

483 (1983) 5 EHRR 347, para 115.

484 Eg, *Leander v Sweden* (1987) 9 EHRR 433, para 82.

485 *Chahal v United Kingdom* (1997) 23 EHRR 413, para 151.

486 (1979–80) 5 EHRR 347, para 116. In *Khan v United Kingdom* (2000) *The Times*, 23 May, the Court held that a complaint to the Police Complaints Authority did not meet the requisite standards of independence.

487 (1979–80) 2 EHRR 214.

a case concerning secret surveillance, the Court stated that an effective remedy meant a remedy that was 'as effective as can be having regard to the restricted scope for recourse inherent in any system of surveillance'.[488]

4.208   Nevertheless, the Court has stated that the remedy required by Article 13 must be 'effective' in practice as well as in law, in particular in the sense that its exercise must not be unjustifiably hindered by the acts or omissions of the authorities of the respondent state.[489] In an appropriate case, Article 13 may require the provision of legal representation, and reasons for the decision challenged.[490]

4.209   Where an individual has an arguable claim to have been tortured.[491] In, the Court held that Article 13 imposes an obligation on states to carry out 'a thorough and effective investigation'.[492]

Article 13 and Article 6(1)

4.210 There is a degree of overlap between the requirements of Article 6(1) (the right to a fair trial) and Article 13. The Court has stated, however, that the requirements of Article 13 are less strict than those of Article 6(1).[493] Where both Article 6(1) and Article 13 apply in respect of an applicant's complaint, the Court will generally decline to consider the matter under Article 13.[494] Importantly, however, the application of Article 6(1) is not co-extensive with that of Article 13. The former applies only to a determinations of either a 'civil rights and obligation' or of a 'criminal charge'. Not all breaches of Convention rights constitute a determination of either kind. They accordingly fall outside the scope of Article 6. In those circumstances, Article 13 provides a valuable additional protection.[495]

---

488 That case concerned alleged breaches of Arts 8 and 10. In *Chahal v United Kingdom* (1997) 23 EHRR 413, paras 150–51, the applicant alleged that a decision to deport him on national security grounds exposed him to a risk of ill treatment contrary to Art 3. The Court held that the requirement of a remedy which is 'as effective as can be' was not appropriate in such a case. The notion of an effective remedy required independent scrutiny of the applicants claim that there existed substantial grounds for fearing a real risk of treatment contrary to Art 3.

489 *Aksoy v Turkey* (1997) 23 EHRR 553, para 95.

490 *Chahal v United Kingdom* (1997) 23 EHRR 413, para 154.

491 *Aydin v Turkey* (1998) 25 EHRR 251, para 103.

492 *Aksoy v Turkey* (1997) 23 EHRR 553, para 98.

493 *Airey v Ireland* (1979–80) 2 EHRR 305, para 35.

494 Eg, *Silver v United Kingdom* (1983) 5 EHRR 347, para 110.

495 See *Golder v United Kingdom* (1979–80) 1 EHRR 524, para 33.

ARTICLE 14: PROHIBITION ON DISCRIMINATION

4.211 Article 14 provides:

> The enjoyment of the rights and freedoms set forth in this Convention shall be secured without discrimination on any grounds such as sex, race, colour, language, religion, political or other opinion, national or social origin, association with a national minority, property, birth or other status.

4.212 Article 14 is not a general prohibition on discrimination. It provides only that there should be no discrimination in the 'enjoyment of' other Convention rights. As such, it has no 'independent existence'.[496] That does not entail, however, that an applicant must establish a breach of such a right to make good a claim under Article 14; if that were so, Article 14 would, in a sense, be redundant. A measure may be in conformity with all other requirements of the Convention, but still amount to a breach of Article 14.[497] As the Court stated in the *Belgian Linguistics* case:[498]

> It is as though [Article 14] formed an integral part of each of the Articles laying down rights and freedoms.[499]

4.213 There can therefore be no breach of Article 14 unless the facts of the case 'fall within the ambit' of one or more of the other substantive provisions of the Convention:[500]

> Article 14 safeguards individuals, placed in similar situations, from any discrimination in the enjoyment of the rights and freedoms set forth in those other provisions.[501]

4.214 Thus, in *Inze v Austria*,[502] the applicant complained that Austrian law had deprived him of an inheritance on the grounds of his illegitimate birth. The applicant did not complain of a breach of Article 1 of Protocol No 1 on its own. The Court found, however, that the facts fell within the ambit of that provision, and taken together with Article 14, a breach was made out.[503]

---

496 *Belgian Linguistics Case* (1979–80) 1 EHRR 252, Pt B1, para 9.

497 *Ibid.*

498 *Ibid.*

499 Cf *R v Secretary of State for Transport ex p Factortame Ltd* [1990] 2 AC 85, p 140, *per* Lord Bridge: the European Communities Act 1972, s 2(1), (4) 'has precisely the same effect as if a section were incorporated [in the domestic legislation] which in terms enacted that [its relevant provisions] were to be without prejudice to the directly enforceable Community rights of nationals of any member state of the EEC'.

500 Eg, *Rasmussen v Denmark* (1985) 7 EHRR 371, para 29.

501 *Marckx v Belgium* (1979–80) 2 EHRR 330, para 32.

502 (1988) 10 EHRR 394.

503 The Court will not, however, generally go on to consider Art 14 where a breach of one of the other Convention rights is made out: *Dudgeon v United Kingdom* (1982) 4 EHRR 149, para 67.

4.215   Importantly, Article 14 extends beyond the minimum guarantees required by the Convention. It includes all provision made by the state in areas with which the Convention is concerned.[504] Thus, in *Abdulaziz, Cabales and Balkandali v United Kingdom*,[505] where the immigration rules permitted the wives of persons settled in the United Kingdom to join their husbands (even though this was not required by the Convention), but did not permit husbands to join wives who were similarly settled, Article 8 was applicable and the question of discrimination under Article 14 arose.[506]

4.216   Where, however, the matter complained of falls outside the scope of the other substantive rights of the Convention, it does not avail an applicant to complain of discrimination.[507] That means, for example, that in the field of employment law, Community law is a far more powerful tool.[508]

4.217   Importantly, not all forms of inequality constitute discrimination within the meaning of Article 14. Such a difference in treatment may be justified:

> ... the principle of equality of treatment is violated if the distinction has no objective and reasonable justification. The existence of such a justification must be assessed in relation to the aim and effects of the measure under consideration, regard being had to the principles which normally prevail in democratic societies. A difference in treatment in the exercise of a right laid down in the Convention must not only pursue a legitimate aim: Article 14 is likewise violated when it is clearly established there is no reasonable relationship of proportionality between the means employed and the aim sought to be realised.[509]

4.218   Contracting States enjoy a margin of appreciation in assessing whether and to what extent differences in treatment may be justified, however. The extent of that margin varies according to the context.[510] In cases of sex discrimination,[511] or differences in treatment of children born in and out of wedlock[512] 'very weighty reasons' are required. Racial discrimination is also treated as especially important.[513] Where differences of treatment are

---

504 *Belgian Linguistics Case* (1979–80) 1 EHRR 252, Pt B1, para 9.

505 (1985) 7 EHRR 471, para 71.

506 See, to similar effect, *Pine Valley Developments Ltd v Ireland* (1992) 14 EHRR 319, paras 61–64 in the context of property development.

507 Discrimination might, however amount to a breach of Art 3: *East African Asians v United Kingdom* (1981) 3 EHRR 76, para 207.

508 This is not to suggest that the Convention cannot apply to relations between an employee and employer; see, especially, Art 11, and *Halford v United Kingdom* (1997) 24 EHRR 523 (Art 8).

509 *Belgian Linguistics* case (1979–80) 1 EHRR 252, Pt B1, para 10.

510 *Rasmussen v Denmark* (1985) 7 EHRR 371, para 40.

511 *Abdulaziz, Cabales and Balkandali v United Kingdom* (1985) 7 EHRR 471, para 78.

512 *Inze v Austria* (1988) 10 EHRR 394, para 41.

513 Eg, *East African Asians v United Kingdom* (1981) 3 EHRR 76, para 207.

established, the state should seek to advance some positive case justifying those differences.[514]

ARTICLE 15: DEROGATION IN TIME OF EMERGENCY

4.219 Article 15 provides:

(1) In time of war or other public emergency threatening the life of the nation any High Contracting Party may take measures derogating from its obligations under this Convention to the extent strictly required by the exigencies of the situation, provided that such measures are not inconsistent with its other obligations under international law.

(2) No derogation from Article 2, except in respect of deaths resulting from lawful acts of war, or from Articles 3, 4 (paragraph 1) and 7 shall be made under this provision.

(3) Any High Contracting Party availing himself of this right of derogation shall keep the Secretary General of the Council of Europe fully informed of the measures which it has taken and the reasons therefor. It shall also inform the Secretary General of the Council of Europe when such measures have ceased to operate and the provisions of the Convention are again being fully executed.

4.220 Article 15 permits Contracting States to derogate from certain Convention rights in time of emergency. The United Kingdom has one current derogation from Article 5(3), concerning the detention of suspected terrorists.[515]

4.221 Article 15 is not amongst the Convention rights expressly given effect to by the Human Rights Act.[516] Section 1(2) of the Human Rights Act provides, however, that those Articles which do fall within the Human Rights Act are to have effect for the purposes of the Human Rights Act subject to any designated derogation or reservation.[517]

4.222 Article 15(1) provides that a derogation is permissible only 'in time of war or other public emergency threatening the life of the nation'. This refers 'to an exceptional situation of crisis or emergency which affects the whole population and constitutes a threat to the organised life of the community of which the state is composed'.[518] The Commission has stated that such a public emergency must be actual or imminent, its effects must involve the whole nation, the continuance of the organised life of the community must be

---

514 *Pine Valley Developments Ltd v Ireland* (1992) 14 EHRR 319, para 64.

515 The derogation is set out in the HRA 1998, Sched 3, Pt I; see Appendix 1.

516 See HRA 1998, s 1(1). The provisions of the HRA 1998 which deal with the issue of derogation are considered at paras 1.102 *et seq.*

517 HRA 1998, s 1(2).

518 *Lawless v Ireland* (1979–80) 1 EHRR 15, para 28. In *Ireland v United Kingdom* (1979–80) 2 EHRR 25, the derogation at issue in fact concerned only Northern Ireland.

threatened, and the crisis or danger must be exceptional, in that the normal measures or restrictions, permitted by the Convention for the maintenance of public safety, health and order, are plainly inadequate.[519]

4.223   Where a public emergency exists, the state may only take such measures as are 'strictly required' in derogation.

4.224   Importantly, the state is, however, permitted a wide margin of appreciation[520] in determining both whether the life of the nation is threatened, and as to the nature and scope of the derogations necessary to avert it.[521] The Strasbourg Court considers that by reason of their direct and continuous contact with the pressing needs of the moment, the national authorities are in principle in a better position than the international judge to decide these questions.[522] Although the Court retains its supervisory role, it has stated that in exercising its supervision, it must give appropriate weight to such relevant factors as the nature of the rights affected by the derogation, the circumstances leading to, and the duration of, the emergency situation.[523]

4.225   Measures taken in derogation from the Convention must not be inconsistent with the state's other obligations under international law. In *Brannigan and McBride v United Kingdom*,[524] the Court considered the compatibility of the United Kingdom's derogation with Article 4 of the ICCPR which requires a public emergency which threatens the life of the nation to be officially proclaimed.[525] The Court held that a statement by the Minister to the House of Commons was 'well in keeping' with this requirement.

4.226   Article 15(2) places limits upon the rights from which a state may derogate. No derogation is permitted in respect of the right to life (save in respect of deaths resulting from lawful acts of war), the prohibition on torture, inhuman or degrading treatment or punishment, the prohibition on slavery and forced labour, and the prohibition on punishment without law.

4.227   Article 15(3) imposes procedural requirements upon the state where it seeks to derogate from a Convention right. It is required to keep the Secretary General of the Council of Europe 'fully informed of the measures it has taken and the reasons therefore'. Such notification must be given 'without delay', although a

---

519 *Greek Case* (1969) 12 YB 1, reiterated in *Brannigan and McBride v United Kingdom* (1994) 17 EHRR 539.

520 See, further, *Brannigan and McBride v United Kingdom* (1994) 17 EHRR 539.

521 *Ireland v United Kingdom* (1979–80) 2 EHRR 25, para 207. The existence of safeguards may be material: see, eg, *Aksoy v Turkey* (1997) 23 EHRR 553.

522 *Ibid*. Cf the *Greek* case (1969) 12 YB 1.

523 *Brannigan and McBride v United Kingdom* (1994) 17 EHRR 539, para 43.

524 *Ibid*.

525 The Commission has said that the Convention imposes a requirement of a 'formal and public act of derogation, such as a declaration of martial law or state of emergency': *Cyprus v Turkey* (1982) 4 EHRR 482, para 527. See, however, *Lawless v Ireland* (1979–80) 1 EHRR 15, para 47: no obligation on the Contracting State to promulgate in its territory the notice of derogation addressed to the Secretary General.

12 day delay has been held to be permissible.[526] The Court will examine of its own motion the question whether a notice of derogation satisfies Article 15(3).[527]

ARTICLE 16: RESTRICTIONS ON POLITICAL ACTIVITY OF ALIENS

4.228 Article 16 provides:

> Nothing in Articles 10, 11 and 14 shall be regarded as preventing the High Contracting Parties from imposing restrictions on the political activity of aliens.

4.229 Article 16 thus permits the state to restrict political activities of aliens which might otherwise be protected by the right to freedom of expression, freedom of thought, conscience and religion and prohibition on discrimination.[528]

4.230 The word 'alien' has been given a narrow meaning. In *Piermont v France*,[529] the applicant was a German MEP expelled from French Polynesia where she had taken part in a pro-independence and anti-nuclear demonstration. She complained (amongst other things) of a breach of Article 10. The French Government sought to rely upon Article 16. The majority of the Court held that, in view of her status as a national of a Member State of the European Union,[530] and an MEP,[531] Article 16 could not be relied upon against her.

4.231 Further provisions concerning the treatment of aliens are to be found in the Fourth and Seventh Protocols to the Convention. The United Kingdom has not ratified those Protocols.[532]

---

526 *Lawless v Ireland* (1979–80) 1 EHRR 15, para 47; *Ireland v United Kingdom* (1979–80) 2 EHRR 25, para 223.

527 *Lawless v Ireland* (1979–80) 1 EHRR 15, para 22; *Aksoy v Turkey* (1997) 23 EHRR 533, para 86.

528 On the face of it at least, Art 16 operates to exclude reliance by an alien on Art 14 whether the basis of discrimination is nationality or otherwise. See, further, *Mathieu-Mohin* and *Clerfayt v Belgium* (1988) 10 EHRR 1, para 54.

529 (1995) 20 EHRR 301.

530 The Court rejected an argument based on 'European citizenship' as the case pre-dated the introduction of the notion of European Citizenship by the Maastricht Treaty.

531 The people of the French Overseas Territories were entitled to vote in European Parliamentary Elections.

532 For an exegesis, see *op cit*, Harris, O'Boyle and Warbrick, fn 1, pp 558 *et seq*.

ARTICLE 17: PROHIBITION OF ABUSE OF RIGHTS

4.232 Article 17 provides:

> Nothing in this Convention may be interpreted as implying for any state, group or person any right to engage in any activity or perform any act aimed at the destruction of any of the rights and freedoms set forth herein or at their limitation to a greater extent than is provided for in the Convention.

4.233 Uniquely, Article 17 provides protection to both the state and the individual. The Court has stated that it purpose is to make it impossible for groups or individuals to derive from the Convention a right or engage or perform any act aimed at destroying any of its rights or freedoms.[533] In *Glimmerveen and Hagenback v Netherlands*,[534] the applicants were members of a political party which advocated an ethnically 'homogeneous population'. They complained (pursuant to Articles 10 and 3 of Protocol No 1) that they had been convicted of distributing leaflets inciting racial hatred and prohibited from standing as candidates in municipal elections. The Commission invoked Article 17, holding that its purpose was to prevent totalitarian groups from exploiting in their own interest the principles enunciated in the Convention[535] and rejected their complaints. In *KPD v Germany*,[536] the Commission held that Article 17 could justify an order which placed an outright ban on the German Communist Party.

4.234 Article 17 is, however, subject to limits. In *Lawless v Ireland*,[537] the Court held that it could not be used to justify depriving a terrorist suspect of rights under Articles 5 and 6 where he had not sought to rely upon the Convention to justify actions which were contrary to its principles. Where Article 17 may be invoked, it applies only to persons who 'threaten the democratic system of Contracting States and then only to the extent strictly proportionate to the seriousness and duration of such a threat'.[538]

---

[533] *Lawless v Ireland* (1979–80) 1 EHRR 15, para 7.

[534] (1982) 4 EHRR 260.

[535] The Court has held that Art 10 protection does not extend to certain forms of racist expression in any event: *Jersild v Denmark* (1995) 19 EHRR 1, para 35.

[536] (1957) 1 YB 222.

[537] (1979–80) 1 EHRR 15, para 7.

[538] *De Becker v Belgium* (1960) 2 YB 214; see, also, the judgment of the Court at (1979–80) 1 EHRR 43.

ARTICLE 18: LIMITATION ON USE
OF RESTRICTIONS ON RIGHTS

4.235 Article 18 provides:

> The restrictions permitted under this Convention to the said rights and freedoms shall not be applied for any purpose other than those for which they have been prescribed.

4.236 As has been seen, most Convention rights are qualified by the language of the Convention itself. Article 18 permits an applicant to contend that those derogations have been applied for an improper purpose. There can be no breach of Article 18 in isolation. A breach can only be made out in conjunction with another substantive Convention right.[539]

4.237 In practice, this provision has proven of little significance; no such allegation has ever succeeded.[540] The burden of demonstrating such an improper purpose is upon the applicant, and accordingly, such allegations have frequently failed for want of evidence.

ARTICLE 1 OF PROTOCOL NO 1:
PROTECTION OF PROPERTY

4.238 Article 1 of Protocol No 1 guarantees a right of property.[541] It provides:

> Every natural or legal person is entitled to the peaceful enjoyment of his possessions. No one shall be deprived of his possessions except in the public interest and subject to the conditions provided by the law and by the general principles of international law.
>
> The preceding provisions shall not, however, in any way impair the right of a state to enforce such laws as it deems necessary to control the use of property in accordance with the general interest or to secure the payment of taxes or other contributions or penalties.

4.239 There are, accordingly, three distinct rules contained in this provision:

> The first rule, which is of a general nature, enunciates the principle of peaceful enjoyment of property; it is set out in the first sentence of the first paragraph.

---

539 *K v France* (1993) 16 EHRR CD 23.

540 Unsuccessful attempts include *Engel v Netherlands* (1979–80) 1 EHRR 647, para 104; *Handyside v United Kingdom* (1979–80) 1 EHRR 737, para 64; *Akdivar v Turkey* (1997) 23 EHRR 143, para 99; *Mentes v Turkey* (1998) 26 EHRR 595, para 96; *Kurt v Turkey* (1999) 27 EHRR 373, para 151.

541 *Marckx v Belgium* (1979–80) 2 EHRR 330, para 63.

The second rule covers deprivation of possessions and subjects it to certain conditions; it appears in the second sentence of the same paragraph. The third rule recognises that the States are entitled, amongst other things, to control the use of property in accordance with the general interest, by enforcing such laws as they deem necessary for the purpose; it is contained in the second paragraph.

The Court must determine, before considering whether the first rule was complied with, whether the last two are applicable.[542]

4.240 The rules shall be considered in turn.

The first rule: peaceful enjoyment of possessions

4.241 'Possessions' has an autonomous Convention meaning,[543] and the concept is broad. It encompasses both corporeal and incorporeal property, such as a lease,[544] a dog,[545] a patent,[546] reputation,[547] a claim for compensation,[548] a judgment debt,[549] the right to emergency assistance under social security legislation,[550] and, possibly, a right in restitution.[551]

4.242 Not all interference with the 'peaceful enjoyment' of possessions will attract the protection of the Convention. Such interference must, however strike a 'fair balance' between the demands of the community and the victim's rights.[552]

4.243 'Deprivation of possessions' and 'control of use' are both sub-sets of interference with the peaceful enjoyment of possessions. The Court may find a breach of the first rule of Article 1 of Protocol No 1 simpliciter where the freedom to use and/or dispose of property has been interfered with, but which cannot be characterised as 'deprivation' or 'control' on use, within the terms of the second and third rules. Thus, in *Sporrong and Lönnroth v Sweden*,[553]

---

542 *Sporrong and Lönnroth v Sweden* (1983) 5 EHRR 35, para 61.

543 *Gasus Dosier-und Födertechnik GmbH v Netherlands* (1995) 20 EHRR 403, para 53.

544 *Mellacher v Austria* (1990) 12 EHRR 391.

545 *Bullock v United Kingdom* (1996) 21 EHRR CD 85.

546 *Smith Kline and French Laboratories Ltd v Netherlands* (1990) 66 DR 70.

547 *Young v Ireland* (1996) 21 EHRR CD 91: the Commission was prepared to assume that reputation fell within the scope of Art 1 of Protocol No 1, without deciding the point.

548 *Pressos Campania Naviera SA v Belgium* (1996) 21 EHRR 301. In that case, the applicants had a mere 'claim for damages which could have been asserted in domestic law' save for the fact that legislation had retrospectively removed their right to do so: para 34. A more stringent test was, however, stated in *Stran Greek Refineries v Greece* (1995) 19 EHRR 293, where the Court held that an arbitration award could amount to a possession: it was 'sufficiently established to be enforceable', as, amongst other things, the judgment was final and binding: paras 59–62.

549 *Ibid*.

550 *Gaygasuz v Austria* (1997) 23 EHRR 364, para 41.

551 *National and Provincial Building Society v United Kingdom* (1998) 25 EHRR 127. The Court proceeded on the assumption that such a right could constitute a possession, but did not express a concluded view: see para 67.

552 *Sporrong and Lönnroth v Sweden* (1983) 5 EHRR 35, para 69.

553 *Ibid*. See, also, *Matos e Silva, Lda v Portugal* (1997) 24 EHRR 573.

'expropriation permits' which authorised the expropriation of the applicants' land but which were never acted upon were held to amount to unlawful interference. Although the permits left the owners' right to use and dispose of their possessions intact in law, they nevertheless in practice significantly reduced the possibility of its exercise.[554] In *Erkner and Hofauer v Austria*,[555] a provisional transfer of land was held to be 'interference' but not deprivation, or control on use.

The second rule: deprivation of possessions

4.244 'Deprivation' is 'the most radical kind of interference with the right of peaceful enjoyment of property'.[556] It has been held to extend to nationalisation of the applicants' assets by the British government,[557] and measures under which monastic land was 'deemed' to be the property of the state.[558] Deprivation may, however, be 'de facto' rather than 'formal' where no legal change of ownership occurs.[559] In *Papamichalopoulos v Greece*,[560] the Court held that de facto appropriation had taken place where a naval base and holiday resort for naval officers had been built on the the applicants' land.

4.245   Deprivation of possessions can only be justified if it is (a) in the public interest; (b) subject to conditions provided by law; and (c) subject to the general principles of international law. These conditions will be considered in turn.

(a) The public interest

4.246 The state is accorded a wide margin of appreciation in determining what is in the public interest. The Court has stated that it would respect the legislature's judgment as to what is 'in the public interest' unless that judgment was manifestly without reasonable foundation: it would not substitute its own assessment.[561] In *James v United Kingdom*,[562] the applicants challenged legislation[563] which had permitted tenants to acquire freeholds, or extended leases. The Court accepted that this amounted to deprivation of the landlord's possessions. Had the transfer of property had been simply for the benefit of a

---

554 See, also, *Matos e Silva, Lda v Portugal* (1997) 24 EHRR 573.

555 (1987) 9 EHRR 464.

556 *James v United Kingdom* (1986) 8 EHRR 123, para 71.

557 *Lithgow v United Kingdom* (1986) 8 EHRR 329.

558 *Holy Monasteries v Greece* (1995) 20 EHRR 1.

559 *Sporrong and Lönnroth v Sweden* (1983) 5 EHRR 35, para 63.

560 (1993) 16 EHRR 440.

561 *James v United Kingdom* (1986) 8 EHRR 123, para 49.

562 *Ibid*.

563 Leasehold Reform Act 1967.

private party, it could not have been in the public interest. If, however, property was taken in pursuance of 'legitimate social, economic or other policies' that could be in the public interest. The aim of the UK legislation was to eliminate social injustice: this could not be characterised as manifestly unreasonable.[564]

4.247 In determining whether a fair balance has been struck, the Court will consider whether alternative solutions are available, although this the mere existence of such an alternative will not render the state's action unjustified.[565] The availability of compensation for such deprivation of property is also likely to be an important element in this equation. It is not an absolute requirement, but deprivation of property in the absence of compensation 'reasonably related' to its value will normally amount to a disproportionate interference with that property.[566] The state is permitted a margin of appreciation in assessing compensation. Legitimate objectives of 'public interest' may call for less than reimbursement of the full market value of the property.[567] The Court has said it will not interfere unless the legislature's judgment unless it was shown to be manifestly without foundation.[568]

(b) Subject to the conditions provided by the law

4.248 Deprivation of property must be in accordance with national law. This requires not only compliance with national law, but also embodies requirements as to the nature of that law. It requires conformity with the rule of law, and an absence of arbitrariness.[569] In *Hentrich v France*,[570] the Court considered the right held by the Revenue to exercise a right of pre-emption over property where it considered the sale price to be too low. It held that the objective – to prevent tax evasion – was legitimate. A breach of the requirement of lawfulness was made out, however, because it the right of pre-emption was exercised 'arbitrarily and selectively'. As such, the French law did not satisfy the Convention requirements of precision and foreseeability.[571]

---

564 *James v United Kingdom* (1986) 8 EHRR 123, para 49.

565 *Ibid*, para 51.

566 *Ibid*, para 54. The failure to pay compensation timeously may so alter the balance between public interest and private rights as to give rise to a breach: *Guillemin v France* (1998) 25 EHRR 435.

567 *James v United Kingdom* (1986) 8 EHRR 123, para 49. See, eg, *Lithgow v United Kingdom* (1986) 8 EHRR 329, para 121.

568 *Ibid*, para 122.

569 *James v United Kingdom* (1986) 8 EHRR 123, para 67; see, further, paras 3.62 *et seq*.

570 *Hentrich v France* (1994) 18 EHRR 440.

571 The Court also criticised the absence of any opportunity to test the issue of underestimation of the price in adversarial proceedings which complied with the principle of equality of arms.

(c) The general principles of international law

4.249 The relevant principle of international law is the requirement that a state pay prompt, adequate and effective compensation where it expropriates the property of foreigners. The Court has declined to extend the protection of this principle to nationals: it has stated that this provision was included in the Convention to enable non-nationals use the Convention to enforce this right without recourse to diplomatic channels, and also to prevent argument that Protocol No 1 had somehow served to cut down this right.[572] In any event, as has already been seen, in most cases, some compensation will be required if deprivation of property from nationals is to be considered proportionate.

The third rule: control of the use of property

4.250 The third rule concerns the 'control [of] the use of property in accordance with the general interest, by enforcing such laws as they deem necessary for the purpose'.[573] Whilst 'control of use' may involve deprivation of property as a constituent element,[574] interference with property falling short of a 'deprivation' may still amount to a 'control'. Rent control legislation,[575] and legislation which suspended residential evictions have been held to be controls on use,[576] as has a prohibition on building on land.[577] Where interference is temporary, without transfer of ownership, that may constitute a control, rather than deprivation.[578] The line between the two is a fine one: sequestration of a flat for breach of planning control was held to be 'control' on grounds that the measure was not designed to deprive the applicant of his property, but only to prevent him from using it.[579] Seizure by customs officers of prohibited goods was held to be a consequence of the prohibition on their importation, and accordingly a measure intended to control their use.[580]

4.251 Control of the use of property is permitted to the extent that it is deemed lawful[581] by the state as necessary either in accordance with the general interest, or to secure the payment of taxes, contributions or penalties.

---

572 *James v United Kingdom* (1986) 8 EHRR 123, para 62, re-affirmed in *Lithgow v United Kingdom* (1986) 8 EHRR 329, para 115.

573 *Sporrong and Lönnroth v Sweden* (1983) 5 EHRR 35, para 61.

574 *AGOSI v United Kingdom* (1987) 9 EHRR 1, para 51.

575 *Mellacher v Austria* (1990) 12 EHRR 391.

576 *Spadea and Scalbrino v Italy* (1996) 21 EHRR 482.

577 *Sporrong and Lönnroth v Sweden* (1983) 5 EHRR 35.

578 *Air Canada v United Kingdom* (1995) 20 EHRR 150, para 33.

579 *Venditelli v Italy* (1995) 19 EHRR 464, para 38.

580 *AGOSI v United Kingdom* (1987) 9 EHRR 1.

581 Eg, *Allan Jacobsson v Sweden* (1990) 12 EHRR 56, para 57. This requirement is discussed at paras 3.62 *et seq*.

(a) The general interest

4.252 The question for the Court is whether there is a reasonable relationship of proportionality, as between the rights of individuals and the general interest.[582] The Court is prepared to take account of a wide range of interests, including, for example, in *Chassagnou v France*,[583] the desire to 'avoid unregulated hunting and encourage the rational management of game stocks'.

4.253 The Court has repeatedly emphasised that in this area, the state enjoys a wide margin of appreciation, both as to the means used by the state to attain its policy objectives, and as to ascertaining whether the consequences are justified in the general interest for the purpose of achieving the object of the law in question.[584] In appropriate case, however, the Court is prepared to find the margin to have been exceeded. In *Chassagnou v France*,[585] it held that found that the compulsory transfer of hunting rights was disproportionate to the legitimate aims pursued (see para 4.232).

4.254 The Court has considered and rejected two challenges to the adequacy of judicial review for the purposes of the second paragraph of Article 1 of Protocol No 1. In *AGOSI v United Kingdom*[586] and *Air Canada v United Kingdom*,[587] the applicants argued that *Wednesbury* judicial review provided insufficient legal safeguards against the exercise of the power of seizure of goods by Customs and Excise. The Court rejected these contentions and concluded that a fair balance had been struck.

(b) Taxes, contributions and penalties

4.255 The wording of Article 1 of Protocol No 1 suggests that taxes, contributions and penalties are all excluded from its protection, provided the laws at issue are deemed necessary by the state. The court has, however, stated that all of Article 1 of Protocol No 1 must be read in the light of its first sentence. Thus, the state must refrain from arbitrary confiscation, and, in addition, it must achieve a fair balance between the demands of the general interest of the community and the requirements of the protection of the individual's fundamental rights.[588] The Court has however stated it will respect the

---

582 *AGOSI v United Kingdom* (1987) 9 EHRR 1, para 52. In *James v United Kingdom* (1986) 8 EHRR 123, para 43, the applicants contended that 'general interest' was broader than where 'deprivation' rather than 'control' had occurred: the Convention granted the state more latitude to control the use of someone's property than it did to deprive him of it. The Court declined to decide the point.

583 (2000) 29 EHRR 615, para 79.

584 *AGOSI v United Kingdom* (1987) 9 EHRR 1, para 52.

585 (2000) 29 EHRR 615, para 85.

586 (1987) 9 EHRR 1.

587 (1995) 20 EHRR 150.

588 *Gasus Dosier-und Fördertechnik GmbH v Netherlands* (1995) 20 EHRR 403, paras 59, 62.

legislature's assessment of such matters unless it is devoid of reasonable foundation.[589]

Application

4.256 The following examples illustrate how Article 1 of Protocol No 1 has been invoked in practice.

Planning

4.257 The Court is reluctant to intervene in planning cases. The Contracting States enjoy a wide margin of appreciation in this area.[590] Where, however, planning decisions lead to long periods of uncertainty as to the fate of land, the Court has found a contravention.[591]

4.258 Where planning permission is granted, and later quashed, this can give rise to breach of Article 1 of Protocol No 1. In this context, the Court uses the language of legitimate expectations, and even estoppel.[592] Breach of legitimate expectations will not, however, invariably constitute a breach of Convention rights. In *Pine Valley Developments Ltd v Ireland*,[593] the applicants purchased land which had outline planning permission. That permission was later held to have been a nullity *ab initio* by the Irish Supreme Court. The Strasbourg Court held that the (effective) withdrawal of planning permission constituted a 'control' of property, and a breach of legitimate expectations, but was a proportionate means by which to preserve the green belt.

Housing

4.259 Article 1 of Protocol No 1 is of limited relevance in housing litigation. There is no positive right to housing under this provision. The wide margin of appreciation which exists where social policy considerations come into play further diminishes its significance.[594] Attempts have, however, been made to contest the legality housing legislation in reliance upon Article 1 of Protocol

---

589 (1995) 20 EHRR 403, para 60.

590 *Sporrong and Lönnroth v Sweden* (1983) 5 EHRR 35, para 69.

591 See *Sporrong and Lönnroth v Sweden* (1983) 5 EHRR 35; *Matos e Silva, Lda v Portugal* (1997) 24 EHRR 573; *Venditelli v Italy* (1995) 19 EHRR 464; *Guillemin v France* (1998) 25 EHRR 435.

592 Eg, *Pine Valley Developments Ltd v Ireland* (1992) 14 EHRR 319, para 51.

593 *Ibid*. See, also, *Guillemin v France* (1998) 25 EHRR 435.

594 ECHR, Art 8 may prove of relevance; see *R v North and East Devon Area Health Authority ex p Coughlan* [2000] 2 WLR 622; *Howard v United Kingdom* (1987) 52 DR 198.

No 1. In *Spadea and Scalbrino v Italy*,[595] for example, the applicants sought to evict the tenants of two adjacent residential flats which they had bought for their own occupation. Possession proceedings were suspended by a succession of legislative decrees. The Court rejected the complaint. It held that the aim of the legislation, to deal with the large number of leases which expired in the relevant period and thereby protect tenants on low incomes and avoid any risk to public order, was legitimate, and the measures adopted, proportionate.

Revenue

4.260 Article 1 of Protocol No 1 expressly permits the state to enforce laws 'to secure the payment of taxes or other contributions', although such measures are subject to some degree of supervision by Strasbourg as set out above (at para 4.255). As a result, it is difficult to challenge such provisions under the Convention.[596] Applicants have, however, successfully invoked the prohibition of discrimination under Article 14 in combination with Article 1 of Protocol No 1: revenue raising measures which are otherwise unimpeachable may contravene the Convention if their effect is discriminatory. The applicant in *Darby v Sweden*[597] was a Finn who worked in Sweden, but was not a permanent resident. He was subject to a tax to the Lutheran Church of Sweden. He could not claim any reduction in this tax unless he was formally registered as resident in Sweden. The Court found the measure had no legitimate aim and that there had been a breach of Article 1 of Protocol No 1 taken together with Article 14.

4.261 Retrospective legislation may infringe the Convention,[598] but, perhaps surprisingly, will not always do so. In *National and Provincial Building Society v United Kingdom*,[599] retrospective legislation was enacted to cure a defect in revenue-raising regulations which had been found by the House of Lords to be *ultra vires*.[600] The Strasbourg Court held that the actions taken by Parliament fell within its margin of appreciation and struck a fair balance; in enacting the retrospective legislation, Parliament was concerned only to reassert its original

---

595 (1996) 21 EHRR 482. See, also, *Mellacher v Austria* (1990) 12 EHRR 391.

596 In a case concerning a challenge to the method of calculating income tax, the Commission held that such regulations should not generally be considered incompatible with Art 1 of Protocol No 1 except where – apart from measures to counter avoidance or fraud – it amounted to *de facto* confiscation of some part of the tax payers' possessions: *X v France* (1983) 32 DR 266.

597 *Darby v Sweden* (1991) 13 EHRR 774. See, also, *Lindsay v United Kingdom* (1986) 49 DR 181.

598 See *Pressos Campania Naviera SA v Belgium* (1996) 21 EHRR 301.

599 *National and Provincial Building Society v United Kingdom* (1998) 25 EHRR 127.

600 *R v Inland Revenue Commissioners ex p Woolwich Equitable Building Society* [1990] 1 WLR 1400, HL.

intention, which had been 'stymied' by the House of Lords by a finding that the regulations were *ultra vires* on 'technical grounds'.[601]

4.262   As has already been seen, the Court has considered applications based upon the seizure of goods by Customs and Excise as a 'control' on the use of property.[602] Even wide ranging powers of this kind may be held to be lawful. In *Air Canada v United Kingdom*,[603] Customs officers seized the applicant's aircraft after finding cannabis on board. The aircraft was returned the next day on payment of a penalty of £50,000. According to the Government, there had been previous occasions when the applicant's procedures had led to the carriage of dangerous drugs; despite promises to improve its procedures, it had failed to do so. The Court found that, whilst the width of the relevant powers was 'striking',[604] the seizure of the aircraft and its release subject to payment were exceptional measures designed to bring about an improvement in the applicant's security procedures, and that a fair balance had been achieved.

Property and Article 6

4.263 Article 6 has been frequently invoked in tandem with Article 1 of the First Protocol. Disputes over property rights fall within the scope of 'civil rights and obligations';[605] penal revenue measures may amount to criminal proceedings.[606] It is frequently contended that protracted litigation over property rights amounts to a breach of Article 6.[607]

ARTICLE 2 OF PROTOCOL NO 1:
RIGHT TO EDUCATION

4.264 Article 2 of Protocol No 1 provides:

> No person shall be denied the right to education. In the exercise of any function which it assumes in relation to education and to teaching, the state shall respect the right of parents to ensure such education and teaching in conformity with their own religious and philosophical convictions.

---

601 (1998) 25 EHRR 127, para 81.

602 *AGOSI v United Kingdom* (1987) 9 EHRR 1, discussed above at para 4.254.

603 *Air Canada v United Kingdom* (1995) 20 EHRR 150.

604 *Ibid*, para 41.

605 *Sporrong and Lönnroth v Sweden* (1983) 5 EHRR 35. See, further, para 4.243.

606 *Bendenoun v France* (1994) 18 EHRR 54.

607 Eg, *Venditelli v Italy* (1995) 19 EHRR 464; *Guillemin v France* (1998) 25 EHRR 435; *Matos e Silva, Lda v Portugal* (1997) 24 EHRR 573 EHRR 435. Other forms of breach of Art 6(1) have been alleged: eg, *Stran Greek Refineries v Greece* (1995) 19 EHRR 293; *Beaumartin v France* (1995) 19 EHRR 485.

Denial of the right to education

4.265 The Court has stated that the first sentence of this provision 'enshrines the right of everyone to education'.[608] The right is, however, couched in negative terms: 'no person shall be denied the right to education'. This drafting has affected the Court's view of its scope. In the *Belgian Linguistics Case*,[609] it held that in view of its negative formulation, Article 2 of Protocol No 1 does not protect such a right to education as would require a state to establish, or subsidise education of any particular type, or at any particular level. There is therefore no right, for example to education in a single sex, or selective school.[610] It has, however, been held to extend to a right of access to the educational institutions in existence at that time.[611] There is a corresponding right to official recognition of studies successfully completed by a student.[612]

4.266 Article 2 of Protocol No 1 may not apply to all types of education. The Commission has said that this provision is primarily concerned with elementary education,[613] although applications have been admitted concerning higher education.[614]

The rights of parents

4.267 The second sentence of Article 2 of Protocol No 1 provides that 'in the exercise of any function which it assumes in relation to education and to teaching, the state shall respect the right of parents to ensure such education and teaching in conformity with their own religious and philosophical convictions'. Not all beliefs fall within the scope of this provision. In *Campbell and Cosans v United Kingdom*,[615] the Court stated that the word 'convictions' is not synonymous with the words 'opinions' or 'ideas' as used in Article 10. It is more akin to the term 'belief' appearing in Article 9, and 'denotes views that attain a certain level of cogency, seriousness, cohesion and importance'. Philosophical convictions are 'such convictions as are worthy of respect in a "democratic society" and are not incompatible with human dignity'.[616] In that case, the Court accepted that an objection to corporal punishment fell within the protection of Article 2 of Protocol No 1; the existence of corporal punishment

---

608 *Kjeldsen, Busk Madsen and Pederson v Denmark* (1970–80) 1 EHRR 711, para 50.
609 *Belgian Linguistics Case* (1979–80) 1 EHRR 252, para B3.
610 *W and DM v United Kingdom* (1989) 37 DR 96.
611 In the case of higher education, a state is permitted to restrict admission to those capable of deriving benefit: *X v United Kingdom* (1980) 23 DR 228.
612 *Belgian Linguistics Case* (1979–80) 1 EHRR 252, para B3.
613 *X v United Kingdom* (1975) 2 DR 50.
614 Eg, *X v United Kingdom* (1980) 23 DR 228.
615 (1982) 4 EHRR 293.
616 *Ibid*, para 36.

at schools attended by the applicants' children violated those rights.[617] By contrast, in the *Belgian Linguistics Case*,[618] the Court stated that it should not be taken to extend to linguistic, or cultural matters, even if they formed part of the 'personalist philosophy' of the applicants.

4.268   The word 'respect' in the second sentence of Article 2 of Protocol No 1 implies some positive obligation on the part of the state.[619] In *Campbell and Cosans*,[620] the Court held that the gradual elimination of corporal punishment was not sufficient to discharge this obligation.[621]

4.269   The Court has stated that the protection provided by Article 2 of Protocol No 1 extends to all functions that the state undertakes in respect of education and teaching, throughout the entire state educational programme.[622] Not all education in apparent conflict with the protected interests of parents will however, give rise to a violation. A Danish law which made sex education compulsory in schools for children between the ages of nine and 11 was unsuccessfully challenged.[623] The Court held that the second sentence of Article 2 of Protocol No 1 aimed at safeguarding pluralism in education. The setting and planning of the curriculum fell in principle within the competence of the Contracting States. Article 2 of Protocol No 1 did not prevent states from imparting through teaching information of a directly or indirectly religious or philosophical kind, provided it is conveyed in an 'objective, critical and pluralistic manner', and not in an attempt to indoctrinate students with a particular moral perspective.[624]

4.270   In the Danish case, the Court held it was material that the state granted assistance to private schools.[625] States are not, however, obliged to subsidise a particular form of education to respect the religious and philosophical convictions of parents. It is sufficient for the state to permit parents to educate their children at home,[626] or to allow the establishment of private schools.[627]

---

617 Corporal punishment is further considered under Art 3: see, para 4.48. It has also been alleged contended, unsuccessfully, that corporal punishment breaches Art 8: *Y v United Kingdom* (1994) 17 EHRR 238; *Costello-Roberts v United Kingdom* (1995) 19 EHRR 112.

618 (1979–80) 1 EHRR 252.

619 *Campbell and Cosans v United Kingdom* (1982) 4 EHRR 293, para 37.

620 *Ibid.*

621 *Ibid.*

622 *Kjelsden, Busk Madsen and Pedersen v Denmark* (1979–80) 1 EHRR 711, paras 50, 51.

623 *Ibid.*

624 See, also, *Valsamis v Greece* (1997) 24 EHRR 294: unsuccessful complaint that the applicants' daughter had been suspended from school for refusing to participate in a parade with 'military overtones'.

625 *Kjelsden, Busk Madsen and Pedersen v Denmark* (1979–80) 1 EHRR 711, para 50.

626 *X v United Kingdom* (1978) 14 DR 179.

627 *W and KL v Sweden* (1985) 45 DR 143. Where there are private schools, the state can in principle be liable for their acts: *Costello-Roberts v United Kingdom* (1995) 19 EHRR 112.

Education and resources

4.271 Much domestic judicial review in the area of education is ultimately driven by questions of resource allocation.[628] Article 2 of Protocol No 1 is of little value in this respect. The Court has made clear that a state is entitled to take the 'needs and resources of the community into account'.[629] The matter is any event put beyond doubt as the United Kingdom made a reservation[630] dealing expressly with the issue of educational resources. It states that the United Kingdom accepts the second sentence of Article 2 of Protocol No 1:

> ... only so far as it is compatible with the provision of efficient instruction and training and the avoidance of unreasonable public expenditure.[631]

4.272 The reservation is accordingly in broadly the same vein[632] as (what is now) s 9 of the Education Act 1996.[633]

4.273   The Commission has repeatedly rejected attempts by parents to challenge the naming of a particular in a statement of special educational needs. Although the authorities must place weight on parents' and pupils' views, a wide measure of discretion is left to the authorities as to how to make use of the resources available to them in the interests of children generally. Thus, it could not be said that the Convention required that an English local authority place a child with special educational needs in a private specialised school where a place was available in an ordinary state school with special facilities.[634]

4.274   The United Kingdom's reservation is however subject to some limits. In *Campbell and Cosans v United Kingdom*,[635] the applicants objected to the use of corporal punishment in schools. The Government contended that it could only meet this objection by setting up a dual system of schools, with and without corporal punishment. That would amount to unreasonable expenditure and was accordingly precluded by the reservation. The Court rejected this argument: there were other solutions which would be less expensive.

---

628 See, in particular, *R v East Sussex County Council ex p Tandy* [1998] AC 714.

629 *Belgian Linguistics Case* (1979–80) 1 EHRR 252.

630 ECHR, Art 57(1) provides: 'Any State may, when signing this Convention or when depositing its instrument of ratification, make a reservation in respect of any particular provision of the Convention to the extent that any law then in force in its territory is not in conformity with the provision. Reservations of a general character are not permitted under this Article.' See, further, *Belilos v Switzerland* (1988) 10 EHRR 466, and ss 15–17 of the HRA 1998 (see paras 1.104 *et seq*).

631 This reservation is set out in full in the HRA 1998, Sched 3, Pt 2. See Appendix 1.

632 See *PD and LD v United Kingdom* (1989) 62 DR 292, p 297.

633 That section provides: '... pupils are to be educated in accordance with the wishes of their parents, so far as that is compatible with the provision of efficient instruction and training and the avoidance of unreasonable public expenditure.'

634 *Simpson v United Kingdom* (1990) 64 DR 188. See, to similar effect, *PD and LD v United Kingdom* (1989) 62 DR 292; *Graeme v United Kingdom* (1990) 64 DR 158.

635 (1982) 4 EHRR 293.

Education and negligence

4.275 In *X v Bedfordshire County Council*,[636] the House of Lords struck out claims which alleged that a local authority had negligently exercised its special educational needs functions, on grounds that it was not fair, just and reasonable to impose a duty of care in respect of these functions. The status of that decision is, however, no longer free from doubt. In *Osman v United Kingdom*,[637] the Strasbourg Court held that the right of access to a court arising under Article 6(1) was breached where the domestic courts conferred a 'blanket immunity' on the police in respect of allegations of negligence in the investigation of crime. An application to Strasbourg brought by the plaintiffs in *X v Bedfordshire*[638] has now been considered by the Commission. It held, by application of the reasoning in the *Osman* case, that a violation of Article 6(1) had occurred.[639]

4.276   The issues raised by *Osman* are considered in detail at paras 5.66 *et seq*.

ARTICLE 3 OF PROTOCOL NO 1: RIGHT TO FREE ELECTIONS

4.277 Article 3 of Protocol No 1 provides:

> The High Contracting Parties undertake to hold free elections at reasonable intervals by secret ballot, under conditions which will ensure the free expression of the opinion of the people in the choice of the legislature.

4.278 The obligations contained in this provision have been described by the Court as being of 'prime importance under the Convention system'.[640] Free elections, together with freedom of expression 'form the bedrock of any democratic system'.[641]

4.279   This provision confers rights on individuals, notwithstanding 'the inter-state colouring' of its wording.[642] Two separate rights are contained within Article 3 of Protocol No 1: the right to vote, and the right to stand for election

---

636 [1995] 2 AC 633.

637 (2000) 29 EHRR 245.

638 *Z v United Kingdom* (1999) 28 EHRR CD 65.

639 In *Phelps v Hillingdon London Borough Council* (2000) *The Times*, 28 July, the House of Lords considered a series of cases which raised questions as to the liability of a local education authority for alleged failure to provide appropriate educational services; it held that such an authority could be vicariously liable for the negligence of teachers and educational psychologists it employed, and that, in some circumstances, a direct claim could arise. The House heard argument on *Osman*, but Lord Slynn expressly stated in his speech (with which Lords Nicholls, Jauncey, Lloyd, Hutton and Millet agreed) that he did not consider that the issue raised in the *Osman* case arose.

640 *Mathieu-Mohan and Clerfayt v Belgium* (1988) 10 EHRR 1, para 47.

641 *Bowman v United Kingdom* (1998) 26 EHRR 1. That case concerned a challenged to restrictive laws on spending during elections by third parties. See para 4.170.

642 *Mathieu-Mohan and Clerfayt v Belgium* (1988) 10 EHRR 1, para 50.

to the legislature.[643] These rights are, however, not absolute, and there is a wide margin of appreciation as to the limits which may be imposed.[644] For example, limitations on the right to vote of persons living abroad may be permissible.[645] As to the right to stand for office, in *Gitonas v Greece*[646] and *Ahmed v United Kingdom*,[647] the Court upheld prohibitions upon public servants standing for elected office. Minimum age requirements for candidates have also been upheld,[648] as has the requirement that candidates provide a deposit.[649]

4.280   Article 3 of Protocol No 1 only applies to the election of the 'legislature'. Where the legislature has two or more chambers, there must be free elections to at least one.[650] 'Legislature' may extend beyond the national parliament; whether it does depends upon the constitutional arrangements in the state in question.[651] In *Matthews v United Kingdom*,[652] the Court held that the European Parliament constituted part of the legislature for the purposes of Article 3; to exclude it 'would risk undermining one of the fundamental tools with which "effective political democracy" can be maintained'.[653]

4.281   There is no right to elections under any specific electoral system, such as proportional representation, or majority voting with one or two ballots. The Court recognises that electoral systems seek to fulfill two competing objectives: '... on the one hand, to reflect fairly faithfully the opinions of the people, and on the other, to channel currents of thought so as to promote the emergence of a sufficiently clear and coherent political will.'[654] Thus, whilst there must be equality of treatment of all citizens in their right to vote and their right to stand for election, it does not follow that all votes must necessarily have equal weight as regards the outcome of the election or that all candidates must have

---

643 *Ibid*, para 51. See, also, *W, X, Y and Z v Belgium* (1975) 2 DR 110.

644 *Mathieu-Mohan and Clerfayt v Belgium* (1988) 10 EHRR 1, para 52.

645 *App No 7566/76 v United Kingdom* (1976) 9 DR 124.

646 (1998) 26 EHRR 691.

647 (2000) 29 EHRR 1.

648 *W, X, Y and Z v Belgium* (1975) 2 DR 110.

649 *Demeules v France* (1990) 67 DR 166.

650 *Mathieu-Mohan and Clerfayt v Belgium* (1988) 10 EHRR 1, para 53.

651 *Ibid*. See, eg, *Timke v Germany* (1995) 82-A DR 158: diets of German Länder held to be legislatures.

652 (1999) 28 EHRR 361. In *Tête v France* (1987) 54 DR 52, the Commission had concluded that in view of the nature of its powers, the European Parliament could not yet be considered a legislature. In *Ahmed v United Kingdom* (2000) 29 EHRR 1, para 76, the question was left open.

653 (1999) 28 EHRR 361, para 43. The implications of this case for the relationship between Convention and Community law are discussed in Chapter 7.

654 *Mathieu-Mohan and Clerfayt v Belgium* (1988) 10 EHRR 1, para 54.

equal chances of victory.[655] In *Liberal Party v United Kingdom*,[656] the Commission left open the question whether a breach of Article 3 of Protocol No 1 might arise in conjunction with the Article 14 prohibition on discrimination 'if religious or ethnic groups could never be represented because there was a clear voting patterns along these lines in the majority'.

ARTICLES 1 AND 2 OF PROTOCOL NO 6: THE DEATH PENALTY

4.282 The Sixth Protocol concerns the death penalty. Article 1 provides:

> The death penalty shall be abolished. No one shall be condemned to such a penalty or executed.

4.283 This prohibition is absolute, save only in time of war. The terms any such exception are set out in Article 2:

> A state may make provision in its law for the death penalty in respect of acts committed in time of war or of imminent threat of war; such penalty shall be applied only in the instances laid down in the law and in accordance with its provisions. The state shall communicate to the Secretary General of Europe the relevant provisions of that law.

4.284 The United Kingdom ratified the Sixth Protocol on 20 May 1999.

---

655 *Mathieu-Mohan and Clerfayt v Belgium* (1988) 10 EHRR 1, para 54. The Court accepts that a system may be suitable for one country, but not another; it 'must be assessed in the light of the political evolution of the country concerned'. See, also, *Liberal Party v United Kingdom* (1980) 21 DR 211; *Tête v France* (1987) 54 DR 52.

656 (1980) 21 DR 21.

CHAPTER 5

ARTICLE 6, JUDICIAL REVIEW
AND NATURAL JUSTICE

OVERVIEW

5.01 The common law doctrine of natural justice contains powerful principles of procedural fairness. The right to a fair trial contained in Article 6 of the ECHR substantially overlaps with those doctrines. As shall be seen, however, the protections provided by Article 6 are, in some respects at least, considerably broader than those provided by the common law. Article 6 does not, though, apply to all areas of the law which fall within the scope of the doctrine of natural justice.

5.02 Article 6 is far more than a mere overlay to natural justice. It will fundamentally affect the nature of judicial review itself, and, controversially, in some circumstances, may impact upon the substantive nature of the law.

5.03 These issues are explored below.

5.04 Article 6 provides:

(1) In the determination of his civil rights and obligations or of any criminal charge against him, everyone is entitled to a fair and public hearing, within a reasonable time by an independent and impartial tribunal established by law. Judgment shall be pronounced publicly but the press and public may be excluded from all or part in the interests of morals, public order or national security in a democratic society, where the interests of juveniles or the protection of the private life of the parties so require, or to the extent necessary in the opinion of the court in special circumstances where publicity would prejudice the interests of justice.

(2) Everyone charged with a criminal offence shall be presumed innocent until proven guilty.

(3) Everyone charged with a criminal offence has the following minimum rights:

(a) to be informed promptly, in a language he understands and in detail of the nature and cause of the allegations against him;

(b) to have adequate time and facilities for the preparation of his defence;

(c) to defend himself in person or through legal assistance of his own choosing, or if he has insufficient means, to be give legal assistance free when the interests of justice so require;

(d) to examine or have examined witnesses against him and to obtain the attendance and examination of witness on his behalf on the same conditions as witnesses against him;

(e) to have the free assistance of an interpreter if he cannot understand or speak the language used in court.

5.05 This chapter deals, first, with the application of Article 6(1) to civil and criminal cases. Secondly, the application of Articles 6(2) and (3) is considered.

APPLICATION OF ARTICLE 6(1)

5.06 Article 6(1) provides a right to a fair trial in respect of some, but not all, civil and criminal litigation. The scope of application of Article 6(1) is not straightforward, however.

Civil cases

5.07 On its face, the only part of Article 6 which applies to civil law is Article 6(1).[1] It applies only in respect of a determination of 'civil rights and obligations'. As shall be seen, however, the Strasbourg case law suggests that much domestic public law would be excluded from the scope of Article 6 protection.

Scope of 'civil rights and obligations'

5.08 In *König v Federal Republic of Germany*,[2] the Strasbourg Court stated that the term 'civil rights' in Article 6(1) has an autonomous Convention meaning. Any other solution, the Court reasoned, 'might lead to results incompatible with the object and purpose of the Convention'. The Court observed:[3]

> Whether or not a right is to be regarded as civil within the meaning of this expression in the Convention must be determined by reference to the substantive contents and effects of the right – and not its legal classification – under the domestic law of the state concerned. In the exercise of its supervisory functions, the Court must also take account of the object and purpose of the Convention and of the national legal systems of the other Contracting States.

5.09 *König* was a case concerned with whether rights which were admittedly in issue in appeal proceedings were 'civil' in character for the purposes of Article 6(1) of the ECHR. The Court's reasoning was, however, expanded upon by the European Commission in *Kaplan v United Kingdom*,[4] so as to embrace the question whether any 'rights' or 'obligations' were involved at all. The Commission concluded that similar considerations applied.

---

1   As shall be seen, in limited circumstances, Art 6(2) and Art 6(3) may apply beyond the scope of criminal law. See para 5.116.
2   (1979–80) 2 EHRR 170, para 88.
3   *Ibid*, para 89.
4   (1982) 4 EHRR 64, paras 133–34.

5.10   The Strasbourg Court has, however, consistently interpreted that this to include all 'private' rights and obligations.[5] So, too, although state designation of a 'right' or 'obligation' as 'public' rather than 'private' is not decisive, it seems clear that where the state characterises such 'right' as 'private' in character then Article 6(1) applies. In order to engage Article 6(1), an applicant need only demonstrate that the alleged right exists on arguable grounds. Thus, if the state itself recognises that the right is 'private', it appears very likely that the Court would accept that it was at least 'arguably' a civil right.

5.11   However, the Court has deliberately refrained from attempting to define the expression,[6] and has, in particular, never been prepared to make explicit the extent to which 'civil' rights and obligations extend beyond rights of a private nature.[7]

5.12   The Strasbourg case law suggests that important areas of English public law which are subject to control by 'ordinary' judicial review do not engage civil rights and obligations, and are, accordingly, outside the scope of Article 6 protection. The following have, for example, all been held by Strasbourg to fall outside its scope: immigration,[8] the categorisation of prisoners,[9] entitlement to elementary education,[10] taxes[11] and detention on remand.[12]

5.13   If, however, a determination is decisive of private rights and obligations, it will fall within the scope of Article 6.[13] The Court has held the following to be within the scope of Article 6(1): expropriation of land,[14] licensing,[15] compensation claims against public authorities,[16] disciplinary proceedings which determine the right to continue to practise a profession,[17] the right of access to a child,[18] the capacity to administer property[19] and entitlement to a pension.[20] As these examples show, the Court readily concludes that Article

---

5   *Ringeisen v Austria* (1979–80) 1 EHRR 455, para 94.

6   See, eg, *Benthem v Netherlands* (1986) 8 EHRR 1, para 35; *Feldbrugge v Netherlands* (1986) 8 EHRR 425, para 27.

7   See, eg, *König v Federal Republic of Germany* (1979–80) 2 EHRR 170, para 95; *Le Compte, Van Leuven and De Meyere v Belgium* (1982) 4 EHRR 1, para 48.

8   *Uppal v United Kingdom* (1981) 3 EHRR 391.

9   *Brady v United Kingdom* (1981) 3 EHRR 297.

10   *X v United Kingdom* (1989) 64 DR 188.

11   *Schouten v Netherlands* (1995) 19 EHRR 432. See, however, *National and Provincial Building Society and Others v United Kingdom* (1998) 25 EHRR 127.

12   *Neumeister v Austria* (1979–80) 1 EHRR 91.

13   *Ringeisen v Austria* (1979–80) 1 EHRR 455, para 94.

14   *Sporrong and Lönnroth v Sweden* (1983) 5 EHRR 35.

15   *Benthem v Netherlands* (1986) 8 EHRR 1.

16   *X v France* (1992) 14 EHRR 483.

17   *König v Federal Republic of Germany* (1979–80) 2 EHRR 170.

18   *W v United Kingdom* (1988) 10 EHRR 29

19   *Winterwerp v Netherlands* (1979–80) 2 EHRR 387.

20   *Massa v Italy* (1994) 18 EHRR 266.

6(1) is engaged where the rights at issue are pecuniary in nature, although this is not strictly a requirement.

5.14   The trend of the Strasbourg case law is, however, to broaden the scope of civil rights and obligations. The matter is powerfully illustrated by the Court's evolving approach to social security. In a series of cases, the Court held that Article 6 protection applied to disputes concerning entitlement to contributory social security benefits.[21] The Court carried out lengthy analyses of the nature of such schemes, and as to whether public or private law features were preponderant. Contributory schemes were held to be personal, economic and individual rights, with a close connection to a contract of employment and affinity with insurance.[22] These types of factors were held to outweigh public law features such as assumption of responsibility by the state, and the compulsory nature of social security contributions.[23]

5.15   The Court has now abandoned this type of analysis. In *Salesi v Italy*,[24] the Court held that a non-contributory statutory scheme fell inside the scope of Article 6 protection. In effect, this was a pure social welfare benefit. By parity of reasoning, it is difficult now to see why adjudication of disputes over (for example) health service provision or education should fall outside the scope of Article 6.

5.16   Further, in the recent case of *Aerts v Belgium*,[25] the Court held that the right to liberty to be a civil right within the meaning of Article 6(1). The Court did not provide any reasoning for this conclusion, but it is difficult to reconcile with its earlier, restrictive approach.

5.17   It is, of course, open to the court in judicial review proceedings to depart from the Strasbourg approach to the scope of the term 'civil' rights so as to encompass all non-criminal rights and obligations. Section 2 of the Human Rights Act 1998 merely requires the court to take the case law of the European Court into account[26] and there are no obvious reasons why, for example, decisions taken in the field of immigration should be excluded from the protection of Article 6(1).

'Dispute'

5.18   The French text of Article 6(1) uses the word 'contestation'. There is no counterpart in the English version. The Strasbourg Court has said, however,

---

21 See, eg, *Feldbrugge v Netherlands* (1986) 8 EHRR 425; *Deumeland v Germany* (1980) 8 EHRR 448 (industrial injury pension).

22 Eg, *Feldbrugge v Netherlands* (1986) 8 EHRR 425, paras 36–39.

23 *Ibid*, paras 31–35.

24 (1998) 26 EHRR 187, followed in *Schüler-Zgraggen v Switzerland* (1993) 16 EHRR 405.

25 (2000) 29 EHRR 50.

26 See paras 1.12 *et seq*.

that the presence of the word 'contestation' means that there must be a dispute as to civil rights and obligations before Article 6(1) is engaged.[27]

5.19   Importantly, the term is not intended to be formalistic. As the European Court observed in *Benthem v Netherlands*:[28]

> Conformity with the spirit of the Convention requires that the word 'contestation' (dispute) should not be 'construed too technically' and should be 'given a substantive rather than a formal meaning'.[29]

5.20   It is in that purposive context that the requirements for a 'dispute' within the meaning of Article 6(1) are to be applied. Those requirements, as enunciated in *Benthem*,[30] are that:

(a) The dispute may relate not only to the actual existence of a right but also to its scope or the manner in which it may be exercised.[31]

(b) Such dispute may concern questions of fact as well as questions of law.

(c) It must be genuine and of a serious nature.[32]

5.21   It follows from the fact that a dispute may relate to the existence of a right that the right itself does not have to be conclusively established before Article 6(1) is triggered. In *H v Belgium*,[33] the Court stated:

> ... Article 6(1) extends only to 'contestations' (disputes) over (civil) 'rights and obligations' which can be said, *at least on arguable grounds,* to be recognised under domestic law ...[34] [Emphasis added.]

5.22   There must, however, be a distinction between a dispute raising an arguable claim to a civil right or obligation and a dispute which raises no truly arguable claim at all and is, therefore, outwith the scope of Article 6(1). Thus, Article 6(1) does not extend to protect a challenge to an exercise of discretion which is lawful as a matter of domestic law:

> If [the applicant] accepts that the opposing party was fully entitled to act as he did, by virtue for instance of powers or rights conferred by statute or contract, then he would have no claim to bring before a court under the applicable domestic law.[35]

---

27 Of the many cases, see, eg, *H v Belgium* (1988) 10 EHRR 339, para 40.

28 (1986) 8 EHRR 1, para 32(a).

29 The phrases there cited are from *Le Compte, Van Leuven and De Meyere v Belgium* (1982) 4 EHRR 1, para 45.

30 (1986) 8 EHRR 1, para 32(b)–(c). Note, too, the further requirement that the dispute must be susceptible to judicial resolution: *Van Marle v Netherlands* (1986) 8 EHRR 183, paras 36–37.

31 See, also, *Le Compte, Van Leuven and De Meyere v Belgium* (1982) 4 EHRR 1, para 49; *Tre Traktorer Aktiebolag v Sweden* (1991) 13 EHRR 309, para 37.

32 (1988) 10 EHRR 339, para 40.

33 *Ibid.*

34 To similar effect, see, eg, *O v United Kingdom* (1988) 10 EHRR 82, para 54; *Baraona v Portugal* (1991) 13 EHRR 329, para 41; *Neves e Silva v Portugal* (1991) 13 EHRR 535, para 37; *Editions Periscope v France* (1992) 14 EHRR 597, para 35.

35 *Kaplan v United Kingdom* (1982) 4 EHRR 64, para 163.

5.23 A dispute may arise, however, if the applicant seeks to challenge the legality of the exercise of such discretion.[36]

5.24   It is by no means obvious that the domestic court would be required to apply the 'dispute' criterion. As has been seen, the requirement of a dispute is founded upon the French rather than the English test of the Convention. The Human Rights Act gives effect to the rights contained in Sched 1 to that Act, which contains the English version of the Convention.[37] Further, even the Strasbourg Court has expressed doubts about the existence of this requirement. In *Moreira de Azevedov v Portugal*,[38] the Court observed as follows:

> ... it [contestation] has no counterpart in the English text of Article 6(1).

> In so far as the French word contestation would appear to require the existence of a dispute, *if indeed it does so at all*, the facts of the case show that there was one ... [Emphasis added.]

5.25 It is respectfully suggested, however, that it is highly likely that the domestic courts will adopt the criterion. Indeed, the Court of Appeal has already invoked this requirement on two occasions, albeit without examination of the issue of its applicability under the English version of the Convention.[39] As has been seen, it serves to prevent the need to extend the protections of Article 6(1) to hopeless cases. The ability of courts to summarily dispose of such cases is to some extent under attack from another line of Strasbourg case law.[40] Further, there are suggestions in the recent case law of the Court that the requirement that a civil right should be 'arguable' (see para 5.21) may be distinct.[41] If so, the status of the 'dispute' test may be academic.

'Directly decisive'

5.26 Article 6(1) applies only to proceedings which are decisive for the civil right or obligation alleged.[42] Civil rights and obligations need not be the sole subject matter of the dispute, but must at least be one of its objects.[43] A tenuous

---

36 *Zander v Sweden* (1994) 18 EHRR 175, para 25.

37 See Appendix 1.

38 (1991) 13 EHRR 721, para 66.

39 *Lightfoot v Lord Chancellor* [2000] HRLR 33; *Monsanto plc v Tilly and Others* (1999) *The Times*, 30 November.

40 *Osman v United Kingdom* (2000) 29 EHRR 245; see paras 5.70 *et seq*.

41 Eg, *Masson and Van Zon v Netherlands* (1996) 22 EHRR 491, para 52; *Jacobsson v Sweden* (1990) 12 EHRR 56, para 69.

42 *Benthem v Netherlands* (1986) 8 EHRR 1, para 32(d); *Ringeisen v Austria* (1979–80) 1 EHRR 455, para 94.

43 *Benthem v Netherlands* (1986) 8 EHRR 1, para 32(d); *Le Compte, Van Leuven and De Meyere v Belgium*, (1982) 4 EHRR 1, para 47; *Winterwerp v Netherlands* (1979–80) 2 EHRR 387, paras 73–76.

connection or remote consequences do not suffice for Article 6(1).[44] The importance of this requirement is illustrated by the case of *R v Secretary of State for Health ex p C*.[45] The Court of Appeal held that inclusion of the applicant's name on the Consultancy Service Index (compiled by the Department of Health in respect of people about whom there were doubts as to their suitability to work with children) was not decisive of any civil right or obligation, notwithstanding the significant impact it had on the applicant's chances of obtaining employment.

Criminal cases

5.27   Article 6(1) engages in respect of a 'determination' of 'any criminal charge'. As shall be seen, although this limb of Article 6(1) extends beyond what would be classified as criminal proceedings in domestic law, not all hearings in the course of criminal proceedings fall within its scope.

5.28   Article 6 covers the whole of the proceedings whereby a criminal charge is determined, including any appeal.[45a] It does not, however, apply to proceedings following conviction, such as the classification of a prisoner;[45b] nor, save exceptionally, to extradition proceedings.[46]

'Criminal'

5.29   As with the concept of civil rights and obligations, the word criminal bears an autonomous Convention meaning. In *Engel v Netherlands*,[47] the Strasbourg Court identified three relevant criteria:

(a) classification of the offence in domestic law;

(b) nature of the offence;

(c) severity of the penalty.

---

44   *Fayed v United Kingdom* (1994) 18 EHRR 393. The link is no less strong merely because the applicant is in the same legal position as many others: *Allan Jacobsson v Sweden* (1990) 12 EHRR 56, para 73.

45   (2000) *The Times*, 1 March.

45a *Eckle v Germany* (1983) 5 EHRR 1.

45b *Detained Persons v Germany* (1968) 11 YB 528.

46   *Soering v United Kingdom* (1989) 11 EHRR 439, para 113.

47   (1979–80) 1 EHRR 647, para 82.

Domestic classification

5.30 Domestic classification of an offence is a starting point but is not conclusive.[48] As the Court observed in *Engel v Netherlands*:

> ... it is first necessary to know whether the provision(s) defining the offence charged belong, according to the legal system of the respondent state, to criminal law, disciplinary law or both concurrently. This however provides no more than a starting point. The indications so afforded have only a formal and relative value and must be examined in the light of the common denominator of the respective legislation of the various Contracting States.[49]

Nature of the offence and severity of penalty

5.313 In examining the nature of an offence, the Strasbourg Court has frequently looked at the other Council of Europe states in order to see how the offence is regarded by those states. One of the most important factors is whether or not the 'offence' applies to the population as a whole or merely to an identifiable sub-group. This criterion has also been used by the Court to justify classification of most forms of disciplinary proceedings as civil in character.[50]

5.32 The nature of the offence is usually considered together with the severity of the penalty imposed.

5.33 In considering the severity of the penalty, the Court also examines its purpose. In particular, the risk of imprisonment and/or deterrent or punitive purpose of the penalty are likely to indicate a criminal offence under the Convention. For example, in *Benham v United Kingdom*,[51] the Court concluded that enforcement proceedings for non-payment of poll tax were criminal in nature, invoking the fact that the penalty for non-payment was three months' imprisonment.

5.34 Cases in which the Court has held that offences/proceedings (despite their domestic classification as civil or disciplinary) are criminal by reference to the nature of the offence and/or the severity of penalty include the following:

(a) severe or intentionally punitive financial penalties for some administrative or regulatory offences;[52]

---

48 The domestic classification may, however, be conclusive where a state classifies an offence as criminal in nature.

49 (1979–80) 1 EHRR 647.

50 Eg, *Weber v Switzerland* (1990) 12 EHRR 508. Not, though, some prison disciplinary hearings which have been classified as criminal by the European Court: see *Campbell and Fell v United Kingdom* (1985) 7 EHRR 165 or, indeed, some military disciplinary hearings which are similarly classified: *Engel v Netherlands* (1979–80) 1 EHRR 647.

51 (1996) 22 EHRR 293, para 56.

52 *Öztürk v Germany* (1984) 6 EHRR 409, paras 50–56; *Bendenoun v France* (1994) 18 EHRR 54, paras 46–47. Contrast *Bendenoun* with *Smith v United Kingdom* (1996) 21 EHRR CD 74 (very small penalty to enforce payment of tax). See, also, *Hodgson v Commissioners of Customs and Excise* [1996] V & TR 200.

(b) some offences relating to the administration of justice[53] and parliamentary privilege;[54]

(c) some disciplinary offences where the penalties involve deprivation of liberty save where such penalty cannot by its nature, duration or manner of execution be appreciably detrimental.[55]

.35 Instances of decisions of the Strasbourg Court (or Commission) ruling that offences/proceedings are not criminal in character include:

(a) a particular charge brought against an electoral candidate for exceeding the limit on campaign expenses;[56]

(b) the imposition of sanctions to enforce an injunction;[57]

(c) mandatory drugs tests in prisons;[58]

(d) forfeiture or ordinary measures to enforce tax payments.[59]

.36 Importantly, the tests for classification of an offence as 'criminal' are not applied in isolation, or mechanistically. Detailed consideration is given to the factual context and other similar cases may fall to be distinguished. For example, in *Ravnsborg v Sweden*,[60] the Court had to determine whether fining a university law lecturer 3,000 Swedish kroner for making improper statements in written pleadings constituted criminal proceedings under Article 6(1).

.37 Applying the three relevant criteria, the Court concluded that although there were indications that the fine formed part of the general corpus of criminal proceedings, there were also contrary indications and the matter could not be conclusively established. The nature of the offence was, essentially, disciplinary and the amount of the fine (although it could, in limited instances, be converted to a term of imprisonment) was low and was not entered on the police register. In the circumstances, therefore, the proceedings were not criminal in nature.

---

53 *Weber v Switzerland* (1990) 12 EHRR 508, paras 29–34. Contrast *Ravnsberg v Sweden* (1994) 18 EHRR 38, paras 32–35.

54 *Demicoli v Malta* (1992) 14 EHRR 47, paras 30–35.

55 *Engel v Netherlands* (1979–80) 1 EHRR 647, para 82. For military discipline classified as civil, see *Engel* itself; for a case involving prison discipline classified as criminal, see *Campbell and Fell v United Kingdom* (1985) 7 EHRR 165, paras 67–73 (570 days loss of remission).

56 *Pierre-Bloch v France* (1998) 26 EHRR 202, paras 53–61.

57 *Krone-Verlag GmbH and Mediaprint Anzeigen GmbH & Co KG v Austria* (1997) 23 EHRR CD 152, para 1(a).

58 *Galloway v United Kingdom* [1999] EHRLR 119.

59 *AGOSI v United Kingdom* (1987) 9 EHRR 1, para 66; *Air Canada v United Kingdom* (1995) 20 EHRR 150, para 52.

60 (1994) 18 EHRR 38.

'Charge'

5.38 The protections of Article 6 apply only from the time at which a criminal charge is imposed. This is the point of 'the official notification given to an individual by the competent authority of an allegation that he has committed a criminal offence'.[61] In practice, the question of whether there is a charge is examined substantively rather than formally and may occur some time before the laying of a formal charge, for example, during preliminary investigation,[62] police questioning[63] or on arrest.[64]

5.39 Once a criminal charge has been finally determined, the protections afforded by Article 6 in respect of criminal matters ceases. These protections extend, however, to cover the whole proceedings and continue to apply until the conclusion of any appeal.[65]

ARTICLE 6(1), ADMINISTRATIVE DECISION MAKING AND JUDICIAL REVIEW

5.40 Much administrative decision making falls below the standard set by Article 6(1). By way of example, decisions taken by public bodies such as local government or health authorities will frequently violate the stipulated requirement of independence,[66] if no other.

5.41 It is, however, fundamental to the operation of Article 6 that it does not prohibit such administrative decision making. The Strasbourg Court recognises both the desirability, and indeed ubiquity, of administrative decision making:

> Demands of flexibility and efficiency, which are fully compatible with the protection of human rights, may justify the prior intervention of administrative or professional bodies and, *a fortiori*, of judicial bodies which do not satisfy the said requirements in every respect.[67]

5.42 Thus, the Court does not require that all administrative decisions which fall within the scope of application of Article 6(1) should be made by the courts, but merely that there should be access to the courts in order that substantial disputes may be fairly determined.[68] The Strasbourg Court considers the

---

61 *Eckle v Germany* (1983) 5 EHRR 1, para 73; *Deweer v Belgium* (1979–80) 2 EHRR 439, para 42.

62 *Funke v France* (1993) 16 EHRR 297, para 44.

63 *Murray v United Kingdom* (1996) 22 EHRR 29, paras 44–45.

64 See Commission decision in *Ewing v United Kingdom* (1988) 10 EHRR 141.

65 *Eckle v Germany* (1983) 5 EHRR 1, paras 76–77.

66 Eg, *Bryan v United Kingdom* (1996) 21 EHRR 342. See paras 5.80 *et seq*.

67 *Le Compte, van Leuven and de Meyere v Belgium* (1982) 4 EHRR 1, para 51.

68 See, eg, *W v United Kingdom* (1988) 10 EHRR 29, para 79.

process by which civil rights, or as the case may be, a criminal charge, has been determined as a whole. Thus, not all stages of the determination need to comply with Article 6 provided that there is a right of appeal.[69] A breach of Article 6 is, generally, capable of being cured by an appeal.[70]

5.43   Such an appellate body must, however, have full jurisdiction to consider the disputed rights.[71] This requirement has been expressly applied by the court to judicial control of administrative decision making.[72]

5.44   In domestic law, in the case of much administrative decision making, the only 'appeal' is by way of judicial review. The question then arises as to whether or not judicial review is a sufficient safeguard to comply with the overall requirements of Article 6. In some cases, the answer is clearly 'no'. As shall be seen, some forms of statutory appeal may also fall foul of Article 6(1).

5.45   The most serious potential 'flaw' in judicial review procedure in respect of the requirements of Article 6(1) is the lack of a full factual enquiry. In *W v United Kingdom*,[73] proceedings arose out of a decision by a local authority to place the applicant's child with foster parents and restrict his access. The Government argued, unsuccessfully, that the applicant's Article 6 rights were satisfied by (amongst other things) the availability of judicial review. The Strasbourg Court rejected this argument, holding that:

> ... on an application for judicial review, the courts will not review the merits of the decision but will confine themselves to ensuring, in brief, that the authority did not act illegally, unreasonably or unfairly ... In a case of the present kind, however, there will in the Court's opinion be no possibility of a 'determination' in accordance with the requirements of Article 6(1) of the parent's right in regard to access ... unless he or she can have the local authority's decision reviewed by a tribunal having jurisdiction to examine the merits of the matter.[74]

5.46   It is, however, necessary to sound a note of caution. In practice, the Court has been prepared to accept a less than comprehensive form of review in many cases concerning administrative decision making. It has stated that in assessing the sufficiency of review:

---

69 *Albert and Le Compte v Belgium* (1983) 5 EHRR 533, para 29; *Le Compte, van Leuven and de Meyere v Belgium* (1982) 4 EHRR 1, para 51.

70 See, eg, *Edwards v United Kingdom* (1992) 15 EHRR 417.

71 *Albert and Le Compte v Belgium* (1983) 5 EHRR 533, para 29.

72 *Fischer v Austria* (1995) 20 EHRR 349, para 28. Where a criminal charge is determined, the appellate body must have power 'to quash in all respects, on questions of law and fact, the decision of the body below': *Umlauft v Austria* (1996) 22 EHRR 76, para 39.

73 (1988) 10 EHRR 29.

74 *Ibid*, para 82. In *Re F (Minors) (Care Proceedings: Contact)* (2000) *The Times*, 22 June, Wall J cautioned against reliance upon cases such as *W* which pre-date the Children Act 1989.

...it is necessary to have regard to matters such as the subject matter of the decision appealed against, the manner in which that decision was arrived at, and the content of the dispute, including the desired and actual grounds of appeal.[75]

5.47　A review of the merits will not therefore be required in all, or even most, cases. Thus, in *Zumbotel v Austria*,[76] a review by the Administrative Court, which lacked full jurisdiction to consider the facts of a case before it was held to satisfy the requirements of Article 6(1) because it in fact was able to consider the submissions made before it 'point by point, without ever having to decline jurisdiction'.[77]

5.48　　　Further, the nature of the underlying decision is important. In *Bryan v United Kingdom*,[78] the Strasbourg Court considered whether the determination by a planning inspector and subsequent challenge by way of appeal to the High Court satisfied the requirements of Article 6(1). The planning inspector, who was a member of the salaried staff of the Department of the Environment, lacked the requisite 'independence' to satisfy Article 6(1) (see, further, paras 5.88–5.89). As to the High Court, the applicant complained that its jurisdiction was confined to errors of law.

5.49　　　The Strasbourg Court rejected the complaint. It noted the 'quasi judicial' nature of the planning inspector's role. Further, the High Court was at least entitled to consider whether inferences based on the inspector's findings of fact were perverse or irrational, and the Strasbourg Court concluded that this was sufficient. It concluded:

> Such an approach by an appeal tribunal on questions of fact can reasonably be expected in specialised areas of the law such as the one at issue, particularly where the facts have already been established in the course of a quasi-judicial procedure governed by many of the safeguards of Article 6(1).[79]

5.50　Thus, the fairness of the original procedure, taken together with its specialised nature, meant that the supervision provided by the High Court was sufficient.[80]

75　*Bryan v United Kingdom* (1996) 21 EHRR 342, para 45.

76　(1994) 17 EHRR 116. The position is otherwise where a determination of a criminal charge is at issue. In *Incal v Turkey* (2000) 29 EHRR 449, the applicant was a political activist convicted of dissemination of separatist propaganda for distribution of a leaflet. The Court held he had a legitimate fear that the court of first instance lacked independence and impartiality. The Strasbourg Court held that the appeal court was 'not able to dispel those concerns' as it lacked full jurisdiction.

77　*Ibid*, para 32.

78　(1996) 21 EHRR 342.

79　*Ibid*, para 47.

80　See, also, *AGOSI v United Kingdom* (1987) 9 EHRR 1; *Air Canada v United Kingdom* (1995) 20 EHRR 150, para 62, where the Court held in a case concerning the seizure of the applicant's aeroplane by Customs and Excise, the applicant could have raised the factual grounds upon which the exercise of the discretion to seize the aeroplane was based.

5.51   The Court's case law therefore provides important qualifications to the requirement that administrative decisions be subject to a review with 'full jurisdiction'. Nevertheless, it appears likely that in some cases at least, the Administrative Court's current approach to factual challenges will prove insufficient to satisfy Article 6(1).

5.52   Judicial review has also been held to be incapable of satisfying Articles 5 and 13 of the Convention in certain circumstances. These issues are discussed elsewhere.[81]

THE SUBSTANCE OF ARTICLE 6(1)

Introduction

5.53   Article 6(1), where applicable,[82] extends both to civil and criminal proceedings. There are additional protections contained in Article 6(2) and (3) which are stated to apply to those charged with a criminal offence.[83] These are considered separately below at paras 5.117 *et seq.*

5.54   The rights protected by Article 6(1) are now analysed and considered against the common law doctrines of natural justice. They are divided into those relating to:

- access to a court;
- other procedural rights going beyond conventional natural justice protection;
- procedural guarantees broadly coincident with natural justice.

5.55   As shall be seen, in addition to those rights which are expressly contained in Article 6(1), the Strasbourg Court has found a series of important protections to be implied by its provisions, stemming from the overall requirement of fairness.[84]

Access to a court

5.56   The right of access to a Court is implicit in the right to a fair hearing under Article 6(1). In *Golder v United Kingdom*,[85] a prisoner sought, but was refused,

---

81   See paras 3.76 *et seq*; paras 4.79 *et seq*; paras 4.79 *et seq*; see, also, para 4.254 (Art 1 of Protocol No 1).

82   For the matters to which Art 6(1) applies, see paras 5.08 *et seq.*

83   In some circumstances, these guarantees apply to the determination of civil rights and obligations; see para 5.116.

84   Whilst the specific guarantees set out in Art 6 are constituent elements of the right to a fair trial, they are not exhaustive. The Court also considers whether, viewed as a whole, proceedings can be considered to have been fair: *Barberà Messegué and Jabaro v Spain* (1989) 11 EHRR 360, para 68.

85   (1979–80) 1 EHRR 524.

permission to consult a solicitor with a view to instituting libel proceedings against a prison officer. The Court held that, although the right of access to a court was not expressly stated in Article 6(1), it was an implied facet of the rights expressly protected in that Article. The Court reasoned:[86]

> Were Article 6(1) to be understood as concerning exclusively the conduct of an action which had already been initiated before a court, a Contracting State could, without acting in breach of that text, do away with its courts, or take away their jurisdiction to determine certain classes of civil actions and entrust it to organs dependent upon the Government ... The fair, public and expeditious character of judicial proceedings are of no value at all if there are no judicial proceedings.

5.57 The Court concluded that the refusal to allow the applicant to consult his solicitor was an unlawful temporary impediment on access to the court.

5.58 Access to a court, where applicable, means effective access which will, in many instances, require the grant of legal representation. Thus, in *Airey v Ireland*,[87] the applicant was held to be entitled to the grant of legal aid in order to obtain legal assistance to seek a decree of judicial separation. The Court observed, materially, that:

> The Convention is intended to guarantee not rights that are theoretical or illusory but rights that are practical and effective. This is particularly so of the right of access to the courts in view of the prominent place held in a democratic society by the right to a fair trial. It must therefore be ascertained whether [the applicant's] appearance before the High Court without the assistance of a lawyer would be effective, in the sense of whether she would be able to present her case properly and satisfactorily.

5.59 Regard must also be had to the severity of any penalty at stake.[88] Whilst the Strasbourg Court emphasised in *Airey*[89] that it was not ruling that legal aid must be granted in all civil proceedings,[90] it is clear that Article 6 may create new entitlements to assistance[91] that the courts have not, to date, been prepared to countenance.[92]

5.60 The right of access to a court may be waived, although any such waiver must be unequivocal.[93]

---

86   (1979–80) 1 EHRR 524, para 35.

87   (1979–80) 2 EHRR 305, para 24.

88   *Benham v United Kingdom* (1996) 22 EHRR 293, para 60; *Perks v United Kingdom* (2000) 30 EHRR 33.

89   (1979–80) 2 EHRR 305.

90   Art 6(3)(c) of the Convention requires it for criminal proceedings.

91   Administrative law does recognise the right of access to the Court and has held that certain negative restrictions or impediments are unlawful. See, eg, *Raymond v Honey* [1983] 1 AC 1; *R v Lord Chancellor ex p Witham* [1997] 2 All ER 779.

92   See, eg, *R v Legal Aid Board and Lord Chancellor's Department ex p Mackintosh Duncan (A Firm)*, 16 February 2000 (unreported); *R v Secretary of State for the Environment ex p Challenger* (2000) *The Times*, 11 July.

93   *Pfeifer and Plankl v Austria* (1992) 14 EHRR 692, para 37.

Procedural limitations

5.61 It is clear that the state is entitled to apply procedural limitations to the right of access to a court. Any limitation upon this right must, however: (a) pursue a legitimate aim; (b) be proportionate to the end sought to be achieved; and (c) not impair the very essence of the right.[94]

5.62 On that basis, for example, limitation periods in personal injury actions have been held to be permissible,[95] as have domestic rules removing a potential defendant from the court's jurisdiction.[96]

5.63 Importantly, too, the fact that a procedural restriction falls within a particular category (for example, limitation period) does not necessarily mean, of itself, that the measure is always either justified or precluded. The question is whether, in the particular circumstances, the measure is permitted. A 'particularly strict' application of a procedural rule may, therefore, breach Article 6(1).[97] Thus, for example, the application of rules relating to seeking security for costs have sometimes been held to be proportionate[98] and, sometimes, to be disproportionate.[99]

5.64 In *Tinnelly and Sons and Others and McElduff and Others v United Kingdom*,[100] the Court held that conclusive evidence certificates issued by the Secretary of State[101] violated Article 6(1) because it removed issues of fact from the determination of the domestic Court and failed to satisfy the proportionality principle.

5.65 In *R v Registrar of Companies ex p Central Bank of India*,[102] the Court of Appeal held that a conclusive evidence clause is unaffected by the principle in *Anisminic v Foreign Compensation Commission*[103] to the effect that statutory clauses ousting[104] the judicial review jurisdiction were, in principle, unlawful

---

94 *Ashingdane v United Kingdom* (1985) 7 EHRR 528, para 57. For the expression of similar principles in Community law, see, eg, *Johnston v Chief Constable of the Royal Ulster Constabulary* [1986] ECR 1651.

95 *Stubbings v United Kingdom* (1997) 23 EHRR 213.

96 *Waite and Kennedy v Germany* (1999) 6 BHRC 499.

97 *Pérez de Rada Cavanilles v Spain* (2000) 29 EHRR 109, para 50.

98 *Tolstoy Miloslavsky v United Kingdom* (1995) 20 EHRR 442, para 62 (security for costs of libel appeal of about £125,000 held permissible).

99 *Ait-Mouhoub v France*, 28 October 1998 (unreported) (security for costs provision impermissible where legal aid refused and applicant had no assets).

100 (1999) 27 EHRR 249.

101 The effect was that the certificate was conclusive in respect of facts certified as true.

102 [1986] QB 1114, especially, pp 1175–76, *per* Slade LJ.

103 [1969] 2 AC 147.

104 By contrast, statutory time clauses preventing supervisory review after a limited time has expired are lawful in domestic law: see, eg, *R v Secretary of State for the Environment ex p Ostler* [1977] QB 122; *R v Cornwall CC ex p Huntington* [1994] 1 All ER 694 and probably, depending on the length of the time period, under the current Strasbourg case law as being a reasonable period of limitation in conformity with proportionality and not impairing the essence of the right in question.

unless stated in the clearest terms. In effect, therefore, conclusive evidence clauses are still capable of ousting judicial review altogether. It is submitted that this decision will fall to be reconsidered in the light of Article 6(1).

New substantive rights

5.66 Perhaps surprisingly, the right of access to a court has been used by the Strasbourg Court to attack the content of substantive domestic law.

5.67   As has been seen, the Court has stated that Article 6(1) applies only to civil rights and obligations which can be said 'at least on arguable grounds, to be recognised under domestic law'.[105] In *James v United Kingdom*,[106] the Court stated:

> ... Article 6(1) extends only to 'contestations' (disputes) over (civil) 'rights and obligations' which can be said, at least on arguable grounds, to be recognised under domestic law: it does not in itself guarantee any particular content for (civil) 'rights and obligations' in the substantive law of the Contracting States.

5.68 It would appear to follow that if a 'right', however desirable, is not recognised by the state then, whatever other remedies may lie for infringement of other Articles of the Convention, the general principle is that Article 6(1) protection cannot be conferred since, to do so, would be effectively to require the state to recognise the right that it had already denied. Thus, for example, in *Masson and Van Zon v Netherlands*,[107] the Court held that Article 6(1) was inapplicable because Dutch civil law recognised no right to a particular form of compensation but merely the most open-ended discretion. Similarly, in *Powell and Rayner v United Kingdom*,[108] the applicants, who owned properties near Heathrow airport, complained of excessive noise levels in connection with the operation of the airport. However, the Court held that the clear effect of s 76(1) of the Civil Aviation Act 1982 was to exclude liability in trespass and nuisance and that the consequence was, therefore, that there was no 'civil right' recognised under domestic law which attracted the application of Article 6(1).

5.69   It does not follow, however, that the state is free to remove areas of established liability from the jurisdiction of the courts – were this so, the protections of Article 6(1) could be readily circumvented. In *Fayed v United Kingdom*,[109] the Court stated:

> ... it would not be consistent with the rule of law in a democratic society or with the basic principle underlying Article 6, para 1 – namely, that civil claims must be capable of being submitted to a judge for adjudication – if ... a state could,

105 *H v Belgium* (1988) 10 EHRR 339, para 40.
106 (1986) 8 EHRR 123, para 81.
107 (1996) 22 EHRR 491, para 51.
108 (1990) 12 EHRR 355, especially para 36.
109 (1994) 18 EHRR 393, para 65.

without restraint or control by the Convention enforcement bodies, remove from the jurisdiction of the courts a whole range of civil claims or confer immunities from civil liability on large groups or categories of persons.

5.70 In the case of *Osman v United Kingdom*,[110] the Strasbourg Court, applying this principle, found a violation of Article 6(1) arising from the substantive law of negligence. In *Osman*, the Court of Appeal had struck out a claim in negligence against the police in respect of their failure to apprehend a man who had harassed one of the applicants, and who eventually shot him, and killed his father. The domestic court applied *Hill v Chief Constable of West Yorkshire*,[111] in which the House of Lords had held that no cause of action lay against the police for failure to apprehend the perpetrator of series of violent crimes on grounds of public policy.

5.71 The Strasbourg Court held there had been a breach of Article 6(1). The Court accepted that the 'exclusionary rule' pursued a legitimate objective – the need to avoid defensive policing and unnecessary wastage of resources, but held that its application without further inquiry into the existence of competing public interest considerations served to confer a 'blanket immunity' and was an unjustifiable restriction on the applicants' right to a determination on the merits. It was necessary for the domestic court to be able to balance competing public interests which may pull the other way. The domestic courts should have been able to take account of the graveness of the allegations and the seriousness of the harm.[112]

5.72 It has been said that, in effect, 'under the cover' of Article 6 the court is 'taking it upon itself to decide what the content of ... civil rights and obligations should be'.[113] On the face of it, the approach taken by the Strasbourg Court simply contradicts its repeated statements to the effect that Article 6(1) does not guarantee any particular content for civil rights and obligations in the substantive law of Contracting States.[114]

5.73 The ostensible reasoning of the Court is, however, capable of being reconciled with its existing case law. The Court said that the UK Government had contended that the 'exclusionary rule' was 'not of an absolute nature and that its application may yield to other public policy considerations' (para 150). In the domestic proceedings, McCowan LJ had stated that *Hill* 'dooms this action to failure',[115] and cited the remarks of Glidewell LJ in *Alexandrou v Oxford*[116] who stated that *Hill* was of general application, and not limited to the facts of the case.

---

110 (2000) 29 EHRR 245.
111 [1989] AC 53.
112 (2000) 29 EHRR 245, para 151.
113 Lord Hoffmann, writing extra-judicially in (1999) 62 MLR 159, p 164.
114 Eg, *James v United Kingdom* (1986) 8 EHRR 123, para 81.
115 *Osman v Ferguson* [1993] 4 All ER 344, p 354.
116 *Ibid*, p 340.

5.74   Thus, in *Osman*,[117] the Strasbourg Court had concluded that notwithstanding the Government's contentions:

> ... it would appear to the Court that in the instant case the Court of Appeal proceeded on the basis that the rule provided a *watertight defence* to the police and that it was *impossible to prise open* an immunity which the police enjoy from civil suit in respect of their acts and omissions in the investigation and suppression of crime. [Emphasis added.]

5.75   It might be said, therefore, that the Strasbourg Court sought only to ensure that the applicants had a fair opportunity to test whether the 'exclusionary rule' applied to their case. Amongst the difficulties with this analysis, however, is, as Lord Browne-Wilkinson stated in *Barrett v London Borough of Enfield*,[118] it appears to be premised on a misunderstanding as to the nature of domestic law:

> In English law, the decision as to whether it is fair, just and reasonable to impose a liability in negligence on a particular class of defendants depends on weighing in the balance the total detriment to the public interest in all cases from holding such class liable in negligence as against the total loss to all would-be plaintiffs if they are not to have a cause of action in respect of the loss they have individually suffered.

5.76   Thus, the kind of 'competing public interests' which are specific to an individual case (such as the gravity of the harm in that particular case) which the Strasbourg Court stated must be taken into consideration – and had not been – are not relevant as a matter of domestic law to whether a duty of care is imposed. The matter depends on the balance of 'total detriment'.

5.77   It would not require a dramatic change in the law of negligence as stated in *Barrett v Enfield*[119] to meet the concerns of the Strasbourg Court in *Osman*. The 'global' balancing exercise identified by Lord Browne-Wilkinson must be modified to admit of consideration of factors which arise in an individual case. In any event, as Auld LJ observed in *Gower v Bromley LBC*:[120]

> ... it was evident even before the recent decision of the ECHR in *Osman v UK*, that such an assessment [fair, just and reasonable] could normally only properly be made after full consideration of the evidence and circumstances at trial. In *E (A Minor) v Dorset CC* [1995] 2 AC 689 ... Sir Thomas Bingham MR indicated at p 694E–F, that if all that remains to a judge hearing a strike-out application is the question whether the claimant has an arguable case that the

---

117 (2000) 29 EHRR 245, para 150.

118 [1999] 3 WLR 79, p 85.

119 *Ibid*, p 85. *Osman* does not necessarily prevent the domestic courts from dealing with such a point (and engaging in the requisite balancing exercise) summarily in a suitable case: *Jarvis v Hampshire County Council* [2000] Ed CR 1, CA. (This case has now been considered by the House of Lords, 27 July 2000, although the issues raised by *Osman* were not addressed by their Lordships.)

120 29 July 1999 (unreported), CA.

duty of care for which he or she contends is fair, just and reasonable in the circumstances, the case is not appropriate for a strike-out.

5.78 It is difficult to escape the conclusion that *Osman* cannot be reconciled with the Strasbourg Court's pre-existing case law on the application of Article 6(1). In effect, the Court has used Article 6(1) to attack the substantive content of the law of negligence. The Strasbourg Court is, however, due to reconsider the issues raised by *Osman*. The unsuccessful claimants *X v Bedfordshire County Council*[121] have applied to Strasbourg, and a violation of Article 6(1) was found by the Commission on *Osman* grounds.[122]

Procedural rights which extend beyond the scope of natural justice

5.79 Article 6(1) provides a number of procedural protections which clearly go beyond the scope of natural justice.

Impartiality

5.80 Conventional natural justice protects against bias that is intrinsic to a court's decision making process by providing objective safeguards similar, but not identical, in nature to the requirement in the Strasbourg case law that, in order to comply with Article 6(1), a court or tribunal must be impartial.

5.81 In domestic judicial review the general test is that laid down in *R v Gough*:[123]

> Having ascertained the relevant circumstances, the court should ask itself whether, having regard to those circumstances, there was a real danger of bias on the part of the relevant member of the tribunal in question, in the sense that he might unfairly regard (or have unfairly regarded) with favour, or disfavour, the case of a party to the issue under consideration by him.[124]

5.82 There are, nonetheless, circumstances in domestic law in which a judge must automatically disqualify himself on the ground of bias. Until the decision of the House of Lords in *R v Bow Street Metropolitan Stipendiary Magistrate ex p Pinochet Ugarte (No 2)*,[125] it was widely thought, however, that the only circumstances in which a judge must automatically disqualify himself in this way was where (s)he had a pecuniary or proprietary interest in the outcome of the litigation.[126] In *Pinochet (No 2)*, it was clarified that the rule was wider than had formerly been supposed. As Lord Browne-Wilkinson observed:

---

121 [1995] 2 AC 633.
122 *Z v United Kingdom* (1999) 28 EHRR CD 65.
123 [1993] AC 646.
124 *Ibid*, p 760F, *per* Lord Goff.
125 [1999] 2 WLR 272.
126 See *Dimes v The Proprietors of the Grand Junction Canal* (1852) 3 HL Cas 759, p 793, *per* Lord Campbell.

... although the cases have all dealt with automatic disqualification on the grounds of pecuniary interest, there is no good reason in principle for so limiting automatic disqualification. The rationale of the whole rule is that a man cannot be a judge in his own cause. In civil litigation, the matters in issue will normally have an economic impact; therefore a judge is automatically disqualified if he stands to make a financial gain as a consequence of his own decision of the case. But if, as in the present case, the matter at issue does not relate to money or economic advantage but is concerned with the promotion of the cause, the rationale disqualifying a judge applies just as much if the judge's decision will lead to the promotion of a cause in which the judge is involved together with one of the parties.[127]

5.83   In *Locabail (UK) Ltd v Bayfield Properties Limited and Others*,[128] the Court of Appeal emphasised that automatic disqualification on the ground of personal interest would (although wider than pecuniary or proprietary interest) be extremely rare and that the fundamental right to a fair hearing, protected by Article 6 and recognised by the Court, was in practice most effectively protected by the rule providing for disqualification if there was a 'real danger' of bias.

5.84   The 'real danger' test is, analytically at least, less demanding than that developed by Strasbourg. In *Piersack v Belgium*,[129] the Court said this:

Whilst impartiality normally denotes absence of prejudice or bias, its existence or otherwise can, notably under Article 6(1) of the Convention, be tested in various ways. A distinction can be drawn in this context between a subjective approach,[130] that is, endeavouring to ascertain the personal conviction of a given judge in a given case, and an objective approach, that is, determining whether he offered guarantees sufficient to exclude any legitimate doubt in this respect.

5.85   The difference in formulation between Strasbourg and domestic law lies in the ostensibly lower threshold, laid down by Strasbourg, that a judge must withdraw unless such guarantees as exclude 'any legitimate doubt' are offered.[131] This may be thought to place a larger measure of responsibility on judges to disqualify themselves than envisaged in *Pinochet (No 2)* and *Locabail*.

---

127 See p 283. See, also, *per* Lord Hutton at p 293.

128 [2000] HRLR 292.

129 [1983] 5 EHRR 169, para 30.

130 Under the subjective test, the personal impartiality of the judge must be presumed unless there is proof to the contrary: *Le Compte, Van Leuven and De Meyere v Belgium* [1981] 4 EHRR 1, para 58.

131 In *McGonnell v United Kingdom* (2000) *The Times*, 22 February, the Strasbourg Court upheld a complaint as to the role of the Deputy Bailiff of Guernsey. He had adjudicated the applicant's complaint in respect of a development plan, but had also presided over the Guernsey legislature when the plan had been adopted. The Court held this cast legitimate doubt over his impartiality in determining the applicant's later complaint. This case accordingly casts doubt over the Lord Chancellor's ability to sit as a judge in cases concerning legislation he has presided over as Speaker in the House of Lords.

5.86   In *Hauschildt v Denmark*,[132] for example, the Strasbourg Court expressed itself thus:

> Under the objective test, it must be determined whether, quite apart from the judge's personal conduct, there are ascertainable facts which may raise doubts as to his impartiality. In this respect even appearances may be of a certain importance. What is at stake is the confidence which the courts in a democratic society must inspire in the public and above all, as far as criminal proceedings are concerned, in the accused. Accordingly, any judge in respect of whom there is a legitimate reason to fear a lack of impartiality must withdraw.

> This implies that in deciding whether in a given case there is a legitimate reason to fear that a particular judge lacks impartiality, the standpoint of the accused is important but not decisive. What is decisive is whether this fear can be held objectively justified.

5.87   Although the Strasbourg formulation demands more of the tribunal than that currently adopted by the domestic courts,[133] many of the cases which have been considered by the Strasbourg Court would probably be decided the same way by a domestic court.[134]

Independence

5.88   The requirement of independence has been developed by the Court as follows:

(a) The court or tribunal in question must be independent both of the executive and of the parties to the proceedings.[135]

(b) In determining whether a court or tribunal is independent in this fashion, regard must be paid to the manner of appointment of its members, the duration of their terms of office, the existence of guarantees against outside pressure and whether the body presents an appearance of independence.[136]

---

132 (1990) 12 EHRR 266, para 48.

133 Note, too, that the Court must investigate a complaint of bias unless such complaint is 'manifestly devoid of merit': see *Remli v France* (1996) 22 EHRR 253, para 48.

134 Cf, eg, *Piersack v Belgium*, (1983) 5 EHRR 169 (violation of ECHR where judge had previously been a member of investigating and prosecution department in respect of the Applicant's case), and *Hauschildt v Denmark*, (1990) 12 EHRR 266 (violation where judge found a 'particularly confirmed suspicion of guilt' during earlier bail applications); with, eg, *Gregory v United Kingdom* (1998) 25 EHRR 577 (no violation where biased juror was excused and trial continued after careful ruling from judge), and *Kraska v Switzerland* (1994) 18 EHRR 188 (no violation where one of the judges had been unable to read whole case file and memorial for lack of time). In *Locabail Ltd v Bayfield Properties Ltd* [2000] HRLR 292, the Court of Appeal declined to decide whether the Strasbourg test was more restrictive, but stated that in the overwhelming majority of cases, the application of the two tests would lead to the same outcome.

135 *Ringeisen v Austria* (1979–80) 1 EHRR 455, para 95.

136 *Campbell and Fell v United Kingdom* (1985) 7 EHRR 165, para 78.

(c) Other factors may also be relevant. For example, a court or tribunal lacks independence if it lacks the power to give a binding decision.[137]

5.89 It has already been noted that much administrative decision making fails to satisfy this requirement. In *V and T v United Kingdom*,[138] the Court held that the role of the Home Secretary in setting the tariff in the case of a child detained during Her Majesty's pleasure gave rise to a breach. Further, the courts may find violations of Article 6(1) caused by a court or tribunal lacking the requisite independence. Already, the Employment Appeal Tribunal has found that there is a 'real and troubling question' as to whether employment tribunals could properly and lawfully adjudicate on claims made against the Secretary of State for Trade and Industry.[139] In Scotland, the High Court of Justiciary, Appeal Court, has held that a person would not have a hearing by an independent and impartial tribunal established by law where the tribunal was a temporary sheriff, holding office at the pleasure of the Lord Advocate, and who therefore had no security of tenure at all.[140]

Hearing within a reasonable time

5.90 There is a further safeguard under Article 6(1) that was not available prior to the Human Rights Act in domestic judicial review. Under Article 6, the hearing must be 'within a reasonable time'.

5.91 In civil cases, several criteria are relevant without any being determinative. These are:

(a) the complexity of the case;

(b) the applicant's conduct;

(c) the conduct of the respondent(s), domestic authorities and of the Court itself;

(d) what is at stake for the applicant.[141]

5.92 The general approach of the Strasbourg Court in civil cases has been to look at the overall length of the proceedings, including time taken on appeal, and make a general assessment of whether it has been conducted within a reasonable time taking into account individual periods of delay with particular emphasis on the conduct of the domestic authorities.[142] The burden is on the

---

137 See, eg, *Findlay v United Kingdom* ((1997) 24 EHRR 221, para 77.

138 (2000) 30 EHRR 121.

139 *Smith v Secretary of State for Trade and Industry* [2000] HRLR 83.

140 *Starrs and Chalmers v Procurator Fiscal (Linlithgow)* [2000] HRLR 191. Cf *Clancy v Caird* 2000 SLT 546.

141 See, especially, *König v Federal Republic of Germany* (1979–80) 2 EHRR 170, paras 99, 102–05 and 107–11; *Buchholz v Germany* (1981) 3 EHRR 597, para 49.

142 See, eg, *Santilli v Italy* (1992) 14 EHRR 421; *Darnell v United Kingdom* (1994) 18 EHRR 205.

judicial authorities to ensure that proceedings progress with the expedition required by Article 6.[143]

5.93   In criminal cases, the relevant factors include the complexity of the matter , the conduct of the applicant and relevant authorities, and 'the point at which the situation of the person concerned has been substantially affected as a result of a suspicion against him'.[144]

5.94   It may be anticipated that the Administrative Court will be prepared to grant relief in respect of decisions where the decision making process has not been conducted expeditiously in accordance with Article 6. Obviously, the context will be important. It is likely that domestic courts will follow Strasbourg's lead in regarding cases involving (for example) children[145] as needing to be conducted particularly expeditiously. It does not follow, however, that, because there is a violation of Article 6, the relief will be in the form of a quashing order. It may, for example, be that time taken to process applications before a Mental Health Review Tribunal will violate Article 6; it does not follow that the decision of the Tribunal will fall to be quashed; rather, the remedy may sound in damages.[146]

Oral and public hearing

5.95   In domestic judicial review, it is well recognised that there is no general right to an oral hearing.[147] The Convention requires that a hearing must, at first instance, be oral in the absence of exceptional circumstances which justify dispensing with it.[148] This is an inevitable concomitant of the requirement, contained in Article 6(1), that the hearing must be public.

5.96   As has been seen at para 5.42, a violation of Article 6(1) may be cured on appeal or review: the Strasbourg Court considers the process by which civil rights, or as the case may be, a criminal charge, has been determined as a whole. Accordingly, it is only exceptionally that an appeal court may deny a right to an oral hearing where that has been refused by the court or tribunal of first instance.[149] There is otherwise no general right to an oral hearing on appeal/review (or permission to appeal or apply for review) from the decision of a first instance court or tribunal. That question will be resolved by reference

---

143 *Buchholz v Germany* (1981) 3 EHRR 597, para 50.

144 *X v Austria* (1967) 24 CD 8, p 18. See, also, *Eckle v Germany* (1983) 5 EHRR 1.

145 *H v United Kingdom* (1988) 10 EHRR 95.

146 As to damages, see Chapter 6.

147 Of the many cases, see, eg, *Lloyd v McMahon* [1987] AC 625; *R v Army Board of the Defence Council ex p Anderson* [1992] QB 169; *R v Criminal Injuries Compensation Board ex p Dickson* [1997] 1 WLR 158.

148 *Fischer v Austria* (1995) 20 EHRR 349, para 44.

149 *Stallinger and Kuso v Austria* (1998) 26 EHRR 81, para 51.

to whether the interests of the applicant have been able to be presented fairly without an oral hearing.[150]

5.97   The requirement of a public hearing is 'to protect litigants from the administration of justice in secret with no public scrutiny' and a means of ensuring that public confidence in the courts is maintained.[151] In applying this limb of Article 6(1), therefore, the domestic courts are likely to be cautious before applying discretion to refuse relief on the basis that an oral hearing would have made no difference.

Reasons

5.98   Article 6(1) requires that courts and tribunals must indicate 'with sufficient clarity the grounds on which they based their decision'.[152] Sufficient reasons must also be given for an administrative decision to make it possible to mount a reasoned challenge.[153]

5.99   It is well established on the domestic authorities that there is no general right to reasons.[154] Although most decisions affecting fundamental rights are required to be reasoned,[155] this is not always so. In particular, magistrates' courts are generally exempt from such a requirement.[156] In *Stefan v General Medical Council*,[157] Lord Clyde stated that the Human Rights Act might bring about 'a re-appraisal of the whole position'. It is submitted that a general right to reasons, in cases falling within the scope of Article 6(1) is all but inevitable in accordance with the Strasbourg case law. Following the advent of the Human Rights Act, the issue is likely to be whether the decision maker has provided adequate reasons, rather than whether reasons are required at all.[158]

---

150 See, eg, *Monnell and Morris v United Kingdom* (1988) 10 EHRR 205, para 68.

151 *Pretto v Italy* (1984) 6 EHRR 182, para 21.

152 *Hadjianastassiou v Greece* (1993) 16 EHRR 219, para 33.

153 *Hentrich v France* (1994) 18 EHRR 440.

154 *Stefan v General Medical Council* [2000] HRLR 1; *R v MOD ex p Murray* [1998] COD 134.

155 See, especially, *R v Higher Education Funding Council ex p Institute of Dental Surgery* [1994] 1 WLR 242; *R v Director of Public Prosecutions ex p Manning* (2000) *The Times*, 19 May: refusal to prosecute following death in custody. ECHR, Art 6 is, of course, concerned not with fundamental rights *per se* but, rather, with the determination of all civil rights and obligations and criminal charges. See paras 5.08 *et seq*.

156 *R v Southend Stipendiary Magistrate ex p Rochford DC* [1995] Env LR 1; *R v Haringey Magistrates ex p Cragg* [1997] COD 160.

157 [2000] HRLR 1, p 10.

158 In *Van de Hurk v Netherlands* (1994) 18 EHRR 481, para 61 the Strasbourg Court stated that courts and tribunals need not give a detailed answer to every argument. In *Stefan v General Medical Council* [2000] HRLR 1, p 13, Lord Clyde stated that, 'in many cases, ... a very few sentences should suffice to give such explanation as is appropriate to the particular situation'.

Disclosure

5.100 Article 6(1) contains a right to disclosure in certain circumstances, implicit in the right to a fair trial. In *Edwards v United Kingdom*,[159] the Court stated:

> ... that it is a requirement of fairness under Article 6(1), indeed one which is recognised under English law, that the prosecution authorities disclose to the defence all material evidence for or against the accused and that the failure to do so in the present case gave rise to a defect in the trial proceedings.

5.101 *Edwards* concerned criminal proceedings, and this statement of principle probably should not be read as extending generally to determinations of civil rights and obligations. Nevertheless, as has been seen at para 5.29, 'criminal' has an autonomous Convention meaning, and may encompass offences which are viewed as regulatory in domestic law. It is further submitted that the scope of the disclosure obligation would be in part determined by the nature of the 'criminal charge' at issue.

5.102 Even in a criminal trial, however, the right to disclosure is not absolute. In *Rowe and Davis v United Kingdom*:[160]

> ... there may be competing interests, such as national security or the need to protect witnesses at risk of reprisals or keep secret police methods, which must be weighed against the rights of the accused. In some cases, it may be necessary to withhold certain evidence from the defence so as to preserve the fundamental rights of another individual or to safeguard an important public inters. However, only such measures restricting the rights of the defence which are strictly necessary are permissible under Article 6(1). Moreover, in order to ensure that the accused receives a fair trial, any difficulties caused to the defence by a limitation on its rights must be sufficiently counterbalanced by the procedures followed by the judicial authorities.

5.103 In that case, the Court held a breach of Article 6 had occurred where information was withheld on public interest grounds without giving the trial judge the opportunity to scrutinise it.[161]

5.104 Where disclosure is sought, the material in question must be at least of potential relevance. In *Bendenoun v France*,[162] a case concerning a prosecution for customs offences, the Court stated it was it was 'necessary, at the very least, that the person concerned should have given, even if only briefly, specific reasons for his request'.

5.105 The right to disclosure also arises under Article 6(3) (see paras 5.136 *et seq*).

---

159 (1992) 15 EHRR 417, para 37.
160 (2000) 30 EHRR 1, para 61.
161 *Ibid*, para 66.
162 (1994) 18 EHRR 54, para 52. See, also, *Schüler-Zgraggen v Switzerland* (1993) 16 EHRR 405.

The right to silence

5.106 In *Funke v France*,[163] the Strasbourg Court held that Article 6(1) contains the general right to anyone charged with a criminal offence to remain silent and not to incriminate himself. This was confirmed in *Murray v United Kingdom*,[164] where the Court observed as follows:

> There can be no doubt that the right to remain silent under police questioning and the privilege against self-incrimination are generally recognised international standards which lie at the heart of the notion of a fair procedure under Article 6. By providing the accused with protection against improper compulsion by the authorities, these immunities contribute to avoiding miscarriages of justices and to securing the aims of Article 6.

5.107 The Court observed, nonetheless, that the right to silence was not absolute. It held that the test for whether the drawing of adverse inferences from silence offended against Article 6(1) was to be determined:

> ... in the light of all the circumstances of the case, having particular regard to the situations where inferences may be drawn, the weight attached to them by the national courts in their assessment of the evidence and the degree of compulsion inherent in the situation.[165]

5.108 In *Saunders v United Kingdom*,[166] the Court held that the essence of the privilege against self-incrimination was to require the prosecution to prove its case without recourse to evidence obtained from the accused through coercion or oppression against his will. The Court held that statements compulsorily obtained by DTI inspectors under s 432(2) of the Companies Act 1985 were inadmissible in subsequent criminal proceedings brought against Mr Saunders. There appears, however, to be a distinction drawn by the Court in *Saunders* between the compulsory obtaining of statements on the one hand (lawful) and the subsequent use of those statements in criminal proceedings (unlawful).[167]

The right to participate in a criminal trial

5.109 In *T and V v United Kingdom*,[168] the Court held that Article 6 guarantees the right of an accused to participate effectively in his criminal trial. In that case,

---

163 (1993) 16 EHRR 297.

164 (1996) 22 EHRR 29, para 45.

165 See *Condron v United Kingdom* (2000) *The Times*, 9 May, where the Court held a direction to a jury on the applicants' silence during interview to give rise to a breach of Art 6(1). The Court of Appeal had held the direction to be deficient, but not to have rendered the convictions unsafe.

166 (1997) 23 EHRR 313. See, also, *R v Hertfordshire County Council ex p Green Industries Ltd* [2000] HRLR 368.

167 *Ibid*, para 67.

168 (2000) 30 EHRR 121.

the Court held that the conditions in which the applicants had been tried for murder whilst children had given rise to a violation.

Rights which are co-extensive with natural justice

5.110 Article 6(1) contains procedural rights which do not clearly extend beyond the scope of the doctrine of natural justice.

Equality of arms

5.111 The principle of equality of arms applies to both civil[169] and criminal proceedings. It requires that everyone who is a party to proceedings must have a reasonable opportunity of presenting his case to the court under conditions which do not place him at a substantial disadvantage vis à vis his opponent.[170] A refusal to permit a party to adduce relevant evidence may violate this requirement.[171] It entitles each party to 'comment effectively' on evidence adduced by the other side,[172] and requires that the witnesses of each side receive equal treatment before the court.[173]

5.112 It does not, however, operate so as to prevent a judge from restricting cross-examination on irrelevant matters. As the Court observed in *Van de Hurk v Netherlands*:[174]

> The effect of Article 6(1) is, *inter alia*, to place the 'tribunal' under a duty to conduct a proper examination of the submissions, arguments and evidence adduced by the parties, without prejudice to its assessment of whether they are relevant to its decision.

5.113 It may accordingly be doubted whether equality of arms extends beyond the scope of natural justice, save perhaps in so far as this doctrine may require disclosure in some circumstances. See, further, paras 5.100 *et seq*.

The right to an adversarial trial

5.114 Although at times treated by the Strasbourg Court as a separate requirement, the right to an adversarial trial overlaps very substantially with the requirement of equality of arms. It requires that each party have the opportunity to have knowledge of and comment on the observations filed or

---

169 Eg, *Dombo Beheer v Netherlands* (1994) 18 EHRR 213.
170 *De Haes and Gijsels v Belgium* (1998) 25 EHRR 1, para 53.
171 *Ibid*.
172 *Mantovanelli v France* (1997) 24 EHRR 370.
173 *Bönisch v Austria* (1987) 9 EHRR 191.
174 (1994) 18 EHRR 481, para 59.

evidence adduced by the other party.[175] Again, it is not clear that this adds to the requirements of the common law.

The rules of evidence

5.115 The Convention does not require that Contracting States adopt any particular rules of evidence; these are matters primarily for national law.[176] The Convention permits the use of illegally obtained evidence,[177] as does domestic law.[178] The domestic law on the use of hearsay in criminal trials has been held to conform with Article 6(1).[179]

GUARANTEES IN CRIMINAL CASES

5.116 Article 6(2) and (3) contains guarantees which expressly apply to those charged with a criminal offence.[180] These guarantees, can, however also apply to civil cases in limited circumstances. In *Albert and Le Compte v Belgium*,[181] the Court held that medical disciplinary proceedings determined civil rights, and declined to decide whether there was a criminal charge. The Court held that the provisions of Article 6(2) and (3) applied *mutatis mutandis* to disciplinary proceedings which were subject to Article 6(1).

Article 6(2): presumption of innocence

5.117 Article 6(2) of the Convention stipulates that:

> Everyone charged with a criminal offence shall be presumed innocent until proved guilty according to law.

5.118 The presumption of innocence contained in Article 6(2) means that, in principle at least, the burden of proof in criminal proceedings lies on the prosecution. This and other consequences of the presumption of innocence were formulated by the Strasbourg Court in *Barbera, Messegue and Jabardo v Spain*[182] as follows:

---

175 Eg, *Ruis-Mateos v Spain* (1993) 16 EHRR 505, para 63.
176 *Schenk v Switzerland* (1991) 13 EHRR 242, para 42.
177 *Ibid*.
178 *R v Khan* [1997] AC 558. The defendant's challenge to Strasbourg failed on this ground: *Khan v United Kingdom* (2000) *The Times*, 23 May.
179 *Blastland v United Kingdom* (1987) 52 DR 273.
180 Certain guarantees found in Art 6(1) may only apply to those charged with a criminal offence. See paras 5.100–5.109.
181 (1983) 5 EHRR 533, para 39.
182 (1989) 11 EHRR 360, para 77.

Paragraph 2 embodies the principle of the presumption of innocence. It requires, *inter alia*, that when carrying out their duties, the members of a court should not start with the preconceived idea that the accused has committed the offence charged; the burden of proof is on the prosecution, and any doubt should benefit the accused. It also follows that it is for the prosecution to inform the accused of the case that will be made against him, so that he may prepare and present his defence accordingly, and to adduce evidence sufficient to convict him.

5.119 Many alleged violations of Article 6(2) will be adjudicated upon not in judicial review proceedings but through appeal. This is because s 29(3) of the Supreme Court Act 1981 precludes judicial review of Crown Court decisions in respect of matters relating to trial on indictment. Neither may decisions to prosecute be challenged by judicial review.[183]

5.120 However, convictions by magistrates' courts and/or decisions of the Crown Court on appeal from magistrates' courts may give rise to judicial review proceedings. Here, difficult issues may sometimes arise in respect of the burden of proof. In *R v Director of Public Prosecutions ex p Kebilene*,[184] for example, the Divisional Court reached a very different conclusion from the House of Lords on whether s 16A of the Prevention of Terrorism (Temporary Provisions) Act 1989 was compatible with Article 6(2).[185]

5.121 Additionally, there will be many contexts in which proceedings that have been classified as 'civil' or 'disciplinary' will constitute criminal proceedings for the purposes of application of Article 6(2) and (3) (see paras 5.29 *et seq*).

5.122 The fact that the burden of proof is on the prosecution does not mean that a specific defence may not fall to be established by the defence at least in circumstances where the prosecution has proved the commission of that which would otherwise constitute a criminal offence. In *Lingens and Leitgens v Austria*,[186] the Commission considered a provision in the Austrian penal code which made it a criminal offence to damage a person's reputation subject to a special defence if the truth of the statement was proved by the person making it. In the view of the Commission:

> The offence as conceived in the applicable provisions of the Penal Code ... can ... be committed by a true statement: what exculpates is not the objective truth of a defamatory statement, but ability to prove its truth.

5.123 Further, despite the burden of proof being borne by the prosecution, there is no necessary violation of Article 6(2) merely because certain presumptions of

---

183 *R v Director of Public Prosecutions ex p Kebilene* [2000] HRLR 93.

184 *Ibid.*

185 Contrast the reasoning of Lord Cooke of Thorndon in the House of Lords (no necessary breach) with that of Lord Bingham in the Divisional Court (a clear incompatibility). In the result, the point did not fall for decision because the House of Lords held that the application (challenging a decision to prosecute) should not have been brought by way of judicial review but should have been ventilated through the criminal justice system.

186 (1982) 4 EHRR 373, para 4.

law or fact are made. In *Salabiaku v France*,[187] the applicant complained of a violation of Article 6(2) in circumstances where he had been charged both with the criminal offence of unlawful importation of narcotics and with the customs offence of smuggling prohibited goods. Although he was awarded the benefit of the doubt on the first charge and acquitted, he was convicted on the second. A presumption of criminal liability was laid down in Article 392(1) of the Customs Code for every person who was found in possession of prohibited goods. The Strasbourg Court held that there was a distinction, of a relative nature, to be drawn between a presumption of accountability and one of guilt and that, since the domestic court had given careful attention to the facts of the case, Article 6(2) was not violated.

5.124   Other cases have followed the *Salabiaku* approach. In *Pham Hoang v France*,[188] the applicant was charged and convicted under French drugs legislation with unlawful importation of narcotics and customs evasion. In respect of the same Article (Article 392) of the French Customs Code as had been considered in *Salabiaku*, the Court held that the presumption of innocence was not violated where the defendant has the opportunity to rebut a presumption of guilt in criminal legislation with evidence to the contrary.

5.125   The standard of proof adopted may also infringe Article 6(2) of the Convention. Undoubtedly, the Convention does not require that where an offence is criminal in nature, proof must be beyond 'reasonable doubt'. However, disciplinary tribunals that are subject to Article 6(2) and (3) (see paras 5.29 *et seq*) would certainly have to apply a standard of proof that was sufficiently high to accord with the presumption of innocence. In *Austria v Italy*,[189] the Commission observed that:

> ... the onus to prove guilt falls on the Prosecution and any doubt is to the benefit of the accused ... In their judgment, [the judges] can find him guilty only on the basis of direct or indirect evidence sufficiently strong in the eyes of the law to establish his guilt.

5.126 Article 6(2) will also be violated where the Court gives voice to an opinion of the accused's guilt in circumstances where there is no conviction at all.[190] For example, in *Moody v United Kingdom*,[191] the trial judge who refused a costs order following acquittal of the accused of selling obscene material on the basis that the material was obscene and that the accused deserved to be penalised were held to be in breach of Article 6(2) of the Convention. So, too, in *Minelli v*

---

187 (1991) 13 EHRR 379. See, further, *R v Lambert* (2000) *The Times*, 5 September.

188 (1993) 16 EHRR 53.

189 (1963) 6 YB 740, p 784. Domestic law may confer equal or greater protection than the Convention in this respect: see, eg, *Re A Solicitor* [1993] QB 69; *R v Police Complaints Board ex p Madden* [1983] 2 All ER 353. Contrast, though, *R v Hampshire County Council ex p Ellerton* [1985] 1 All ER 599.

190 *Minelli v Switzerland* (1983) 5 EHRR 554.

191 22613/93 (Rep) 16 January 1996.

Switzerland,[192] the Court found a violation of Article 6(2) where the domestic court ordered the applicant to pay part of the private prosecutor's costs on the basis that had the case proceeded to full trial he would 'very probably' have been convicted.

5.127   In practice, this may be a fertile ground for applications for judicial review, at least in circumstances where s 29(3) of the Supreme Court Act 1981 does not apply (see para 5.119). Given the prohibition in s 9(1) of the Human Rights Act of challenging judicial acts other than by way of appeal or such other procedure as may be prescribed by rules, it may be that s 29(3) of the 1981 Act will have to be construed more liberally than it has been in the past to permit such a challenge. In the past an expression of view adverse to the accused in the course of any hearing otherwise susceptible to judicial review could not have been challenged immediately by way of judicial review on the ground of prematurity since an acquittal might still follow. Given the terms of Article 6(2), it may be that judicial review will lie so that declaratory relief is granted that the statements should not have been made and breached Article 6(2).

5.128   Further, Article 6(2) may be breached by public authorities other than the courts as, for example, by unqualified public statements that induce prejudging of an accused's guilt. In *Allenet de Ribemont v France*,[193] for example, the applicant (then in police custody) was described at a press conference by the police as being the instigator of the murder under investigation. This was held to violate Article 6(2), even though no court had made such a finding or voiced such an opinion.

Article 6(3): additional minimum safeguards in criminal cases

5.129 Article 6(3) provides as follows:

Everyone charged with a criminal offence has the following minimum rights:

(a) to be informed promptly, in a language which he understands and in detail, of the nature and cause of the accusation against him;

(b) to have adequate time and facilities for the preparation of his defence;

(c) to defend himself in person or through legal assistance of his own choosing or, if he has not sufficient means to pay for legal assistance, to be given it free when the interests of justice so require;

(d) to examine or have examined witnesses against him and to obtain the attendance and examination of witnesses on his behalf under the same conditions as witnesses against him;

(e) to have the free assistance of an interpreter if he cannot understand or speak the language used in court.

---

192 (1983) 5 EHRR 554.
193 (1995) 20 EHRR 557, especially para 41.

5.130 In most cases, an alleged violation of Article 6(3) will fall to be addressed through the appeal system rather than by way of judicial review because of the terms of s 29(3) of the Supreme Court Act 1981 (see para 5.119). However, judicial review will lie for breaches of Article 6(3) occurring in hearings before magistrates' courts, before the Crown Court on appeal from magistrates' courts and before other courts or tribunals that are conducting criminal rather than civil proceedings within the Convention meaning of 'charged with a criminal offence' (see paras 5.38–5.39).

5.131   Article 6(3)(a) requires information about the charge. The accused must be informed in a language that he understands.[194] It has also been suggested by the Strasbourg Court that a defendant who is unfamiliar with the national language should be provided with a written translation of the charge.[195]

5.132   Article 6(3)(a) is applied more rigorously than the corresponding provision in Article 5(2) which requires the reasons for arrest to be given in order to be in a position to challenge the legality of a detention; the requirement in Article 6(3)(a) is, by contrast, intended to enable the accused's defence to be prepared.[196] Thus, in principle, the service of an indictment is important. As the Court held in *Kamasinski v Austria*:[197]

> An indictment plays a crucial role in the criminal process, in that it is from the moment of its service that the defendant is formally put on notice of the factual and legal basis of the charge against him ...

5.133 However, the critical feature is always whether prejudice has occurred. In *Kamasinski*, it had not because the defendant had requested that the indictment be served upon his defence counsel who had been appointed by the national court because he was fluent in English. In *Brozicek v Italy*,[198] on the other hand, there was prejudice because only a summary notification of the charges was sent to the defendant who had informed the Italian authorities in unequivocal terms of his lack of knowledge of Italian. In *Pélissier and Sassi v France*,[199] the Strasbourg Court also found a breach of Article 6(3)(a) where the information set out in the indictment was insufficiently detailed so as to ensure that the applicants were aware that an alternative verdict of 'aiding and abetting' (requiring proof of additional matters) was available in respect of the charged offence of criminal bankruptcy.

5.134   There is a close relationship between Article 6(3)(a) and Article 6(3)(b). The latter provision is designed to ensure 'the right of the accused to have at his

---

194 *Brozicek v Italy* (1990) 12 EHRR 371.
195 *Kamasinski v Austria* (1991) 13 EHRR 36. On the facts, though (see text), an oral translation of the charges was held to be sufficient.
196 *GSM v Austria* (1983) 34 DR 119.
197 (1991) 13 EHRR 36, para 80.
198 (1990) 12 EHRR 371.
199 Judgment of 25 March 1999.

disposal, for the purpose of exonerating himself or to obtain a reduction in his sentence, all relevant elements that have been or could be collected by the competent authorities'.[200] Its requirements will depend upon the circumstances of each case.

5.135   Article 6(3)(b) provides a right to disclosure in some circumstances. See further paras 5.100 *et seq.*

5.136   The requirement of adequate time for the preparation of a defence in Article 6(3)(b) has been invoked where prosecution evidence has been produced late or there has been a last minute change of counsel. Again, the approach of the Strasbourg Court is to look at each case on its facts. Extremely short time limits that prejudice the preparation of the defence will, clearly, violate Article 6(3)(b).

5.137   The Strasbourg Court's interpretation of Article 6(3)(c) (right to choose legal assistance) is narrow. It is clear that legally aided defendants are not entitled to absolute choice. As the Court observed in *Croissant v Germany*:[201]

> It is true that Article 6(3)(c) entitles 'everyone charged with a criminal offence' to be defended by counsel of his choosing. Nevertheless, and notwithstanding the importance of a relationship of confidence between lawyer and client, this right cannot be considered to be absolute. It is necessarily subject to certain limitations where free legal aid is concerned and also where, as in the present case, it is for the courts to decide whether the interests of justice require that the accused be defended by counsel appointed by them. When appointing defence counsel, the national courts must certainly have regard to the defendant's wishes ... However, they can override those wishes when there are relevant and sufficient grounds for holding that this is necessary in the interests of justice.

5.138 Further, the poor performance of a selected representative must be 'manifest' before the accused person will be allowed to replace him. In *Kamasinski v Austria*,[202] for example, the applicant complained that his lawyer had failed to acquaint himself with the evidence but the Court held that this was insufficient and that a failure by legal aid counsel had to be manifest or brought to the attention of the Court in some other way. A similar complaint was held not even to be admissible in *F v United Kingdom*.[203] On the other hand, the Court held, in *Goddi v Italy*,[204] that there was a breach of Article 6(3)(c) where the defendant and his lawyer were unable to be present and where the court appointed lawyer was not acquainted with the case and was given no time to prepare for it.

---

200 *Jespers v Belgium* (1981) 27 DR 61.
201 (1993) 16 EHRR 135, para 29.
202 (1991) 13 EHRR 36.
203 (1993) 15 EHRR CD 32.
204 (1984) 6 EHRR 457.

5.139   The second important issue in relation to Article 6(3)(c) is the stage at which legal representation in criminal cases must be granted. This may certainly extend to the committal hearing if the case is sufficiently complex or important for the accused person.[205] It is also capable of arising at an earlier time, such as the stage of police questioning in circumstances where there was the danger of an adverse inference arising from his silence.[206] A delay in obtaining access to legal assistance whilst in custody may give rise to a breach of Article 6(3).[207]

5.140   Article 6(3)(d) of the Convention confers a minimum right on an accused person to examine and have cross-examined witnesses. Generally, all witnesses must be available for cross-examination and a conviction will not be upheld if the evidence of a witness who has not been questioned forms the principal basis of any conviction.

5.141   This aside, however, whether or not a particular witness must be available for cross-examination will depend upon a balancing exercise. As the Strasbourg Court observed in *Doorson v Netherlands*:[208]

> It is true that Article 6 does not explicitly require the interests of witnesses in general, and those of victims called upon to testify in particular, to be taken into consideration. However, their life, liberty and security of person may be at stake, as may interests coming generally within the ambit of Article 8 of the Convention. Such interests of witnesses and victims are in principle protected by other, substantive provisions of the Convention, which imply that Contracting States should organise their criminal procedure in such a way that those interests are not unjustifiably imperilled.

5.142 So far as defence witnesses are concerned, although Article 6(3)(d) does not require the attendance and examination of every defence witness,[209] it does require equality of arms to be observed (see above) and also that the defence case is heard.

5.143   Finally, Article 6(3)(e) guarantees the right to an interpreter. The scope of this right was considered by the Strasbourg Court in *Luedicke, Belkacem and Koç v Germany*.[210] In that case, the Court held that 'the right protected by Article 6(3)(e) entails, for anyone who cannot speak or understand the language used in court, the right to receive the free assistance of an interpreter, without subsequently having claimed back from him payment of the costs thereby

---

205 *Benham v United Kingdom* (1996) 22 EHRR 293, para 64.

206 *Murray v United Kingdom* (1996) 22 EHRR 29.

207 See *Magee v United Kingdom* (2000) *The Times*, 20 June; *Averill v United Kingdom* (2000) *The Times*, 20 June.

208 (1996) 22 EHRR 330, para 70.

209 *Vidal v Belgium* (1992) A 235.

210 (1979–80) 2 EHRR 149.

incurred'.[211] The Court also observed that the right of free assistance extends to free assistance 'for the translation or interpretation of all those documents or statements in the proceedings instituted against him which it is necessary for him to understand in order to have the benefit of a fair trial'.[212]

---

211 (1979–80) 2 EHRR 149, para 46.

212 (1979–80) 2 EHRR 149, para 48. As already seen, this right extends to the communication of the charge: *Kamasinski v Austria* (1991) 13 EHRR 36, para 74; see para 5.131.

CHAPTER 6

DAMAGES

INTRODUCTION

6.01 There is no general right to damages for misuse of public law powers in English law. CPR Pt 54.3(2) provides that a claim for judicial review may include a claim for damages but may not seek damages alone. Section 31(4) of the Supreme Court Act 1981 further provides that, on an application for judicial review, the court has a discretion to award damages to the applicant, if satisfied that:

> ... if the claim had been made in an action begun by the applicant at the time of making his application, he could have been awarded damages.

6.02 Thus, damages may only be awarded in judicial review proceedings where there also exists a freestanding claim to damages under some other head of claim. As shall be seen, the Human Rights Act 1998 provides such a head of claim.

6.03 There is, further, a perceptible judicial trend towards the widening of the availability of claims for compensation in respect of the actions of public bodies. Restitutionary remedies against public bodies are bound to become of increasing importance now that the courts have recognised payment under a mistake of law as a ground of restitution.[1] Claims for damages can also be pursued against public authorities for misfeasance in public office.[2] Further, the immunities enjoyed by public authorities from actions in negligence in respect of their statutory functions are being eroded,[3] in part because of the Convention case law.[4]

6.04 Where rights in Community law are infringed, different principles apply. In certain circumstances, the state must make good loss and damage caused to individuals by breaches of Community law for which it is responsible. Not all breaches of Community law will, however, give rise to a right to reparation:

---

1 *Kleinwort Benson Ltd v Lincoln City Council and Others* [1999] 2 AC 349. See, also, *R v Inland Revenue Commissioners ex p Woolwich Equitable Building Society* [1990] 1 WLR 1400.

2 *Bourgoin SA v Minister of Agriculture, Fisheries and Food* [1986] QB 716 and *Three Rivers District Council v Bank of England (No 3)* (2000) *The Times*, 19 May.

3 See *X v Bedfordshire County Council* [1995] 2 AC 633; *Barrett v Enfield Borough Council* [1999] 3 WLR 79; *Phelps v Hillingdon London Borough Council* (2000) *The Times*, 28 July.

4 *Osman v United Kingdom* (1999) 29 EHRR 245. This case is discussed at paras 5.70 *et seq.*

whether this is so depends upon the nature of the breach of Community law giving rise to the loss and damage complained of.[5] The leading case is now *Brasserie du Pêcheur and Factortame*.[6] For a right to reparation to arise in Community law, three conditions must be met: the rule of law infringed must be intended to confer rights on individuals; the breach must be sufficiently serious, and there must be a direct causal link between the breach of the obligation resting on the state and the damage sustained by the injured party.[7] If those criteria are satisfied, Community law requires 'full' compensation for breach of Community rights.[8] The reparation provided to the applicants must be 'commensurate with the loss or damage sustained so as to ensure the effective protection for their rights'.[9]

6.05   The Human Rights Act introduces the possibility of awards of damages for breach of Convention rights. The principles which the domestic court must apply when deciding whether to make such an award, and how much to award, are set out below. As shall be seen, it is likely that such awards of damages will fall short of full compensation in many cases.[10]

6.06   The result still leaves an unfortunate lacuna in the law. Claimants for judicial review who are unable to articulate their grievance in either Convention or Community law terms will generally be unable to claim compensation, even where a justiciable wrong has been established.

DAMAGES UNDER THE HUMAN RIGHTS ACT

6.07 The Human Rights Act makes express provision for the award of damages in certain circumstances. It enjoins the courts to take into account the 'principles applied' by the Strasbourg Court when deciding whether to award damages, or the amount of damages to be awarded.[11]

---

5   *Francovich and Bonifaci v Italy* (C-6 and 9/90) [1991] ECR I-5357, para 38.

6   Cases C-46 and 48/93 [1996] ECR I-1029.

7   *Ibid*, para 51.

8   Case C-271 *Marshall v Southampton and South West Hampshire Health Authority (Teaching) (No 2)* [1993] ECR I-4367.

9   Cases C-46 and 48/93 *Brasserie du Pêcheur and Factortame* [1996] ECR I- 1029, para 82. See, however, Case C-66/95 *R v Secretary of State for Social Security ex p Sutton* [1997] ECR I-2163.

10   Where, therefore, a claim that Convention rights have been breached falls within the scope of Community law, it may be preferable to pursue a claim in Community law, rather than pursuant to the HRA 1998. See, further, Chapter 7.

11   HRA 1998, s 8(4).

The power to award damages

6.08 Although Convention rights may be relied upon in any legal proceedings,[12] it does not follow that damages for breach of Convention rights may be awarded by any court or tribunal. Section 8 of the Human Rights Act provides:

(1) In relation to any act (or proposed act) of a public authority which the court finds is (or would be) unlawful, it may grant such relief or remedy, or make such order, within its powers as it considers just an appropriate.

(2) But damages may be awarded only by a court which has power to award damages, or to order the payment of compensation, in civil proceedings.

6.09 Elementarily, there are statutory tribunals which lack any such power, such as, for example, the Immigration Appeal Tribunal. Lest there be any doubt about it, s 8(2) provides:

... damages may be awarded only by a court which has power to award damages, or to order the payment of compensation, in civil proceedings.

6.10 In this context, 'court' is defined so as to include a tribunal.[13] Thus, on the face of it, only a court or tribunal with the power to at least make some form of order for the payment of compensation, such as employment tribunals, may make an award of damages for breach of Convention rights.

6.11 It appears clear that a tribunal which lacks any such compensatory power which the Act can 'piggy back' upon does not acquire a power to award damages from the Act itself.[14]

6.12 Section 7(11) of the Act provides for a possible expansion in the remedies available:

The Minister who has power to make rules in relation to a particular tribunal may, to the extent he considers it necessary to ensure that the tribunal can provide an appropriate remedy in relation to an act (or proposed act) of a public authority which is (or would be) unlawful as a result of s 6(1), by order add to:

(a) the relief or remedies which the tribunal[15] may grant; or

(b) the grounds on which it may grant any of them.

---

12 HRA 1998, s 7(1)(b).

13 *Ibid*, s 8(6).

14 Although the Act requires such tribunals to take into account the Strasbourg case law when determining a question in connection with a 'Convention right' (*ibid*, s 2(1)), such rights are however defined so as to exclude ECHR, Art 13 (right to an effective remedy) and Art 41 (just satisfaction).

15 *Ibid*, s 7(11) refers only to the power of the minister to make rules for a 'tribunal'. In several sections of the Act, 'tribunal' is defined to include 'court', eg, s 8(6). No such definition appears in s 7.

6.13 At the date this book went to press, no such orders had been made. The Lord Chancellor's Department consultation paper on the proposed rules of court[16] provides that there is no intention at present to use this power.

6.14 The Consultation Paper makes further proposals as to where a claim for damages under the Convention should be pursued:

> We propose that a free-standing case under s 7(1)(a)[17] of the Act should be brought in the following ways:
>
> • using the existing judicial review procedures;
>
> • in the county court or in the High Court where a claim for damages is made (unless this is associated with a claim for judicial review).

6.15 No such express rule has been included in CPR Pt 54 to date. The effect of the rules is, it is submitted, that a damages claim can be pursued outside the Administrative Court, but, if judicial review relief is also sought (that is, where the victim of breach of Convention rights also seeks a quashing order or another prerogative remedy) the claim must be brought within the bounds of CPR Pt 54.

Civil proceedings only

6.16 Section 8(2) of the Act expressly precludes the possibility that a criminal court might make an award of damages. Such claims should be pursued through the civil courts.[18]

Discretionary nature of award of damages

6.17 There is no entitlement to an award of damages for breach of Convention rights even where harm can be proven; s 8(1) of the Act makes it plain that all remedies under the Act are discretionary. Further, as shall be seen at para 6.25, domestic courts and tribunals are required to 'take into account the principles of the European Court of Human Rights'. That Court too regards the award of damages as a matter of discretion.[19]

6.18 Section 8(3) of the Human Rights Act specifies a number of factors which must be taken into account by the courts when exercising the discretion to award damages:

---

16 *Human Rights Act 1998: Rules and Practice Directions*, 13 March 2000.

17 HRA 1998, s 7(1)(a) provides that a person who claims that a public authority has acted (or proposes to act) in a way which is incompatible with a Convention right may bring proceedings under the Act in an appropriate court or tribunal.

18 See *Hansard*, HL, 24 November 1997, col 855, *per* the Lord Chancellor.

19 *Sunday Times v United Kingdom* (Art 50) (1981) 3 EHRR 317, para 15; *Guzzardi v Italy* (1981) 3 EHRR 333, para 114.

No award of damages is to be made unless, taking account of all the circumstances of the case, including:

(a) any other relief or remedy granted, or order made, in relation to the act in question (by that or any other court); and

(b) the consequences of any decision (of that or any other court) in respect of that act,

the court is satisfied that the award is necessary to afford just satisfaction to the person in whose favour it is made.

6.19 The court must be satisfied that an award of damages is 'necessary to afford just satisfaction' to the claimant. As shall be seen at paras 6.27 *et seq*, this is the test which the Strasbourg Court applies when considering an award of damages.

6.20 The Act requires that the factors set out in s 8(3)(a) and (b) are expressly taken into account when considering such an award.

6.21 The principal rationale for the first limb, (a), may be to ensure that a court awarding damages takes account of any award made under 'ordinary' domestic law. If, for example, Article 5 is prayed in aid in a false imprisonment case, domestic case law provides for compensation.[20] It may, therefore, be asked why the courts should make any further award in such a case. Section 8(3)(a) of the Human Rights Act appears aimed at discouraging them from doing so. This limb may also be intended to encourage the courts to adopt a specific doctrine of the Strasbourg Court. That Court frequently declines to make any award of damage on the grounds that the 'judgment itself offers sufficient reparation' (see, further, paras 6.56 *et seq*) even in cases where damage is unequivocally shown to have occurred.

6.22 The second limb, (b), is more opaque. It may be, however, that where, for example, a domestic court disapplies subordinate legislation, it is envisaged that a court could invoke this limb in holding that the relief given is sufficient without further award of damages.

Damages for 'judicial acts'

6.23 The Human Rights Act erects a further hurdle for applicants seeking to obtain damages where the breach of Convention rights complained of was committed by a court. Section 9(3) states:

In proceedings under this Act in respect of a judicial act done in good faith, damages may not be awarded otherwise than to compensate a person to the extent required by Article 5(5) of the Convention.[21]

---

20 See, further, *Thompson v Commissioner of Police for the Metropolis* [1998] QB 498.

21 ECHR, Art 5(5) provides for an enforceable right to compensation where there has been arrest or detention in contravention of the Convention.

6.24 The Act provides that a 'judicial act' means a judicial act of a court,[22] 'Court' is defined to include a tribunal.[23] Where a challenge is brought to a judicial act, damages will not be awarded in the absence of bad faith. In practice, this is likely to be of wide ranging importance in view of the large number of administrative bodies which fall within the ordinary meaning of 'tribunal'. The Strasbourg Court does not apply any such restrictions.[24] As shall be seen at paras 6.37 *et seq*, where there are good policy reasons for refusing an award of damages, the inherent flexibility of the Convention approach to damages provides ample scope to decline to make any award.

The role of the Strasbourg case law

6.25 The Human Rights Act makes clear that the Strasbourg case law will be central to the assessment of damages for the breach of Convention rights. Section 8(4) provides:

> In determining:
>
> (a) whether to award damages; or
>
> (b) the amount of an award,
>
> the court must take into account the principles applied by the European Court of Human Rights in relation to the award of compensation under Article 41 of the Convention.

6.26 The approach of the Strasbourg Court is considered below.

THE STRASBOURG CASE LAW

6.27 The Strasbourg Court is not bound by any national legal rule in respect of the award of compensation.[25] The award of compensation is governed by Article 41[26] of the Convention, which provides:

> If the Court finds that there has been a violation of the Convention or the protocols thereto, and if the internal law of the High Contracting Party concerned allows only partial reparation to be made, the Court shall, if necessary afford just satisfaction to the injured party.

---

22 HRA 1998, s 9(5).

23 *Ibid*, s 9(5). Thus, there is no prospect that the courts will apply the broad approach to the meaning of judicial act to be found in *Ridge v Baldwin* [1964] AC 40, which provides that any exercise of power which affects rights or interests is 'judicial' and must accordingly be exercised fairly. Such a wide interpretation of the provisions of the HRA 1998 would have removed much of the utility of the remedy of damages.

24 See, eg, *Dombo Beheer BV v Netherlands* (1994) 18 EHRR 213, para 40; the claim for just satisfaction arising out of breach of Art 6 by a court failed, but only as a matter of evidence.

25 *Sunday Times v United Kingdom* (Art 50) (1981) 3 EHRR 317, para 15.

26 Formerly, Art 50.

5.28 The concept of 'just satisfaction' is central to the Strasbourg Court's approach, and, as has been seen, the Human Rights Act provides that this is the test that the domestic courts must apply in considering an award of damages.[27] In addition, the Act expressly requires domestic courts to take into account the principles applied by the Strasbourg Court in relation to an award of compensation under Article 41.

5.29 It has become trite to say that there are no such 'principles' which the domestic courts could take into account in considering an award of damages. This is, however, over-simplistic. There are inconsistencies and anomalies in the approach of the Strasbourg Court to the award of compensation. Nevertheless, there are governing principles which the Court applies – and which may be invoked before a domestic court. They are considered below.

Who can receive just satisfaction

5.30 Only a victim of a breach of Convention rights can claim just satisfaction. The meaning of 'victim' is analysed elsewhere.[28] In order to obtain just satisfaction, the 'victim' must, however, be one of the applicants named in the petition to the Court. Thus, in *Olsson v Sweden*,[29] where applicant parents established that their children had been taken into care in breach of the Convention, no award of just satisfaction could be made to their children who were not parties.

5.31 Claims before the Strasbourg Court are sometimes permitted to continue notwithstanding the death of the applicant (see paras 2.45 *et seq*). The Court has accepted that as a matter of principle a claim for just satisfaction vested in a deceased person may survive for the benefit of his estate, at least in respect of pecuniary damage, and costs.[30] Whilst there is no express prohibition upon an award in respect of non-pecuniary damage suffered by a deceased applicant, the Court is more reluctant to make such an award. In *Deweer v Belgium*,[31] the Court entertained the claim in principle, but declined to make any award of just satisfaction beyond the finding of violation. In *X v United Kingdom*,[32] the applicant had been detained unlawfully in a mental hospital. He had died before his case was heard by the Court. The Court held that no award would be made to his estate for injuries of a 'purely personal nature'. By contrast, in

---

27 HRA 1998, s 8(3), see para 6.18.
28 See paras 2.12 *et seq*. The lawyer of a successful applicant cannot pursue a claim for fees or expenses under Art 50: *Leudicke, Belkacem and Koç v Germany (No 2)* (1979–80) 2 EHRR 433, para 15.
29 (1989) 11 EHRR 259, para 101.
30 *Deweer v Belgium* (1979–80) 2 EHRR 439.
31 *Ibid.*
32 (1982) 4 EHRR 188.

X v France,[33] the applicant died in the course of proceedings for compensation arising out of the supply of contaminated blood which caused him to become HIV positive. The Court awarded FF150,000 in respect of non-pecuniary injury.[34]

Proof of loss

6.32 The Court will not consider the question of just satisfaction of its own motion.[35] The applicant must advance details of any claimed pecuniary losses.[36] The Court is sometimes prepared to infer the existence of non-pecuniary loss, but will not always do so.[37]

Pecuniary and non-pecuniary loss

6.33 The Strasbourg Court generally distinguishes pecuniary and non-pecuniary loss. These measures are broadly equivalent to general and special damages in domestic law, although as shall be explained the meaning is not precisely the same. The distinction between these categories is not treated by the Court as an entirely rigid one.[38] The Court sometimes makes global awards which combine elements of compensation for pecuniary and non-pecuniary loss without apportioning the figure between these elements.[39]

6.34 The Court makes awards of compensation for non-pecuniary loss for a wide range of non-fiscal harms, including frustration,[40] feelings of injustice[41]

---

33 (1992) 14 EHRR 483. See, also, *McCann v United Kingdom* (1996) 21 EHRR 97 where an award of just satisfaction was refused to terrorist suspects killed by the SAS without determining the issue of principle.

34 It appears from the judgment that *X v United Kingdom* was not cited to the Court, and the underlying issue of principle is not explored in the judgment.

35 *Sunday Times v United Kingdom* (Art 50) (1981) 3 EHRR 317 restated on numerous occasions; eg, *Inze v Austria* (1988) 10 EHRR 394, para 46.

36 Eg, *H v Belgium* (1988) 10 EHRR 339, para 72. An 'equitable award' may however be made even in the absence of clear evidence. See *Open Door Counselling and Dublin Well Woman v Ireland* (1993) 15 EHRR 244, para 6.42.

37 Contrast, eg, *Artico v Italy* (1981) 3 EHRR 1, para 47 and *Pakelli v Germany* (1984) 6 EHRR 1, para 46.

38 Eg, in *Darnell v United Kingdom* (1994) 18 EHRR 205, para 24, an award was made for serious damage to the applicant's 'professional career' as a result of time lost due to prolonged disciplinary proceedings under the head of non-pecuniary loss.

39 Eg, *Lechner and Hess v Austria* (1987) 9 EHRR 490; *Allenet de Ribemont v France* (1995) 20 EHRR 557.

40 *Philis v Greece* (1991) 13 EHRR 741.

41 *Keegan v Ireland* (1994) 18 EHRR 342, para 68.

stress and anxiety[42] caused by unlawful actions, fear,[43] inconvenience,[44] humiliation,[45] a 'distressing sensation of isolation, confusion and neglect',[46] feelings of defencelessness,[47] and the adverse effect on the applicant's reputation.[48]

6.35   The Court is sometimes willing to infer that on the circumstances of a particular case, such harm must have occurred;[49] on other occasions, it has rejected such claims for want of proof.[50] Even where the Court finds such harm to have occurred, it does not always make an award of compensation for it.[51]

6.36   It appears that in principle awards for non-pecuniary damage may be made to non-natural persons. In *Matos e Silva, Lda v Portugal*,[52] the applicant company claimed non-pecuniary damage on the basis of feelings of 'frustration, powerlessness, suffering and revolt' arising from its dispute with the state.[53] The Court did not rule upon the respondent's submission that only 'individuals'[54] could suffer under these heads, but made an equitable award of damages, without distinguishing between pecuniary and non-pecuniary losses, taking into account the uncertainty created by the prolonged proceedings. In *Pressos Compania SA v Belgium*,[55] the Court rejected a claim for non-pecuniary loss by the applicant company but did so on the basis that the judgment offered sufficient reparation in this respect – not as a matter of principle.

The compensatory approach

6.37 The Court has at times adopted a truly compensatory approach to the award of damages. In *Papamichalopoulos v Greece*,[56] it cited with approval the words of the Permanent Court of International Justice:[57]

---

42 *H v France* (1990) 12 EHRR 74, para 73.
43 *Van der Leer v Netherlands* (1990) 12 EHRR 567, para 42.
44 *Olsson v Sweden* (1989) 11 EHRR 259, para 102.
45 *Young, James and Webster v United Kingdom* (just satisfaction) (1983) 5 EHRR 201, para 12.
46 *Artico v Italy* (1981) 3 EHRR 1, para 47.
47 *Ibid.*
48 *Brincat v Italy* (1993) 16 EHRR 591, para 26.
49 Eg, *Artico v Italy* (1981) 3 EHRR 1, para 47.
50 Eg, *Pakelli v Germany* (1984) 6 EHRR 1 para 46.
51 *Abdulaziz and Others v United Kingdom* (1985) 7 EHRR 471, para 96.
52 (1997) 24 EHRR 573.
53 *Ibid*, para 98.
54 *Ibid*, para 99.
55 (just satisfaction) 26 June 1997.
56 (1996) 21 EHRR 439, para 36.
57 *Case concerning the factory at Chorzów*, Series A No 17, p 47.

... reparation must, as far as possible, wipe out all the consequences of the illegal act and re-establish the situation which would, in all probability, have existed if that act had not been committed. Restitution in kind, or, if this is not possible, payment of a sum corresponding to the value which a restitution in kind would bear; the award, if need be, of damage for loss sustained which would not be covered by restitution in kind or payment in place of it – such are the principles which should serve to determine the amount of compensation due for an act contrary to international law.

6.38 The Strasbourg Court accordingly held that an award of just satisfaction would be made where the state has not,[58] or cannot, effect *restitutio in integrum*.[59] In the *Papamichalopoulos* case, the Court expressly sought to put the applicants 'as far as possible in a situation equivalent to the one in which they would have been had there not been a breach'[60] of the Convention.

6.39 These statements of principle are broadly equivalent to the 'tortious' measure of damages in domestic law. They must, however, be put in proper context. As has already been seen, the Court considers the award of just satisfaction to be discretionary.[61] It does not generally explicitly endorse or apply any tortious, or compensatory rule, even where invited to do so.[62] Where the Court has awarded full compensation, it has generally done so where the measure of such damages was clear or obvious. Thus, in *Darby v Sweden*,[63] the applicant was a Finnish citizen working in Sweden. He complained successful that he had been subjected to a tax to finance the religious activities of the Church of Sweden. The Court awarded him the full amount of the tax he had paid, plus interest. Similarly, in *Schmidt v Germany*,[64] the applicants successfully challenged a requirement that all male adults should either serve as firemen or pay a levy in lieu. The Court ordered repayment of the levy.

6.40 There are, however, many cases in which restitution was possible and instead, the Court has preferred the imprecision of an 'equitable' award.

---

58 For the effect of partial, or total, reparation by the state, see para 6.47.

59 *Papamichalopoulos v Greece* (just satisfaction) (1996) 21 EHRR 439, para 34.

60 *Ibid*, para 38.

61 *Sunday Times v United Kingdom* (Art 50) (1981) 3 EHRR 317, para 15; *Guzzardi v Italy* (1981) 3 EHRR 333, para 114.

62 In *Matos e Silva v Portugal* (1997) 24 EHRR 573, the applicant submitted that this tortious measure should apply. The Court in fact applied an 'equitable' measure (discussed further below) but did not seek to suggest that this measure of damages could not be applied in principle.

63 (1991) 13 EHRR 774.

64 (1994) 18 EHRR 513.

The equitable approach

6.41 As has been seen, the Court regards the award of damages as a matter of discretion. It generally makes 'equitable' awards in respect of losses, both pecuniary and otherwise. The Court has made equitable awards in respect of pecuniary damages when faced by complex calculations. In *Pine Valley v Ireland*,[65] a case concerned with the value of land, the Court reserved its judgment on just satisfaction,[66] gave a reasonably detailed analysis of arguments on quantum advanced by both sides but eventually made an equitable award in any event. In *Sporrong and Lönnroth v Sweden*,[67] the Court declared the methods of calculation proposed by the parties to be inadequate, but stated that it did not consider it had to establish another.

6.42 An equitable award of damages may however, sometimes work to the applicant's advantage. In *Open Door Counselling v Ireland*,[68] the applicant clinic claimed IR£62,172 loss of earnings arising out of an Irish law which prohibited it from providing information about abortion clinics outside Ireland. The Court held that the applicant had 'not indicated how these losses were calculated or sought to substantiate them'.[69] Nevertheless, the Court concluded that there must have been some damage, and awarded IR£25,000 on an equitable basis.

Quantum

6.43 There is some justification in the frequent observation that awards of damages by the Strasbourg Court are generally small.[70] Nevertheless, the Court has made large awards in some cases. In *Pine Valley Developments Ltd v Ireland*,[71] the Court awarded IR£1.2 million in respect of the loss of value of land. In *Vermiere v Belgium*,[72] it awarded Bfr22,000,000 for loss of inheritance due to an illegitimate child.

---

65 (1992) 14 EHRR 319.

66 Judgment of 9 February 1993.

67 Judgment on just satisfaction, 18 December 1984. See, similarly, *Matos e Silva, Lda v Portugal* (1997) 24 EHRR 573.

68 (1993) 15 EHRR 244.

69 *Ibid*, para 87.

70 Extremely helpful quantum tables can be found in Karen Reid, *A Practitioner's Guide to the European Convention of Human Rights*, 1998, London: Sweet & Maxwell.

71 (just satisfaction) (1993) 16 EHRR 379. In *Papamichalopoulos v Greece* (just satisfaction) (1996) 21 EHRR 439, the Court awarded 4,200 million drachmas, again in respect of the value of land.

72 (1990) A 270-A.

6.44   The Court has sanctioned the use of experts to assess quantum. In *Papamichalopoulos v Greece*,[73] the applicants' land had been deprived of the use of land. The Court ordered the parties to nominate agreed experts to value the disputed land; the costs of the experts was to be born by the Greek state.[74] In *Pressos Compania SA and Others v Belgium*,[75] however, the Court refused to extend the use of experts to a case where it was necessary to establish primary liability, as well as quantum of damage.

6.45   Where the applicant restricts his claim to a modest[76] or 'token'[77] sum the Court may simply award it in full.

6.46   As to awards of non-pecuniary damage, the Court does not appear to apply a clearly identifiable tariff, and such awards are highly unpredictable.[78]

Mitigation

6.47   The acts of an infringing state may serve to mitigate the harm suffered by the victim of a breach of the Convention.[79] Article 41 of the Convention permits the Strasbourg Court to make an award of just satisfaction only 'if the internal law of the High Contracting Party concerned allows only partial reparation to be made'. Awards of damages,[80] or other forms of reparation including ex gratia payments[81] and even an apology[82] may be taken into account.

6.48   Where damages are claimed for unlawful detention, the Court takes into account any remission provided by the state against other periods of lawful detention.[83]

---

73   (just satisfaction) (1996) 21 EHRR 439.

74   It assessed the experts' fees on an equitable basis: judgment on just satisfaction, para 54.

75   (just satisfaction) 26 June 1997.

76   *Salesi v Italy* (1998) 26 EHRR 187.

77   *Canea Catholic Church v Greece* (1999) 27 EHRR 521.

78   See, eg, cases on unlawful detention: *Quinn v France* (1996) 21 EHRR 529; *De Jong, Baljet and Van den Brink v Netherlands* (1986) 8 EHRR 20.

79   As to the question whether full reparation by national authorities may deprive an applicant of the status of 'victim', see para 2.33.

80   Eg, *Inze v Austria* (1988) 10 EHRR 394, para 47.

81   Eg, *A and Others v Netherlands* (1996) 22 EHRR 458.

82   *Darnell v United Kingdom* (1994) 18 EHRR 205.

83   See, amongst others, *Neumeister v Austria* (1979–80) 1 EHRR 136, para 40; *Ringeisen v Austria (No 2)* (1979–80) 1 EHRR 504, para 21; *Engel v Netherlands (No 2)* (1979–80) 1 EHRR 706, para 10. The Court has sometimes accepted that some non-pecuniary harm remains in any event, eg, *De Jong, Baljet and Van den Brink v Netherlands* (1986) 8 EHRR 20, para 65.

Conduct of the applicant

6.49 The Court takes account of the conduct of the applicant in assessing non-pecuniary loss. Thus, in *McCann v United Kingdom*,[84] which concerned the shooting by the SAS of three suspected IRA terrorists in Gibraltar, the Court declined to make an award of damages on the basis that it did not consider it 'appropriate' as the victims had intending to plant a bomb.

6.50 The doctrine can also apply on less extreme facts. In *Johnson v United Kingdom*,[85] the applicant was awarded £10,000 for three years unlawful detention in a mental hospital. The Court expressly took account of his 'negative attitude towards his rehabilitation' and refusal to cooperate in finding a placement. Similarly, in *A and Others v Netherlands*,[86] the Court award for non-pecuniary damage arising out of the length of proceedings, but took into account the contribution by the applicants to that delay. Hansard reveals that the government had this particular feature of the Strasbourg case law in mind in requiring tribunals to take account of the Strasbourg case law in determining whether to award damages, or the amount of an award pursuant to s 8(4) of the Human Rights Act.[87]

Causation – lost opportunities and procedural unfairness

6.51 The Court frequently emphasises the need to establish a causal link between the breach of Convention rights and the damage claimed. Claims are often rejected for want of it.[88]

6.52 Where, however, a claim is made for 'lost opportunities' which the Court considers do not readily lend themselves to precise quantification, an award may be made.[89] In *Gaygasuz v Austria*,[90] the applicant, who was Turkish but lived in Austria, had been refused an advance on his pension by way of emergency assistance because he did not have Austrian nationality. The applicant claimed on the basis of six years assistance that he had been deprived of. He in fact had left Austria within weeks of his application, but contended that this had been because of the non-payment. The Strasbourg Court stated it did not wish to speculate as to his situation after the date of his

---

84 (1996) 21 EHRR 97.
85 (1999) 27 EHRR 296, para 77.
86 (1996) 22 EHRR 458.
87 See statement of Mike O'Brien MP (Parliamentary Under Secretary of State for the Home Department) *Hansard*, HC, 24 June 1998, col 1113.
88 Se, eg, *Mauer v Austria* (1998) 25 EHRR 91.
89 Eg, *Inze v Austria* (1988) 10 EHRR 394.
90 (1997) 23 EHRR 361.

departure awarded him one-quarter of what he had claimed on an equitable basis. [91]

6.53   Where the complaint is one of procedural unfairness, the question which arises is whether the applicant would have suffered the loss complained of had he received a fair trial. The Court's approach to this question is not consistent. In such cases, the Court frequently declines to 'speculate' at to what the outcome of proceedings would have been in the absence of a breach of the Convention.[92] *Dombo Beheer BV v Netherlands*[93] typifies this approach. The applicant complained that a decision by a Dutch judge to preclude it calling certain evidence in the course of a civil trial amounted to a breach of natural justice. It claimed just satisfaction, on the basis that it would have won the trial. The Court concluded that it could not determine whether this would indeed have been the outcome had evidence been heard and declined to award any compensation in respect of this loss. Similarly, in *Fredin v Sweden*,[94] the applicants complained of the revocation of a license granted to them to exploit a gravel pit which they owned. The Court found that the absence of any available form of judicial review breached Article 6(1). The applicants sought consequential economic losses of Skr28,000,000. The Court held that no causal link had been established between the violation of Convention rights and the alleged harm.

6.54   On the other hand, where it appears that the applicant's claim appears to be less conjectural, the Court has been prepared to make an award. In *Martins Moriera v Portugal*,[95] the Court found that civil proceedings arising out of a road traffic accident had exceeded a reasonable length. The defendant company had become insolvent before judgment against it could be enforced, and as a result, the applicant claimed to have been deprived of the chance to recover damages. The Strasbourg Court concluded that although it was not certain he would have recovered the entirety of the judgment debt had the domestic proceedings been terminated earlier, it was reasonable to conclude he had suffered a loss of opportunities. The Court has made such awards without requiring that the applicant must establish that the outcome would have been different on the balance of probabilities. In *Goddi v Italy*,[96] the applicant complained that neither he nor his lawyer had been present during a criminal appeal at which a custodial sentence imposed by a lower court was increased.

---

91 See, similarly, *Pressos Compania SA and Others v Belgium* (just satisfaction) 26 June 1997.

92 See, amongst others, *Håkansson and Sturesson v Sweden* (1991) 13 EHRR 1, para 72; *Fredin v Sweden* (1991) 13 EHRR 784, para 65; *Findlay v United Kingdom* (1997) 24 EHRR 221, para 88.

93 (1994) 18 EHRR 213.

94 (1991) 13 EHRR 784.

95 (1991) 13 EHRR 517.

96 (1984) 6 EHRR 457. See, to similar effect, *Colozza v Italy* (1985) 7 EHRR 516 (trial and conviction in absentia).

A court appointed lawyer had acted in his absence. The Court rejected the applicant's assertion that had his lawyer been present 'he would certainly have received a lighter sentence', but found that the outcome 'might possibly have been different' if he had the benefit of a 'practical and effective' defence. It accordingly awarded L5 million to reflect the loss of an opportunity and non-pecuniary damage suffered.

6.55 A claim for non-pecuniary damage arising from procedural failure ought not to face such difficulties over causation. The applicant in *H v Belgium*[97] was a disbarred lawyer who successfully contended that there had been a breach of Article 6 in the conduct of his application for readmission. He was awarded Bfr250,000 for non-pecuniary loss, without the Court even reaching an express finding that he had lost any real opportunity to affect the outcome of his case.[98]

Judgment as sufficient reparation

6.56 The Strasbourg Court frequently holds that the judgment of the Court itself offers sufficient reparation in itself.[99] The 'sufficient reparation' doctrine is superficially akin to the domestic doctrine of nominal damage.[100] Such a finding does not imply that no harm has occurred. In *Dudgeon v United Kingdom*,[101] for example, the Court accepted that the applicant had suffered 'distress, anxiety, suffering and inconvenience' on account of a police investigation into his (then) illegal homosexual acts. The Court had held that the law in question breached the applicant's Article 8 rights, but held the prejudice complained of did not warrant an award of compensation. Ostensibly at least, the sufficient reparation doctrine is invoked where the Court considers that the judgment is itself compensation for that harm. The Court has made such a finding in cases where it is apparent that the suffered is relatively slight.[102] It is, however, applied where it appears that more

---

97 See, amongst many examples, *H v Belgium* (1988) 10 EHRR 339; *Fredin v Sweden* (1991) 13 EHRR 784; *De Moor v Belgium* (1994) 18 EHRR 372;

98 Compare, however, *Le Compte, Van Leuven and De Meyere v Belgium (Art 50)* (1983) 5 EHRR 183, where judgment was held to be sufficient reparation for non-pecuniary losses allegedly flowing from procedural unfairness in the course of professional disciplinary proceedings.

99 The Court may, however, decline to make award without reference to this doctrine: *Bunkate v Netherlands* (1995) 19 EHRR 477, para 25.

100 The Strasbourg Court has also awarded nominal damages, Eg, *Engel v Netherlands (No 2)* (1979–80) 1 EHRR 706.

101 (Art 50) (1983) 5 EHRR 573. See, also, Fox, *Campbell and Hartley v United Kingdom* (just satisfaction) (1992) 14 EHRR 108.

102 *Koster v Netherlands* (1992) 14 EHRR 396.

significant harm has been suffered.[103] Judgment has also been held to be sufficient reparation in cases which are superficially comparable to others where monetary awards have been made.[104]

Non-compensatory awards

6.57 There are indications that the Court will take into account a non-compensatory element in assessing an award. In *Halford v United Kingdom*,[105] the applicant established a breach of Article 8 where calls from her office telephone had been intercepted by her employer, the police. The Court took into account that this had been the 'primary purpose' of the interception was to gather evidence for use in sex discrimination proceedings brought by her, and that this was a 'serious infringement' of her rights. It also accepted that there was no evidence to suggest that the stress she had suffered was directly attributable to the calls, rather than to her other conflicts with the police. It awarded her £10,000 in non-pecuniary loss on a just and equitable basis.[106] It appears therefore that to some extent the award reflected the perceived gravity of the breach, the gravity itself being in part a function of the intentions of the respondent state. Similarly, in *Allenet de Ribemont v France*,[107] the Court expressly took into account the 'reprehensible' nature of the state's conduct in making an award.

Interest

6.58 A truly compensatory approach to the award of damages requires the award of interest in an appropriate case. Sometimes, the Strasbourg Court makes such an award. In *Stran Greek Refineries v Greece*,[108] the applicants had received an arbitration award which had been rendered invalid and unenforceable by legislation. The Strasbourg Court held that a breach of Article 1 of Protocol No 1 was made out and that the applicants were entitled both to reimbursement of the arbitration awards, together with interest, as without it 'the adequacy of the compensation would be diminished'.[109] Ten years had elapsed since the original arbitration award. Similarly, in *Darby v Sweden*,[110] it

---

103 Eg, *Zimmerman and Steiner v Switzerland* (1984) 6 EHRR 17 (three and a half year delay in administrative proceedings); *Dudgeon v United Kingdom* (Art 50) (1983) 5 EHRR 573 (police investigation into homosexual activities); *Amuur v France* (1996) 22 EHRR 533 (17 days unlawful detention for asylum seekers).

104 Compare *Le Compte, Van Leuven and De Meyere v Belgium* (Art 50) (1983) 5 EHRR 183 and *H v Belgium* (1988) 10 EI IRR 339.

105 (1997) 24 EHRR 523.

106 *Ibid*, para 76.

107 (1995) 20 EHRR 557.

108 (1995) 19 EHRR 293.

109 *Ibid*, para 82.

110 (1991) 13 EHRR 774, para 37. The facts are summarised at para 6.39.

awarded the applicant interest calculated 'in the light of the interest rates in Sweden at the time' calculated from the date in which the applicant paid taxes (held by the Court to be contrary to the Convention) to the date on which they were to be reimbursed.

6.59　　The practice of the Strasbourg Court is not consistent, however. It frequently makes no award of interest at all, or may even make an equitable award of interest.[111]

6.60　　The Court does, however, usually award 'default' interest to run if the respondent fails to pay the award of just satisfaction[112] within the time ordered by the Court. Where it does so, it usually applies the measure of interest applicable in national law.[113]

Costs and expenses

6.61　Costs and expenses are recoverable in principle as 'just satisfaction'.[114] This extends to both the proceedings before the national court, and those at Strasbourg. The injured party is not, however, entitled to costs as of right; the Court applies an 'equitable' or discretionary approach to such awards,[115] just as otherwise in considering an award of just satisfaction.

6.62　　The Court asks whether the sums claimed were 'actually[116] incurred, were necessarily incurred and were also reasonable as to quantum'.[117] In practice, it carries out a form of summary taxation. It frequently awards less than the full amount claimed by lawyers,[118] although not invariably.[119]

6.63　　Where the Court substitutes its own figure, on an 'equitable basis' the effect can be drastic. In *Matos e Silva, Lda v Portugal*,[120] the applicants claimed costs of

---

111 *Schüler-Zgraggen v Switzerland* (just satisfaction) (1995) A 305-A.

112 Such an order generally extends to awards of costs and expenses.

113 See, eg, *Matos e Silva v Portugal* (1997) 24 EHRR 573; *Bowman v United Kingdom* (1998) 26 EHRR 1. In *Mentes v Turkey* (1997) 26 EHRR 595, however, the Court applied the English measure of interest.

114 The Court will, however, deduct any legal aid received from the Council of Europe, eg, *Open Door Counselling v Ireland* (1993) 15 EHRR 244, para 90.

115 *Sunday Times v United Kingdom (Art 50)* (1981) 3 EHRR 317, para 15.

116 The requirement that costs be 'actually' incurred has been held by the Court to exclude the award of any sum in respect of a contingency fee arrangement under which was unenforceable and where in fact the fees were paid by a third party in any event: *Dudgeon v United Kingdom* (Art 50) (1983) 5 EHRR 573, para 22.

117 *Sunday Times v United Kingdom* (Art 50) (1981) 3 EHRR 317, para 23.

118 See, eg, *Inze v Austria* (1988) 10 EHRR 394, para 55; *Darby v Sweden* (1991) 13 EHRR 774, para 41. The Court does not consider itself bound by domestic scales and practices, but is prepared to consider them: *König v Germany* (1979–80) 2 EHRR 469, recently re-affirmed in *Tolstoy Miloslavsky v United Kingdom* (1995) 20 EHRR 442, para 77.

119 Eg, *Findlay v United Kingdom* (1997) 24 EHRR 221, para 91.

120 (1997) 24 EHRR 573, para 105.

PTE320,000,000; the Court awarded PTE6,000,000. The Court may disallow a claimed head of expenses in its entirety.[121]

6.64　　　Where the applicant's claim only succeeds in part, a reduction in the award of costs and expenses may be made to reflect this,[122] just as under CPR r 44.3.

---

121 Eg, *Mentes v Turkey* (1997) 26 EHRR 595, para 107: claim to the costs of assistance by the Kurdish Human Rights Project by applicants who complained of actions by the Turkish security forces, rejected by the Court. See, also, *Open Door Counselling and Dublin Well Woman v Ireland* (1993) 15 EHRR 244, para 90.

122 Eg, *Benham v United Kingdom* (1996) 22 EHRR 293, para 71.

CHAPTER 7

THE CONVENTION AND COMMUNITY LAW

OVERVIEW

7.01 The relationship between European Community law, the European Convention on Human Rights and the Human Rights Act 1998 is complex. Three fundamental questions arise:

(1) On what basis are the principles underlying the ECHR part of Community law?

(2) To what *extent* are these principles part of Community law?

(3) How should the High Court, on judicial review, approach human rights issues where Community law is involved?

7.02 This chapter addresses each of these questions in turn. Three preliminary points are emphasised.

7.03 First, the nature and extent of ECHR principles as part of Community law are a matter for determination by the European Court of Justice in Luxembourg ('ECJ') rather than the European Court of Human Rights in Strasbourg[1] or, indeed, the national court. This legal reality, elementary in the context of Community law, is relevant to the general priority that the High Court must accord to the ECJ over Strasbourg where Convention issues arise in the course of a determination as to whether a breach of fundamental rights has given rise to a breach of Community law.[2]

7.04 Secondly, as shall be seen, the Court in Luxembourg has, at times, reached a different view from that taken in Strasbourg as to the interpretation of Convention rights. The ECJ applies the Convention as a tool for the interpretation of fundamental rights in Community law. The Convention itself is not a part of Community law. Thus, in a case within the scope of Community law, a finding that there has been no breach of fundamental rights does not preclude a claimant from establishing a breach of Convention rights by reliance upon the Human Rights Act.

---

1   As will be seen, however, the Strasbourg case law is, increasingly, referred to by the ECJ. See paras 7.14 *et seq*.

2   This is subject to the possibility, considered below, of whether as a matter of Community law Strasbourg judgments could take precedence over those of the ECJ itself.

7.05   Lastly, whilst s 4 of the Human Rights Act prevents the High Court from disapplying primary legislation that is incompatible with the ECHR, where the legislation is incompatible with Community law the same legislation would, it is submitted, have to be disapplied even where the basis of the Community law challenge is fundamental rights.

7.06   There is, therefore, considerable potential for inconsistency in the application of human rights law between cases which fall within the scope of Community law and those which do not.

THE ECHR IN COMMUNITY LAW

The initial position

7.07   For some time, there was resistance in Luxembourg to the notion that the ECHR had any part to play in Community law. Early cases such as *Stork*,[3] *Geitling*[4] and *Sgarlata*[5] stressed, in different ways, that the protection of fundamental rights as recognised in the constitutions of certain Member States was neither intrinsic to the EC Treaty nor part of the general principles of Community law.[6]

7.08   This position reflected the tension, as between domestic law and Community law, inherent in the then developing concept of Community law supremacy as developed by the ECJ (see, for example, *Costa v ENEL*;[7] *Simmenthal*)[8] and direct effect (*Van Gend en Loos*).[9] If Convention law could trump Community law, then, axiomatically, Community law could not be 'supreme'.

Stages of change

7.09   Analysis of the subsequent case law demonstrates that the ECJ has edged its way, in a process that is even now incomplete, towards a recognition that the ECHR must be given effect as part of the general principles of Community law.

---

3   Case 1/58 *Stork v High Authority* [1959] ECR 17
4   Joined Cases 36-38 and 40/59 *Geitling v High Authority* [1960] ECR 423.
5   Case 40/64 *Sgarlata v Commission* [1965] ECR 215.
6   Professor Noreen Burrows detects in these cases merely a delimitation of the ECJ's jurisdiction as not trespassing upon domestic law (see Brice Dickson (ed), *Human Rights and the European Convention*, 1997, London: Sweet & Maxwell, Chapter 2, pp 30–31). But see, eg, *Geitling v High Authority* [1960] ECR 423, p 439.
7   Case 6/64 *Costa v ENEL* [1964] ECR 585.
8   Case 92/78 *Simmenthal v Commission* [1979] ECR 777.
9   Case 26/62 *Van Gend en Loos* [1963] ECR 1.

7.10   The starting point is *Stauder v City of Ulm*.[10] Although Mr Stauder's claim was dismissed, its importance lay in the ECJ's statement that the allegedly offending Community provision did not infringe 'the fundamental human rights enshrined in the general principles of Community law and protected by the Court'.[11] For the first time, therefore (albeit without reference to the ECHR), the ECJ accepted, by necessary implication, that a Community measure that infringed a fundamental human right could, in principle at least, be unlawful.

7.11   A similar approach was taken in *Internationale Handelsgesellschaft*[12] where the ECJ, after observing that it could not apply domestic constitutional provisions, stated (again, without reference to the ECHR) that the protection of fundamental rights formed an integral part of the general principles of law but that 'the protection of such rights, whilst inspired by the constitutional traditions common to the Member States, must be ensured within the framework of the structure and objectives of the Community'.[13]

7.12   *Nold*[14] was the first case in which the ECJ made direct reference to international human rights treaties, to which Member States were signatories as affording guidelines. Although the Court did not expressly refer to the ECHR (on which the applicant had relied for an asserted breach of property rights by a Commission decision), it did hold that 'international treaties for the protection of human rights on which the Member States have collaborated or of which they are signatories, can supply guidelines which should be followed within the framework of Community law'.[15]

7.13   In *Rutili*,[16] the ECJ made its first reference both to the ECHR and to specific Convention Articles. The case concerned freedom of movement. The ECJ concluded that a particular provision of Community law (Article 39(3) of the EC Treaty) was a 'specific manifestation of the more general principle' enshrined in Articles 8–11 of, and Article 2 of Protocol 4 to, the ECHR justifying limitation on free movement on limited public policy grounds.[17] As Jacobs and White observe,[18] the decision is especially significant because the

---

10   Case 29/69 [1969] ECR 419.

11   *Ibid*, p 425, para 7.

12   Case 11/70 *Internationale Handelsgesellschaft mbH v Einfuhr- und Vorratsstelle für Getreide und Futtermittel* [1970] ECR 1125.

13   [1970] ECR 1125, p 1134, paras 3–4.

14   Case 4/73 *Nold v Commission of the European Communities* [1974] ECR 491.

15   [1974] ECR 491, p 507, para 13.

16   Case 36/75 *Rutili v Ministre de l'Intérieur* [1975] ECR 1219.

17   See para 32 of the judgment in *Rutili* summarising the effect of the cited ECHR provisions as being that 'no restrictions in the interests of national security or public safety shall be placed on the rights secured ... other than such as are necessary for the protection of those interests in a democratic society'.

18   See Francis G Jacobs and Robin CA White, *The European Convention on Human Rights*, 2nd edn, 1996, Clarendon, p 411.

recognition of the relevance of the ECHR provisions was unnecessary for the Court's ruling.

The modern view

7.14 Since *Rutili*, the Convention has become firmly established as an analytical tool of the ECJ. The ECJ has even subjected its own procedures to scrutiny on Convention grounds. In *Emesa Sugar v Aruba*,[19] it considered and rejected a challenge to the role of the Advocate General based upon Article 6(1) of the ECHR.

7.15 Although the ECJ has advised in Opinion 2/94 on Accession by the Community to the ECHR[20] that the Community lacks competence to accede to the ECHR, that Court's Opinion contains a clear summary of the status of the ECHR in Community law. Materially, the ECJ observes thus:

> It is well settled that fundamental rights form an integral part of the general principles of law whose observance the Court ensures. For that purpose, the Court draws inspiration from the constitutional traditions common to the Member States and from the guidelines supplied by international treaties for the protection of human rights on which the Member States have collaborated or of which they are signatories. In that regard, the Court has stated that the Convention has special significance ...[21]

7.16 Three essential propositions can be derived from this formulation. The first is that the ECHR is not, of itself, a source of Community law. It is, rather, an indicator of common values of the Member States.[22] That means that it is not formally binding.

7.17 Secondly, the corollary is that the ECJ treats its fundamental rights doctrine as autonomous. As Advocate General Trabucchi observed in *Watson v Belmann*:[23]

> ... some learned writers have felt justified in concluding that the provisions of the said Convention [on Human Rights] must be treated as forming an integral part of the Community legal order, whereas it seems clear to me that the spirit of the judgment [in *Rutili*] did not involve any substantive reference to the provisions themselves but merely to the general principles of which, like the Community rules with which the judgment drew an analogy, they are a specific expression.
>
> In fact, in that judgment, the Court substantially reaffirmed the principle which had already emerged from its previous decisions that the fundamental human

---

19 Case C-17/98 *Emesa Sugar (Free Zone) NV v Aruba* (2000) *The Times*, 29 February.

20 [1996] ECR I-1759.

21 See para 33 of the Opinion.

22 Contrast Lord Browne-Wilkinson 'The infiltration of a Bill of Rights' [1992] PL 397, p 401, who suggests that, in the Community context, the ECHR has already been directly incorporated into English domestic law.

23 Case 118/75 *Watson v Bellmann* [1976] ECR 1185, p 1207.

rights recognized under the constitutions of the Member States are also an integral part of the Community legal order.

The extra-Community instruments under which those states have undertaken international obligations in order to ensure better protection for those rights can, without any question of their being incorporated as such in the Community order, be used to establish principles which are common to the states themselves.

7.18 Thirdly, the ECHR has a 'special significance'.[24] Its significance, however, lies in the assistance in interpreting the fundamental rights which are themselves part of the Community legal order.

Approach of the ECJ to the Strasbourg case law

7.19 Whilst the autonomous doctrine of fundamental rights in Community law embraces other international instruments apart from the ECHR,[25] it is not, however, the use of these instruments that gives the EU human rights case law its distinctiveness. The Strasbourg Court also draws on other international sources of human rights jurisprudence. That which, in truth, distinguishes the ECJ jurisprudence is where either the ECJ interprets the ECHR in a manner different to that of the European Court of Human Rights or where there is a conflict between Community law and the ECHR itself.

7.20   Constitutionally, the position seems clear. It is the ECJ that must determine the scope and extent of fundamental rights in Community law. Article 220 (formerly, Article 164) of the EC Treaty makes the ECJ the final arbiter of Community law by providing, as it does, that the ECJ 'shall ensure that in the interpretation and application of this Treaty the law is observed'. As has been observed, this general mandate would be 'seriously impaired' if, for example, a parallel fundamental rights jurisdiction could be set up by the Member States.[26] So, too, Article 292 (formerly, Article 219) excludes other forms of judicial settlement between Member States and stipulates the obligation undertaken by the Member States 'not to submit a dispute concerning the interpretation or application of the Treaty to any method of settlement other than those provided for therein'. Further, as Advocate General Jacobs emphasised in *Konstantinidis*,[27] the European Court of Human Rights has

---

24 Apart from Opinion 2/94, see, eg, *Ter Voort* [1992] ECR I-5485, para 34.

25 Eg, the International Covenant on Civil and Political Rights of 19 December 1966; the European Social Charter of 18 October 1961; the Universal Declaration on Human Rights of 10 December 1948; the International Covenant on Economic, Social and Cultural Rights of 19 December 1966.

26 See N Reich (1996) 7 EJIL 103, pp 110–11.

27 Case C-168/91 *Konstantinidis v Stadt Altensteig-Standesamt and Landratsamt Calw, Ordnungsant* [1993] ECR I-1191, at para 50 of the AG's Opinion.

always accepted that its jurisdiction is subsidiary and that it is primarily for the national authorities and the national courts to apply the ECHR.[28]

7.21 The ECJ itself has stressed that it is not required to follow rulings of the European Court of Human Rights. For example, in *Orkem v Commission*,[29] the ECJ observed thus:

> This Court may ... adopt, with respect to provisions of the Convention, an interpretation which does not coincide exactly with that given by the Strasbourg authorities, in particular the European Court of Human Rights. It is not bound, in so far as it does not have systematically to take into account, as regards fundamental rights under Community law, the interpretation of the Convention given by the Strasbourg authorities ...

7.22 It is, however, possible that Strasbourg judgments (and indeed the Convention itself) may have a higher priority in Community law than has been suggested. Article 307 (formerly, Article 234) of the EC Treaty stipulates that the Treaty is subject to any pre-existing international obligation. Plainly, at the time of ratifying the EC Treaty, the United Kingdom had already ratified the European Convention on Human Rights. It may be, therefore, that, as a matter of Community law, the ECJ should defer to Strasbourg. This issue has never been determined by the ECJ, however, and it is clearly for the ECJ (as opposed to Strasbourg) to decide the question.

7.23 In practice, the ECJ seeks to avoid inconsistency with Strasbourg. In *Prais v Council*,[30] Advocate General Warner regretted the absence from the ECHR of any power in the ECJ or in national courts to refer questions of interpretation of the Convention for a preliminary ruling comparable to that allowing references to the ECJ under Article 234 (formerly, Article 177) of the EC Treaty.

7.24 Inevitably, though, inconsistencies have occurred. For example, in *Grogan*,[31] Advocate General Van Gerven considered that a prohibition against dissemination of information in Ireland about UK abortion services would not (even if justiciable in EC law) be a breach of Article 10 of the ECHR. By contrast, the European Court of Human Rights, on substantially the same facts, held exactly the opposite in *Open Door Counselling and Dublin Well Woman v Ireland*.[32] In *Hoechst*,[33] the ECJ held that Article 8 of the ECHR did not extend to business premises. The opposite conclusion was reached by the European Court of Human Rights in *Niemeitz v Germany*.[34]

---

28 See, eg, *Belgian Linguistics Case* (1979–80) 1 EHRR 252; *Handyside v United Kingdom* (1979–80) 1 EHRR 737; *Eckle v Germany* (1983) 5 EHRR 1.

29 [1989] ECR 3283, para 140.

30 Case 130/75 [1976] ECR 1589.

31 Case C-159/90 *SPUC v Grogan* [1991] ECR I-4685.

32 (1993) 15 EHRR 97.

33 Cases 46/87 and 227/88 *Hoechst AG v Commission* [1989] ECR 2859.

34 (1993) 16 EHRR 97.

7.25   It is also important to have regard to the fact that the ECHR is, in Community law, being mediated through a legal system with its own distinct priorities.

7.26   Thus, in *Commission v Germany*,[35] the ECJ was careful to observe that:

> ... such [fundamental] rights are not absolute privileges, but may be subject to restrictions, provided that the latter actually promote the objectives of general interest pursued by the Community and are not, by reference to such objectives, disproportionate and intolerable to such an extent that they would interfere with the very substance of the rights thus safeguarded ...

7.27   It is, therefore, by reference to Community objectives that the legality of interference with Convention rights will be evaluated. For example, in *National Panasonic v Commission*,[36] the ECJ had to consider whether Article 8(2) of the ECHR justified infringement of the right to privacy. After citing Article 8(2), the ECJ applied it against the Community background and held that:

> ... The exercise of the powers given to the Commission by Regulation 17 contributes to the maintenance of the system of competition intended by the Treaty which undertakings are absolutely bound to comply with. In these circumstances it does not therefore appear that Regulation 17, by giving the Commission the powers to carry out investigations without previous notification, infringes the right invoked by the applicant.

7.28   Further, whilst Community and ECHR protection of fundamental rights may sometimes coincide, in Community law, concepts such as 'margin of appreciation' and 'proportionality' may have a different meaning to that applied by the Strasbourg Court.[37]

7.29   The Strasbourg Court has addressed the question as to the priority that should be afforded to Convention rights as against Community law provisions. In *Matthews v United Kingdom*[38] the applicant, a British citizen resident in Gibraltar, successfully complained to the Strasbourg Court that she had been unable to vote in the 1994 elections to the European Parliament and that, in consequence, there had been a violation of Article 3 of Protocol No 1. The Government submitted that her real objection was to a Council Decision and to a Community Act which governed the elections to the European Parliament.

7.30   In constitutional terms, the issue was whether, despite the fact that the Convention extended to Gibraltar, the quality of elections to the European Parliament (itself an organ of the EC) could be challenged before the Strasbourg Court. Strasbourg held that although the acts of the EC, as such, could not be challenged before the Court since the EC was not a Contracting Party, and although nothing in the Convention prevented the transfer of

---

35   Case C-62/90 [1992] ECR I-2575.

36   C-136/79 [1980] ECR 2033.

37   See, eg, Case 44/79 *Hauer v Land Rheinland-Pfalz* [1979] ECR 3727. See, further, Takis Tridimas, *The General Principles of EC Law*, 1999, Oxford.

38   (1999) 28 EHRR 361, especially, paras 30–32.

competences to international organisations, the United Kingdom was, as an individual Contracting Party, still bound under its Convention obligations to comply with Article 3 of Protocol No 1.

7.31   Thus, the Strasbourg Court's view is that it is no answer to a breach of a person's rights under the Convention to assert that such breach is either permitted or required by Community law. This raises the possibility, at least, of a direct conflict between Strasbourg and Luxembourg should the ECJ reach a contrary view as to the content of the rights at issue.

THE SCOPE OF HUMAN RIGHTS PROTECTION IN COMMUNITY LAW

The regulating principle

7.32 It is clear that the scope of the doctrine of fundamental rights in Community law extends to the legality of Community measures.[39] The doctrine also applies to domestic law in so far as domestic law is itself within the scope of Community law. In *ERT*, the ECJ said:[40]

> As the Court has held, it has no power to examine the compatibility with the European Convention on Human Rights of national rules which do not fall within the scope of Community law. On the other hand, where such rules do fall within the scope of Community law, and reference is made to the Court for a preliminary ruling, it must provide all the criteria of interpretation needed by the national court to determine whether those rules are compatible with the fundamental rights the observance of which the Court ensures and which derive in particular from the European Convention on Human Rights.

7.33 The question as to what falls within the scope of Community law in the human rights context has not yet been decisively resolved.[41] The ECJ's existing case law, however, provides some indication of where clear lines can be drawn.

Cases falling outside the scope of Community law

7.34 Community law may not be relied upon with respect to a purely internal situation.[42] Further, a connection with Community law that is considered to be contrived or incidental falls outside Community human rights protection. In

---

39   See Opinion 2/94 on Accession by the Community to the ECHR, para 34.

40   Case C-260/89 *Elliniki Radiophonia Tileorassi AE v Dimotiki Etairia Pliroforissis* [1991] ECR I-2925, at para 42.

41   See *R v Ministry of Agriculture, Fisheries and Food ex p First City Trading Ltd* [1997] 1 CMLR 250; *R v Customs and Excise Commissioners ex p Lunn Poly Ltd* [1998] STC 649, DC; and *R v Ministry of Agriculture, Fisheries and Food ex p British Pig Industry Support Group* 27 July 2000 (unreported), in which Richards J expressed 'real doubts' about the correctness of *First City Trading*.

42   C-132/93 *Volker Steam v Deutsche Bundespost (No 2)* [1994] I ECR 2715.

Kremzow,[43] Mr Kremzow's claim for compensation for unlawful detention consequent upon a sentence of life imprisonment imposed after a trial found to be in breach of Article 6 of the ECHR was held not to fall within the scope of Community law. The Austrian Court that rejected the compensation claim referred the case to the ECJ on the basis of Mr Kremzow's argument that his right to freedom of movement under the EC Treaty had been infringed by his sentence of imprisonment. The ECJ held that the purely hypothetical prospect of exercising the right of free movement did not establish a sufficient connection with Community law. Further, Mr Kremzow's sentence was under a domestic law which was not designed to secure compliance with any rule of Community law.

7.35   In *Demirel,*[44] the ECJ held that it did not possess jurisdiction to determine whether the wife of a Turkish worker must be allowed to remain with her husband whose residence in the Member State was regulated by the subsidiary legislation of the EEC/Turkey Association Agreement. The asserted breach of Article 8 of the ECHR was not within the scope of Community law because rights to family reunification were not, at that time, covered by the Agreement and the national law lay outside the Court's jurisdiction.

Cases within the scope of Community law

7.36   It is well established that the legislation of Member States may be assessed on the basis of Community fundamental rights in two situations. The first is where the national legislation implements Community rules. As the ECJ has stated:

> ... the requirements flowing from the protection of fundamental rights in the Community legal order are also binding on Member States when they implement Community rules and that the Member States must therefore, as far as possible, apply those rules in accordance with those requirements.[45]

7.37   Secondly, the Community law fundamental rights doctrine also applies where a Member State implements measures to derogate from Community provisions.

7.38   In *ERT*[46] (above), the ECJ was asked to consider a reference seeking a preliminary ruling as to the lawfulness of a television monopoly which the

---

43   Case C-299/95 *Kremzow v Austria* [1997] ECR I-2405.

44   Case 12/86 *Demirel v Stadt Schwäbisch Gmünd* [1987] ECR 3719.

45   Case C-2/92 *R v MAFF ex p Bostock* [1994] ECR I-955, para 16; Cases 201 and 202/85 *Marthe Klensch v Secrétaire d'État à l'Agriculture et à la Viticulture* [1986] ECR 3477, para 8; Case 5/88 *Hubert Wachauf v Federal Republic of Germany* [1989] ECR 2609, para 19.

46   *Elliniki Radiophonia Tileorassi AE v Dimotiki Etairia Pliroforissis* [1991] ECR I-2925.

Member State sought to justify under Articles 46 and 55 (formerly, Articles 56 and 66).[47] The ECJ observed:[48]

> In particular, where a Member State relies on the combined provisions of Articles 56 and 66 in order to justify rules which are likely to obstruct the exercise of the freedom to provide services, such justification, provided for by Community law, must be interpreted in the light of the general principles of law and in particular of fundamental rights. Thus the national rules in question can fall under the exceptions provided for by the combined provisions of Articles 56 and 66 only if they are compatible with the fundamental rights the observance of which is ensured by the Court.

7.39 The difficult unresolved question is what other situations may be said to fall within the scope of Community law for the purposes of fundamental human rights protection.[49]

Extent of substantive ECHR protection in the ECJ cases

7.40 The fact that Community law confers protection of fundamental rights in the areas analysed above may not mean that those availing themselves of such protection are entitled to the protection of all the substantive provisions of the ECHR.

7.41 In *Konstantinidis*, Advocate General Jacobs said this:[50]

> In my opinion, a Community national who goes to another state as a worker or self-employed person under Articles 48, 52 or 59 of the Treaty is entitled not just to pursue his trade or profession and to enjoy the same living and working conditions as nationals of the host state; he is in addition entitled to assume that, wherever he goes to earn his living in the European Community, he will be treated in accordance with a common code of fundamental values, in particular those laid down in the European Convention on Human Rights. In other words, he is entitled to say '*civis europeus sum*' and to invoke that status in order to oppose any violation of his fundamental rights.

7.42 However, nothing in the Court's judgment endorsed such a broad approach; a fact noted by Advocate General Gulman when disagreeing with Advocate General Jacobs and giving his Opinion in *R v Ministry of Fisheries, Agriculture and Food ex p Bostock*.[51] The true analysis may, it is submitted, be that any

---

47 EC Treaty, Art 46(1) provides that the Treaty provisions concerning freedom of establishment shall not prejudice rules of law which provide for special treatment for foreign nationals on grounds of public policy, public security or health. EC Treaty, Art 55 applies the same rule to the Treaty provisions concerning freedom to provide services.

48 *Elliniki Radiophonia Tileorassi AE v Dimotiki Etairia Pliroforissis* [1991] ECR I-2925, para 43.

49 See para 7.33.

50 Case C-168/91 *Konstantinidis v Stadt Altensteig-Standesamt and Landratsamt Calw, Ordnungsant* [1993] ECR I-1191, para 46.

51 [1994] ECR I-955, p 971.

applicable ECHR protection as part of the Community fundamental rights doctrine extends only so far as is necessary to protect the Community right in question. If the position were otherwise, Community fundamental rights protection would extend beyond the scope of Community law as analysed in the above mentioned case law.

7.43   The following Table provides examples of cases in which the Convention has been deployed by the ECJ.

Article 2 (right to life)	Case C-159/90 *SPUC v Grogan* [1991] ECR I-4605
Article 3 (protection from torture etc)	Cases 115 and 116/81 *Adoui and Another v Belgian State* [1982] ECR 1665
Article 5 (right to liberty/security)	Case C-299/95 *Kremzow v Austria* [1997] ECR I-2405
Article 6 (right to a fair hearing)	Case 222/86 *UNECTEF v Heylens* [1987] ECR 4097
Article 7 (non-retroactive punishment)	Case 63/83 *R v Kent Kirk* [1984] ECR 2689
Article 8 (right to respect for private and family life, etc)	Case 53/85 *AKZO Chemie BV and AKZO Chemie UK Limited v Commission* [1986] ECR 2585
Article 9 (freedom of thought, etc)	Case 130/75 *Prais v Council* [1976] ECR 1589
Article 10 (freedom of expression)	Case C353/89 *Commission v The Netherlands* [1991] ECR I-4069
Article 11 (freedom of assembly/association)	Case C-415/93 *Union Royale Belge des Societes de Football v Bosman* [1995] ECR I-4921
Article 12 (right to marry)	Case 236/87 *Bergemann v Bundesanstalt für Arbeit* [1988] ECR 5125
Article 13 (right to an effective remedy)	Case C-70/88 *Parliament v Council (Radioactive Food)* [1991] ECR 1-4529
Article 14 (non-discrimination)	Case 149/77 *Defrenne v SABENA* [1978] ECR 1365
Article 1, Protocol 1 (right to property)	Case 5/88 *Wachauf v The State* [1989] ECR 2609

Article 2, Protocol 4 (liberty of movement within territory of Contracting State)	Case 36/75 *Rutili v Ministere de l'Intérieur* [1975] ECR 121
Article 3 Protocol 4 (prohibition of expulsion of nationals)	Case C-370/90 *R v IAT and Surinder Singh ex p Secretary of State for the Home Department* [1992] ECR I-4265

7.45 As the Table shows, the ECJ has considered Convention rights contained in the Fourth Protocol, which has not been ratified by the United Kingdom. This does not prevent the ECJ from applying those fundamental rights as part of Community law in a suitable UK case.

FUNDAMENTAL RIGHTS IN COMMUNITY LAW AND THE HUMAN RIGHTS ACT

7.46 As the above analysis shows, there may be important differences between the approach to fundamental rights of the ECJ and the Strasbourg Court. The question that arises, therefore, is which approach the domestic court should follow. Section 2 of the Human Rights Act requires a court or tribunal determining issues connected with a Convention right to 'take into account' all material from Convention institutions that is, in its opinion, relevant. This contrasts strongly with s 3(1) of the European Communities Act 1972 which requires the Court to treat questions as to the meaning or effect of Treaty provisions 'as a question of law ... for determination ... in accordance with the principles laid down by and any relevant decision of the European Court'.

7.47 As has already been observed at para 1.16, s 2 of the Human Rights Act appears to confer on UK judges a power to give a different interpretation to the ECHR than that accorded by the Strasbourg Court. By contrast, in cases engaging fundamental rights within the scope of Community law, s 3(1) of the European Communities Act requires the English Court to determine the question in accordance with the ECJ rulings.

7.48 There is no necessary conflict between s 2 of the Human Rights Act and s 3(1) of the 1972 Act. Where the domestic court is seeking to decide whether a breach of fundamental rights in Community law has occurred, s 3(1) of the 1972 Act and the ECJ's case law prevails. Nevertheless, the same facts may give rise to an allegation that a breach of Convention rights, and accordingly s 6(1) of the Human Rights Act has also taken place. In determining the latter claim, the domestic court must apply the cannons of construction contained in the Human Rights Act and take account of the Strasbourg case law. It is at least possible that a different conclusion may be reached.

7.49   To this somewhat stark theoretical position there are some qualifications. First, there are very few cases in which the conflict has, thus far, occurred. In any event, there is considerable scope for distinguishing past cases on their facts. It is central to the approach of the Strasbourg Court that it confines its determinations to concrete factual situations.[52] It is not itself bound by a doctrine of precedent.

7.50   Secondly, where there is a divergence between the two Courts, it is open to the national court to request the ECJ to give a preliminary ruling by way of reference under Article 234 (formerly Article 177) of the EC Treaty.

7.51   Whilst as a matter of practice human rights claims within the scope of Community law will, where possible, be couched both in terms of Community law and under the Human Rights Act, in such a case, the Human Rights Act may have only limited importance because of the more powerful remedies available in Community law.

7.52   At the time of writing, there are proposals for an EU Charter of Fundamental Rights. A decision as to whether it will be legally binding is due in December 2000. The current draft of the Charter contains fifty rights including, amongst others, rights broadly approximating to those contained in the Convention. If the Charter is enacted in the proposed form, then it may further reduce importance of the Human Rights Act within the scope of Community law.[53]

---

52 Eg, *Salabiaku v France* (1991) 13 EHRR 379, para 30.

53 See Sandra Fredman, Christopher McCrudden and Mark Freedland, 'An EU charter of fundamental rights' [2000] PL 178.

THE HUMAN RIGHTS ACT 1998

INTRODUCTION

The Convention Rights

1 (1) In this Act 'the Convention rights' means the rights and fundamental freedoms set out in –

(a) Articles 2 to 12 and 14 of the Convention;

(b) Articles 1 to 3 of the First Protocol; and

(c) Articles 1 and 2 of the Sixth Protocol,

as read with Articles 16 to 18 of the Convention.

(2) Those Articles are to have effect for the purposes of this Act subject to any designated derogation or reservation (as to which see sections 14 and 15).

(3) The Articles are set out in Schedule 1.

(4) The Secretary of State may by order make such amendments to this Act as he considers appropriate to reflect the effect, in relation to the United Kingdom, of a protocol.

(5) In sub-section (4) 'protocol' means a protocol to the Convention –

(a) which the United Kingdom has ratified; or

(b) which the United Kingdom has signed with a view to ratification.

(6) No amendment may be made by an order under sub-section (4) so as to come into force before the protocol concerned is in force in relation to the United Kingdom.

Interpretation of Convention rights

2 (1) A court or tribunal determining a question which has arisen in connection with a Convention right must take into account any –

(a) judgment, decision, declaration or advisory opinion of the European Court of Human Rights;

(b) opinion of the Commission given in a report adopted under Article 31 of the Convention;

(c) decision of the Commission in connection with Article 26 or 27(2) of the Convention; or

(d) decision of the Committee of Ministers taken under Article 46 of the Convention, whenever made or given, so far as, in the opinion of the court or tribunal, it is relevant to the proceedings in which that question has arisen.

(2) Evidence of any judgment, decision, declaration or opinion of which account may have to be taken under this section is to be given in proceedings before any court or tribunal in such manner as may be provided by rules.

(3) In this section 'rules' means rules of court or, in the case of proceedings before a tribunal, rules made for the purposes of this section –

(a) by the Lord Chancellor or the Secretary of State, in relation to any proceedings outside Scotland;

(b) by the Secretary of State, in relation to proceedings in Scotland; or

(c) by a Northern Ireland department, in relation to proceedings before a tribunal in Northern Ireland –

(i) which deals with transferred matters; and

(ii) for which no rules made under paragraph (a) are in force.

LEGISLATION

Interpretation of legislation

3 (1) So far as it is possible to do so, primary legislation and subordinate legislation must be read and given effect in a way which is compatible with the Convention rights.

(2) This section –

(a) applies to primary legislation and subordinate legislation whenever enacted;

(b) does not affect the validity, continuing operation or enforcement of any incompatible primary legislation; and

(c) does not affect the validity, continuing operation or enforcement of any incompatible subordinate legislation if (disregarding any possibility of revocation) primary legislation prevents removal of the incompatibility.

Declaration of incompatibility

4 (1) Sub-section (2) applies in any proceedings in which a court determines whether a provision of primary legislation is compatible with a Convention right.

(2) If the court is satisfied that the provision is incompatible with a Convention right, it may make a declaration of that incompatibility.

(3) Sub-section (4) applies in any proceedings in which a court determines whether a provision of subordinate legislation, made in the exercise of a power conferred by primary legislation, is compatible with a Convention right.

(4) If the court is satisfied –

    (a) that the provision is incompatible with a Convention right; and

    (b) that (disregarding any possibility of revocation) the primary legislation concerned prevents removal of the incompatibility,

it may make a declaration of that incompatibility.

(5) In this section 'court' means –

    (a) the House of Lords;

    (b) the Judicial Committee of the Privy Council;

    (c) the Courts-Martial Appeal Court;

    (d) in Scotland, the High Court of Justiciary sitting otherwise than as a trial court or the Court of Session;

    (e) in England and Wales or Northern Ireland, the High Court or the Court of Appeal.

(6) A declaration under this section ('a declaration of incompatibility') –

    (a) does not affect the validity, continuing operation or enforcement of the provision in respect of which it is given; and

    (b) is not binding on the parties to the proceedings in which it is made.

Right of Crown to intervene

5   (1) Where a court is considering whether to make a declaration of incompatibility, the Crown is entitled to notice in accordance with rules of court.

   (2) In any case to which sub-section (1) applies –

    (a) a Minister of the Crown (or a person nominated by him);

    (b) a member of the Scottish Executive;

    (c) a Northern Ireland Minister;

    (d) a Northern Ireland department,

is entitled, on giving notice in accordance with rules of court, to be joined as a party to the proceedings.

   (3) Notice under sub-section (2) may be given at any time during the proceedings.

   (4) A person who has been made a party to criminal proceedings (other than in Scotland) as the result of a notice under sub-section (2) may, with leave, appeal to the House of Lords against any declaration of incompatibility made in the proceedings.

   (5) In sub-section (4) –

'criminal proceedings' includes all proceedings before the Courts-Martial Appeal Court; and

'leave' means leave granted by the court making the declaration of incompatibility or by the House of Lords.

PUBLIC AUTHORITIES

Acts of public authorities

6 (1) It is unlawful for a public authority to act in a way which is incompatible with a Convention right.

(2) Sub-section (1) does not apply to an act if –

(a) as the result of one or more provisions of primary legislation, the authority could not have acted differently; or

(b) in the case of one or more provisions of, or made under, primary legislation which cannot be read or given effect in a way which is compatible with the Convention rights, the authority was acting so as to give effect to or enforce those provisions.

(3) In this section 'public authority' includes –

(a) a court or tribunal; and

(b) any person certain of whose functions are functions of a public nature,

but does not include either House of Parliament or a person exercising functions in connection with proceedings in Parliament.

(4) In sub-section (3) 'Parliament' does not include the House of Lords in its judicial capacity.

(5) In relation to a particular act, a person is not a public authority by virtue only of sub-section (3)(b) if the nature of the act is private.

(6) 'An act' includes a failure to act but does not include a failure to –

(a) introduce in, or lay before, Parliament a proposal for legislation; or

(b) make any primary legislation or remedial order.

Proceedings

7 (1) A person who claims that a public authority has acted (or proposes to act) in a way which is made unlawful by section 6(1) may –

(a) bring proceedings against the authority under this Act in the appropriate court or tribunal; or

(b) rely on the Convention right or rights concerned in any legal proceedings,

but only if he is (or would be) a victim of the unlawful act.

(2) In sub-section (1)(a) 'appropriate court or tribunal' means such court or tribunal as may be determined in accordance with rules; and proceedings against an authority include a counterclaim or similar proceeding.

(3) If the proceedings are brought on an application for judicial review, the applicant is to be taken to have a sufficient interest in relation to the unlawful act only if he is, or would be, a victim of that act.

(4) If the proceedings are made by way of a petition for judicial review in Scotland, the applicant shall be taken to have title and interest to sue in relation to the unlawful act only if he is, or would be, a victim of that act.

(5) Proceedings under sub-section (1)(a) must be brought before the end of –

   (a) the period of one year beginning with the date on which the act complained of took place; or

   (b) such longer period as the court or tribunal considers equitable having regard to all the circumstances,

but that is subject to any rule imposing a stricter time limit in relation to the procedure in question.

(6) In sub-section (1)(b) 'legal proceedings' includes –

   (a) proceedings brought by or at the instigation of a public authority; and

   (b) an appeal against the decision of a court or tribunal.

(7) For the purposes of this section, a person is a victim of an unlawful act only if he would be a victim for the purposes of Article 34 of the Convention if proceedings were brought in the European Court of Human Rights in respect of that Act.

(8) Nothing in this Act creates a criminal offence.

(9) In this section 'rules' means –

   (a) in relation to proceedings before a court or tribunal outside Scotland, rules made by the Lord Chancellor or the Secretary of State for the purposes of this section or rules of court;

   (b) in relation to proceedings before a court or tribunal in Scotland, rules made by the Secretary of State for those purposes;

   (c) in relation to proceedings before a tribunal in Northern Ireland –

      (i) which deals with transferred matters; and

      (ii) for which no rules made under paragraph (a) are in force,

   rules made by a Northern Ireland department for those purposes,

   and includes provision made by order under section 1 of the Courts and Legal Services Act 1990.

(10) In making rules, regard must be had to section 9.

(11) The Minister who has power to make rules in relation to a particular tribunal may, to the extent he considers it necessary to ensure that the tribunal can provide an appropriate remedy in relation to an act (or proposed act) of a public authority which is (or would be) unlawful as a result of section 6(1), by order add to –

   (a) the relief or remedies which the tribunal may grant; or

   (b) the grounds on which it may grant any of them.

(12) An order made under sub-section (11) may contain such incidental, supplemental, consequential or transitional provision as the Minister making it considers appropriate.

(13) 'The Minister' includes the Northern Ireland department concerned.

Judicial remedies

8 (1) In relation to any act (or proposed act) of a public authority which the court finds is (or would be) unlawful, it may grant such relief or remedy, or make such order, within its powers as it considers just and appropriate.

(2) But damages may be awarded only by a court which has power to award damages, or to order the payment of compensation, in civil proceedings.

(3) No award of damages is to be made unless, taking account of all the circumstances of the case, including –

(a) any other relief or remedy granted, or order made, in relation to the act in question (by that or any other court); and

(b) the consequences of any decision (of that or any other court) in respect of that act,

the court is satisfied that the award is necessary to afford just satisfaction to the person in whose favour it is made.

(4) In determining –

(a) whether to award damages; or

(b) the amount of an award,

the court must take into account the principles applied by the European Court of Human Rights in relation to the award of compensation under Article 41 of the Convention.

(5) A public authority against which damages are awarded is to be treated –

(a) in Scotland, for the purposes of section 3 of the Law Reform (Miscellaneous Provisions) (Scotland) Act 1940 as if the award were made in an action of damages in which the authority has been found liable in respect of loss or damage to the person to whom the award is made;

(b) for the purposes of the Civil Liability (Contribution) Act 1978 as liable in respect of damage suffered by the person to whom the award is made.

(6) In this section –

'court' includes a tribunal;

'damages' means damages for an unlawful act of a public authority; and

'unlawful' means unlawful under section 6(1).

Judicial acts

9 (1) Proceedings under section 7(1)(a) in respect of a judicial act may be brought only –

(a) by exercising a right of appeal;

(b) on an application (in Scotland a petition) for judicial review; or

(c) in such other forum as may be prescribed by rules.

(2) That does not affect any rule of law which prevents a court from being the subject of judicial review.

(3) In proceedings under this Act in respect of a judicial act done in good faith, damages may not be awarded otherwise than to compensate a person to the extent required by Article 5(5) of the Convention.

(4) An award of damages permitted by sub-section (3) is to be made against the Crown; but no award may be made unless the appropriate person, if not a party to the proceedings, is joined.

(5) In this section –

'appropriate person' means the Minister responsible for the court concerned, or a person or government department nominated by him;

'court' includes a tribunal;

'judge' includes a member of a tribunal, a justice of the peace and a clerk or other officer entitled to exercise the jurisdiction of a court;

'judicial act' means a judicial act of a court and includes an act done on the instructions, or on behalf, of a judge; and

'rules' has the same meaning as in section 7(9).

REMEDIAL ACTION

Power to take remedial action

10 (1) This section applies if –

(a) a provision of legislation has been declared under section 4 to be incompatible with a Convention right and, if an appeal lies –

(i) all persons who may appeal have stated in writing that they do not intend to do so;

(ii) the time for bringing an appeal has expired and no appeal has been brought within that time; or

(iii) an appeal brought within that time has been determined or abandoned; or

(b) it appears to a Minister of the Crown or Her Majesty in Council that, having regard to a finding of the European Court of Human Rights made after the coming into force of this section in proceedings against the United Kingdom, a provision of legislation is incompatible with an obligation of the United Kingdom arising from the Convention.

(2) If a Minister of the Crown considers that there are compelling reasons for proceeding under this section, he may by order make such amendments to the legislation as he considers necessary to remove the incompatibility.

(3) If, in the case of subordinate legislation, a Minister of the Crown considers –

(a) that it is necessary to amend the primary legislation under which the subordinate legislation in question was made, in order to enable the incompatibility to be removed; and

(b) that there are compelling reasons for proceeding under this section, he may by order make such amendments to the primary legislation as he considers necessary.

(4) This section also applies where the provision in question is in subordinate legislation and has been quashed, or declared invalid, by reason of incompatibility with a Convention right and the Minister proposes to proceed under paragraph 2(b) of Schedule 2.

(5) If the legislation is an Order in Council, the power conferred by subsection (2) or (3) is exercisable by Her Majesty in Council.

(6) In this section 'legislation' does not include a Measure of the Church Assembly or of the General Synod of the Church of England.

(7) Schedule 2 makes further provision about remedial orders.

OTHER RIGHTS AND PROCEEDINGS

Safeguard for existing human rights

11 A person's reliance on a Convention right does not restrict –

(a) any other right or freedom conferred on him by or under any law having effect in any part of the United Kingdom; or

(b) his right to make any claim or bring any proceedings which he could make or bring apart from sections 7 to 9.

Freedom of expression

12 (1) This section applies if a court is considering whether to grant any relief which, if granted, might affect the exercise of the Convention right to freedom of expression.

(2) If the person against whom the application for relief is made ('the respondent') is neither present nor represented, no such relief is to be granted unless the court is satisfied –

(a) that the applicant has taken all practicable steps to notify the respondent; or

(b) that there are compelling reasons why the respondent should not be notified.

(3) No such relief is to be granted so as to restrain publication before trial unless the court is satisfied that the applicant is likely to establish that publication should not be allowed.

(4) The court must have particular regard to the importance of the Convention right to freedom of expression and, where the proceedings relate to material which the respondent claims, or which appears to the court, to be journalistic, literary or artistic material (or to conduct connected with such material), to –

(a) the extent to which –

(i) the material has, or is about to, become available to the public; or

(ii) it is, or would be, in the public interest for the material to be published;

(b) any relevant privacy code.

(5) In this section –

'court' includes a tribunal; and

'relief' includes any remedy or order (other than in criminal proceedings).

Freedom of thought, conscience and religion

13 (1) If a court's determination of any question arising under this Act might affect the exercise by a religious organisation (itself or its members collectively) of the Convention right to freedom of thought, conscience and religion, it must have particular regard to the importance of that right.

(2) In this section 'court' includes a tribunal.

DEROGATIONS AND RESERVATIONS

Derogations

14 (1) In this Act 'designated derogation' means –

(a) the United Kingdom's derogation from Article 5(3) of the Convention; and

(b) any derogation by the United Kingdom from an Article of the Convention, or of any protocol to the Convention, which is designated for the purposes of this Act in an order made by the Secretary of State.

(2) The derogation referred to in sub-section (1)(a) is set out in Part I of Schedule 3.

(3) If a designated derogation is amended or replaced it ceases to be a designated derogation.

(4) But sub-section (3) does not prevent the Secretary of State from exercising his power under sub-section (1)(b) to make a fresh designation order in respect of the Article concerned.

(5) The Secretary of State must by order make such amendments to Schedule 3 as he considers appropriate to reflect –

(a) any designation order; or

(b) the effect of sub-section (3).

(6) A designation order may be made in anticipation of the making by the United Kingdom of a proposed derogation.

Reservations

15 (1) In this Act 'designated reservation' means –

(a) the United Kingdom's reservation to Article 2 of the First Protocol to the Convention; and

(b) any other reservation by the United Kingdom to an Article of the Convention, or of any protocol to the Convention, which is designated for the purposes of this Act in an order made by the Secretary of State.

(2) The text of the reservation referred to in sub-section (1)(a) is set out in Part II of Schedule 3.

(3) If a designated reservation is withdrawn wholly or in part it ceases to be a designated reservation.

(4) But sub-section (3) does not prevent the Secretary of State from exercising his power under sub-section (1)(b) to make a fresh designation order in respect of the Article concerned.

(5) The Secretary of State must by order make such amendments to this Act as he considers appropriate to reflect –

(a) any designation order; or

(b) the effect of sub-section (3).

Period for which designated derogations have effect

16 (1) If it has not already been withdrawn by the United Kingdom, a designated derogation ceases to have effect for the purposes of this Act –

(a) in the case of the derogation referred to in section 14(1)(a), at the end of the period of five years beginning with the date on which section 1(2) came into force;

(b) in the case of any other derogation, at the end of the period of five years beginning with the date on which the order designating it was made.

(2) At any time before the period –

(a) fixed by sub-section (1)(a) or (b); or

(b) extended by an order under this sub-section,

comes to an end, the Secretary of State may by order extend it by a further period of five years.

(3) An order under section 14(1)(b) ceases to have effect at the end of the period for consideration, unless a resolution has been passed by each House approving the order.

(4) Sub-section (3) does not affect –

(a) anything done in reliance on the order; or

(b) the power to make a fresh order under section 14(1)(b).

(5) In sub-section (3) 'period for consideration' means the period of forty days beginning with the day on which the order was made.

(6) In calculating the period for consideration, no account is to be taken of any time during which –

(a) Parliament is dissolved or prorogued; or

(b) both Houses are adjourned for more than four days.

(7) If a designated derogation is withdrawn by the United Kingdom, the Secretary of State must by order make such amendments to this Act as he considers are required to reflect that withdrawal.

Periodic review of designated reservations

17 (1) The appropriate Minister must review the designated reservation referred to in section 15(1)(a) –

    (a) before the end of the period of five years beginning with the date on which section 1(2) came into force; and

    (b) if that designation is still in force, before the end of the period of five years beginning with the date on which the last report relating to it was laid under sub-section (3).

  (2) The appropriate Minister must review each of the other designated reservations (if any) –

    (a) before the end of the period of five years beginning with the date on which the order designating the reservation first came into force; and

    (b) if the designation is still in force, before the end of the period of five years beginning with the date on which the last report relating to it was laid under sub-section (3).

  (3) The Minister conducting a review under this section must prepare a report on the result of the review and lay a copy of it before each House of Parliament.

JUDGES OF THE EUROPEAN COURT OF HUMAN RIGHTS

Appointment to European Court of Human Rights

18 (1) In this section 'judicial office' means the office of –

    (a) Lord Justice of Appeal, Justice of the High Court or Circuit judge, in England and Wales;

    (b) judge of the Court of Session or sheriff, in Scotland;

    (c) Lord Justice of Appeal, judge of the High Court or county court judge, in Northern Ireland.

  (2) The holder of a judicial office may become a judge of the European Court of Human Rights ('the Court') without being required to relinquish his office.

  (3) But he is not required to perform the duties of his judicial office while he is a judge of the Court.

  (4) In respect of any period during which he is a judge of the Court –

    (a) a Lord Justice of Appeal or Justice of the High Court is not to count as a judge of the relevant court for the purposes of section 2(1) or 4(1) of the Supreme Court Act 1981 (maximum number of judges) nor as a judge of the Supreme Court for the purposes of section 12(1) to (6) of that Act (salaries, etc);

(b) a judge of the Court of Session is not to count as a judge of that court for the purposes of section 1(1) of the Court of Session Act 1988 (maximum number of judges) or of section 9(1)(c) of the Administration of Justice Act 1973 ('the 1973 Act') (salaries, etc);

(c) a Lord Justice of Appeal or judge of the High Court in Northern Ireland is not to count as a judge of the relevant court for the purposes of section 2(1) or 3(1) of the Judicature (Northern Ireland) Act 1978 (maximum number of judges) nor as a judge of the Supreme Court of Northern Ireland for the purposes of section 9(1)(d) of the 1973 Act (salaries, etc);

(d) a Circuit judge is not to count as such for the purposes of section 18 of the Courts Act 1971 (salaries, etc);

(e) a sheriff is not to count as such for the purposes of section 14 of the Sheriff Courts (Scotland) Act 1907 (salaries, etc);

(f) a county court judge of Northern Ireland is not to count as such for the purposes of section 106 of the County Courts Act Northern Ireland) 1959 (salaries, etc).

(5) If a sheriff principal is appointed a judge of the Court, section 11(1) of the Sheriff Courts (Scotland) Act 1971 (temporary appointment of sheriff principal) applies, while he holds that appointment, as if his office is vacant.

(6) Schedule 4 makes provision about judicial pensions in relation to the holder of a judicial office who serves as a judge of the Court.

(7) The Lord Chancellor or the Secretary of State may by order make such transitional provision (including, in particular, provision for a temporary increase in the maximum number of judges) as he considers appropriate in relation to any holder of a judicial office who has completed his service as a judge of the Court.

PARLIAMENTARY PROCEDURE

Statements of compatibility

19 (1) A Minister of the Crown in charge of a Bill in either House of Parliament must, before Second Reading of the Bill –

(a) make a statement to the effect that in his view the provisions of the Bill are compatible with the Convention rights ('a statement of compatibility'); or

(b) make a statement to the effect that although he is unable to make a statement of compatibility the government nevertheless wishes the House to proceed with the Bill.

(2) The statement must be in writing and be published in such manner as the Minister making it considers appropriate.

SUPPLEMENTAL

Orders, etc, under this Act

20 (1) Any power of a Minister of the Crown to make an order under this Act is exercisable by statutory instrument.

(2) The power of the Lord Chancellor or the Secretary of State to make rules (other than rules of court) under section 2(3) or 7(9) is exercisable by statutory instrument.

(3) Any statutory instrument made under section 14, 15 or 16(7) must be laid before Parliament.

(4) No order may be made by the Lord Chancellor or the Secretary of State under section 1(4), 7(11) or 16(2) unless a draft of the order has been laid before, and approved by, each House of Parliament.

(5) Any statutory instrument made under section 18(7) or Schedule 4, or to which sub-section (2) applies, shall be subject to annulment in pursuance of a resolution of either House of Parliament.

(6) The power of a Northern Ireland department to make –

(a) rules under section 2(3)(c) or 7(9)(c); or

(b) an order under section 7(11),

is exercisable by statutory rule for the purposes of the Statutory Rules (Northern Ireland) Order 1979.

(7) Any rules made under section 2(3)(c) or 7(9)(c) shall be subject to negative resolution; and section 41(6) of the Interpretation Act Northern Ireland) 1954 (meaning of 'subject to negative resolution') shall apply as if the power to make the rules were conferred by an Act of the Northern Ireland Assembly.

(8) No order may be made by a Northern Ireland department under section 7(11) unless a draft of the order has been laid before, and approved by, the Northern Ireland Assembly.

Interpretation, etc

21 (1) In this Act –

'amend' includes repeal and apply (with or without modifications);

'the appropriate Minister' means the Minister of the Crown having charge of the appropriate authorised government department (within the meaning of the Crown Proceedings Act 1947);

'the Commission' means the European Commission of Human Rights;

'the Convention' means the Convention for the Protection of Human Rights and Fundamental Freedoms, agreed by the Council of Europe at Rome on 4th November 1950 as it has effect for the time being in relation to the United Kingdom;

'declaration of incompatibility' means a declaration under section 4;

'Minister of the Crown' has the same meaning as in the Ministers of the Crown Act 1975;

'Northern Ireland Minister' includes the First Minister and the deputy First Minister in Northern Ireland;

'primary legislation' means any –

(a) public general Act;

(b) local and personal Act;

(c) private Act;

(d) Measure of the Church Assembly;

(e) Measure of the General Synod of the Church of England;

(f) Order in Council –

    (i) made in exercise of Her Majesty's Royal Prerogative;

    (ii) made under section 38(1)(a) of the Northern Ireland Constitution Act 1973 or the corresponding provision of the Northern Ireland Act 1998; or

    (iii) amending an Act of a kind mentioned in paragraph (a), (b) or (c),

and includes an order or other instrument made under primary legislation (otherwise than by the National Assembly for Wales, a member of the Scottish Executive, a Northern Ireland Minister or a Northern Ireland department) to the extent to which it operates to bring one or more provisions of that legislation into force or amends any primary legislation;

'the First Protocol' means the protocol to the Convention agreed at Paris on 20th March 1952;

'the Sixth Protocol' means the protocol to the Convention agreed at Strasbourg on 28th April 1983;

'the Eleventh Protocol' means the protocol to the Convention (restructuring the control machinery established by the Convention) agreed at Strasbourg on 11th May 1994;

'remedial order' means an order under section 10;

'subordinate legislation' means any –

(a) Order in Council other than one –

(i) made in exercise of Her Majesty's Royal Prerogative;

(ii) made under section 38(1)(a) of the Northern Ireland Constitution Act 1973 or the corresponding provision of the Northern Ireland Act 1998; or

(iii) amending an Act of a kind mentioned in the definition of primary legislation;

(b) Act of the Scottish Parliament;

(c) Act of the Parliament of Northern Ireland;

(d) Measure of the Assembly established under section 1 of the Northern Ireland Assembly Act 1973;

(e) Act of the Northern Ireland Assembly;

(f) order, rules, regulations, scheme, warrant, byelaw or other instrument made under primary legislation (except to the extent to which it operates to bring one or more provisions of that legislation into force or amends any primary legislation);

(g) order, rules, regulations, scheme, warrant, byelaw or other instrument made under legislation mentioned in paragraph (b), (c), (d) or (e) or made under an Order in Council applying only to Northern Ireland;

(h) order, rules, regulations, scheme, warrant, byelaw or other instrument made by a member of the Scottish Executive, a Northern Ireland Minister or a Northern Ireland department in exercise of prerogative or other executive functions of Her Majesty which are exercisable by such a person on behalf of Her Majesty;

'transferred matters' has the same meaning as in the Northern Ireland Act 1998; and

'tribunal' means any tribunal in which legal proceedings may be brought.

(2) The references in paragraphs (b) and (c) of section 2(1) to Articles are to Articles of the Convention as they had effect immediately before the coming into force of the Eleventh Protocol.

(3) The reference in paragraph (d) of section 2(1) to Article 46 includes a reference to Articles 32 and 54 of the Convention as they had effect immediately before the coming into force of the Eleventh Protocol.

(4) The references in section 2(1) to a report or decision of the Commission or a decision of the Committee of Ministers include references to a report or decision made as provided by paragraphs 3, 4 and 6 of Article 5 of the Eleventh Protocol (transitional provisions).

(5) Any liability under the Army Act 1955, the Air Force Act 1955 or the Naval Discipline Act 1957 to suffer death for an offence is replaced by a liability to imprisonment for life or any less punishment authorised by those Acts; and those Acts shall accordingly have effect with the necessary modifications.

Short title, commencement, application and extent

22 (1) This Act may be cited as the Human Rights Act 1998.

(2) Sections 18, 20 and 21(5) and this section come into force on the passing of this Act.

(3) The other provisions of this Act come into force on such day as the Secretary of State may by order appoint; and different days may be appointed for different purposes.

(4) Paragraph (b) of sub-section (1) of section 7 applies to proceedings brought by or at the instigation of a public authority whenever the act in question took place; but otherwise that sub-section does not apply to an act taking place before the coming into force of that section.

(5) This Act binds the Crown.

(6) This Act extends to Northern Ireland.

(7) Section 21(5), so far as it relates to any provision contained in the Army Act 1955, the Air Force Act 1955 or the Naval Discipline Act 1957, extends to any place to which that provision extends.

SCHEDULES

SCHEDULE 1

THE ARTICLES

PART I

THE CONVENTION

RIGHTS AND FREEDOMS

ARTICLE 2

RIGHT TO LIFE

1 Everyone's right to life shall be protected by law. No one shall be deprived of his life intentionally save in the execution of a sentence of a court following his conviction of a crime for which this penalty is provided by law.

2 Deprivation of life shall not be regarded as inflicted in contravention of this Article when it results from the use of force which is no more than absolutely necessary:

(a) in defence of any person from unlawful violence;

(b) in order to effect a lawful arrest or to prevent the escape of a person lawfully detained;

(c) in action lawfully taken for the purpose of quelling a riot or insurrection.

ARTICLE 3

PROHIBITION OF TORTURE

No one shall be subjected to torture or to inhuman or degrading treatment or punishment.

ARTICLE 4

PROHIBITION OF SLAVERY AND FORCED LABOUR

1 No one shall be held in slavery or servitude.

2 No one shall be required to perform forced or compulsory labour.

3   For the purpose of this Article the term 'forced or compulsory labour' shall not include:

   (a) any work required to be done in the ordinary course of detention imposed according to the provisions of Article 5 of this Convention or during conditional release from such detention;

   (b) any service of a military character or, in case of conscientious objectors in countries where they are recognised, service exacted instead of compulsory military service;

   (c) any service exacted in case of an emergency or calamity threatening the life or well-being of the community;

   (d) any work or service which forms part of normal civic obligations.

ARTICLE 5

RIGHT TO LIBERTY AND SECURITY

1   Everyone has the right to liberty and security of person. No one shall be deprived of his liberty save in the following cases and in accordance with a procedure prescribed by law:

   (a) the lawful detention of a person after conviction by a competent court;

   (b) the lawful arrest or detention of a person for non-compliance with the lawful order of a court or in order to secure the fulfilment of any obligation prescribed by law;

   (c) the lawful arrest or detention of a person effected for the purpose of bringing him before the competent legal authority on reasonable suspicion of having committed an offence or when it is reasonably considered necessary to prevent his committing an offence or fleeing after having done so;

   (d) the detention of a minor by lawful order for the purpose of educational supervision or his lawful detention for the purpose of bringing him before the competent legal authority;

   (e) the lawful detention of persons for the prevention of the spreading of infectious diseases, of persons of unsound mind, alcoholics or drug addicts or vagrants;

   (f) the lawful arrest or detention of a person to prevent his effecting an unauthorised entry into the country or of a person against whom action is being taken with a view to deportation or extradition.

2   Everyone who is arrested shall be informed promptly, in a language which he understands, of the reasons for his arrest and of any charge against him.

3   Everyone arrested or detained in accordance with the provisions of paragraph 1(c) of this Article shall be brought promptly before a judge or other officer authorised by law to exercise judicial power and shall be entitled to trial within a reasonable time or to release pending trial. Release may be conditioned by guarantees to appear for trial.

4 Everyone who is deprived of his liberty by arrest or detention shall be entitled to take proceedings by which the lawfulness of his detention shall be decided speedily by a court and his release ordered if the detention is not lawful.

5 Everyone who has been the victim of arrest or detention in contravention of the provisions of this Article shall have an enforceable right to compensation.

ARTICLE 6

RIGHT TO A FAIR TRIAL

1 In the determination of his civil rights and obligations or of any criminal charge against him, everyone is entitled to a fair and public hearing within a reasonable time by an independent and impartial tribunal established by law. Judgment shall be pronounced publicly but the press and public may be excluded from all or part of the trial in the interest of morals, public order or national security in a democratic society, where the interests of juveniles or the protection of the private life of the parties so require, or to the extent strictly necessary in the opinion of the court in special circumstances where publicity would prejudice the interests of justice.

2 Everyone charged with a criminal offence shall be presumed innocent until proved guilty according to law.

3 Everyone charged with a criminal offence has the following minimum rights:

(a) to be informed promptly, in a language which he understands and in detail, of the nature and cause of the accusation against him;

(b) to have adequate time and facilities for the preparation of his defence;

(c) to defend himself in person or through legal assistance of his own choosing or, if he has not sufficient means to pay for legal assistance, to be given it free when the interests of justice so require;

(d) to examine or have examined witnesses against him and to obtain the attendance and examination of witnesses on his behalf under the same conditions as witnesses against him;

(e) to have the free assistance of an interpreter if he cannot understand or speak the language used in court.

ARTICLE 7

NO PUNISHMENT WITHOUT LAW

1 No one shall be held guilty of any criminal offence on account of any act or omission which did not constitute a criminal offence under national or international law at the time when it was committed. Nor shall a heavier penalty be imposed than the one that was applicable at the time the criminal offence was committed.

2   This Article shall not prejudice the trial and punishment of any person for any act or omission which, at the time when it was committed, was criminal according to the general principles of law recognised by civilised nations.

ARTICLE 8

RIGHT TO RESPECT FOR PRIVATE AND FAMILY LIFE

1   Everyone has the right to respect for his private and family life, his home and his correspondence.

2   There shall be no interference by a public authority with the exercise of this right except such as is in accordance with the law and is necessary in a democratic society in the interests of national security, public safety or the economic well-being of the country, for the prevention of disorder or crime, for the protection of health or morals, or for the protection of the rights and freedoms of others.

ARTICLE 9

FREEDOM OF THOUGHT, CONSCIENCE AND RELIGION

1   Everyone has the right to freedom of thought, conscience and religion; this right includes freedom to change his religion or belief and freedom, either alone or in community with others and in public or private, to manifest his religion or belief, in worship, teaching, practice and observance.

2   Freedom to manifest one's religion or beliefs shall be subject only to such limitations as are prescribed by law and are necessary in a democratic society in the interests of public safety, for the protection of public order, health or morals, or for the protection of the rights and freedoms of others.

ARTICLE 10

FREEDOM OF EXPRESSION

1   Everyone has the right to freedom of expression. This right shall include freedom to hold opinions and to receive and impart information and ideas without interference by public authority and regardless of frontiers. This Article shall not prevent States from requiring the licensing of broadcasting, television or cinema enterprises.

2   The exercise of these freedoms, since it carries with it duties and responsibilities, may be subject to such formalities, conditions, restrictions or penalties as are prescribed by law and are necessary in a democratic society, in the interests of national security, territorial integrity or public safety, for the prevention of disorder or crime, for the protection of health or morals, for the protection of the reputation or rights of others, for preventing the disclosure of information received in confidence, or for maintaining the authority and impartiality of the judiciary.

ARTICLE 11

FREEDOM OF ASSEMBLY AND ASSOCIATION

1 Everyone has the right to freedom of peaceful assembly and to freedom of association with others, including the right to form and to join trade unions for the protection of his interests.

2 No restrictions shall be placed on the exercise of these rights other than such as are prescribed by law and are necessary in a democratic society in the interests of national security or public safety, for the prevention of disorder or crime, for the protection of health or morals or for the protection of the rights and freedoms of others. This Article shall not prevent the imposition of lawful restrictions on the exercise of these rights by members of the armed forces, of the police or of the administration of the State.

ARTICLE 12

RIGHT TO MARRY

Men and women of marriageable age have the right to marry and to found a family, according to the national laws governing the exercise of this right.

ARTICLE 14

PROHIBITION OF DISCRIMINATION

The enjoyment of the rights and freedoms set forth in this Convention shall be secured without discrimination on any ground such as sex, race, colour, language, religion, political or other opinion, national or social origin, association with a national minority, property, birth or other status.

ARTICLE 16

RESTRICTIONS ON POLITICAL ACTIVITY OF ALIENS

Nothing in Articles 10, 11 and 14 shall be regarded as preventing the High Contracting Parties from imposing restrictions on the political activity of aliens.

ARTICLE 17

PROHIBITION OF ABUSE OF RIGHTS

Nothing in this Convention may be interpreted as implying for any State, group or person any right to engage in any activity or perform any act aimed at the destruction of any of the rights and freedoms set forth herein or at their limitation to a greater extent than is provided for in the Convention.

ARTICLE 18

LIMITATION ON USE OF RESTRICTIONS ON RIGHTS

The restrictions permitted under this Convention to the said rights and freedoms shall not be applied for any purpose other than those for which they have been prescribed.

PART II

THE FIRST PROTOCOL

ARTICLE 1

PROTECTION OF PROPERTY

Every natural or legal person is entitled to the peaceful enjoyment of his possessions. No one shall be deprived of his possessions except in the public interest and subject to the conditions provided for by law and by the general principles of international law.

The preceding provisions shall not, however, in any way impair the right of a State to enforce such laws as it deems necessary to control the use of property in accordance with the general interest or to secure the payment of taxes or other contributions or penalties.

ARTICLE 2

RIGHT TO EDUCATION

No person shall be denied the right to education. In the exercise of any functions which it assumes in relation to education and to teaching, the State shall respect the right of parents to ensure such education and teaching in conformity with their own religious and philosophical convictions.

ARTICLE 3

RIGHT TO FREE ELECTIONS

The High Contracting Parties undertake to hold free elections at reasonable intervals by secret ballot, under conditions which will ensure the free expression of the opinion of the people in the choice of the legislature.

PART III

THE SIXTH PROTOCOL

ARTICLE 1

ABOLITION OF THE DEATH PENALTY

The death penalty shall be abolished. No one shall be condemned to such penalty or executed.

ARTICLE 2

DEATH PENALTY IN TIME OF WAR

A State may make provision in its law for the death penalty in respect of acts committed in time of war or of imminent threat of war; such penalty shall be applied only in the instances laid down in the law and in accordance with its provisions. The State shall communicate to the Secretary General of the Council of Europe the relevant provisions of that law.

SCHEDULE 2

REMEDIAL ORDERS

Orders

1 – (1) A remedial order may –

    (a) contain such incidental, supplemental, consequential or transitional provision as the person making it considers appropriate;

    (b) be made so as to have effect from a date earlier than that on which it is made;

    (c) make provision for the delegation of specific functions;

    (d) make different provision for different cases.

  (2) The power conferred by sub-paragraph (1)(a) includes –

    (a) power to amend primary legislation (including primary legislation other than that which contains the incompatible provision); and

    (b) power to amend or revoke subordinate legislation (including subordinate legislation other than that which contains the incompatible provision).

  (3) A remedial order may be made so as to have the same extent as the legislation which it affects.

(4) No person is to be guilty of an offence solely as a result of the retrospective effect of a remedial order.

Procedure

2   No remedial order may be made unless –

(a) a draft of the order has been approved by a resolution of each House of Parliament made after the end of the period of 60 days beginning with the day on which the draft was laid; or

(b) it is declared in the order that it appears to the person making it that, because of the urgency of the matter, it is necessary to make the order without a draft being so approved.

Orders laid in draft

3 – (1) No draft may be laid under paragraph 2(a) unless –

(a) the person proposing to make the order has laid before Parliament a document which contains a draft of the proposed order and the required information; and

(b) the period of 60 days, beginning with the day on which the document required by this sub-paragraph was laid, has ended.

(2) If representations have been made during that period, the draft laid under paragraph 2(a) must be accompanied by a statement containing –

(a) a summary of the representations; and

(b) if, as a result of the representations, the proposed order has been changed, details of the changes.

Urgent cases

4 – (1) If a remedial order ('the original order') is made without being approved in draft, the person making it must lay it before Parliament, accompanied by the required information, after it is made.

(2) If representations have been made during the period of 60 days beginning with the day on which the original order was made, the person making it must (after the end of that period) lay before Parliament a statement containing –

(a) a summary of the representations; and

(b) if, as a result of the representations, he considers it appropriate to make changes to the original order, details of the changes.

(3) If sub-paragraph (2)(b) applies, the person making the statement must –

(a) make a further remedial order replacing the original order; and

(b) lay the replacement order before Parliament.

(4) If, at the end of the period of 120 days beginning with the day on which the original order was made, a resolution has not been passed by each House approving the original or replacement order, the order ceases to have effect

(but without that affecting anything previously done under either order or the power to make a fresh remedial order).

Definitions

5   In this Schedule –

'representations' means representations about a remedial order (or proposed remedial order) made to the person making (or proposing to make) it and includes any relevant Parliamentary report or resolution; and

'required information' means –

> (a) an explanation of the incompatibility which the order (or proposed order) seeks to remove, including particulars of the relevant declaration, finding or order; and

> (b) a statement of the reasons for proceeding under section 10 and for making an order in those terms.

Calculating periods

6   In calculating any period for the purposes of this Schedule, no account is to be taken of any time during which –

> (a) Parliament is dissolved or prorogued; or

> (b) both Houses are adjourned for more than four days.

SCHEDULE 3

DEROGATION AND RESERVATION

PART I

DEROGATION

The 1988 notification. The United Kingdom Permanent Representative to the Council of Europe presents his compliments to the Secretary General of the Council, and has the honour to convey the following information in order to ensure compliance with the obligations of Her Majesty's Government in the United Kingdom under Article 15(3) of the Convention for the Protection of Human Rights and Fundamental Freedoms signed at Rome on 4 November 1950. There have been in the United Kingdom in recent years campaigns of organised terrorism connected with the affairs of Northern Ireland which have manifested themselves in activities which have included repeated murder, attempted murder, maiming, intimidation and violent civil disturbance and in bombing and fire raising which have resulted in death, injury and widespread destruction of property. As a result, a public emergency within the meaning of Article 15(1) of the Convention exists in the United Kingdom. The Government found it necessary in 1974 to introduce and since then, in cases concerning persons reasonably suspected of involvement in terrorism connected with the affairs of Northern Ireland, or of certain offences under the legislation, who have been detained for 48 hours, to exercise powers enabling further detention without charge, for periods of up to five days, on the authority of the Secretary of State. These powers are at present to be found in Section 12 of the Prevention of Terrorism (Temporary Provisions) Act 1984, Article 9 of the Prevention of Terrorism (Supplemental Temporary Provisions) Order 1984 and Article 10 of the Prevention of Terrorism (Supplemental Temporary Provisions) (Northern Ireland) Order 1984. Section 12 of the Prevention of Terrorism (Temporary Provisions) Act 1984 provides for a person whom a constable has arrested on reasonable grounds of suspecting him to be guilty of an offence under Section 1, 9 or 10 of the Act, or to be or to have been involved in terrorism connected with the affairs of Northern Ireland, to be detained in right of the arrest for up to 48 hours and thereafter, where the Secretary of State extends the detention period, for up to a further five days. Section 12 substantially re-enacted Section 12 of the Prevention of Terrorism (Temporary Provisions) Act 1976 which, in turn, substantially re-enacted Section 7 of the Prevention of Terrorism (Temporary Provisions) Act 1974. Article 10 of the Prevention of Terrorism (Supplemental Temporary Provisions) (Northern Ireland) Order 1984 (SI 1984/417) and Article 9 of the Prevention of Terrorism (Supplemental Temporary Provisions) Order 1984 (SI 1984/418) were both made under Sections 13 and 14 of and Schedule 3 to the 1984 Act and substantially re-enacted powers of detention in Orders made under the 1974 and 1976 Acts. A person who is being examined under Article 4 of either Order on his arrival in, or on seeking to leave, Northern Ireland or Great Britain for the purpose of determining whether he is or has been involved in terrorism connected with the affairs of Northern Ireland, or whether there are grounds for suspecting that he has committed an offence under Section 9 of the 1984 Act, may be detained under Article 9 or 10, as appropriate, pending the conclusion of his examination. The period of this examination may exceed 12 hours if an examining officer has reasonable grounds for suspecting him to be or to have been involved in acts of terrorism connected with the affairs of Northern Ireland. Where such a person is detained under the said Article 9 or 10 he may be detained for up to 48 hours on the authority of an examining officer and thereafter, where the Secretary of State extends the detention period, for up to a further five days. In its judgment of 29 November 1988 in the Case of *Brogan and Others*, the European Court of Human Rights held that there had been a violation of Article 5(3) in respect of each of the applicants, all of whom had been detained under Section 12 of the 1984 Act. The Court held that even the shortest of the four periods of detention concerned, namely four days and six hours, fell outside the constraints as to time permitted by the first part of Article 5(3). In addition, the Court held that there had been a violation of Article 5(5) in the case of each applicant. Following this judgment, the Secretary of State for the Home Department informed Parliament on 6 December 1988 that, against the background of the terrorist campaign, and the over-riding need to bring terrorists to justice, the Government did not believe that the maximum period of detention should be reduced. He informed Parliament that the Government were examining the matter with a view to responding to the judgment. On 22 December 1988, the Secretary of State further informed Parliament that it remained the Government's wish, if it could be achieved, to find a judicial process under which extended detention might be reviewed and where appropriate authorised by a judge or other judicial officer. But a further period of reflection and consultation was necessary before the Government could bring forward a firm and final view. Since the judgment of 29 November 1988 as well as previously, the Government have found it necessary to continue to exercise, in relation to terrorism connected with the affairs of Northern Ireland, the powers described above enabling further detention without charge for periods of up to 5 days, on the authority of the Secretary of State, to the extent strictly required by the exigencies of the situation to enable necessary enquiries and investigations properly to be completed in order to decide whether criminal proceedings should be instituted. To the extent that the exercise of these powers may be inconsistent with the obligations imposed by the Convention the Government has availed itself of the right of derogation conferred by Article 15(1) of the Convention and will continue to do so until further notice. Dated 23 December 1988.

The 1989 notification. The United Kingdom Permanent Representative to the Council of Europe presents his compliments to the Secretary General of the Council, and has the honour to convey the following information. In his communication to the Secretary General of 23 December 1988, reference was made to the introduction and exercise of certain powers under section 12 of the Prevention of Terrorism (Temporary Provisions) Act 1984, Article 9 of the Prevention of Terrorism (Supplemental Temporary Provisions) Order 1984 and Article 10 of the Prevention of Terrorism (Supplemental Temporary Provisions) (Northern Ireland) Order 1984. These provisions have been replaced by section 14 of and paragraph 6 of Schedule 5 to the Prevention of Terrorism (Temporary Provisions) Act 1989, which make comparable provision. They came into force on 22 March 1989. A copy of these provisions is enclosed. The United Kingdom Permanent Representative avails himself of this opportunity to renew to the Secretary General the assurance of his highest consideration. 23 March 1989.

PART II

RESERVATION

At the time of signing the present (First) Protocol, I declare that, in view of certain provisions of the Education Acts in the United Kingdom, the principle affirmed in the second sentence of Article 2 is accepted by the United Kingdom only so far as it is compatible with the provision of efficient instruction and training, and the avoidance of unreasonable public expenditure. Dated 20 March 1952. Made by the United Kingdom Permanent Representative to the Council of Europe.

SCHEDULE 4

JUDICIAL PENSIONS

Duty to make orders about pensions

1 – (1) The appropriate Minister must by order make provision with respect to pensions payable to or in respect of any holder of a judicial office who serves as an ECHR judge.

(2) A pensions order must include such provision as the Minister making it considers is necessary to secure that –

(a) an ECHR judge who was, immediately before his appointment as an ECHR judge, a member of a judicial pension scheme is entitled to remain as a member of that scheme;

(b) the terms on which he remains a member of the scheme are those which would have been applicable had he not been appointed as an ECHR judge; and

(c) entitlement to benefits payable in accordance with the scheme continues to be determined as if, while serving as an ECHR judge, his salary was that which would (but for section 18(4)) have been payable to him in respect of his continuing service as the holder of his judicial office.

Contributions

2   A pensions order may, in particular, make provision –

(a) for any contributions which are payable by a person who remains a member of a scheme as a result of the order, and which would otherwise be payable by deduction from his salary, to be made otherwise than by deduction from his salary as an ECHR judge; and

(b) for such contributions to be collected in such manner as may be determined by the administrators of the scheme.

Amendments of other enactments

3   A pensions order may amend any provision of, or made under, a pensions Act in such manner and to such extent as the Minister making the order considers necessary or expedient to ensure the proper administration of any scheme to which it relates.

Definitions

4   In this Schedule –

'appropriate Minister' means –

(a) in relation to any judicial office whose jurisdiction is exercisable exclusively in relation to Scotland, the Secretary of State; and

(b) otherwise, the Lord Chancellor;

'ECHR judge' means the holder of a judicial office who is serving as a judge of the Court;

'judicial pension scheme' means a scheme established by and in accordance with a pensions Act;

'pensions Act' means –

(a) the County Courts Act Northern Ireland) 1959;

(b) the Sheriffs' Pensions (Scotland) Act 1961;

(c) the Judicial Pensions Act 1981; or

(d) the Judicial Pensions and Retirement Act 1993; and

'pensions order' means an order made under paragraph 1.

THE EUROPEAN CONVENTION ON HUMAN RIGHTS

The governments signatory hereto, being members of the Council of Europe,

Considering the Universal Declaration of Human Rights proclaimed by the General Assembly of the United Nations on 10th December 1948;

Considering that this Declaration aims at securing the universal and effective recognition and observance of the Rights therein declared;

Considering that the aim of the Council of Europe is the achievement of greater unity between its members and that one of the methods by which that aim is to be pursued is the maintenance and further realisation of human rights and fundamental freedoms;

Reaffirming their profound belief in those fundamental freedoms which are the foundation of justice and peace in the world and are best maintained on the one hand by an effective political democracy and on the other by a common understanding and observance of the human rights upon which they depend;

Being resolved, as the governments of European countries which are like-minded and have a common heritage of political traditions, ideals, freedom and the rule of law, to take the first steps for the collective enforcement of certain of the rights stated in the Universal Declaration,

Have agreed as follows:

ARTICLE 1 – OBLIGATION TO RESPECT HUMAN RIGHTS

The High Contracting Parties shall secure to everyone within their jurisdiction the rights and freedoms defined in Section I of this Convention.

SECTION I – RIGHTS AND FREEDOMS

ARTICLE 2 – RIGHT TO LIFE

1. Everyone's right to life shall be protected by law. No one shall be deprived of his life intentionally save in the execution of a sentence of a court following his conviction of a crime for which this penalty is provided by law.

2. Deprivation of life shall not be regarded as inflicted in contravention of this article when it results from the use of force which is no more than absolutely necessary:

   a. in defence of any person from unlawful violence;

   b. in order to effect a lawful arrest or to prevent the escape of a person lawfully detained;

   c. in action lawfully taken for the purpose of quelling a riot or insurrection.

ARTICLE 3 – PROHIBITION OF TORTURE

No one shall be subjected to torture or to inhuman or degrading treatment or punishment.

ARTICLE 4 – PROHIBITION OF SLAVERY AND FORCED LABOUR

1. No one shall be held in slavery or servitude.

2. No one shall be required to perform forced or compulsory labour.

3. For the purpose of this article the term "forced or compulsory labour" shall not include:

   a. any work required to be done in the ordinary course of detention imposed according to the provisions of Article 5 of this Convention or during conditional release from such detention;

   b. any service of a military character or, in case of conscientious objectors in countries where they are recognised, service exacted instead of compulsory military service;

   c. any service exacted in case of an emergency or calamity threatening the life or well-being of the community;

   d. any work or service which forms part of normal civic obligations.

ARTICLE 5 – RIGHT TO LIBERTY AND SECURITY

1. Everyone has the right to liberty and security of person. No one shall be deprived of his liberty save in the following cases and in accordance with a procedure prescribed by law:

   a. the lawful detention of a person after conviction by a competent court;

   b. the lawful arrest or detention of a person for non-compliance with the lawful order of a court or in order to secure the fulfilment of any obligation prescribed by law;

   c. the lawful arrest or detention of a person effected for the purpose of bringing him before the competent legal authority on reasonable suspicion of having committed an offence or when it is reasonably considered necessary to prevent his committing an offence or fleeing after having done so;

d. the detention of a minor by lawful order for the purpose of educational supervision or his lawful detention for the purpose of bringing him before the competent legal authority;

e. the lawful detention of persons for the prevention of the spreading of infectious diseases, of persons of unsound mind, alcoholics or drug addicts or vagrants;

f. the lawful arrest or detention of a person to prevent his effecting an unauthorised entry into the country or of a person against whom action is being taken with a view to deportation or extradition.

2. Everyone who is arrested shall be informed promptly, in a language which he understands, of the reasons for his arrest and of any charge against him.

3. Everyone arrested or detained in accordance with the provisions of paragraph 1.c of this article shall be brought promptly before a judge or other officer authorised by law to exercise judicial power and shall be entitled to trial within a reasonable time or to release pending trial. Release may be conditioned by guarantees to appear for trial.

4. Everyone who is deprived of his liberty by arrest or detention shall be entitled to take proceedings by which the lawfulness of his detention shall be decided speedily by a court and his release ordered if the detention is not lawful.

5. Everyone who has been the victim of arrest or detention in contravention of the provisions of this article shall have an enforceable right to compensation.

ARTICLE 6 – RIGHT TO A FAIR TRIAL

1. In the determination of his civil rights and obligations or of any criminal charge against him, everyone is entitled to a fair and public hearing within a reasonable time by an independent and impartial tribunal established by law. Judgment shall be pronounced publicly but the press and public may be excluded from all or part of the trial in the interests of morals, public order or national security in a democratic society, where the interests of juveniles or the protection of the private life of the parties so require, or to the extent strictly necessary in the opinion of the court in special circumstances where publicity would prejudice the interests of justice.

2. Everyone charged with a criminal offence shall be presumed innocent until proved guilty according to law.

3. Everyone charged with a criminal offence has the following minimum rights:

a. to be informed promptly, in a language which he understands and in detail, of the nature and cause of the accusation against him;

b. to have adequate time and facilities for the preparation of his defence;

c. to defend himself in person or through legal assistance of his own choosing or, if he has not sufficient means to pay for legal assistance, to be given it free when the interests of justice so require;

d. to examine or have examined witnesses against him and to obtain the attendance and examination of witnesses on his behalf under the same conditions as witnesses against him;

e. to have the free assistance of an interpreter if he cannot understand or speak the language used in court.

ARTICLE 7 – NO PUNISHMENT WITHOUT LAW

1. No one shall be held guilty of any criminal offence on account of any act or omission which did not constitute a criminal offence under national or international law at the time when it was committed. Nor shall a heavier penalty be imposed than the one that was applicable at the time the criminal offence was committed.

2. This article shall not prejudice the trial and punishment of any person for any act or omission which, at the time when it was committed, was criminal according to the general principles of law recognised by civilised nations.

ARTICLE 8 – RIGHT TO RESPECT FOR PRIVATE AND FAMILY LIFE

1. Everyone has the right to respect for his private and family life, his home and his correspondence.

2. There shall be no interference by a public authority with the exercise of this right except such as is in accordance with the law and is necessary in a democratic society in the interests of national security, public safety or the economic well-being of the country, for the prevention of disorder or crime, for the protection of health or morals, or for the protection of the rights and freedoms of others.

ARTICLE 9 – FREEDOM OF THOUGHT, CONSCIENCE AND RELIGION

1. Everyone has the right to freedom of thought, conscience and religion; this right includes freedom to change his religion or belief and freedom, either alone or in community with others and in public or private, to manifest his religion or belief, in worship, teaching, practice and observance.

2. Freedom to manifest one's religion or beliefs shall be subject only to such limitations as are prescribed by law and are necessary in a democratic society in the interests of public safety, for the protection of public order, health or morals, or for the protection of the rights and freedoms of others.

ARTICLE 10 – FREEDOM OF EXPRESSION

1. Everyone has the right to freedom of expression. This right shall include freedom to hold opinions and to receive and impart information and ideas without interference by public authority and regardless of frontiers. This article shall not prevent States from requiring the licensing of broadcasting, television or cinema enterprises.

2. The exercise of these freedoms, since it carries with it duties and responsibilities, may be subject to such formalities, conditions, restrictions or penalties as are prescribed by law and are necessary in a democratic society, in the interests of national security, territorial integrity or public safety, for the prevention of disorder or crime, for the protection of health or morals, for the protection of the reputation or rights of others, for preventing the disclosure of information received in confidence, or for maintaining the authority and impartiality of the judiciary.

ARTICLE 11 – FREEDOM OF ASSEMBLY AND ASSOCIATION

1. Everyone has the right to freedom of peaceful assembly and to freedom of association with others, including the right to form and to join trade unions for the protection of his interests.

2. No restrictions shall be placed on the exercise of these rights other than such as are prescribed by law and are necessary in a democratic society in the interests of national security or public safety, for the prevention of disorder or crime, for the protection of health or morals or for the protection of the rights and freedoms of others. This article shall not prevent the imposition of lawful restrictions on the exercise of these rights by members of the armed forces, of the police or of the administration of the State.

ARTICLE 12 – RIGHT TO MARRY

Men and women of marriageable age have the right to marry and to found a family, according to the national laws governing the exercise of this right.

ARTICLE 13 – RIGHT TO AN EFFECTIVE REMEDY

Everyone whose rights and freedoms as set forth in this Convention are violated shall have an effective remedy before a national authority notwithstanding that the violation has been committed by persons acting in an official capacity.

ARTICLE 14 – PROHIBITION OF DISCRIMINATION

The enjoyment of the rights and freedoms set forth in this Convention shall be secured without discrimination on any ground such as sex, race, colour, language, religion, political or other opinion, national or social origin, association with a national minority, property, birth or other status.

ARTICLE 15 – DEROGATION IN TIME OF EMERGENCY

1. In time of war or other public emergency threatening the life of the nation any High Contracting Party may take measures derogating from its

obligations under this Convention to the extent strictly required by the exigencies of the situation, provided that such measures are not inconsistent with its other obligations under international law.

2. No derogation from Article 2, except in respect of deaths resulting from lawful acts of war, or from Articles 3, 4 (paragraph 1) and 7 shall be made under this provision.

3. Any High Contracting Party availing itself of this right of derogation shall keep the Secretary General of the Council of Europe fully informed of the measures which it has taken and the reasons therefor. It shall also inform the Secretary General of the Council of Europe when such measures have ceased to operate and the provisions of the Convention are again being fully executed.

ARTICLE 16 – RESTRICTIONS ON POLITICAL ACTIVITY OF ALIENS

Nothing in Articles 10, 11 and 14 shall be regarded as preventing the High Contracting Parties from imposing restrictions on the political activity of aliens.

ARTICLE 17 – PROHIBITION OF ABUSE OF RIGHTS

Nothing in this Convention may be interpreted as implying for any State, group or person any right to engage in any activity or perform any act aimed at the destruction of any of the rights and freedoms set forth herein or at their limitation to a greater extent than is provided for in the Convention.

ARTICLE 18 – LIMITATION ON USE OF RESTRICTIONS ON RIGHTS

The restrictions permitted under this Convention to the said rights and freedoms shall not be applied for any purpose other than those for which they have been prescribed.

SECTION II – EUROPEAN COURT OF HUMAN RIGHTS

ARTICLE 19 – ESTABLISHMENT OF THE COURT

To ensure the observance of the engagements undertaken by the High Contracting Parties in the Convention and the Protocols thereto, there shall be set up a European Court of Human Rights, hereinafter referred to as "the Court". It shall function on a permanent basis.

ARTICLE 20 – NUMBER OF JUDGES

The Court shall consist of a number of judges equal to that of the High Contracting Parties.

ARTICLE 21 – CRITERIA FOR OFFICE

1. The judges shall be of high moral character and must either possess the qualifications required for appointment to high judicial office or be jurisconsults of recognised competence.
2. The judges shall sit on the Court in their individual capacity.
3. During their term of office the judges shall not engage in any activity which is incompatible with their independence, impartiality or with the demands of a full-time office; all questions arising from the application of this paragraph shall be decided by the Court.

ARTICLE 22 – ELECTION OF JUDGES

1. The judges shall be elected by the Parliamentary Assembly with respect to each High Contracting Party by a majority of votes cast from a list of three candidates nominated by the High Contracting Party.
2. The same procedure shall be followed to complete the Court in the event of the accession of new High Contracting Parties and in filling casual vacancies.

ARTICLE 23 – TERMS OF OFFICE

1. The judges shall be elected for a period of six years. They may be re-elected. However, the terms of office of one-half of the judges elected at the first election shall expire at the end of three years.
2. The judges whose terms of office are to expire at the end of the initial period of three years shall be chosen by lot by the Secretary General of the Council of Europe immediately after their election.
3. In order to ensure that, as far as possible, the terms of office of one-half of the judges are renewed every three years, the Parliamentary Assembly may decide, before proceeding to any subsequent election, that the term or terms of office of one or more judges to be elected shall be for a period other than six years but not more than nine and not less than three years.
4. In cases where more than one term of office is involved and where the Parliamentary Assembly applies the preceding paragraph, the allocation of the terms of office shall be effected by a drawing of lots by the Secretary General of the Council of Europe immediately after the election.
5. A judge elected to replace a judge whose term of office has not expired shall hold office for the remainder of his predecessor's term.
6. The terms of office of judges shall expire when they reach the age of 70.

7. The judges shall hold office until replaced. They shall, however, continue to deal with such cases as they already have under consideration.

ARTICLE 24 – DISMISSAL

No judge may be dismissed from his office unless the other judges decide by a majority of two-thirds that he has ceased to fulfil the required conditions.

ARTICLE 25 – REGISTRY AND LEGAL SECRETARIES

The Court shall have a registry, the functions and organisation of which shall be laid down in the rules of the Court. The Court shall be assisted by legal secretaries.

ARTICLE 26 – PLENARY COURT

The plenary Court shall:

a. elect its President and one or two Vice-Presidents for a period of three years; they may be re-elected;

b. set up Chambers, constituted for a fixed period of time;

c. elect the Presidents of the Chambers of the Court; they may be re-elected;

d. adopt the rules of the Court, and

e. elect the Registrar and one or more Deputy Registrars.

ARTICLE 27 – COMMITTEES, CHAMBERS AND GRAND CHAMBER

1. To consider cases brought before it, the Court shall sit in committees of three judges, in Chambers of seven judges and in a Grand Chamber of seventeen judges. The Court's Chambers shall set up committees for a fixed period of time.

2. There shall sit as an *ex officio* member of the Chamber and the Grand Chamber the judge elected in respect of the State Party concerned or, if there is none or if he is unable to sit, a person of its choice who shall sit in the capacity of judge.

3. The Grand Chamber shall also include the President of the Court, the Vice-Presidents, the Presidents of the Chambers and other judges chosen in accordance with the rules of the Court. When a case is referred to the Grand Chamber under Article 43, no judge from the Chamber which rendered the judgment shall sit in the Grand Chamber, with the exception of the President of the Chamber and the judge who sat in respect of the State Party concerned.

ARTICLE 28 – DECLARATIONS OF INADMISSIBILITY BY COMMITTEES

A committee may, by a unanimous vote, declare inadmissible or strike out of its list of cases an application submitted under Article 34 where such a decision can be taken without further examination. The decision shall be final.

ARTICLE 29 – DECISIONS BY CHAMBERS ON ADMISSIBILITY AND MERITS

1. If no decision is taken under Article 28, a Chamber shall decide on the admissibility and merits of individual applications submitted under Article 34.
2. A Chamber shall decide on the admissibility and merits of inter-State applications submitted under Article 33.
3. The decision on admissibility shall be taken separately unless the Court, in exceptional cases, decides otherwise.

ARTICLE 30 – RELINQUISHMENT OF JURISDICTION TO THE GRAND CHAMBER

Where a case pending before a Chamber raises a serious question affecting the interpretation of the Convention or the protocols thereto, or where the resolution of a question before the Chamber might have a result inconsistent with a judgment previously delivered by the Court, the Chamber may, at any time before it has rendered its judgment, relinquish jurisdiction in favour of the Grand Chamber, unless one of the parties to the case objects.

ARTICLE 31 – POWERS OF THE GRAND CHAMBER

The Grand Chamber shall:

a. determine applications submitted either under Article 33 or Article 34 when a Chamber has relinquished jurisdiction under Article 30 or when the case has been referred to it under Article 43; and
b. consider requests for advisory opinions submitted under Article 47.

ARTICLE 32 – JURISDICTION OF THE COURT

1. The jurisdiction of the Court shall extend to all matters concerning the interpretation and application of the Convention and the protocols thereto which are referred to it as provided in Articles 33, 34 and 47.
2. In the event of dispute as to whether the Court has jurisdiction, the Court shall decide.

ARTICLE 33 – INTER-STATE CASES

Any High Contracting Party may refer to the Court any alleged breach of the provisions of the Convention and the protocols thereto by another High Contracting Party.

ARTICLE 34 – INDIVIDUAL APPLICATIONS

CHART OF DECLARATIONS UNDER FORMER ARTICLES 25 AND 46 OF THE ECHR

The Court may receive applications from any person, non-governmental organisation or group of individuals claiming to be the victim of a violation by one of the High Contracting Parties of the rights set forth in the Convention or the protocols thereto. The High Contracting Parties undertake not to hinder in any way the effective exercise of this right.

ARTICLE 35 – ADMISSIBILITY CRITERIA

1. The Court may only deal with the matter after all domestic remedies have been exhausted, according to the generally recognised rules of international law, and within a period of six months from the date on which the final decision was taken.

2. The Court shall not deal with any application submitted under Article 34 that:

   a. is anonymous; or

   b. is substantially the same as a matter that has already been examined by the Court or has already been submitted to another procedure of international investigation or settlement and contains no relevant new information.

3. The Court shall declare inadmissible any individual application submitted under Article 34 which it considers incompatible with the provisions of the Convention or the protocols thereto, manifestly ill-founded, or an abuse of the right of application.

4. The Court shall reject any application which it considers inadmissible under this Article. It may do so at any stage of the proceedings.

ARTICLE 36 – THIRD PARTY INTERVENTION

1. In all cases before a Chamber or the Grand Chamber, a High Contracting Party one of whose nationals is an applicant shall have the right to submit written comments and to take part in hearings.

2. The President of the Court may, in the interest of the proper administration of justice, invite any High Contracting Party which is not a party to the proceedings or any person concerned who is not the applicant to submit written comments or take part in hearings.

ARTICLE 37 – STRIKING OUT APPLICATIONS

1. The Court may at any stage of the proceedings decide to strike an application out of its list of cases where the circumstances lead to the conclusion that:

   a. the applicant does not intend to pursue his application; or

   b. the matter has been resolved; or

   c. for any other reason established by the Court, it is no longer justified to continue the examination of the application.

   However, the Court shall continue the examination of the application if respect for human rights as defined in the Convention and the protocols thereto so requires.

2. The Court may decide to restore an application to its list of cases if it considers that the circumstances justify such a course.

ARTICLE 38 – EXAMINATION OF THE CASE AND FRIENDLY SETTLEMENT PROCEEDINGS

1. If the Court declares the application admissible, it shall:

   a. pursue the examination of the case, together with the representatives of the parties, and if need be, undertake an investigation, for the effective conduct of which the States concerned shall furnish all necessary facilities;

   b. place itself at the disposal of the parties concerned with a view to securing a friendly settlement of the matter on the basis of respect for human rights as defined in the Convention and the protocols thereto.

2. Proceedings conducted under paragraph 1.b shall be confidential.

ARTICLE 39 – FINDING OF A FRIENDLY SETTLEMENT

If a friendly settlement is effected, the Court shall strike the case out of its list by means of a decision which shall be confined to a brief statement of the facts and of the solution reached.

ARTICLE 40 – PUBLIC HEARINGS AND ACCESS TO DOCUMENTS

1. Hearings shall be in public unless the Court in exceptional circumstances decides otherwise.

2. Documents deposited with the Registrar shall be accessible to the public unless the President of the Court decides otherwise.

ARTICLE 41 – JUST SATISFACTION

If the Court finds that there has been a violation of the Convention or the protocols thereto, and if the internal law of the High Contracting Party concerned allows only partial reparation to be made, the Court shall, if necessary, afford just satisfaction to the injured party.

ARTICLE 42 – JUDGMENTS OF CHAMBERS

Judgments of Chambers shall become final in accordance with the provisions of Article 44, paragraph 2.

ARTICLE 43 – REFERRAL TO THE GRAND CHAMBER

1. Within a period of three months from the date of the judgment of the Chamber, any party to the case may, in exceptional cases, request that the case be referred to the Grand Chamber.
2. A panel of five judges of the Grand Chamber shall accept the request if the case raises a serious question affecting the interpretation or application of the Convention or the protocols thereto, or a serious issue of general importance.
3. If the panel accepts the request, the Grand Chamber shall decide the case by means of a judgment.

ARTICLE 44 – FINAL JUDGMENTS

1. The judgment of the Grand Chamber shall be final.
2. The judgment of a Chamber shall become final:
   a. when the parties declare that they will not request that the case be referred to the Grand Chamber; or
   b. three months after the date of the judgment, if reference of the case to the Grand Chamber has not been requested; or
   c. when the panel of the Grand Chamber rejects the request to refer under Article 43.
3. The final judgment shall be published.

ARTICLE 45 – REASONS FOR JUDGMENTS AND DECISIONS

1. Reasons shall be given for judgments as well as for decisions declaring applications admissible or inadmissible.
2. If a judgment does not represent, in whole or in part, the unanimous opinion of the judges, any judge shall be entitled to deliver a separate opinion.

ARTICLE 46 – BINDING FORCE AND EXECUTION OF JUDGMENTS

1. The High Contracting Parties undertake to abide by the final judgment of the Court in any case to which they are parties.
2. The final judgment of the Court shall be transmitted to the Committee of Ministers, which shall supervise its execution.

ARTICLE 47 – ADVISORY OPINIONS

1. The Court may, at the request of the Committee of Ministers, give advisory opinions on legal questions concerning the interpretation of the Convention and the protocols thereto.
2. Such opinions shall not deal with any question relating to the content or scope of the rights or freedoms defined in Section I of the Convention and the protocols thereto, or with any other question which the Court or the Committee of Ministers might have to consider in consequence of any such proceedings as could be instituted in accordance with the Convention.
3. Decisions of the Committee of Ministers to request an advisory opinion of the Court shall require a majority vote of the representatives entitled to sit on the Committee.

ARTICLE 48 – ADVISORY JURISDICTION OF THE COURT

The Court shall decide whether a request for an advisory opinion submitted by the Committee of Ministers is within its competence as defined in Article 47.

ARTICLE 49 – REASONS FOR ADVISORY OPINIONS

1. Reasons shall be given for advisory opinions of the Court.
2. If the advisory opinion does not represent, in whole or in part, the unanimous opinion of the judges, any judge shall be entitled to deliver a separate opinion.
3. Advisory opinions of the Court shall be communicated to the Committee of Ministers.

ARTICLE 50 – EXPENDITURE ON THE COURT

The expenditure on the Court shall be borne by the Council of Europe.

ARTICLE 51 – PRIVILEGES AND IMMUNITIES OF JUDGES

The judges shall be entitled, during the exercise of their functions, to the privileges and immunities provided for in Article 40 of the Statute of the Council of Europe and in the agreements made thereunder.

SECTION III – MISCELLANEOUS PROVISIONS

ARTICLE 52 – INQUIRIES BY THE SECRETARY GENERAL

On receipt of a request from the Secretary General of the Council of Europe any High Contracting Party shall furnish an explanation of the manner in which its internal law ensures the effective implementation of any of the provisions of the Convention.

ARTICLE 53 – SAFEGUARD FOR EXISTING HUMAN RIGHTS

Nothing in this Convention shall be construed as limiting or derogating from any of the human rights and fundamental freedoms which may be ensured under the laws of any High Contracting Party or under any other agreement to which it is a Party.

ARTICLE 54 – POWERS OF THE COMMITTEE OF MINISTERS1

Nothing in this Convention shall prejudice the powers conferred on the Committee of Ministers by the Statute of the Council of Europe.

ARTICLE 55 – EXCLUSION OF OTHER MEANS OF DISPUTE SETTLEMENT

The High Contracting Parties agree that, except by special agreement, they will not avail themselves of treaties, conventions or declarations in force between them for the purpose of submitting, by way of petition, a dispute arising out of the interpretation or application of this Convention to a means of settlement other than those provided for in this Convention.

ARTICLE 56 – TERRITORIAL APPLICATION

1. Any State may at the time of its ratification or at any time thereafter declare by notification addressed to the Secretary General of the Council of Europe that the present Convention shall, subject to paragraph 4 of this Article, extend to all or any of the territories for whose international relations it is responsible.

2. The Convention shall extend to the territory or territories named in the notification as from the thirtieth day after the receipt of this notification by the Secretary General of the Council of Europe.

3. The provisions of this Convention shall be applied in such territories with due regard, however, to local requirements.

4. Any State which has made a declaration in accordance with paragraph 1 of this article may at any time thereafter declare on behalf of one or more of the territories to which the declaration relates that it accepts the competence of the Court to receive applications from individuals, non-governmental organisations or groups of individuals as provided by Article 34 of the Convention.

ARTICLE 57 – RESERVATIONS

1. Any State may, when signing this Convention or when depositing its instrument of ratification, make a reservation in respect of any particular provision of the Convention to the extent that any law then in force in its territory is not in conformity with the provision. Reservations of a general character shall not be permitted under this article.

2. Any reservation made under this article shall contain a brief statement of the law concerned.

ARTICLE 58 – DENUNCIATION

1. A High Contracting Party may denounce the present Convention only after the expiry of five years from the date on which it became a party to it and after six months' notice contained in a notification addressed to the Secretary General of the Council of Europe, who shall inform the other High Contracting Parties.

2. Such a denunciation shall not have the effect of releasing the High Contracting Party concerned from its obligations under this Convention in respect of any act which, being capable of constituting a violation of such obligations, may have been performed by it before the date at which the denunciation became effective.

3. Any High Contracting Party which shall cease to be a member of the Council of Europe shall cease to be a Party to this Convention under the same conditions.

4. The Convention may be denounced in accordance with the provisions of the preceding paragraphs in respect of any territory to which it has been declared to extend under the terms of Article 56.

ARTICLE 59 – SIGNATURE AND RATIFICATION

1. This Convention shall be open to the signature of the members of the Council of Europe. It shall be ratified. Ratifications shall be deposited with the Secretary General of the Council of Europe.

2. The present Convention shall come into force after the deposit of ten instruments of ratification.

3. As regards any signatory ratifying subsequently, the Convention shall come into force at the date of the deposit of its instrument of ratification.

4. The Secretary General of the Council of Europe shall notify all the members of the Council of Europe of the entry into force of the Convention, the names of the High Contracting Parties who have ratified it, and the deposit of all instruments of ratification which may be effected subsequently.

Done at Rome this 4th day of November 1950, in English and French, both texts being equally authentic, in a single copy which shall remain deposited in the archives of the Council of Europe. The Secretary General shall transmit certified copies to each of the signatories.

INDEX

A

Abortion 88

Abuse of rights 148–49

Access to courts
    access to legal advice 178
    conclusive evidence
        clauses 179–80
    exclusionary rule 181–82
    fair trials .177–83
    legal aid 178
    legal representation 178
    legality 65–66
    negligence 181–83
    police, negligence of 181–83
    procedural limitations 179–80
    proportionality 179
    public interests 182
    remedies 180
    security for costs 179
    substantive rights, new 180–83
    time limits 179
    waiver 178

Access to legal advice 178

Access to records 120

Administrative action 15–16

Administrative Court 10, 187, 204

Administrative
    decision making
        appeals 175
        fair trials .174–77
        judicial review 174–77

Adversarial trials, right to 191–92

Adverse inferences 190

Alcoholics 102–04

Aliens, political rights of 148

Anton Piller orders 127

Appeals
    administrative
        decision making 175
    fair trials in criminal
        proceedings 196

Appropriation 152

Armed forces
    homosexuals in 55–56, 123
    remedies,
        effectiveness of 55–56

Arrest
    deportation 104–05
    extradition 104–05
    fair trials in criminal
        proceedings 196
    mental disabilities 106–07
    reasons 196
    right to liberty
        and security 100–01,
                        104–07

Assembly, freedom of 137–38

Association, freedom of 138–39

Associations, standing of 34–35

Asylum
    legality 66
    remedies,
        effectiveness of 56, 58
    right to liberty
        and security 106

B

Bail 109

Bills of Rights 5

Blasphemy 134

Breach
    damages 17, 216
    EC law 219, 226

European Convention
on Human Rights,
UK law in 11–17, 54–55
legislation .11–17
statutory defence 16–17
torture, inhuman or
degrading treatment 89–90

Broadcasting 136–37

C

Capital punishment 86, 164

Care, children in 120

Causes of action 9–10

Certainty 66

Charges 174

Children and young persons
access 119–20
care, in 120
custody .119–20
delay 119
detention 102
educational supervision 102
fair trials 119
right to liberty
and security 102
right to respect for
private and family life 118–20

Civil cases,
See, also, Fair trials in
civil cases 204

Compensation,
See, also, Damages
expropriation 153–54
property, protection of 153–54
right to liberty
and security 113

Compulsory purchase 152

Confidentiality 124–25

Conscience,
See Freedom of thought,
conscience and religion

Contributions .155

Convention rights,
See, also, Freedom of
expression 83–164
EC law 225
interference with 61–65, 68–69
democratic
values, for 69–70
legitimate
aims, for 68–69
legitimate aims,
restrictions for 68–69
limitation on use of
restrictions on 149–50
meaning of .1–2
prescribed by law,
interference 63–64
proportionality 71–74
respect for human
rights obligation 84
restrictions on 140–50

Corporal punishment 95, 159–60

Costs
access to courts 179
damages .217–18
security for .179

Courts,
See, also, Access to courts;
European Court
of Human Rights;
Fair trials
Administrative Court 10, 187, 204
damages 203, 206
European Court
of Justice 219, 222,
223–26, 228–30
independence 185–86
judicial review 45–46

meaning .109, 203
public authorities 45–46, 49
right to be brought
    promptly before 107

Criminal offences,
  See, also, Fair trials in
  criminal cases
  immigration 121–22
  retrospectivity 114–15

Cross-examination 198

Custody of children 119–20

D

Damages,
  See, also, Compensation 201–18
  Administrative Court 204
  breach 17, 216
  causation 213–15
  Civil Procedure Rules 1998 204
  civil proceedings 204
  compensatory approach 209–10
  conduct of the applicant 213
  costs 217–18
  courts 203, 206
  death of applicants 207
  detention 212
  discretion 204–05
  EC law 201–02
  equitable approach 211
  European Court of
    Human Rights,
    case law of 206–18
  expenses 217–18
  fair trials 214
  Human Rights Act 1998 201–06
  interest 216–17
  judgment as
    sufficient reparation 215–16
  judicial acts 205–06
  judicial review 201
  just satisfaction 207–08, 210

loss of opportunity 213–15
mitigation 212
natural justice 214
non-compensatory
  awards 216
non-pecuniary
  loss 208–09, 213, 215
pecuniary loss 208–09
power to award 203–04
procedural unfairness 213–15
proof of loss 208
public authorities 201
quantum 211–12
tribunals 203–04, 206
victims 207

Data protection 124–25

Death of applicants 33, 207

Death penalty 86, 164

Declarations of
  incompatibility 11–14, 15

Defence, statutory 16–17

Defendants 8–9, 37–47
  consensual element 40
  European Convention
    on Human Rights,
    case law of 41–42
  Governmental
    functions 39–40
  Human Rights
    Act 1998 .38
  functions subject to
    challenge under 42–47
  judicial review,
    susceptibility to 38–40
  public authorities 38, 41
  public functions 39
  regulatory bodies 42
  source of power 39

Delay
  children 118

fair trials 186–87
    criminal cases, in 187
judicial review 186–87
right to liberty
    and security 108–09

Democratic values 69–70

Demonstrations 137–38

Deportation
    arrest 104–05
    national security 112
    remedies,
        effectiveness of 55
    right to liberty
        and security 104–05, 112

Deprivation of
    possessions 152–54

Derogations 19–20

Detention,
    See, also, Prisoners'
    rights
    alcoholics 102–04
    children and
        young persons 102
    conditions 91–92
    convictions by
        competent court 99–100
    damages 212
    deportation 104–05
    drug addicts 102–04
    emergencies 111
    extradition 104–05
    hospitals in 98
    infectious diseases 102–04
    injuries sustained
        whilst in 91
    legality 66–67
    medical treatment 91–92
    mental disabilities 66–67, 98,
                102–04, 106–07,
                110–11

non-compliance
    with lawful
        orders of court 100
    reviews of 109–10, 112–13
    right to liberty
        and security 98–100,
                     102–113
    suspicion of having
        committed offence or
            fleeing afterwards 100–01
    torture, inhuman or
        degrading treatment 91–92
    unauthorised entry 104–05
    vagrants .102–04

Disabled persons,
    See, also, Mental
    disabilities 87

Disciplinary proceedings 193

Disclosure .189, 197

Discrimination 143–45
    education 164
    illegitimacy 144
    immigration 144–45
    margin of
        appreciation 146
    property,
        protection of 157
    racial discrimination 145
    taxation 157
    torture, inhuman or
        degrading treatment 94

Drug addicts 102–04

E

EC law
    breach 219, 226
    cases outside scope of 227
    cases within scope of 227–28
    Convention rights 225
    damages 201–02

elections 225–26
European Convention
    on Human Rights 219–31
    accession to 222
European Court of
    Human Rights,
      case law of 223–26
European Court
    of Justice 219, 222,
               223–26, 228–30
European Parliament,
    elections to 225–26
freedom of
    movement 221–22, 227
fundamental rights 219–23,
               226–27, 230–31
Human Rights
    Act 1998 230–31
inconsistencies 224
interpretation 5, 219,
                  223, 230
legislation 220
margin of appreciation 225
proportionality 225
regulating principle 226–28
scope of protection 226–30
stages of change 220–21
substantive protection 228–30
supremacy of 220
treaties on human rights 221

Education 158–62
corporal punishment 159–60
denial of right to 159
negligence 162
parents' rights 159–60
religion .159, 160
resources 161
special educational
    needs statements 161, 162
supervision .102

Effectiveness of
domestic remedies 2, 53–61,
                   140–43

Elections
discrimination 164
electoral systems 163
European Parliament 225–26
margin of appreciation 163
right to free 162–64

Emergencies
derogations in time of 146–47
detention 111
margin of
    appreciation 147
procedural requirements 147
right to liberty
    and security 111
terrorism 146

Emissions 75–76

Environment
nuisance .127–28
right to life 89
right to respect for
    private and family life 127–28

Equality of arms 191

European Convention on
    Human Rights,
    See, also, Convention
    rights
breach 11–17, 54–55
concepts under 49–82
    application of 62–78
    approach of
      court to 78–82
derogations 19–20
EC law and 219–31
horizontal effect of 47
implementation of 2
interpretation 3–7, 50–62
living instrument, as 59
positive obligations 62–63, 74–78,
                  84, 117–18
reservations 19–20
restrictions 62
treaty, as .51–52

European Court of
Human Rights
burden of proof 82
case law,
    departing from 3–4, 50
Convention concepts
informing
    approach of 78–82
damages 206–18
defendants 41–42
EC law 223–26
fourth instance
    principle 80
individual right
    of petition 21
interpretation 3–7, 50–62
margin of
    appreciation 78–79
precedent...................4, 21, 59
public authorities 44–45
role of 21
subsidiarity 80
victims 81–82

European Court
of Justice 219, 222,
                    223–26, 228–30

European Parliament 225–26

European Union,
See EC law

Euthanasia 88

Evidence
access to courts 179–80
conclusive evidence
    clauses 179–80
fair trials 192

Executions 86, 164

Exhaustion of
domestic remedies 21, 113

Expenses 217–18

Expropriation 153–54

Expulsion 93–94

Extradition
arrest 104–05
detention 104–05
remedies,
    effectiveness of 56–57
right to liberty
    and security 104–05
torture, inhuman or
    degrading treatment 92–93

F

Fair trials,
See, also, Fair trials in
civil cases; Fair trials in
criminal cases 113, 165–99
access to courts 177–83
administrative
    decision making 174–77
adversarial trials,
    right to 191–92
application of right 166–74
children 119
damages 214
delay 186–87
disclosure 189
equality of arms 191
evidence......................192
impartiality 183–85
independence 185–86
judicial review 165, 174–77
natural justice 165
co-extensive
    with, rights 191–92
procedural rights
    extending beyond 183–91
oral hearings 187–88
procedural unfairness 213–15
public hearings 187–88
reasons 188
substance of right 177–92

Fair trials in civil cases 166–71
  'civil rights and
     obligations' 166–68
  contestation 169–70
  criminal proceedings 193
  'directly decisive' 170–71
  'disputes' .168–70
  equality of arms 191
  judicial review 167, 168
  'private rights and
     obligations' 167–68

Fair trials in criminal cases 171–74
  adverse inferences 190
  appeals 196
  arrest, reasons for 196
  burden of proof 192–94
  charge
     information on 196
     meaning .174
  civil proceedings 193
  'criminal' 171
  delay 187
  'determination' 171
  disciplinary proceedings 193
  disclosure 189, 197
  domestic classification 172
  equality of arms 191
  fines 172–73
  guarantees in 192–99
  interpreters 198–99
  judicial review 196
  legal representation 197–98
  nature of the offence 172–73
  participate in, right to 190–91
  penalties, severity of 172–73
  prejudice 196
  presumption of
     innocence 192–95
  right to silence 190
  self-incrimination,
     privilege against 190
  standard of proof 194
  witnesses,
     cross-examination of 198

Family life,
  See Right to respect
  for private and family life

Fines 172–73

Force,
  See Use of force

Forced labour .95–96

Forum 9–10

Fourth instance principle 80

Freedom of assembly 137–38

Freedom of association 137, 138–39

Freedom of expression 131–37
  artistic expression 134
  blasphemy 134
  broadcasting 136–37
  commercial
     expression 133, 136
  injunctions 18–19, 135–36
  journalists' sources 134–35
  judiciary 135
  margin of
     appreciation 133–34
  press 134–35
  restrictions 132
  scope of 131–32
  special protection for 18–19
  subject matter 133–34

Freedom of information 76–77, 132

Freedom of movement 221–22, 227

Freedom of thought,
  conscience and religion 129–30
  education 159, 160
  'manifestation' 130
  prisoners' rights 130
  special protection for 18–19

Fundamental rights
  under EC law 219–23,
              226–27, 230–31

G

Gender reassignment 123, 139–40

General principles of
international law 153–54

Government
bodies 35–36
functions .39–40

H

Habeus corpus 105–06, 110–13

Health 87–89

Hearings,
See, also, Courts;
Fair trials
fair 177–78
oral 187–88
public 187–88

'Home' 116–17

Homosexuals
armed forces in 55–56, 123
margin of
appreciation 122
proportionality 71
remedies,
effectiveness of 55–56
right to respect for
private and family life 122–24
sado-masochism 123
same sex couples 123

Housing 156–57

Human Rights Act 1998
damages .201–06
exclusions from 2
horizontal effect 78, 81
interpretation 49, 81
public authorities,
functions subject
to challenge 42–47
retrospectivity 10

standing 26–37
time limits 10
victims 26–37, 81–82

Hunger strikes 91–92

I

Illegitimacy 76, 144

Immigration
criminal offences 121–22
discrimination 144–45
right to respect for
private and family life 121–22
torture, inhuman or
degrading treatment 93–94

Immunities 201

Impartiality
fair trials 183–85
judicial review 183
judiciary 183–85
natural justice 183

Independence
administrative
decision making 186
courts 185–86
fair trials 185–86
tribunals 185–86

Infectious diseases 102–04

Information, freedom of 76–77

Inhuman or degrading
treatment,
See Torture, inhuman
or degrading treatment

Injunctions 18–19, 135–36

Innocence,
presumption of 192–95

Interception of
communications,
See Surveillance

Interest on damages 216–17

Interpretation,
See, also, Statutory
interpretation 4
aids to 52
autonomous meaning of
Convention terms 60–61
EC law 219, 223, 230
effectiveness
principle 2, 53–61
European Convention
on Human Rights 3–7, 50–62
European Court of
Human Rights 3–7, 50–62
exceptions,
strictly construed 61–62
Human Rights Act 1998 . . . . .49, 81
precedent .59–60
public international law 51–52
up to date .59–60
victims 81
Vienna Convention 52–53
Wednesbury
unreasonableness 55–56

Interpreters .198–99

Intervention 37

Investigations 125–27

J

Journalists' sources 134–35

Judicial review
bodies subject to 38–47
courts 45–46
damages 201
delay 186–87
effectiveness of 55
fair trial 174
Parliament .46–47
planning 176

presumption
of innocence 193, 195
property,
protection of 155
public authorities,
susceptibility to 38–47
regulatory bodies 42, 45
right to liberty
and security 105–06, 110–13
standing 23–24
sufficient interest 23–24, 175–76
susceptibility to 38–47
tribunals 45–46
utilities 43–44

Judiciary
damages .205–06
impartiality 183–85

L

Legal representation
access to 178
fair trials in criminal
proceedings 197–98

Legality 63–68
access to courts 65–66
asylum 66
certainty 66
detention .66–67
interference with
Convention rights 63–65
prisoners' rights 67–68
surveillance 65
telephone tapping 63–64
unlawful state action 66

Legislation,
See, also, Statutory
interpretation
amending 14
breach 11–17
declarations of
incompatibility 11–14

EC law 220

fast track process
 for amending 13, 14

primary 11–14

remedial orders 12–13

retrospectivity 157

subordinate 15

Legitimate aims 68–69

Liberty,
 See Right to liberty
 and security

Life, right to,
 See Right to life

Limitation periods,
 See Time limits

Locus standi,
 See Standing

Loss of opportunity 213–15

M

Margin of appreciation 4, 62

 discrimination 145

 EC law 225

 education 163

 emergencies 147

 European Court of
  Human Rights'
  approach to 78–79

 freedom of expression 133, 135

 homosexuals 122

 planning 156

 property,
  protection of 152–53,
          155, 156

 proportionality 72–74

Marriage 139–40

Media 134–37

Medical treatment

 best interests 92

 compulsory 129

 detention, whilst in 91–92

 disabled persons 87

 refusal of 88

 right to life 87–89

 right to respect for
  private and family life 129

 screening 129

 torture, inhuman or
  degrading treatment 91–92

Mental disabilities

 arrest 106–07

 detention 66–67, 98,
        102–04, 106–07,
            110–11

 right to liberty
  and security 98, 102–04,
         106–07, 110–11

Minors,
 See Children and
 young persons

Misfeasance in
 public office 201

Mitigation 212

N

National security 112

Nationalisation 152

Natural justice

 fair trials 165, 183–91

 impartiality 183

 procedural rights
  extending beyond 183–91

 rights co-extensive with 191–92

Negligence

 access to courts 181–83

 education 162

 police 181–83

New Zealand 5

Non-governmental
 organisations 35–36, 41

Non-natural persons,
standing of 31–32

Nuisance 127–28

O

Oral hearings 187–88

P

Parents' rights 159–60

Parliament
judicial review 46–47
public authorities 46–47
sovereignty 6–7
statutory interpretation 6–7

Peaceful enjoyment
of possessions 151–52

Penalties
fair trials in
criminal cases 172–73
property, protection of 155

Planning 156, 176

Police negligence 181–83

Positive obligations 62–63, 74–78,
84, 117–18

Possessions
deprivation of 152–54
peaceful enjoyment of 151–52

Precedent 4, 21, 59–60

Prejudice 30–31, 196

Press 134–35

Pressure groups
standing 25–26, 34–35, 37
victims 34–35, 37

Presumption of
innocence 192–95

Prisoners' rights,
See, also, Detention
correspondence 55, 68–69, 128
interference with 68–69
legality 67–68
freedom of thought,
conscience and
religion 130
remedies, right to
an effective 142
right to respect for
private and family life 128

Private life,
See Right to respect for
private and family life

Privilege against
self-incrimination 190

Procedural unfairness 213–15

Property, protection of 150–58
application of
principle 156–58
compensation 153–54
compulsory
purchase 152, 153–54
conditions
prescribed by law 153
contributions 155
control of use 151–52, 154–55
deprivation of
possessions 152–54
discrimination 157
expropriation 153–54
general interest 154–55
general principles of
international law 153–54
housing 156–57
judicial review 155
margin of
appreciation 152, 153,
155, 156
nationalisation 152

peaceful enjoyment
   of possessions 151–52
penalties 155
planning 156
proportionality 154
public interest 152–53
retrospectivity 157
seizure 157–58
taxation 155, 157–58

Proportionality 71–74
   access to courts 179
   EC law 225
   homosexual conduct 71
   margin of appreciation 72–74
   property, protection of 154

Public authorities
   courts 45–46, 49
   damages 201
   definition 8, 45
   European Court of
      Human Rights 44–45
   Human Rights Act 1998,
      functions subject to
         challenge under 42–47
   immunities 201
   judicial review,
      susceptibility to 38–47
   misfeasance in
      public office 201
   Parliament 46–47
   positive obligations 77–78
   public law powers 8–9
   public/private functions 43
   standing 35–36
   statutory interpretation 6–7
   subsidiarity 80
   tribunals 45–46
   victims 1, 35–36, 81

Public hearings 187–88

Public interest
   access to courts 182

disclosure 189
property, protection of 152–53
standing 34–35
victims 35

Public international law 51–52

Public law 8–9

Public/private functions 43

Punishment, without
   law, no 114–15

Q

Quantum of damages 211–12

R

Racial discrimination 145

Reasonableness,
   See Wednesbury
   unreasonableness

Reasons 188

Records, access to 120

Regulatory bodies 42, 45

Religion,
   See Freedom of thought,
   conscience and religion

Remedial orders 12–13

Remedies,
   See, also, Compensation;
   Damages
   access to courts 180
   arguable violation 141
   asylum 56, 58
   deportation 55
   effectiveness
      principle 2, 53–61,
                  140–43
   exhaustion of local 21, 113

extradition .56–57
homosexuals, armed
  forces in 55–56
injunctions 18–19, 135–36
prisoners' rights 142
sufficient remedy,
  nature of 141–43
surveillance 142
torture 143
Wednesbury
  unreasonableness 55–58

Reservations .19–20

Retrospectivity
Human Rights Act 1998 11
no punishment
  without law 114–15
property, protection of 157

Right to liberty and
security .96–113
alcoholics .102–04
arrest 100–01, 104–07
asylum 106
bail 109
compensation 113
convictions by
  competent court 99–100
court
  convictions by
    competent 99–100
  meaning of 109–10
  right to be brought
    promptly before 107–09
delay 108–09
deportation 104–05, 112
deprivation of liberty,
  prohibition on 98
  permissible 98–110
detention . . . .
  alcoholics 102–04
  children and
    young persons 102

convictions by
  competent court 99–100
deportation 104–05
drug addicts 102–04
emergencies 111
extradition 104–05
hospitals in 98
infectious diseases 102–04
mental disabilities 98, 102–04,
                                      106–07,
                                      110–11
non-compliance
  with lawful orders
    of court 100
reviews of 109–10,
                                      112–13
suspicion of having
  committed offence or
    fleeing afterwards 100–01
unauthorised entry 104–05
vagrants 102–04
drug addicts 102–04
extradition 104–05
habeus corpus 105–06, 110–13
infectious diseases 102–04
judicial review 105–06, 110–13
meaning 97–98
mental disabilities 102–04, 106–07,
                                      110–11
release pending trial 107–09
remedies, exhaustion
  of local 113
trial, release pending 108–09
vagrants 102–04

Right to life 85–89
abortion 88
death penalty 86
disabled persons 87
environment .89
euthanasia 88
failure to act 85–86

health and
  medical issues 87–89
medical treatment 87–89
  refusal of 88
use of force 86–87
warnings of health risks 88

Right to marry 139–40

Right to respect for private
and family life 115–29
  balancing exercise 118
  children 118–20
  correspondence 117
  data protection 124–25
  definitions 116–17
  divorce 120–21
  environment 127–28
  'home' 116–17
  immigration 121–22
  investigations 125–27
  medical treatment 129
  positive obligations 117–18
  prisoners' rights 128
  search and seizure 127
  sexual orientation 122–24
  surveillance 125–27

Right to silence 190

S

Sado-masochism 123

Same sex couples 123

Searches
  Anton Piller orders 127
  right to respect for
    private and family life 127
  safeguards 127

Security,
  See, also, National security;
  Right to liberty and security
  costs, for 179

Seizure
  property, protection of 157–58
  right to respect for
    private and family life 127
  safeguards 127
  taxation 157–58
  Wednesbury
    unreasonableness 58

Self-incrimination,
  privilege against 190

Servitude 95–96

Sexual orientation,
  See Homosexuals

Silence, right to 190

Slavery 95–96

Sovereignty of Parliament 6–7

Special educational
  needs statements 161–62

Standing 23–37
  actio popularis 28
  associations 34–35
  death of the applicant 33
  domestic law narrower
    than Convention law 34
  future events 28–29
  government bodies 35–36
  Human Rights Act 1998 26–37
  impugned measure,
    potential effect of 29–30
  indirect effect 31
  judicial review 23–26, 27
  merits, examination of 24
  non-governmental
    organisations 35–36
  non-natural persons 31–32
  prejudice .30–31
  pressure groups 25–26,
    34–35, 37
  prima facie cases 28
  public authorities 35–36

public interest
    challenges 34–35
    sufficient interest 23–26
    relatives 31
    third party
        intervention 37
    victims 7–8, 26–37
    Wednesbury
        unreasonableness 27

State security 113

Statutory interpretation
    aids to 6
    Bill of Rights 5
    EC law 5
    New Zealand 5
    Parliamentary
        sovereignty 6–7
    public authorities 6–7
    UK, in 4–6

Subordinate legislation 15

Subsidiarity 80

Supremacy of EC law 220

Surveillance
    legality 63–65
    remedies, right to
        an effective 142
    right to respect for
        private and family life 125–26
    safeguards 126–27
    telephone tapping 63–64

T

Taxation
    discrimination 157
    property,
        protection of 155, 157–58
    seizure 157–58

Terrorism 146, 149

Third parties, standing of 37

Time limits
    access to courts 179
    extension of 10
    Human Rights Act 1998 10

Thought, freedom of,
    See Freedom of thought,
    conscience and religion

Torture, inhuman or
    degrading treatment 89–95
    breach 89–90
    corporal punishment 95
    discrimination 94
    detention,
        conditions of 91–92
    expulsion 93–94
    extradition 92–93
    hunger strikes 91–92
    immigration 93–94
    meaning 90–91
    medical treatment
        best interests of patient 91–92
        failure to provide 91
    remedies, right
        to effective 143
    therapeutic environment,
        failure to provide 92

Trade unions 138–39

Transsexuals 123–24,
                    139–40

Trials,
    See Courts; Fair trials

Tribunals
    damages 203–04, 206
    independence 185–86
    judicial review 45–46
    public authorities 45–46

U

Unreasonableness,
See Wednesbury
unreasonableness

Use of force
right to life .86–87
torture, inhuman or
degrading treatment 91

Utilities 43–44

V

Vagrants 102–04

Victims
damages 207
European Court of
Human Rights'
approach to 81–82
Human Rights
Act 1998 . . . . .26–37, 81–82
interpretation 81
judicial review 27
pressure groups 34–35, 37
public authorities 1, 35–36, 81

public interest .35
standing 7–8, 26–37

Vienna Convention on
the Law of Treaties 52–53

W

Warnings on
health issues .88

Wednesbury
unreasonableness
judicial review 27
prisoners' rights 55
remedies,
effectiveness of 55–58
seizure 58
standing 27

Witnesses 198

Y

Young persons,
See Children and
young persons